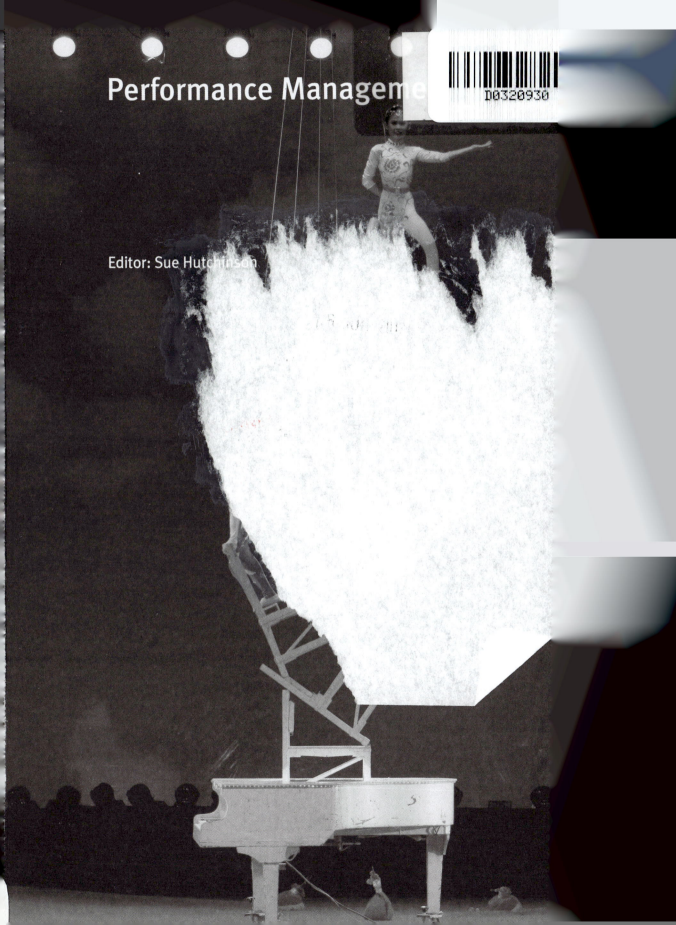

Performance Manageme

Editor: Sue Hutchinson

The Chartered Institute of Personnel and Development is the leading publisher of books and reports for personnel and training professionals, students, and all those concerned with the effective management and development of people at work. For details of all our titles, please contact
the publishing department:
tel: 020 8612 6204
email: publishing@cipd.co.uk
The catalogue of all CIPD titles can be viewed on the CIPD website:
www.cipd.co.uk/bookstore

Performance Management

Editor: Sue Hutchinson

Chartered Institute of Personnel and Development

Published by the Chartered Institute of Personnel and Development
151, The Broadway, London, SW19 1JQ

This edition first published 2013

© Chartered Institute of Personnel and Development, 2013

All rights reserved. No part of this publication may be reproduced, stored in a retrieval system, or transmitted, in any form or by any means, electronic, mechanical photocopying, recording, or otherwise, without the prior written permission of the publisher.

This publication may not be sold, lent, hired out or otherwise dealt with in the course of trade or supplied in any form of binding or cover other than that in which it is published without the prior written permission of the publisher.

No responsibility for loss occasioned to any person acting or refraining from action as a result of any material in this publication can be accepted by the editor, authors or publisher.

Designed and Typeset by Exeter Premedia Services, India
Printed in Great Britain by Bell & Bain, Glasgow

British Library Cataloguing in Publication Data
A catalogue of this publication is available from the British Library

ISBN 978 1 84398 305 7

The views expressed in this publication are the authors' own and may not necessarily reflect those of the CIPD.

The CIPD has made every effort to trace and acknowledge copyright holders. If any source has been overlooked, CIPD Enterprises would be pleased to redress this in future editions.

Chartered Institute of Personnel and Development
151 The Broadway, London SW19 1JQ
Tel: 020 8612 6200
Email: cipd@cipd.co.uk
Website: www.cipd.co.uk
Incorporated by Royal Charter
Registered Charity No. 1079797

ST. HELENS
COLLEGE

658·314
HUT

131695

Oct 13

LIBRARY

Contents

List of figures and tables

Contributor biographies

Sue Hutchinson, Academic FCIPD, is Associate Professor in HRM at the University of the West of England (UWE), where she is also Associate Head of the HRM teaching and research group. She teaches on a range of HRM postgraduate modules, including performance management, and is actively involved in research. Her main research interests focus on the link between people management and performance, and the role of line managers in HRM, and she has published extensively in these fields. Previous work experiences include research and teaching at Bath University, policy adviser for the CIPD, and industrial relations adviser in the paper industry.

John Neugebauer is a Senior Lecturer in HRM and Knowledge Exchange at Bristol Business School, University of the West of England. In addition to lecturing on HRM, his role includes consultation to a range of commercial, public sector and not-for-profit organisations. His previous experience has included senior roles in employee relations, global reward, global HRD, and HR business partnering to MDs in UK and international banking, and in hospital management. He holds trustee and non-executive directorships in a number of charities, and is external examiner for postgraduate HRM and MBA programmes at Plymouth Business School. He is a Chartered Fellow of the CIPD.

Graeme Mather is a Senior Lecturer in HRM at Bristol Business School, University of the West of England. He is also a member of the Centre for Employment Studies Research at UWE. He teaches on a range of postgraduate HRM modules including Employee Relations and Performance Management, and is currently undertaking part-time doctoral studies at Cardiff Business School, Cardiff University. His research interests include HRM and industrial relations in the public sector, with a particular focus on the nature and impact of performance management for those working on the front line in public sector settings.

Jane Moore, MCIPD, is a Senior Lecturer in HRM and responsible for postgraduate HRM programmes at the University of the West of England. She is a Chartered Member of the CIPD and Educational Adviser for the West of England Branch. Her current teaching interests include resourcing and talent management and applied HRM and business skills at postgraduate level. Prior to working at the University, Jane worked as an HR practitioner within the electricity supply industry and as an independent training consultant.

Acknowledgements

We are grateful to the following organisations for allowing us to use case study material based on their organisation: Ministry of Defence, Artizan hairdressers, Space Engineering, and the General Dental Council. We would also like to thank XpertHR for allowing us to use tables from their surveys and other adapted case study material.

We are also grateful to the following for permission to use copyright material:

Figure 1.1 *Linking HR practices to competitive strategy* from Peter Boxall and John Purcell (2011) *Strategy and Human Resource Management*, published by Palgrave Macmillan; Figure 1.2 *The people management–performance causal chain* from John Purcell and Sue Hutchinson (2007) in 'Front-line managers as agents in the HRM performance causal chain: theory, analysis and evidence', *Human Resource Management Journal*, Vol.17, No.1: 3–20, published by John Wiley; Table 1.1 *ACAS, the theory and practice*, from ACAS (www.acas.org.uk); Table 1.2 *Implicit and explicit promises*, from the article by Rob Briner and Neil Conway in *People Management*; Dennis Organ for the quote in Chapter 1 from *Organizational Citizenship Behaviour: The Good Soldier Syndrome* (1988), published by Lexington Books; Table 2.2 published in *Organizational Dynamics*, R. Miles and C. Snow *Designing human resource systems*, pp36–52, copyright Elsevier (1984); Chapter 5, the extract from John Shields, page 128 in *Managing Employee Performance and Reward* (2007), published by Cambridge University Press; Chapter 6, the extract from S. Brutus, C. Fletcher and C. Baldry (2009) 'The influence of independent self-construal on rater self-efficacy in performance appraisal', *International Journal of Human Resource Management*, Vol.20, No. 9: 1999–2011, published by Taylor & Francis Ltd, (www.informaworld.com); Chapter 9, the quote from P. Cressey and J. MacInnes (1980) 'Voting for Ford: industrial democracy and the control of labour', *Capital and Class*, Vol.11: 5–33, published by Sage Publications; Chapter 9, the quote from J. Storey (1983) *Management Prerogative and the Question of Control*, published by Taylor & Francis; Figures 11.1 and 11.2 from the Cranet survey; Table 11.2 in Chapter 11 adapted from Figure 1 by M. Harvey and M. Novecevic (2001) 'Selecting expatriates for increasingly complex global assignments', *Career Development International*, Vol.6, No.2: 69–87, published by Emerald Group Publishing; Chapter 11, the quote from A. Varma, S. Budhwar and A. DeNisi (2008) *Performance Management Systems: A global perspective*, Routledge, page 260, reprinted by Taylor & Francis Books.

We would also like to thank all the reviewers who provided detailed and invaluable feedback, and all the team at the CIPD for their support and consideration. Sue would also like to add a very special thanks to her husband Mark and children Fi, Laura and Chris, for their unending support and patience.

CIPD qualifications map

If you are studying the Performance Management module, the following table may be useful in determining how the learning outcomes of that module map onto the chapters of this book.

CIPD learning outcomes	Mapped to chapters in this book
1	Systematically decide and communicate strategic performance aims, objectives, priorities and targets	Chapter 1: Setting the scene: HRM and performance Chapter 2: Strategic performance management Chapter 3: Motivation at work Chapter 4: The role of line managers in managing performance Chapter 7: Integrating learning and performance Chapter 11: International performance management
2	Plan effective performance management policies and practices to improve organisational and employee performance	Chapter 2: Strategic performance management Chapter 4: The role of line managers in managing performance Chapter 5: Defining and measuring individual work performance Chapter 6: Performance appraisal and feedback Chapter 7: Integrating learning and performance Chapter 11: International performance management
3	Devise and sustain arguments for using appropriate performance management techniques, rewards and sanctions to improve performance	Chapter 4: The role of line managers in managing performance Chapter 5: Defining and measuring individual work performance Chapter 7: Integrating learning and performance Chapter 8: Performance-related rewards Chapter 9: Managing under-performance Chapter 10: Absence management
4	Demonstrate the communication skills required when managing achievement and under-achievement	Chapter 4: The role of line managers in managing performance Chapter 6: Performance appraisal and feedback Chapter 9: Managing under-performance Chapter 12: Developing performance management
5	Critically evaluate the effectiveness of performance management	Chapter 1: Setting the scene: HRM and performance Chapter 6: Performance appraisal and feedback Chapter 7: Integrating learning and performance Chapter 8: Performance-related rewards Chapter 12: Developing performance management

Walkthrough of textbook features and online resources

LEARNING OUTCOMES

At the beginning of each chapter, a bulleted set of learning outcomes summarises what you can expect to learn from the chapter, helping you to track your progress.

LEARNING OUTCOMES

By the end of this chapter you should be able to:

- identify and explain the different ways in which performance management can be defined and interpreted
- consider developments in performance management
- understand the relationship between performance management and organisational strategy
- critically review the balanced scorecard approach
- review the performance management process
- consider the role of the HR function with respect to performance management

CASE STUDIES

A range of case studies illustrate how key ideas and theories are operating in practice, with accompanying questions or activities.

CASE STUDY 3.5

REWARD AMONG GENERATION Y: CASH IS KING

Until recently it was widely considered that Generation Y people (teenagers and young adults) valued flexible working, travel, and a good work–life balance above pay. However, a survey conducted by *Personnel Today* and Ipsos Mori in 2008 suggests that this may no longer be the case. The findings revealed that those aged between 18 and 28 considered money to be the most important benefit for Generation Y people. The most important employee benefits in five to ten years' time are felt likely to be:

- learning and development – 10%
- flexible working – 9%
- other financial benefits – 6%
- childcare benefits – 4%
- holiday entitlement – 3%.

Furthermore, 85% of respondents said they would prefer their employer to offer cash as an incentive to boost performance. Heavy student debt, difficulties in getting onto the property ladder and rises in the cost of living are likely contributory factors.

Source: *Berry* (2008)

ACTIVITIES

In each chapter, a number of questions and activities will help you to check on your understanding of the key concepts and reflect on what you have just read.

ACTIVITY 3.5

Teams and Motivation

Theories on work motivation are premised on the assumption of workers as individual actors. It can be argued that group motivation to work is informed by individual motivation to do work. So if a person finds a job boring and demotivating, his/her perspective of that job will not change because he/she must now perform it with others. However, it could be argued that team members motivate and demotivate each other. Theory on collective efficacy (Bandura, 1986), which is based on the shared belief of team members that their team's capacity to perform is important, is relevant here. Theory on team social identity also provides useful insights into the motivation of teams. In a sports team setting, for example, in-group identity can be a powerful motivator for improving performance,

CRITICAL REFLECTION 1.4

Can commitment be managed?

Commitment is affected by other factors in addition to HR policies – such as personality, job role experiences, work experiences, and structural factors (Legge, 2005). This has led writers such as Conway and Monks (2009) to ask if commitment can be managed. Some of the arguments cited by Conway and Monks are that employees may not be ideologically disposed to commitment; that there may be resistance from unions (for instance, in relation to participation); and that line managers may inhibit commitment because they 'may have their own misguided assumptions about what motivates employees as well as how to manage them' (Iverson and Buttigieg, 1999).

1   Do you agree with this view?

2   What are the implications for performance management?

CRITICAL REFLECTION

Critical Reflection boxes encourage you to pause and reflect on what you have just read and explore important concepts and issues in greater depth.

EXPLORE FURTHER

Boselie, P., Dietz, G. and Boon, C. (2005) 'Commonalities and contradictions in HRM and performance research', *Human Resource Management Journal*, Vol.15, No.3: 67–94

Boxall, P. and Purcell, J. (2011) *Strategy and Human Resource Management*, 3rd edition. Basingstoke: Palgrave Macmillan

Combs, C., Liu, Y., Hall, A. and Kitchen, D. (2006) 'How much do high-performance work systems matter? A meta-analysis of their effects on organisational performance', *Personnel Psychology*, Vol.59, No.3: 501–28

Conway, E. and Monks, K. (2009) 'Unravelling the complexities of high commitment: an employee-level analysis', *Human Resource Management Journal*, Vol.19, No.2: 140–58

Guest, D. E. (2011) 'Human resource management and performance: still searching for some answers', *Human Resource Management Journal*, Vol.21, No.1: 3–13

Macky, K. and Boxall, P. (2007) 'The relationship between "high-performance work practices" and employee attitudes: an investigation of additive and interaction

EXPLORE FURTHER

Explore further boxes contain suggestions for further reading and useful websites, encouraging you to delve further into areas of particular interest.

ONLINE RESOURCES FOR STUDENTS

- Annotated web-links – access a wealth of useful sources of information in order to develop your understanding of the issues in the text

ONLINE RESOURCES FOR TUTORS

- PowerPoint slides – design your programme around these ready-made lectures, including figures and tables from the text

- Lecturer's Guide – provides guidance on how to use the book in your teaching, discussing the context of each chapter and responses to in-text learning features.

To access the online resources for this textbook www.cipd.co.uk/olr

CHAPTER 1

Setting the Scene: HRM and Performance

SUE HUTCHINSON

LEARNING OUTCOMES

By the end of this chapter you should be able to:

- explain and critique the research on HRM and performance
- understand and explain key theories that seek to explain the link between HR policies and individual and organisational performance
- appreciate the importance of the role of the line manager
- evaluate the role of employee attitudes and behaviours necessary for effective HRM and performance management
- begin evaluating issues for effective performance management.

INTRODUCTION

Performance management has many different meanings, but in essence it is about improving performance, and usually refers to a range of management initiatives which seek to make performance more 'manageable'. It can be viewed from a diverse range of perspectives including strategy, organisational behaviour, operations management, economics and accounting, and HRM. This book adopts the latter perspective, and is focused on how to improve performance through the management of people. In this context performance management is generally portrayed as an integrated process in which managers engage with employees to set expectations, measure and review results, agree improvement plans, and sometimes reward performance (Den Hartog *et al*, 2004). As such, it involves aligning a range of interrelated HR activities, such as induction, training and development, performance appraisal, and performance-related pay, with the aim of affecting individual and organisational performance. The same emphasis can be found in the strategic human resource management (SHRM) literature, which emphasises the importance of a system of HR work practices that leads to better performance (eg Appelbaum *et al*, 2000). Performance management can therefore be seen as a microcosm of SHRM (Boselie, 2010).

Before embarking on the theories, activities and debates surrounding performance management it is important to consider the basic premise that HR or people management activities can and do lead to improved organisational performance. The relationship between HRM and organisational performance has proved a fertile ground for academic research, and although significant progress has been made, there still remain many unanswered questions about the nature of this link, such as how HR policies work, and why there is a relationship. This has come to be known as 'the black box' problem (Purcell *et al*, 2003; Wright and Gardner, 2004).

The purpose of this chapter is to review recent research in this area and provide some insight into the causal relationships between HRM and performance. This is necessary if we are to understand how performance management works. The chapter begins with an overview and critique of the research on HRM and performance, and then moves on to explore theory and research on the 'how' and the 'why' of this relationship. A model of the HR causal chain is presented which proposes a linked sequence of events to explain the connection between HR practices, employee outcomes and performance in which emphasis is given to the effectiveness of HR policies and their implementation. The role of line managers, the psychological contract, and key employee attitudes and behaviour are considered. The chapter concludes with a framework for managing performance.

HRM AND PERFORMANCE: KEY THEORIES

Searching for a causal link between HRM and organisational performance has dominated academic research in the field of HRM over the last few decades (Purcell and Kinnie, 2007). Although stimulated by research by US academics (eg Huselid, 1995; Pfeffer, 1998a), studies have tested this relationship in different countries, different sectors, different-sized organisations, with different units of analysis and using different performance outcomes (Boselie, 2010). Overall, the conclusion from this vast body of work is that HRM is positively related to performance, albeit modestly (Boselie *et al*, 2005; Combs *et al*, 2006). This led the CIPD to confidently claim in 2001 that that there is 'no room to doubt that a clear link between people management and performance exists' (CIPD, 2001: 4). Others, however, remain more cautious. Guest, for example, maintains that although a large majority of the published studies show an association between HRM and performance, the analysis provides evidence of an association rather than of causation (Guest, 2011).

This research into the link between HRM and performance has been primarily dominated by two schools of thought: 'best practice', and 'best fit'. More recently, a third approach has entered the debate based on the resource-based view of the firm. These debates are very well covered elsewhere in the HRM literature (see list below), and so are only briefly considered here.

Review articles/chapters of the research on HRM and performance

Boselie, P., Dietz, G. and Boon, C. (2005) 'Commonalties and contradictions in research on human resource management and performance', *Human Resource Management Journal*, Vol.15, No.3: 67–94

Boxall, P. and Macky, K. (2009) 'Research and theory in high-performance work systems: progressing the high-involvement stream', *Human Resource Management Journal*, Vol.19: No. 1: 3–23

Guest, D. (2011) 'Human resource management and performance: still searching for some answers', *Human Resource Management Journal*, Vol.21, No.1: 3–13

Marchington, M. and Grugulis, I. (2000) '"Best practice" human resource management: perfect opportunity or dangerous illusion?', *International Journal of Human Resource Management*, Vol.11, 6 December: 1104–24

Marchington, M. and Wilkinson, A. (2012) *Human Resource Management at Work*, 5th edition. CIPD (Chapters 3, 4, 15)

Purcell, J. (1999) 'The search for best practice and best fit in human resource management: chimera or cul de sac?', *Human Resource Management Journal*, Vol.9, No.3: 26–41

Wall, T. and Wood, S. (2005) 'The romance of HRM and business performance, and the case for big science', *Human Relations*, Vol.58, No.4: 429–62

Wood, S. (1999) 'Human resource management and performance', *International Journal of Management Review*, Vol.1, No.4: 367–413

BEST PRACTICE

Best practice advocates that there is a distinctive set of HR practices which can be adopted by any organisation, irrespective of setting, which will result in improved performance. Various other terms are used to describe this approach, including 'high-commitment management' (eg Wood and de Menezes, 1998), 'high-involvement management' (eg Lawler, 1986) and 'high-performance work systems' (eg Appelbaum *et al*, 2000). A common theme in all of these studies is that combining HR practices into a coherent and integrated 'bundle' has stronger effects on performance than individual practices (Combs *et al*, 2006; Boxall and Macky, 2009). This is based on the assumption that firstly, practices have an additive effect (MacDuffie, 1995), and secondly, that synergies occur when one practice reinforces another. For example, training enhances participation programmes because employees are better equipped to make decisions that participation programmers empower them to make (in Combs *et al*, 2006). It is also possible for HR practices to reduce organisational performance by producing 'deadly combinations', wherein practices work against each other (Becker *et al*, 1997). The classic example is teamworking and performance-related pay which rewards highly individual behaviour.

There are many different lists of what the HR practices should be. One of the best known is presented by Pfeffer (1998a), who identifies seven practices, distilled from a previous list of 16. This includes employment security, selective hiring, extensive training, self-managed teams, high compensation contingent on organisational performance, reduction in status differentials and information-sharing. Arthur's (1994) study of small steel mills contains six type of practices (training, empowerment, high wages, performance-based reward, collective participation and skill development). Wood and de Menezes (1998) add recruitment, appraisal and job security to Arthur's list. There are many more – for instance, Guest and Hoque (1994) list 23 practices, MacDuffie (1995) has 11 practices, and Lawler (1986) four types of practices. Appelbaum *et al*'s study (2000) uses a range of practices based on three components of high-performance work systems: opportunity to participate, skill enhancement and incentives to increase motivation (see the box below). Whatever the list, the common assumption is that these practices are universally applicable and successful.

Appelbaum *et al*'s research on high-performance work systems (HPWSs)

Appelbaum and colleagues (2000) researched the links between high-performance working practices and organisational performance in 44 US manufacturing sites in steel, clothing and medical electronics equipment in the mid-1990s. Unlike many other studies, their research involved surveys of worker responses to HR initiatives rather than managerial responses. HR practices included autonomy in decision-making, development of self-directed teams, offline team membership, communication, formal and informal training, and extrinsic and intrinsic rewards (such as pay, employment security, promotion opportunities, work–life balance). Employee outcomes included workers' trust, intrinsic satisfaction, commitment, job satisfaction and stress. Overall, the research found that the introduction of HPWSs leads to a win/win outcome for manufacturing plants and workers (2000: 115). Plant performance was higher, and there was consistent evidence of positive links between greater use of various HR practices and positive employee outcomes. The researchers discerned little support for the view that these systems have a 'dark side', with no evidence of 'speed up' or work intensification and higher levels of stress. The research also highlighted the importance of positive discretionary effort as the critical behaviour that can give an organisation its competitive advantage, as discussed later in this chapter.

Although this approach has a strong intuitive appeal, it has been criticised on a number of grounds, not least for its approach that there is 'one best way' of managing people, and for its failure to acknowledge the importance of contexts at the national, sectoral and organisational level (Boxall and Purcell, 2011). Why, for example, would it be appropriate for a large global restaurant chain operating in a highly competitive market on the basis of cost to adopt the same HR practices as a small UK-based knowledge-intensive firm? Differences in national culture, institutional frameworks, sector, the cost of labour, the organisation's competitive position and its size are all ignored. Performance-related pay may work in a Westernised setting but not sit well in other more collectivist cultures (Trompenaars and Hampden-Turner, 1997). Research also shows that different groups can be managed in significantly different ways (Lepak and Snell, 1999; Kinnie *et al*, 2005).

There is also a lack of consensus over what the HR practices actually are, and the importance of certain practices. Pfeffer's work, for example, attaches high importance to job security, which is not included on the list of many others. The role of employee voice and performance-related pay is also hotly contested. There are also debates about whether you need all the practices or just a core, and whether they should be applied to all employees or just to those with key skills, as proposed in Lepak and Snell's (1999) HR architecture model. The idea that HPWSs can benefit employees has also been challenged, involving claims that it can lead to work intensification, stress and more insidious forms of control (eg White *et al*, 2003; Ramsey *et al*, 2000; Marchington and Grugulis, 2000). Some forms of teamwork, for example, undermine, rather than enhance, autonomy.

The research also has a number of methodological shortcomings. It has been dominated by organisation-based surveys looking at the impact of HR policies on organisational outcomes (such as turnover, productivity and financial measures), and gathering data from single respondents (normally the HR manager) who are expected to represent the whole of the firm. Crucially, this ignores the impact on employees (those at the receiving end of the HR practices) and only captures the practices as intended rather than those experienced by employees (Purcell, 1999; Guest, 1999). The research also fails to adequately address the issue of causality (do high-commitment HR practices lead to improved organisational performance, or is it that high-performing organisations can afford to invest in high-commitment HRM?), which can only be analysed in longitudinal research (Purcell, 1999).

CRITICAL REFLECTION 1.1

Marchington and Grugulis's critique of best practice asserts that the practices are far less 'best' than might be hoped. Focusing on the seven practices in Pfeffer's (1998a) model, they argue that certain HR practices – such as self-managed teams and teamworking, which 'conveys images of working together, equality and management by peers, utilising expertise to the full and being able to make more contributions' (2000: 1109) – may not actually offer such universal benefits but increase management control and stress, and not increase involvement. Boxall and Macky (2009: 17) raise concerns about the interaction between involvement and work intensification, stating that 'it would be extremely unwise for anyone to argue that any particular practice, such as teamwork, automatically enhances employee autonomy and leads on to positive levels of trust, satisfaction and commitment'.

1   Are there any other 'best' HR practices which might also be criticised for having a negative impact on employees?

BEST FIT

Derived from the contingent view, the 'best fit' approach argues that the effectiveness of HR practices depends on how closely they are aligned to the internal and external environment of the organisation (Boxall and Purcell, 2011). In contrast to the best practice approach, it does not accept that there is one best way of managing people but avers that account must be taken of factors such as the organisation's strategy, location, sector, size and the nature of work. As with best practice, however, there are variations in the theory. For example, some believe that HR practices must fit the life-cycle of the organisation (eg Baird and Meshoulam, 1988; Kochan and Barocci, 1985), others the competitive strategy (eg Miles and Snow, 1984).

Figure 1.1 Linking HR practices to competitive strategy

Source: adapted from Schuler and Jackson (1987, as cited in Boxall and Purcell, 2011)

Schuler and Jackson (1987) have developed the approach to show how different kinds of role behaviours are needed for different competitive strategies (see Figure 1.1). Based on the three strategic options outlined by Porter (1985) of cost leadership, quality enhancement and innovation, they identify the types of HR practices which are necessary to achieve the desired behaviours linked to the firm's strategy. For instance, a strategy of innovation will require behaviours focused on risk-taking, creativity and co-operation. Appropriate HR techniques would include selecting highly skilled staff, appraisals based on individual and team performance, a high level of discretion and broad career paths. On the other hand, a strategy based on cost reduction will require predictable behaviours, a short-term focus and concern for quantity rather than quality. HR policies and practices focused on a concern for results, flexible working (eg the high use of contingent labour), low investment in training, and tightly defined jobs would be more appropriate.

Critics of this approach point to the fact that organisations may pursue a mix of competitive strategies (leading to confusion over which is the most appropriate combination of HR practices), that not all firms have a clearly identifiable strategy (Purcell, 1999), and that the approach is not sufficiently flexible for the increasingly volatile environment that organisations have to operate in. Despite the logic of the contingent approach, there is little empirical evidence to support the idea that matching HR practices to strategy leads to positive outcomes (in Truss *et al*, 2012), and all the empirical evidence favours a universality model (Combs *et al*, 2006). The research is also subject to many of the methodological shortcomings identified with the best practice research.

THE RESOURCE-BASED VIEW

A rather different approach to conceptualising the theory about how HR practices impact on organisational performance is based on Barney's (1991) resource-based view (RBV) of the firm, which has been developed and applied to HRM by such authors as Wright *et al* (1994), Lepak and Snell (1999) and others. The RBV takes an 'inside-out' approach, focusing on the internal organisation resource, in contrast to the 'outside-in' approach of best fit (Paauwe and Boselie, 2003). The basic argument, as explained by Truss *et al* (2012: 107), is that 'HRM impacts on performance because a firm's HR meet the RBV criteria for a "resource", and therefore the role of SHRM is to deploy those resources effectively in such a way that sustained competitive advantage accrues to the firm.' HR can contribute to sustained competitive advantage by meeting the following RBV criteria for resources:

- **value** – the resource must be capable of adding value to the firm. For instance, employees with high levels of skills are shown to be those that bring the most value to the firm (Wright *et al*, 1994).
- **rarity** – the resources and capabilities of the firm should be different from those of its competitors. Highly skilled people are rare.
- **imitability** – the resources must be very difficult to copy. Even if people have the same skills across organisations, there will be differences in the way people deploy their skills and are managed.
- **substitutability** – the resources must not be easily substitutable by other factors.

The practical application of the RBV rests on defining and developing core competences. This is discussed further in Chapter 7. It also emphasises the importance of culture and values, which is explored in Chapter 2. However, there are a number of serious shortcomings with the RBV, including its status as a theory (it does not really explain how organisations work or predict which will do better than others over time), its failure to take account of the external environment, and its applicability to all kinds of organisations (Paauwe and Boselie, 2003). Critics have also noted the absence of empirical studies that test out the theory and its lack of detail for practitioners. More recently, other approaches have been 'grafted' on to the RBV (Truss *et al*, 2012: 116), including the institutional perspective (Paauwe, 2004), which takes account of the fact that organisations are part of a wider social and institutional environment.

A MODEL OF THE HR CAUSAL CHAIN

One of the critical limitations of all this research is that it fails to explain the relationship between HR practices and individual and organisational performance. As Purcell and Kinnie note (2007: 539), this is the problem of theory – we do not know how and why a mix of HR policies and practices influences performance. How and why, for instance, do job design, enhanced selection, training, participation and performance appraisal linked to compensation positively relate to labour productivity, corporate financial performance and lower employee turnover? As Huselid claims (1995: 667):

> The magnitude of the returns on high performance work practices is substantial. A 1 per cent standard deviation increase in such practices is associated with a 7.05 per cent decrease in labour turnover and, on a per employee basis, US $27,044 more in sales and $18,641 and $3,814 more in market value and profits respectively.

For obvious reasons this has been referred to as 'the black box' problem (Purcell *et al*, 2003; Wright and Gardner, 2004).

Looking inside the black box requires specifying the HR causal chain (Purcell and Kinnie, 2007), and in recent years a number of theories have been put forward to explain the process by which HRM impacts on performance (eg Becker *et al*, 1997; Guest, 1997; Appelbaum *et al*, 2000; Bowen and Ostroff, 2004; Wright and Nishii, 2004; Boxall and Macky, 2009; Nishii *et al*, 2008; Paauwe and Richardson, 1997). These look beyond the mere presence of HRM, and focus on the effectiveness of HR practices by considering the impact on employee attitudes and behaviours.

One of the principal models which explain these links is that developed by Wright and Nishii (2004). Their HR causal chain has five critical steps, moving from (1) intended HR practices, leading to (2) actual practices, leading to (3) perceived practices, leading to (4) employee reactions, and finally to (5) performance outcomes. Wright and Nishii's model has been developed further by Purcell and colleagues (Purcell and Kinnie, 2007; Purcell and Hutchinson, 2007a) to subdivide employee reactions into employee attitudes and behaviour (see Figure 1.2).

Figure 1.2 The people management–performance causal chain

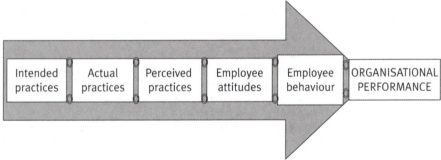

Source: Purcell and Hutchinson (2007a)

The key features of the model are:

- **Intended HR practices** – These are the HR policies and practices designed by the organisation and contained in strategy and policy documents, and concern employees' ability, motivation and opportunity to participate (discussed later in the chapter). They are influenced by the nature of the business, the organisation's strategy and values, and its work structures. Den Hartog *et al* (2004) refer to HRM practices as 'signals' of the organisation's intentions towards its employees, which are interpreted as such by employees.
- **Actual HR practices** – These are the practices which are actually applied or implemented in the workplace, more often than not by line managers (discussed in

more detail below). Research suggests that there is frequently a gap between intended and implemented HR practices, and that when intended and implemented practices are congruent, employee satisfaction and organisational performance is higher (Khilji and Wang, 2006). This gap can be minimised by addressing the role and effectiveness of line managers in delivering HRM (Truss, 2001; Hutchinson and Purcell, 2003; Khilji and Wang, 2006).

- **Perceived HR practice**s – How employees perceive HR practices will be judged through the lens of fairness, organisational justice and the psychological contract. Individual perceptions of HR practices will vary according to the organisational climate, individuals' expectations and evaluations of their employer, their beliefs, and previous and current job experiences (eg effort, autonomy, stress) (Bowen and Ostroff, 2004; Den Hartog *et al*, 2004). Positive perceptions of HR practices are thought to directly influence attitudes and employee behavioural outcomes, and is suggested by social exchange theory (Blau, 1967). This posits that there is a 'norm of reciprocity' – in other words, if people are treated well by a person or entity, they will feel a sense of obligation to reciprocate. In the HRM context, this means that perceived investments in HR practices can give employees a feeling that the organisation values their contributions and cares for their wellbeing, which will elicit positive employee attitudes and behaviour. So if people have very positive perceptions about their training or career opportunities, it can be expected to affect their job satisfaction and commitment to the organisation. In Khilji and Wang's analysis HR satisfaction emerges as a powerful indicator of organisational performance, leading them to assert (2006: 1185) that 'it is employee satisfaction with HRM, not the mimicry of HR practices, which translates into improved organisational performance'. More recently, Nishii *et al* (2008) have used attribution theory to explore the way in which workers interpret HR practices and show how these interpretations can shape employee responses (see *Attribution theory* box below).

- **Attitudinal outcomes** – These include job satisfaction, involvement, morale, and commitment. In theory, we would expect highly committed and satisfied employees to be more productive and flexible than those with low commitment and dissatisfaction. Boxall and Macky (2009) suggest including other attitudes such as motivation and trust (in management and in peers) and argue that different HR practices may influence different attitudes. Atkinson and Hall (2011) make the case for including 'happiness' as an important attitude, returning to the rather neglected 'happy/productive worker' thesis (Wright, 2006), which makes the case for linking happiness with wellbeing and job performance (discussed later in this chapter).

- **Behavioural outcomes** – Performance-related behaviours are assumed to flow from attitudes. This includes discretionary behaviour, organisational citizenship behaviours and 'engagement', which has recently been used by some as an indicator of positive behaviour. Dysfunctional work behaviours could also be included here, such as counterproductive work behaviour (ie behaviour which harms employees, such as bullying or discrimination, or the organisation, such as sabotage) and withdrawal work behaviour, such as absence, lateness and turnover (Fuchs, 2010). These types of behaviours are discussed further in Chapters 5 and 9.

- **Performance outcomes** – These are seen in a raft of measures such as profit, market value, market share, sales, service quality, financial performance and customer satisfaction, sometimes referred to as distal outcomes (Paauwe and Richardson, 1997; Guest, 1997). Also relevant here are critical HR goals such as productivity, legitimacy and flexibility (Boxall and Purcell, 2011). Guest (1997) and others make a case for using proximal outcomes of performance in studying HRM, which includes HR goals, since these are directly or almost directly affected by HR practices. Distal outcomes will be influenced by other factors outside HRM. This debate is returned to later in the chapter.

REFLECTIVE ACTIVITY 1.1

Critical HR goals

Boxall and Purcell (2008, 2011) identify a number of critical HR goals, covering economic and socio-political goals. They include:

- cost effective labour
- organisational flexibility
- social legitimacy and employment citizenship.

The latter concerns the legitimacy of the organisation to the outside environment (eg society, consumers, trade unions, government) but also to its employees. Nike's use of child

labour some years ago directly affected its social legitimacy, impacting negatively on its corporate image, with potentially damaging consequences for consumer behaviour.

1   What other HR activities might impact on each of these three goals?

2   Discuss the potential tension between these three goals in organisations. How can they be reconciled?

3   Can you think of any other critical HR goals that might be included?

Attribution theory

Nishii *et al* (2008) use attribution theory to explore the 'why' of HR practices, arguing that the attribution employees make has an impact on their attitudes and behaviours. 'Attributions' in this context are defined as the 'causal explanations that employees make regarding management's motivation for using particular HR practices' (p507). There are five possible attributions: compliance with the union, employee wellbeing, exploiting employees, a focus on quality of service, and a focus on cost reduction.

Based on a survey of departmental managers and employees in a large supermarket chain, the researchers found that the attribution that HR practices are motivated by the organisation's concern for enhancing service quality and employee wellbeing was positively associated with employee attitudes. However, the attributions that centred on reducing costs and exploiting employees were negatively associated with attitudes, and the attribution associated with union compliance was not significantly associated with attitudes either way. Also of significance was the finding that the same set of HR practices may not exhibit the same response within the same organisation.

On a practical level the study suggests that organisations should assess HR attributions if they want to know why their HR policies have or have not achieved the organisational goals intended.

(Source: Nishii, Lepak and Schneider, 2008)

In sum, this model makes significant contributions to our understanding of the link between HRM and performance. It suggests that the effect of HR policies and practices on performance is not automatic and is not always as intended. Instead, the effect depends on the effectiveness of HR practices and their implementation. The model also emphasises the important role of employee attitudes and behaviours.

Researchers are now starting to pay attention to these issues. In a recent study of senior and HR managers, Guest and Conway (2011) found that when the presence of HR practices was compared with their effectiveness, it was the effectiveness which had the stronger impact on most outcomes (eg labour productivity, financial performance, quality of products/services) – ie effectiveness is more important than the presence of practices in determining outcomes. Research for the CIPD by Purcell and colleagues (Purcell *et al*,

2003), which sought to 'unlock the black box', broke new ground by focusing attention on the employee in explaining the HR–performance link. One of their findings was that differences between the intended HR policies and the practices that are delivered by management can have potentially damaging consequences for employee attitudes and behaviour, and ultimately for organisational performance.

The rest of this chapter considers some elements of this chain of events, beginning with the AMO framework, which provides a useful starting point from which to explain how HR practices might impact on performance. The role of line managers, the psychological contract and then some potentially influential attitudes and behaviours are discussed.

THE AMO THEORY OF PERFORMANCE

The ability, motivation and opportunity (AMO) model, initially proposed by Bailey (1993) and developed by Appelbaum *et al* (2000), has become a commonly accepted framework to explain how HR policies might work and impact on performance, and is helpful in deciding which HR policies should be developed and implemented. According to Macky and Boxall (2007), most of the studies on high-performance working practices use the AMO framework either explicitly or implicitly (for example, Huselid, 1995; Appelbaum *et al*, 2000; MacDuffie, 1995; Purcell *et al*, 2003). The model proposes that HR practices contribute to improved employee performance by developing employees' abilities (A) and skills to do their job, improving an employee's motivation (M) for discretionary effort, and providing employees with the opportunity (O) to make full use of their skills and be motivated.

Examples of how HR practices can achieve this are:

- **A (ability)** can be influenced by recruitment and selection to ensure that capable employees are recruited in the first instance, and by training, learning and development. Competency frameworks are a useful tool to express and assess abilities and skills (discussed further in Chapter 7).
- **M (motivation)** is influenced by extrinsic (eg financial) and intrinsic rewards (eg interesting work), performance reviews, feedback, career development, employment security and work–life balance. Motivation is explored in Chapter 3.
- **O (opportunity)** is influenced by involvement initiatives, teamworking, autonomy, communication, job design and job rotation. Many researchers claim that this is the distinctive feature that marks high-performance working practices out from other HR practices (Appelbaum *et al*, 2000; Wood and Wall, 2007; Boxall and Macky, 2009).

 REFLECTIVE ACTIVITY 1.2

Thinking about your own work experiences, what HR policies do you think would influence AMO?

In Appelbaum *et al*'s model of performance, HR practices contribute to improved employee performance by encouraging employees to exhibit positive discretionary behaviours (Figure 1.3). Purcell *et al*'s work took a similar approach, developing it further in their study for the CIPD (Purcell *et al*, 2003). 'Discretionary behaviours' refers to the degree of choice people have over how they perform their job, and recognises that employees can contribute more to the organisation than simply enough to get the job done (see *What is discretionary behaviour?* box below). It is closely related to organisational citizenship behaviours discussed in more detail later in this chapter.

Figure 1.3 The AMO model of performance

Source: adapted from Appelbaum *et al* (2000)

What is discretionary behaviour?

Discretionary behaviour refers to the degree of choice people have over how they perform their tasks and responsibilities (Purcell *et al*, 2003). Significantly, it is something that is undertaken voluntarily and cannot be forced. Interest in discretionary behaviour is not new and can be traced back to the work of Fox (1974), who argued that 'every job contains both prescribed and discretionary elements'. Positive discretionary behaviours are associated with working beyond the basic requirements of the job and 'going the extra mile' for the organisation. Examples include taking on additional tasks, covering for an absent colleague, helping new employees learn the job, mentoring, being polite to a customer. These behaviours are particularly important in service industries such as banking, retail, and the hotel industry where relationships between the customer and employees make a vital difference to service quality. It is this which can give an organisation a distinct competitive advantage. This view contrasts with traditional Taylorist systems of management (see Chapter 3) which give emphasis to limiting discretion through tightly prescribed jobs and tasks, and close supervision.

(Source: adapted from Purcell *et al*, 2003)

Implicit in the AMO model is an assumption that managing employees at the individual level brings together a range of HRM policies and practices which are interrelated, are mutually supportive, and can be bundled, similar to the best practice model. If any of the key components (A, M, and O) are missing, discretionary effort is unlikely to be forthcoming. For example, an employee may have the ability, skills and the motivation to perform well, but if not empowered to make decisions, if restricted by the job description, or if not given the right information, performance is likely to be inhibited.

Exactly what these HR policies are will vary from sector to sector and organisation to organisation. Appelbaum *et al*'s research, for example, found that the HR practices associated with AMO had different effects in different industries. In the clothing industry, for instance, they found that self-directed teams were highly influential (raising sewing time by 94 per cent and leading to considerable cost savings); in medical equipment the opportunity to participate was closely associated with profits, value added and quality. Michael West's study (West *et al*, 2002) illustrates how AMO can work in practice in the health sector (see the case study *A matter of life and death* below).

It should be noted, however, that other factors in addition to HRM affect the AMO components (Boxall and Purcell, 2011), as discussed later in this chapter.

 A MATTER OF LIFE AND DEATH

CASE STUDY 1.1

In a study of 61 hospitals in England, Michael West and colleagues (West *et al*, 2002) found strong associations between HR practices and patient mortality. Chief executive and HR directors completed a questionnaire asking them about their hospital characteristics, HRM strategy, employee involvement strategy and practices, and other HR policies and practices covering the main occupational groups, such as doctors, nurses and midwives, professions allied to medicine, ancillary staff, professional and technical staff, administrative and clerical, and managers. Data was also collected on the number of deaths following emergency and non-emergency surgery, admission for hip fractures, admission for heart attacks, and re-admission rates. Care was taken not to bias the data and account was taken of the size and wealth of each hospital and of local health needs.

Their analysis found a strong link between HRM practices overall and patient mortality. Three practices in particular appeared to be significant:

- appraisal – this had the strongest relationship with patient mortality. In other words, if satisfaction with appraisal improves, patient mortality falls
- training policies that are well developed
- the extent of teamworking.

The relationship was even stronger where the HR director was a full voting member of the hospital board.

One of their conclusions was that 'If you have HR practices that focus effort and skill, that develop people's skills, and that encourage co-operation, collaboration, innovation and synergy for most if not all employees, the whole system functions and performs better.'

Source: West, 2002

A similar model to AMO is the PIRK rubric (power, information, knowledge, reward) (Vandenberg *et al*, 1999) which can be mapped onto AMO – power being similar to opportunity, information and knowledge to ability, and reward to motivation (Cox *et al*, 2011). Like the AMO components, the four dimensions are mutually reinforcing. However, the causal chain is slightly different. Rather than explaining improved performance through increased discretionary effort, the model suggests a 'direct' route whereby HR processes directly improve performance by allowing employees to do their job better, and an 'indirect' path by which HR processes increase job satisfaction, commitment and lower quit rates (Boxall and Purcell, 2011).

It is, however, the AMO framework that is referred to regularly throughout this book because it is more commonly used in the HRM–performance literature.

THE ROLE OF LINE MANAGERS

Over the last few decades line managers have been expected to take on greater responsibility for HRM, and in most organisations it is the line manager, not HR specialists, who implement HRM (Larsen and Brewster, 2003; Hutchinson and Wood, 1995; Hutchinson and Purcell, 2007; Perry and Kulik, 2008; IRS, 2008). Recent studies show how the behaviour of line managers mediates the effect of HR practices on attitudes and behaviour (Purcell *et al*, 2003; Purcell and Hutchinson, 2007; Truss, 2001). For example, Purcell and colleagues show that the way line managers implement and enact HRM, or 'bring policies to life' and show leadership, strongly influences employees' attitudes. In analysing the role of front-line managers (FLMs) – those at the lower levels of the management hierarchy – they find (Hutchinson and Purcell, 2003: 14) that:

> The higher employees rate FLMs in terms of the way they manage people, the more committed and satisfied those employees will be, and the higher their levels of (self-reported) job discretion.

In a subsequent paper they go further and argue (Purcell and Hutchinson, 2007a: 4) that:

> Poorly designed or inadequate policies can be 'rescued' by good management behaviour in much the same way as 'good' HR practice can be negated by poor front-line management behaviour or weak leadership.

The gap between intended and actual practices can be largely explained by the problems line managers face in implementing HR practices, such as work overload, lack of competence and skill, lack of willingness, and inadequate support (Purcell *et al*, 2008/9; Perry and Kulik, 2008; Maxwell and Watson, 2006; Nehles *et al*, 2006). Table 1.1, adapted from the ACAS guide for FLMs, illustrates how the difference between theory and practice may manifest itself in the workplace.

Research on leader–member exchange, perceived supervisory and organisational support, the psychological contract and interactional and procedural justice also highlights the importance of manager–employee relationships and role of the line managers in implementing HRM (eg Uhl-Bien *et al*, 2000; Rhoades and Eisenberger, 2002; Guest and Conway, 2002). Chapter 4 specifically explores the critical role of line managers in performance management, the barriers they face, and the supportive conditions necessary for effective line management behaviours in performance management.

Table 1.1 ACAS: the theory and the practice

The theory	The practice
Your policy is that FLMs should meet quarterly	Do your FLMs: ● meet only when there is a problem? ● have an ongoing dialogue with their staff that negates the need for formal meetings? ● meet their staff quarterly to discuss performance – but only for five minutes?

The theory	The practice
Your attendance policy is that FLMs have 'return-to-work discussions' with all absent employees on the day they return	Do your FLMs: • hold return-to-work meetings only if they don't know why an individual is absent? • hold return-to-work meetings only if they feel the employee will be comfortable talking about personal issues? • insist that the employee give a full account of their absence no matter what the reason?
Your policy on communication and consultation is that FLMs should talk to their staff about all changes to the way their teams are run	Do your FLMs: • give staff a chance to express their views before a decision is made? • present changes as a *fait accompli* but offer to be sympathetic about their concerns? • discuss changes with one or two people in the team and hope they'll tell their colleagues?

Source: ACAS (2009a)

THE PSYCHOLOGICAL CONTRACT

The concept of the psychological contract is particularly helpful to our understanding of how employees perceive HR practices and of their reactions in terms of attitudinal and behavioural outcomes. The idea of the psychological contract (PC) was first discussed in the 1960s (Argyris, 1960), but reconceptualised in the 1990s when it re-emerged as a popular concept in HRM following the work of Rousseau (1995). This has resulted in two different interpretations of the concept. The first is based on the work of Argyris (1960) and Schein (1978: 48), who define it as

> a set of unwritten reciprocal expectations between an individual employee and the organisation.

The second is based on the work of Rousseau who takes a different perspective and views it from the employee perspective, defining it (Rousseau, 1995: 6) as:

> individual beliefs, shaped by the organisation, regarding terms of an exchange between individuals and their organisation.

Rousseau therefore positions it as subjective, individual and 'in the eye of the beholder'. Rousseau further distinguished between transactional contracts and relational contracts. The former are based primarily on economic incentives such as pay, and focus on short-term exchanges, whereas relational contracts are less tangible and focus on broad, open-ended exchanges (eg loyalty in return for job security) and are longer-term. It is relational contracts that are often considered more important since they can signify increased commitment and strong identification with the organisation and its goals (Tietze and Nadin, 2011). Rousseau suggested that HR practices send out strong messages to individuals regarding what the organisation expects of them and what they can expect in return (for example, during the recruitment process or in performance appraisals), and it is this perspective which is particularly useful in explaining the HR causal chain.

An important point about the psychological contract is that it is based on expectations believed by the employee to be part of the relationship with the employer and can be inferred from action in the past as well as statements and promises made by employers (Conway and Briner, 2004). Promises can be explicit and implicit, written and unwritten. Some examples of mutual promises are given Table 1.2.

Table 1.2 Implicit and explicit promises

Employees might promise to:	Employers might promise to:
<ul><li>work hard</li><li>show loyalty to the company</li><li>act as 'ambassadors' for the organisation and uphold its reputation</li><li>maintain good attendance and punctuality</li><li>put in extra effort when necessary</li><li>be flexible with regard to tasks, duties and hours when required</li><li>learn new skills and update existing ones</li><li>be courteous to customers and colleagues</li><li>be honest</li><li>make suggestions for improvement</li></ul>	<ul><li>deliver pay commensurate with performance</li><li>offer an attractive benefits package</li><li>provide training and development opportunities</li><li>provide opportunities for promotion</li><li>give recognition</li><li>provide reasonable job security</li><li>provide interesting work</li><li>provide a safe place to work</li><li>give feedback on performance</li></ul>

Source: Conway and Briner (2004)

In their work for the CIPD, Guest and Conway (2002) propose a causal relationship between HR practices, the psychological contact, employee attitudes and behavioural outcomes. These outcomes are also influenced by contextual factors such as individual and organisational characteristics, and policies concerning organisational support, control and change (Figure 1.4). They refer to the 'state' of the psychological contract, which is viewed through the lens of fairness, trust and 'delivery of the deal'. When the contract is positive (ie expectations are met and promises fulfilled), increased employee commitment, satisfaction and motivation will result and have a positive impact on behaviour and business performance. However, if the psychological contract is breached or violated, employee commitment and motivation will be undermined, resulting in negative work behaviours such as reduced discretionary effort, absence or resignation. Conway and Briner's research found that broken and exceeded promises occurred regularly at work (69 per cent of participants reported at least one broken promise over the period of analysis) and in relation to many aspects of work. Line managers were the main agents for this.

Figure 1.4 The psychological contract model

Background factors	Policy influences	The state of the psychological contract	The outcomes
Individual • age • gender • education • union membership • level in organisation • type of work • hours worked • employment contract • marital status • number of children • ethnicity • tenure • income • whether disabled *Organisational* • sector • organisation size • establishment size • location	• HR policy and practice • direct participation • job alternatives • organisational support • working centrally • surveillance • organisational charge • suitably qualified • promise made	• fairness • trust • delivery of the deal	*Attitudinal consequences* • organisational commitment • life satisfaction • work satisfaction • work–life balance • satisfaction • job security • motivation • stress *Behavioural consequences* • intention to stay/quit • knowledge-sharing

Source: adapted from Guest and Conway (2002)

The psychological contract is therefore a key link in the HR causal chain because it focuses on employees' perceptions of HR practices which impact on employee attitudes and behaviour (Guest, 2007). Performance management practices which communicate the terms of the psychological contract include induction, performance appraisals, training and development, and performance-related pay. These topics are addressed in detail in subsequent chapters.

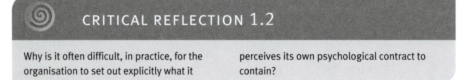

CRITICAL REFLECTION 1.2

Why is it often difficult, in practice, for the organisation to set out explicitly what it perceives its own psychological contract to contain?

EMPLOYEE ATTITUDES

The assumption made in the model is that attitudes influence behaviours, and that attitudes can be changed. The popularity of attitude surveys suggests practitioners also hold this belief. However, the extent to which attitudes predict behaviour is not as obvious as the model assumes, and the relationship is far more complex than that. In this section two of the more traditional key attitudes are considered: job satisfaction, and organisational commitment. Motivation – which can be described as both an attitude and a behaviour – is explored in a separate chapter.

JOB SATISFACTION

Job satisfaction has been described as a 'pleasurable or positive emotional state resulting from the appraisal of one's job or job experiences' (Locke, 1976: 1304). 'Satisfaction' can refer to a variety of aspects of the job – the extrinsic (eg pay, career opportunities, working conditions) and the intrinsic (eg the job itself, responsibility) – and is often used as one indicator of employee wellbeing. The 1998 UK Workplace Employee Relations Survey (WERS) used a combination of key intrinsic and extrinsic aspects of the job to record job satisfaction, including satisfaction with the amount of influence, the sense of achievement in the job, the level of pay and the respect received from management. In 'searching for the happy workplace', Riccardo Peccei (2004) combined these measures with perceptions of job stress to measure wellbeing or happiness (high job satisfaction, low levels of stress).

It is generally assumed that satisfied employees are productive employees ('a happy worker is a productive worker'), and that job satisfaction is a predictor of job performance – ie that people perform better when they are more satisfied with their job. However, there is no strong compelling evidence that this is the case, and it is possible to find dissatisfied employees who are very productive and satisfied employees who are not particularly productive. It could also be that people are more satisfied with their job because they work harder or are more successful at it. On balance, however, the research suggests a positive, but moderate, relationship between job satisfaction and job performance, and that this is stronger for professional jobs (Judge *et al*, 2001). There is also evidence that job satisfaction is negatively correlated with voluntary turnover (eg Harter *et al*, 2002), and that job dissatisfaction is an antecedent of an intention to quit (Griffeth *et al*, 2000). Nevertheless, the extent to which job satisfaction affects performance remains unclear, partly because a multitude of factors can influence a person's job, such as personality, education, ability and organisational factors (leadership style, work relationships, organisational change, and HR policies and practices).

CRITICAL REFLECTION 1.3

Can an unhappy worker display positive discretionary behaviour ?

COMMITMENT

Organisational commitment is associated with the relative strength of an employee's identification with, and involvement in, an organisation (Mowday *et al*, 1979) and generally considered to be something that employers want from their employees, and at the heart of models of HRM (eg Guest, 1997; Storey, 2007). Commitment, however, is complex and multifaceted. Three forms of commitment have been identified (Meyer and Allen, 1991):

- **Affective commitment** relates to an individual's emotional attachment to the organisation such that people continue employment because they want to. It is this type of commitment to which people are normally referring when they talk of 'organisational commitment'.
- **Continuance commitment** is more calculating and is about a person's perception of the costs and risks associated with leaving the employer. Employees who remain in the

organisation because they need to (eg because they cannot find a job elsewhere) display continuance commitment.

- **Normative commitment** reflects an individual's feeling of obligation to the organisation as his or her employer – that is, they remain in the organisation because they feel they ought to. This may be because of attachment to work colleagues, to the line manager, or to customers.

Such distinctions are important because research suggests that a positive commitment–performance link is most likely to stem from affective commitment, as opposed to normative or continuance commitment. Affective commitment has been found to be associated with higher productivity, organisational citizenship behaviours (OCBs), an intention to stay, attendance and better health, but also stress (Meyer *et al*, 1989; Meyer *et al*, 2002). Employees who show this form of commitment are likely to engage in less counterproductive behaviour than those who are less committed (Wright *et al*, 2003). This is discussed further in Chapter 9.

The other two forms of commitment tend to be associated with negative outcomes. For example, continuance commitment has been negatively associated with organisational citizenship behaviour (Shore and Wayne, 1993) and job satisfaction (Hackett *et al*, 1994). This seems to make sense. High continuance commitment based on a perception of lack of employment opportunities elsewhere may simply be because people are not good at their job. Continuance commitment may also be a reflection of particularly high pay or good benefits, known as 'golden chains'. If an employee becomes dissatisfied with his or her work or simply wants to move on and do something else, the 'chains of gold' may become a source of frustration and demotivation as the individual is faced with having to choose between either moving on or staying just for the super benefit. Normative commitment arises out a sense of moral obligation to continue in a job, not because of any sense of motivation, and may also result in negative outcomes.

The notion of commitment is further complicated by the fact that employees can feel multiple commitments at work. A nurse, for instance, can feel commitment to the organisation, the profession, the team/department and the patient. Becker *et al* (1996) found that commitment to the supervisor is more highly correlated to job performance than is organisational commitment.

Despite the assumed importance of commitment in the HRM literature, the links between attitudes to HR practices and commitment are a surprisingly under-researched area (Conway and Monks, 2009; Edwards and Wright, 2001). Among those who have studied this are Purcell *et al* (2003), who found that employee satisfaction with certain HR practices – such as reward and recognition, communication and work–life balance – were consistently linked to organisational commitment. However, they also found that other practices might be tailored to the particular needs of certain job categories (employees, managers and professions) (Kinnie *et al*, 2005). For instance, employee satisfaction with career opportunities was only important for commitment of managers, and satisfaction with performance appraisal was only linked to the commitment of professionals. This is relevant to the debate on the HR architecture model developed by Lepak and Snell (1999).

A few other studies have examined the impact of employee attitudes towards HR practices on the different types of commitment. Conway and Monks' (2009) study shows that attitudes towards particular HR practices positively influence affective commitment, but there was no clear evdience that this was the case for continuance and normative commitment. Pay has been positively associated with continuance commitment (Iverson and Buttigieg, 1999), attitudes towards career management have been related to affective and normative commitment (Iverson and Buttigieg, 1999; Taormina, 1999), and attitudes towards transferable skills and promotion prospects have been shown to be negatively associated with continuance commitment (Meyer *et al*, 1989; Allen and Meyer, 1990). There is also evidence that affective commitment is influenced by strategies aimed towards corporate social responsibility (or CSR), such as the ethical treatment of employees (Brammer *et al*, 2007).

CRITICAL REFLECTION 1.4

Can commitment be managed?

Commitment is affected by other factors in addition to HR policies – such as personality, job role experiences, work experiences and structural factors (Legge, 2005). This has led writers such as Conway and Monks (2009) to ask if commitment can be managed. Some of the arguments cited by Conway and Monks are that employees may not be ideologically disposed to commitment; that there may be

resistance from unions (for instance, in relation to participation); and that line managers may inhibit commitment because they 'may have their own misguided assumptions about what motivates employees as well as how to manage them' (Iverson and Buttigieg, 1999).

1   Do you agree with this view?

2   What are the implications for performance management?

EMPLOYEE BEHAVIOURS

ORGANISATIONAL CITIZENSHIP BEHAVIOURS

Organisation citizenship behaviours (OCBs) are closely linked to discretionary behaviour and associated with positive outcomes for organisational performance and efficiency. This concept has grown in popularity in the last few decades because it is considered a good indicator of a person's willingness to perform in the interests of the organisation and may therefore be particularly useful when organisations are under pressure. The presence of OCBs is thought to decrease the need for formal and costly mechanisms of control (in Becton *et al*, 2008). Organ, who has been instrumental in defining and researching OCBs, defines it thus (Organ, 1988: 4):

> behaviour that is discretionary, not directly or explicitly recognised by the formal reward system, and that in aggregate promotes the effective functioning of the organisation… the behaviour is not an enforceable requirement of the role of the job description… the behaviour is a matter of personal choice.

Examples would be helping and co-operating with others, showing consideration, courtesy and tact in relation to others, general support for the organisation, and putting in extra effort despite individual conditions. Commonly used measures of OCBs are (Coyle-Shapiro *et al*, 2004):

- making suggestions to improve work of the department
- always attending monthly team meetings
- keeping up with developments that are happening in the organisation
- participating in activities that help the image of the organisation.

OCBs can be viewed as a form of employee reciprocity whereby employees engage in OCBs to reciprocate perceived fair or good treatment from their employer (Coyle-Shapiro *et al*, 2004). The converse is also true: employees may withhold those behaviours in response to perceived poor treatment. This is relevant when we consider under-performance, discussed in Chapter 9. Accordingly, perceptions of justice are strong predictors of OCB. For example, Coyle-Shapiro *et al* (2004) show that procedural and interactional justice (discussed further in Chapter 3) are positively associated with mutual commitment that in turn is related directly to OCB. Furthermore, mutual commitment also influences OCB indirectly through expanding the boundaries of an individual's job. This is similar to Snape and Redman's (2010) research, which found a positive impact of HRM practices on OCB through an effect on perceived job influence/discretion. Job satisfaction is also linked to OCB (eg Bateman and Organ, 1983), although it has been suggested that this is more a consequence of perceived fairness. The implications for practice are that organisations have to effectively manage the treatment of employees procedurally, pay attention to how well managers interact with employees, and provide employees with some role autonomy. In the performance management context this means, for example, giving employees a chance to voice their views in the performance review, ensuring that judgements on performance are based on meaningful and accurate information, and looking at work design.

ENGAGEMENT

Employee engagement is a relatively new concept which has received increasing attention in recent years as a key determinant of performance (Gruman and Saks, 2011). Much of this seems to have been initiated by consultancy firms who have developed their own research instruments to measure engagement (such as Gallup's Q12) and who make strong claims for its positive outcomes. More recently, the UK government has taken an interest in the concept, commissioning an independent report on the issue. It concluded that a wider take-up of engagement approaches could impact positively on UK competitiveness and performance (MacLeod and Clarke, 2009).

The academic research in this area, however, is thin, although academics are just starting to take an interest in the subject (Truss *et al*, 2012). One of the difficulties is that there are many ways of conceptualising engagement, and little consensus on its definition and measurement. MacLeod and Clarke (2009: 8), for example, found over 50 different definitions of 'engagement', and views differ as to whether it is an attitude, a behaviour, an activity – or all three. In reviewing the definition of 'engagement', Truss *et al* (2012) conclude that it is generally believed that engagement is characterised by positive emotions, intellectual focus and energetic behaviour directed towards task performance. It has also been suggested that positive social connections are a feature of engagement. It is therefore a multidimensional construct which comprises feelings, cognitions and behaviours. In this respect it differs from other constructs such as job satisfaction and commitment.

INDIVIDUAL AND ORGANISATIONAL PERFORMANCE

The proposed HR causal chain model involves individual performance that affects organisational performance, but this impact is mostly assumed rather than tested, and the relationship is complex (Den Hartog *et al*, 2004; DeNisi, 2000). DeNisi makes the point that although performance at a higher level (ie the organisation) is in part due to performance at a lower level (eg an individual, a team), it is much more than that, and changing individual performance may be insufficient to guarantee improved organisational performance. The opposite is also true – in other words, changing variables at the organisation level may constrain individual performance.

The fact is that the HRM causal chain does not take place in a vacuum, and as Bowen and Ostroff (2004) state in setting out their case for strong HR systems, attention must be paid to the context within which HR practices are enacted. The organisation's culture and values, emphasised in the resource-based view of strategy, and the employee relations climate are critical in determining the choice of HR policies, management behaviour and how HR practices are perceived by employees. These issues are discussed further in Chapters 2 and 11. Technology, other work practices and the external environment also affect organisational performance. Individual performance is in addition affected by other factors such as personal characteristics (eg drive and ambition), experiences in previous job roles, organisational tenure, age, work and personal relationships. Thus to understand and change individual and organisational performance one has to understand other organisational contextual factors and individual employee characteristics outside the HR causal chain. This is also why, when studying the impact of HRM outcomes, it makes more sense to measure proximal outcomes which are closely related to HR practices.

Figure 1.5 develops the HR causal chain (see Figure 1.2) to take account of these and other issues discussed in this chapter, plus the potential for reverse causality – ie how high performance or poor performance affects HRM.

Figure 1.5 The people management–performance causal chain, as developed

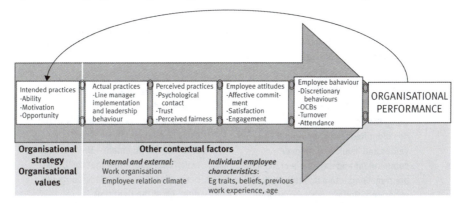

Source: adapted from Purcell and Hutchinson (2007a); Purcell and Kinnie (2007); Boselie (2010)

CASE STUDY 1.2

EMPLOYEE COMMITMENT AND THE IMPORTANCE OF VALUES AT NATIONWIDE BUILDING SOCIETY

Employee commitment is seen as key to success at the Nationwide Building Society, one of the UK's largest financial services organisations, and the world's largest building society. Committed employees are believed to display discretionary effort, are more likely to achieve sales targets, more likely to remain in the organisation, and more likely to want to work in the organisation and gain/retain customer commitment.

The Society has developed a human capital model 'genome', so called because it is likened to the human genome – in other words, our DNA. It seeks to find out what makes

Nationwide employees 'tick' to enable the company to develop employee commitment, or the behaviours which might influence customer commitment and business performance. Employee commitment is measured using the annual employee survey 'Viewpoint', using the following statements:

● 'In my opinion, Nationwide is a good employer'
● 'Nationwide is where I want to work'
● 'I intend to still be working for Nationwide in 12 months'
● 'I am proud to say I work for Nationwide'
● 'I would apply for a job at Nationwide again'

- 'Based upon my experience, I would recommend Nationwide as an employer to my friends.'

Nationwide has a strong set of values which seek to drive employee behaviours and shape the organisation's culture. These values distinguish Nationwide from its competitors, and underpin its commitment to its status as a mutual organisation.

The values are summarised by the 'PRIDE' initiative:

- Putting members first
- Rising to the challenge
- Inspiring confidence
- Delivering best values
- Exceeding expectations.

Using the genome model, Nationwide has identified a link between these core values and levels of employee commitment and engagement, which are translated into a positive customer experience. Individuals whose values set is aligned with the organisation's are more likely to display greater discretionary effort.

Analysing employee commitment

When analysing the results of the genome project, Nationwide divided its workforce into three levels of employee commitment – top, middle and bottom. It found that, when compared with the bottom third, those who are in the 'top' ranking of employee commitment displayed the following characteristics:

- they are less likely to have applied for another job in the previous 12 months
- they put in higher levels of discretionary effort
- they are more likely to be happy with their line manager

- they are more likely to have a positive view of senior management/leadership
- they are more likely to be happy with their training
- they are more likely to be happy with their pay and reward
- they are more likely to be happy with the way their career is progressing.

Drivers of commitment

The model identified five key drivers of employee commitment:

- pay – employees' perceptions about fair pay and the value of the reward package
- length of service – longer-serving staff are more productive and more committed
- coaching – equipping people with the skills to do their job
- resource management – the extent to which employees feel that the right person is in the right place doing the right job at the right time
- values – the belief in the society's values, as encapsulated in its PRIDE programme.

Subsequent research identified a further positive relationship between commitment and corporate social responsibility (Purcell *et al*, 2008/9).

Sources: IDS HR studies 846 and 871; Purcell *et al*, 2008/9

Question

1   Based on your understanding of the HR causal chain and the information given here, what advice would you give to Nationwide to improve organisational performance?

CONCLUSION

This chapter provides the foundation for a book on performance management by exploring the relationship between HR or people management policies and practices and by providing a theoretical framework for managing performance. It began by considering the basic premise that HRM links to organisational performance by critically reviewing some of the research in this area. In doing so it briefly considered the three main models: best practice, best fit and the resource-based view of the firm, concluding that there is a positive relationship although the direction of that relationship remains inconclusive, and it would be reasonable to suppose that the relationship is iterative (Wright *et al*, 2005). Together these models highlight the need to achieve horizontal and vertical fit or integration, and emphasise the importance of organisational culture and values, key themes which are developed in this book. The chapter then moved on to consider more recent research that seeks to 'unlock the black box' and explain how and why HR practices impact on performance. A model of the HR causal chain was presented which has made significant inroads into our thinking about the process by which HRM impacts on performance, and asserts the critical point that it is not just the design of HR policies that is important but the effectiveness of these policies and their implementation. Employees' perceptions of HR policies, and line management behaviour in enacting HRM, are key mediating variables through which HR policies and practices influence performance. At the heart of this model is the AMO theory of performance, which argues that positive discretionary behaviours are the key to driving higher performance, and that it is the role of HRM to influence and develop employees' abilities and skills to do their job, improve motivation for discretionary effort and provide employees with the opportunity to make full use of their skills and be motivated.

Persuasive as this theory might be, however, it has its limitations. For other factors impact on organisational performance which can limit the effect of changes in individual performance (and vice versa). This highlights the importance of context in managing performance – another theme running throughout this book.

EXPLORE FURTHER

Boselie, P., Dietz, G. and Boon, C. (2005) 'Commonalities and contradictions in HRM and performance research', *Human Resource Management Journal*, Vol.15, No.3: 67–94

Boxall, P. and Purcell, J. (2011) *Strategy and Human Resource Management*, 3rd edition. Basingstoke: Palgrave Macmillan

Combs, C., Liu, Y., Hall, A. and Kitchen, D. (2006) 'How much do high-performance work systems matter? A meta-analysis of their effects on organisational performance', *Personnel Psychology*, Vol.59, No.3: 501–28

Conway, E. and Monks, K. (2009) 'Unravelling the complexities of high commitment: an employee-level analysis', *Human Resource Management Journal*, Vol.19, No.2: 140–58

Guest, D. E. (2011) 'Human resource management and performance: still searching for some answers', *Human Resource Management Journal*, Vol.21, No.1: 3–13

Macky, K. and Boxall, P. (2007) 'The relationship between "high-performance work practices" and employee attitudes: an investigation of additive and interaction effects', *International Journal of Human Resource Management*, Vol.18, No.4: 537–67

Purcell, J., Kinnie, N., Hutchinson, S., Rayton, B. and Swart, J. (2003) *Understanding the People and Performance Link: Unlocking the black box*. London: Chartered Institute of Personnel and Development.

CHAPTER 2

Strategic Performance Management

SUE HUTCHINSON

LEARNING OUTCOMES

By the end of this chapter you should be able to:

- identify and explain the different ways in which performance management can be defined and interpreted
- consider developments in performance management
- understand the relationship between performance management and organisational strategy
- critically review the balanced scorecard approach
- review the performance management process
- consider the role of the HR function with respect to performance management.

INTRODUCTION

The term 'performance management' is ambiguous, with many different facets and meanings. To some it is the formal performance appraisal process; to others it is synonymous with performance-related pay or performance measurement. These are all activities associated with managing performance – but it is much more than that. As we saw in the previous chapter, the conceptual foundation of performance management is partly based on the view that performance is a function of ability, motivation and opportunity, and that a range of interrelated HR policies (such as appraisal, training and development, and reward) contribute to this. The contemporary view of performance management is that it must also align processes and policies with organisational strategy and objectives. Positioned as a strategic and integrated management approach makes it more relevant to the business, and organisational performance can be enhanced.

The aim of this chapter is to consider the 'ideal' of performance management as a strategic tool. The chapter begins by examining some of the definitions of performance management, and considers how interpretations and the practice of the concept have changed over time. It then goes on to explore how performance management can be strategic and integrated, and some of the challenges in operationalising this model. One of the key difficulties is how to translate strategy into action, and the **balanced scorecard** is a recent development which helps managers demonstrate the strategic linkages. The chapter takes a critical look at this approach and then moves on to consider how performance management should work at the operational level – in other words, as a process of interlinked HR activities. The potential benefits of performance management as a strategic management tool are summarised, before the chapter concludes with a look at the role of the HR function in strategic performance management.

WHAT IS PERFORMANCE MANAGEMENT?

The use of the term 'performance management' varies enormously, and in the HRM literature a vast array of definitions are offered, ranging from the very simple – 'Performance management is managing the business' (Mohrman and Mohrman, 1995) – to the more sophisticated. For DeNisi (2000), it is a broad range of activities that an organisation engages in to enhance the performance of individuals, with the ultimate aim of improving organisational effectiveness. Others go further describing it as a strategic and integrated process which aligns individual, team and organisational goals. For example, Aguinis (2009):

> a continuous process of identifying, measuring and developing the performance of individuals and teams and aligning performance with the strategic goals of the organisation.

Armstrong and Baron (in CIPD, 2009a) describe performance management as:

> a process which contributes to the effective management of individuals and teams in order to achieve high levels of organisational performance. As such, it establishes shared understanding about what is to be achieved and an approach to leading and developing people which will ensure that it is achieved.

They also add that it is:

> a strategy which relates to every activity of the organisation set in the context of its human resources policies, culture, style and communications systems. The nature of the strategy depends on the organisational context and can vary from organisation to organisation.

Armstrong also emphasises that 'It is owned and driven by line management' (Armstrong, 2009: 9).

Taken together these definitions inform us that, from an HRM perspective, the principal features of performance management are that it should be:

- **strategic** – in other words, it is concerned with achieving the long-term goals of the organisation.
- **integrated** – it should link individual and team/departmental objectives to the organisation's strategy and goals (vertical integration). Integration also requires complementary HR policies and practices to enhance organisational effectiveness, such as induction, development, reward and recognition, performance appraisal, career management, and capability procedures (horizontal integration). The rationale for integrating HR policies and practices, or 'bundling', was described in Chapter 1.
- **shared** – it should develop a shared understanding of corporate goals and values which results not only in improved organisational performance but in enhanced employee motivation, satisfaction and identification with the organisation.
- **a continuous process** which incorporates informal as well as formal activities. It is not a discrete one-off event like the formal performance appraisal.
- **specific** to the organisation, its culture and values, its relationship with employees and the types of jobs that people do (Hendry *et al*, 1997). The implication, therefore, is that performance management must be designed and implemented within the context of the organisation. It must be tailor-made, and cannot be bought 'off the shelf' or borrowed from another organisation.

- **flexible** – the approach to performance management must be flexible and enable organisations to respond to the changing economic and competitive environment.
- **delivered and owned by line managers** who are responsible on a day-to-day basis for such activities as observing and reviewing performance, conducting appraisals, providing feedback, and supporting underperformers (see Chapters 1 and 4). There is a role for HR professionals, as discussed later in the chapter, but it is the line manager who enacts the policy.

Conceptualised in this way, performance management has elements of best fit, best practice and the resource-based view of the firm (Chapter 1). Tailoring performance management to the context of each organisation (internal and external) implies a best fit approach, and allows for flexibility in the system. The need for alignment and internal cohesion of HR practices is similar to the concept of 'bundling' in best practice. The RBV, with its emphasis on the strategic potential of human resource capabilities and the importance of process (eg the role of line managers), is also evident.

To understand more clearly what is meant by performance management today it is helpful to track its history.

DEVELOPMENTS OF PERFORMANCE MANAGEMENT IN THE UK

Performance management has its roots in performance appraisal, which has been around for a very long time. Examples can be traced as far back as the Wei dynasty in China (AD 220–65) to the 'imperial raters' whose task it was to assess the performance of the ruling family (Armstrong and Baron, 2005). In the UK, early developments of monitoring were evident in the textile mills during the Industrial Revolution (Armstrong, 2009; Redman, 2009), and in the USA appraisal has its origins in the formal monitoring systems which evolved out of the work of Taylor in the 1920s (Chapter 3). Subsequent approaches – such as merit rating (which came to the fore in the 1950s and 1960s) and management by objectives (Drucker, 1955), popularised in the 1960s and 1970s (but subsequently discredited) – can still be found in performance management practices today.

It was not until the 1980s, however, that the term 'performance management' emerged as a new management concept in the USA, and by the late 1980s/early 1990s it had entered the vocabulary of human resource management in the UK (Armstrong, 2009). Since that time, interest in the subject has grown, although the emphasis and practice of performance management has changed considerably over the years. Guest and Conway (1998) argue that there has been a marked shift in performance management from a top-down approach, with a focus on content, evaluation by the supervisor, performance-related pay, and ownership by the HR function, to a focus on process, joint evaluation, multi-source feedback, development and ownership by the line manager.

Sparrow (2008) tracks the main developments in practice in UK organisations through a series of stages driven by successive concerns for cost-effectiveness, competence, commitment and coherence, concluding that today 'the field of PMS [performance management systems] in the UK is a mature one' (2008: 143):

- In the 1980s a concern for cost-effectiveness led to the development of top-down-based systems with a focus on narrow performance specifications measured through outputs such as objectives, targets and standards.
- By the early to mid-1990s a more developmental approach had evolved, focused on the enablement of competence and the measurement of behaviours.
- By the late 1990s there was concern about the need to establish mutual employer–employee understanding of, and commitment to, performance. PMS were seen as a means for enabling a more open and honest communication between managers and individuals, developing mutual trust, and a means of engaging the workforce.

- By the early 2000s concern that broader strategic initiatives might be constrained by poorly designed PMS shifted attention to the need to integrate PMS with other HR initiatives such as talent management and total reward management.

A summary of all these developments is shown in Table 2.1. Although there is little research on the impact of the recent economic recession on performance management, it seems reasonable to surmise that there has been a greater focus on managing under-performance.

Table 2.1 The development of performance management in the UK

Before the mid/late 1990s	After the mid/late 1990s
A top-down system	Shared ownership: a joint process of evaluation and dialogue
Attention to the content and system	Attention to the underlying process
No link with organisational goals or strategy	Clearer link with organisational strategy and objectives
Backward-looking	Forward-looking
Focus on objectives and results	Focus on behaviours and competence
Often linked to pay-for-performance	Focus on development
Appraisal by direct supervisor	Multi-source feedback
One-off (annual) event	On-going process
Isolated HR practices	Integrated, mutually-reinforcing HR practices
Owned by HR	Owned by line managers

Source: adapted from Stiles *et al* (1997), Guest and Conway (1998) and Armstrong (2009)

The two approaches shown in Table 2.1 can be seen in the 'hard' and 'soft' approaches to performance management. The hard approach, with its focus on employer interests, is associated with evaluation, measurement and close supervision, and perceived as more judgemental. In contrast, the soft version is focused more on the employee, and emphasises development, motivation and involvement and communication. Of course, these are two extremes, and in practice some organisations try to operate a mixture of both (see Chapter 6).

Performance management is now widely practised in one form or other in most sectors and at many staff levels. It has spread from private to public sector, as exemplified by the explosion of performance indicators, targets and league tables witnessed in the health sector, schools and local and national government (Bach, 2009). Performance management was very much part of new public management reform, and seen as a means of improving the efficiency and effectiveness of services, and demonstrating value for money. At the time of writing, up-to-date information on the up-take of performance management is lacking. The most comprehensive data available is from the 2005 CIPD survey on performance management, which shows that 87 per cent of respondents operated a formal performance management process (37 per cent of which were new systems). More than three-quarters (78.9 per cent) of respondents linked team and organisation objectives, and 71 per cent agreed that the focus of performance management is developmental.

DEVELOPING A STRATEGIC APPROACH TO PERFORMANCE MANAGEMENT

So in its purest and most recent form, performance management is presented as a strategic management tool, integrating individual and group contributions with organisational aims and priorities, and aligning various HRM practices into a coherent and integrated 'bundle'. It is often portrayed as a systematic cascade process linking business and individual objectives, underpinned by a range of performance management practices, as shown in Figure 2.1. Although often depicted as a top-down rational process, the upward arrows highlight the importance of feedback in the process.

Figure 2.1 Strategic performance management

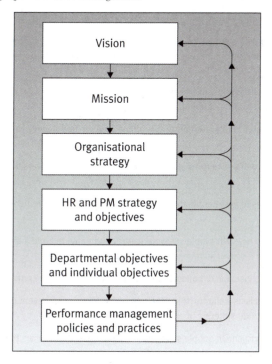

To understand more fully what 'strategic performance management' is and how it works we must be clear what is meant by 'strategy'. There is a vast and confusing array of definitions and interpretations to be found in the literature. To Porter (1985), for example, strategy means finding a competitive advantage, or making a choice over how to compete (see Chapter 1). Others see it as a process or set of actions through which an organisation develops and uses resources (eg Haberberg and Rieple, 2008). Truss *et al* (2012: 45) suggest that:

> Strategy is a plan that integrates an organisation's vision, mission, goals and objectives and determines how resources will be used.

It is this definition which seems most appropriate to our understanding of strategic performance management. The starting point, then, for developing a strategic approach to performance management is the organisation's vision and mission statement, which are useful ways of capturing and communicating what the organisation is about and its future direction. A vision statement is normally a formula of inspirational words about what the organisation will look like in the future, whereas a mission statement focuses on the organisation's present state, although in practice organisations often blend the two (see the *Examples* box below). These statements are said to be most effective when expressed clearly and simply (eg Truss *et al*, 2012). For example, Easyjet's vision 'to be the best low-fare airline in the world' succinctly captures what the business is about. These statements can be underpinned by value statements, which can set overarching principles for the psychological contract (Stiles *et al*, 1997), and can signal which attitudes and behaviours are important for organisational effectiveness, and are particularly important when behavioural change is required (Biron *et al*, 2011).

Examples of mission and value statements

Coca-Cola: Our Mission

Our Roadmap starts with our mission, which is enduring. It declares our purpose as a company and serves as the standard against which we weigh our actions and decisions –

- to refresh the world
- to inspire moments of optimism and happiness
- to create value and make a difference.

Virgin Atlantic's mission is to grow a profitable airline … where people love to fly … and where people love to work.

Google's mission is to organise the world's information and make it universally accessible and useful.

Facebook's mission is to give people the power to share and make the world more open and connected.

Amazon's vision is to be earth's most customer-centric company; to build a place where people can come to find and discover anything they might want to buy online.

Co-operative Group's vision is to build a better society by excelling in everything we do.

The RSPCA's mission is as a charity [that it] will, by all lawful means, prevent cruelty, promote kindness to and alleviate suffering of animals.

The BBC's mission is to enrich people's lives with programmes and services that inform, educate and entertain; its vision is to be the most creative organisation in the world.

Statements on their own, however, are not enough. They have to be well communicated and acted upon, so that employees understand and are committed to what the organisation stands for and are motivated to play their part in achieving it. This emphasises the importance of having a strongly integrated management approach. Purcell and colleagues (2003), in their research on the link between people management and organisational performance, use the concept of the 'Big Idea' – a mission underpinned by strong values and a culture, to illustrate this point.

The Big Idea

The Big Idea was described as 'a clear mission underpinned by values and a culture expressing what the organisation stands for and is trying to achieve'. In Jaguar, for example, the Big Idea is quality; in Nationwide, it is mutuality.

The Big Idea has five distinct elements by which it is described – it is:

- embedded
- connected
- enduring
- collective
- measured and managed.

This means that the values are spread through the organisation so that they are embedded in policies and practices. These values interconnect the relationships with customers (both internal and external), culture and behaviour, and provide the basis upon which employees should be managed (particularly important in customer-facing organisations). The values must also be enduring or long-lasting even during difficult times, and provide a stable basis on which policies can be built and changed. The Big Idea is also a collective endeavour or a sort of glue binding the people and processes together for one common goal. Finally, the Idea can be managed and measured, providing not just the means of measuring performance but also a way of integrating different functional areas of the business, both horizontally and vertically.

(Source: Purcell *et al*, 2003: ix–x)

The organisation's HR and performance management strategy must also support and reinforce the organisation's strategy. For example, to support the idea of quality, Jaguar Car's HR strategy might be expected to focus on recruiting and selecting highly skilled engineers and designers, continuous improvement, teamworking, and training and development. Performance management might be based on a mix of evaluation (based on quality) and development to improve skills. For innovative organisations a performance management strategy with a developmental orientation and focus on involvement and participation would seem to be most appropriate and might include a competence-based approach to performance assessment.

The organisation's strategic objectives and goals have to translate into departmental, team and individual objectives. In this way the performance of employees is aligned with the needs of the business, and employees have a 'line of sight' between what they do and what the organisation seeks to achieve (Lawler, 1986). If an individual can identify and understand the contribution his or her job makes, he or she is more likely to be committed and engage in positive discretionary behaviours (Chapter 1).

Supporting these links is a range of performance management policies which must be mutually supportive and consistent and must fit. The 2009 CIPD survey on performance management lists the following activities under the banner of performance management (the percentages listed represent the proportion of respondents who practised the performance management activity):

- performance appraisal (83 per cent)
- objective- or target-setting (75 per cent)
- regular review meetings to assess progress (63 per cent)
- development opportunities discussions (50 per cent)
- performance-related pay (30 per cent)
- career development meetings (20 per cent)
- 360-degree feedback (19 per cent).

REFLECTIVE ACTIVITY 2.1

Choose one of the organisations in the *Examples* box above, and look at its website.

1   How does the organisation's strategy link to the vision and /or mission of the organisation?

2   What performance management strategy, policies and practices might support the organisation's strategy and vision?

In summary, then, for performance management to be strategic requires integration both vertically and horizontally. Individual and group contributions must be integrated with organisational aims and priorities, and various performance management practices must be aligned into a coherent and integrated 'bundle' to support and reinforce the organisation's strategy.

The BIG Lottery Fund (see Case Study 2.1) is an example of one organisation which appears to have successfully aligned its approach to performance management with its mission and values.

CASE STUDY 2.1

THE GOLDEN THREAD AT THE BIG LOTTERY FUND

Following a merger in 2004, the BIG Lottery Fund (the largest UK lottery distributor) developed a new performance management initiative to help unify the newly merged workforce. The organisation's mission is to 'Bring together improvements to communities and the lives of people most in need', and this is supported by three core values:

- making the best use of lottery money
- using knowledge and evidence
- being supportive and helpful.

These are aligned to the organisation's corporate objectives (to be efficient, effective, customer-focused and well managed), which together feed into the overall mission. This alignment is intended to run all the way through the organisation as a 'golden thread' from business objectives to an individual's objectives.

Underpinning the PM scheme is a competency framework which identifies four key behaviours derived from the organisation's values and intended to align with the organisation's overall corporate strategy. The four behaviours are:

- leadership
- working together
- customer service
- continuous improvement.

These behaviours are broken down into four groups, reflecting the main types of role in the organisation (business delivery, professional, people and process, operational, function, departmental management, strategic and corporate), and supported by a series of behavioural indicators. The competency framework is also used in the recruitment and selection process, to fit roles within a new job family structure and link training course to competencies.

Source: adapted from IDS HR Studies 938 (2011a)

This is all very prescriptive and, of course, a gross oversimplification of what happens in practice: operationalising these linkages is hugely challenging. For a start, developing a corporate strategy is problematic even for well-known brands which have a clearly defined vision and/or mission. Organisational strategy can be difficult to set in complex and dynamic markets, and priorities can conflict with each other (Hamel, 2012; McDonnell and Gunnigle, 2009). Pulakos and O'Leary (2011) maintain that organisational goals are often 'lofty and broad', which can create confusion and frustration when managers attempt to cascade them down to individuals. In practice, business strategies often evolve over time, and many organisations never have clear strategies (Boxall and Purcell, 2011). As Truss *et al* conclude in their chapter on strategic management (2012: 56):

> the reality is that the internal contexts of organisations tend to be messy, ambiguous and conflict-laden, while external environments range from the relatively stable to highly unstable. This means that the practice of strategic management is highly problematic. It is one thing to state an organisation's strategic direction but a totally different matter to turn this intent into action.

Stiles *et al*'s (1997) research on performance management in three large UK organisations found that three factors impeded operationalising the link between strategy, values and the objective-setting – namely, the short-term focus of the organisation, the degree of change being experienced, and the nature of the objective-setting process itself. The short-term demands of the business meant that targets set in terms of corporate values (eg teamwork or innovation) were given a low priority by managers – who felt that their real goal was to meet financial or budgetary targets – and this gave conflicting messages to employees (Stiles *et al*, 1997: 60). Change often meant that some targets were inappropriate or unattainable, and objectives were often imposed by management rather than as a result of joint negotiation.

A further challenge is to integrate human resource plans and policy with the organisation's strategy to ensure that the right kinds of impact on organisational performance are being achieved (Holbeche, 2009). This, as Legge notes, is 'a highly complex and iterative process much dependent on the interplay and resources of different stakeholders' (Legge, 2005: 171). If strategies are emergent, their integration with HRM is similarly tentative and exploratory. The 'best fit' HRM model (Chapter 1) suggests a number of approaches to 'matching'. Schuler and Jackson's framework outlined in Chapter 1 is one such approach which emphasises the importance of aligning essential employee behaviours with HR policies and strategy. Another well-known model was developed by Miles and Snow (1984), which uses three types of strategic behaviour that are associated with HR strategies: these they term 'defender', 'prospector' and 'analyser' (see Table 2.2).

Table 2.2 Strategic behaviours associated with HR strategies

Organisational characteristics	Defenders	Prospectors	Analysers
Competitive strategies	• Stable product line • Growth through market penetration, with emphasis on efficiency	• Broad, changing product line • Growth through product and market development • Emphasis on effectiveness of product design	• Stable and changing product lines • Growth mostly through market development • Some focus on efficiency

Organisational characteristics	Defenders	Prospectors	Analysers
Staffing and development strategies	• Emphasis on 'make': extensive training focused on skill development • Little recruitment above entry level	• Emphasis on 'buy': recruitment, limited training • Sophisticated recruitment at all levels	• Mixed approach of 'make' *and* 'buy' • Mixed recruitment and selection, extensive training
Performance appraisal	• Process-oriented – eg critical incident or production targets • Identification of training needs • Individual/group performance assessments	• Results-oriented linked to rewards – eg management by objectives • Identification of staffing needs • Division/company performance evaluation	• Mostly process-oriented • Identification of training and staffing needs • Individual/group/division performance evaluation
Reward policies	• Focused on internal equity	• Focused on external competitiveness	• Concerned with both internal equity and external competitiveness

Source: adapted from Miles and Snow (1984)

Another challenge is to align individual and team objectives in a way which is meaningful, relevant and measurable. As Pulakos and O'Leary (2011) note, the whole process of cascading goals through multiple levels is time-consuming, necessitating many meetings that are contingent on the previous level's completing the cascade. HR and performance management practices also have to align with each other, and this is often ignored in practice. It is not uncommon, for example, to find the 'deadly combination' of individual performance-related pay and teamworking practised together (see Chapters 1 and 8).

One way in which organisations can show some of the strategic linkages is by using the 'balanced scorecard' approach.

THE BALANCED SCORECARD

The 'balanced scorecard', developed by Kaplan and Norton in the 1990s, provides a framework to help managers translate strategy into action. Initially envisaged as a performance measurement tool, it has developed into a strategic management system used to link an organisation's long-term strategy to individual and business objectives/actions (Kaplan and Norton, 1992; 1993; 1996a). The approach seeks to move away from performance evaluations based purely on financial measures to a more rounded and comprehensive view of performance by recognising multiple stakeholder interests in organisational success. In the traditional model, performance is assessed on four stakeholder perspectives:

- **customers** (How do customers see us?) – Customer value includes cost, quality, service, time and innovations.
- **financial** (How do we look to shareholders?) – Typically this includes profitability, growth, risk, assets and value-creation.
- **internal business processes** (What must we excel at?) – This has three aspects: the values that drive the business, the support process which delivers the values, and the

good citizenship process which seeks to maintain effective relationship with stakeholders.

- **learning and growth** (How can we continue to improve and create value?) – This covers strategic competencies (skills and knowledge) as well as technologies (eg information systems) and 'climate for action' or the cultural shifts needed to motivate, empower and align employees behind the organisation's strategies. Such a perspective is largely about HR activities and is consistent with the AMO model of performance and the resource-based view of the firm (Boxall and Purcell, 2011), outlined in the previous chapter.

Figure 2.2 The balanced scorecard

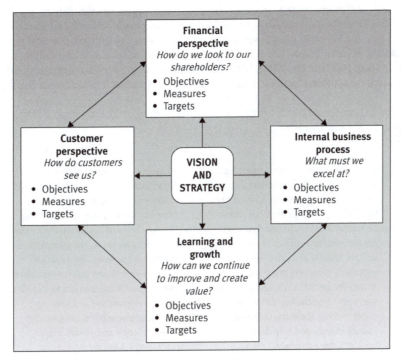

Source: Kaplan and Norton (1996a)

Short-term measurable objectives and actions are identified for each perspective, which are linked to the achievement of the organisation's strategy and vision (Figure 2.2). The model implicitly assumes that the various stakeholders of an organisation will have different views on which measures are most important. All the perspectives are equally weighted and integrated. The idea is that this encourages a 'balanced' approach to management by forcing managers to consider all the measures together and make connections between changes in one area to another. For example, improved financial results could have an adverse impact on the customer if achieved through cutting staffing levels. In the NHS, a department may have a financial target to reduce costs by maintaining high vacancies, but this would be to the detriment of waiting times and the patient experience.

Shields (2007) believes that the balanced scorecard is 'undoubtedly one of the most comprehensive and cohesive models of "best-practice" performance management to have emerged in recent decades' (Shields, 2007: 138). Although a 'best practice' approach, the model can be adapted to different organisational circumstances, and indeed there are wide variations on the application of this model. The advantages are that it provides a direct line of sight between employee goals, business unit objectives and the organisation's objectives, and attempts to balance long-term and short-term requirements. In this way it 'makes strategy everyone's everyday job' (Kaplan and Norton, 2001). It avoids a focus on purely financial and/or operational results, and helps integrate all key functional areas, thus discouraging the setting of functional boundaries and 'silo'-type mentality. Links between cause and effect are more apparent, as illustrated earlier, and it can facilitate a change in culture such as a greater focus on the customer and people, as demonstrated by the creation and use of 'the Tesco Wheel' (see Figure 2.3 and Case Study 2.2). As Boxall and Purcell (2011) note, it recognises that outcomes matter to other *stake*holders (eg customers and employees) besides *stock*holders, and opens up the debate about what makes the organisation successful or could make it successful (Boxall and Purcell, 2011: 329f). Sears, the US retail giant, used the idea to show that the organisation will become a 'compelling place to invest' if it is a 'compelling place to shop' and a 'compelling place to work' (Kaplan and Norton, 2001). Often organisations have their balanced scorecard goals pre-printed on appraisal forms so that indivuduals can set objectives under each category.

 TESCO AND THE TESCO WHEEL

CASE STUDY 2.2

In the 1990s, Tesco – the largest food retailer in the UK – underwent a culture change, moving from a business that was driven purely by financial and operational factors to one that gave greater emphasis to a customer-facing culture. Quality and price were perceived to be very much the same across the sector, and quality of service was seen to be the key differentiator. In order to bring about the required culture change and help define the business more strongly, Tesco developed its own version of Kaplan and Norton's balanced scorecard (Purcell et al 2003). The scorecard was translated into a graphic representation of a 'steering wheel' initially with four quadrants (people, finance, customers and operations), each quadrant having a set of objectives or key performance indicators (KPIs) attached to it. In 2006 a fifth perspective was added to reflect the community (see Figure 2.3). Every Tesco store has its own individual Tesco Wheel, and each store's performance is measured against targets set against every one of these objectives. The measures are updated every quarter and link to corporate measures which underpin the organisation's strategic objectives, its vision and values. In 2012 the company's vision was stated as: 'for Tesco to be most highly valued by the customers we serve, the communities in which we operate, our loyal and committed staff and our shareholders; to be a growth company; a modern and innovative company and winning locally, applying our skills globally' (www.tescoplc.com/index.asp [accessed 5 August 2012]).

The Wheel is highly visible to Tesco's staff (displayed in back-office staff areas) and uses a traffic-light system of red, green and amber to show if performance is below, above, or on target. Individuals' objectives are linked to the store Wheel, and in every store employees use a 'plan and review' document to think about how their work relates to the five perspectives and to develop objectives that are consistent with the needs of the Wheel (Witcher and Chau, 2008). The remuneration of senior management is determined by the KPIs, their bonuses varying according to the level of their store's overall achievement.

Sir Terry Leahy, former chief executive of Tesco, has publicly attributed much of the success of the company to the balanced scorecard approach, which has brought about a much greater focus on people and customer issues in stores.

Questions

1 Identify some KPIs for each quadrant of the steering wheel.

2 How do these measures help deliver Tesco's vision?

Figure 2.3 The Tesco Wheel

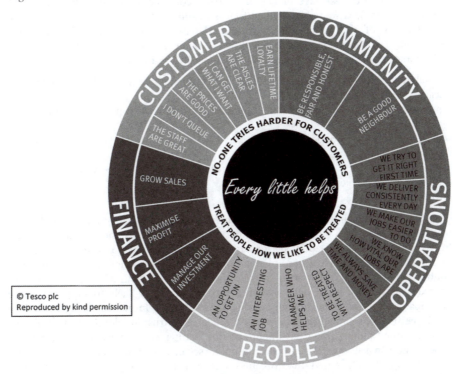

© Tesco plc
Reproduced by kind permission

Critics (eg Voelpel *et al*, 2006), however, point to the rigidity of the system in limiting the number of perspectives that can be used, ignoring, for example, external suppliers and the external environment. This is well illustrated by the collapse of Eastman Kodak. The company adapted the balanced scorecard as a means of improving its cost competiveness, but a preoccupation with process improvements in the manufacture of high-quality films 'blinded it to the threat and opportunity of digital photographs' (Shields, 2007). The system's inflexibility in volatile climates, a focus on strategic alignment which inevitably means that it is perceived as a top-down rather than participative practice, and the linear causal relationship between the main perspectives are also open to question. Some have also argued that it gives comparatively little direct attention to the people/employee issues. There are also very practical difficulties – it is ambiguous, and time-consuming to develop and implement, and there remain the challenges of translating organisational goals into individual goals, as discussed earlier in the chapter.

Although it has been applied by some high-profile organisations (including Motorola, American Express, Mobile, BMW, the NHS and Tesco), a CIPD survey (2005) found that only 4 per cent of respondents use the balanced scorecard to link team and organisational objectives.

CONTEXTUAL FACTORS

It is not only the strategy that an organisation pursues that affects performance management: many other contextual factors play a major role (Murphy and Cleveland, 1991; Levy and Williams, 2004; Den Hartog *et al*, 2004; Aycan, 2005; Murphy and DeNisi, 2008; Haines and St-Onge, 2012). Other internal organisational factors are important, such as culture, the employee relations climate, organisational structure, sector and size. External constraints also have to be considered (economic, national culture, political, legal, competition), as well as individual factors relating to the nature of the job and the characteristics of the person. Murphy and DeNisi's (2008) framework for global performance management systems identifies a range of key factors that can affect performance management. These are grouped under five main headings:

- distal factors (norms: industry, national, and cultural; strategy and firm performance; legal system; technology)
- proximal factors (purpose of the appraisal, organisational norms, acceptance of appraisal systems)
- judgement factors (opportunities to observe, availability of standards, recall of performance, time pressure)
- intervening factors (frequency and source of appraisal, supervisor–subordinate relationships and rater motivation), and
- distortion factors (eg reward systems).

Organisations operating in fast-changing environments, with fairly flat hierarchies in which employees have a high degree of autonomy (eg advanced technology and computer firms) are more likely to adopt performance management schemes which are flexible, informal and offer a high degree of involvement and participation. A command-and-control type of management style is likely to be associated with a top-down directive approach in contrast to an open management style which is likely to support a more participative, non-directive and empowering approach to performance management. The employee relations climate will influence the degree of trust employees and employers have in one another, and is important for setting and managing performance expectations. In a study of 312 private and public sector organisations in Canada, Haines and St-Onge (2012) found that organisations which have a constructive employee relations climate provide more performance management training and employee recognition, and are likely to have more effective schemes.

National culture will influence the approach to appraisal and reward, as is explored further in Chapter 12. For example, individual-based appraisal schemes are likely to be avoided in collectivist cultures which are likely to prefer group feedback. Technology can influence the type of performance measurements gathered and how that information is used. Electronic monitoring (eg in call centres), for example, facilitates the collection of quantitative data on performance quickly and efficiently. The purpose of performance management (developmental or evaluative) will influence the choice of performance criteria, whether ratings are used, and reward outcomes. Judgemental factors affect employee perceptions of equity and organisational justice, and are critical to the effectiveness of performance appraisal (as considered further in Chapters 3 and 6). Intervening factors similarly impact on employee attitudes and outcomes, in particular the behaviour of line managers, which can affect the quality of performance management activities, and the relationship an employee has with his or her boss (see Chapters 4 and 6). Any link between performance and reward can also determine the efffectiveness of any outcomes, as is discussed in Chapter 8.

REFLECTIVE ACTIVITY 2.2

Contextual factors

How might union presence influence an organisation's approach to performance management?

CASE STUDY 2.3

MANAGING PEOPLE AT THE EDEN PROJECT

The Eden Project is a botanical garden built in a former china-clay pit near St Austell in Cornwall, which opened in March 2001. It is an educational charity, tourist attraction and social enterprise. In addition to attracting visitors, activities include running transformational social and environmental projects, education and learning, research into plants and conservation, and making sure that the Project is run and operated in a 'green' way. In 2013 Eden employed around 400 core staff, in addition to 200 seasonal workers and around 150 volunteers. Staff are wide-ranging and include horticulturalists, chefs, teachers, artists, technicians, stewards, publishers, scientists, fundraisers, designers, sales staff and storytellers. The Project is a major employer in Cornwall, and the majority of employees are recruited locally. Since 2011, the Eden Project has received around 13 million visitors and contributed £1 billion to the local economy. Its mission is 'To inspire people to create Eden wherever they live'.

(Source: Eden Project sustainability report, 2010–2011)

The project has a clear identity and set of values. Critical to this is the engagement of employees and their ability to live and communicate the values of the organisation. Under the leadership of Tim Smit, the chief executive, the Project has introduced a set of unique management practices termed 'monkey practices' to help engage employees in its culture (MacLeod and Clarke, 2009). This includes saying hello to 20 colleagues before starting work in the morning as a way of getting to know people and supporting the team spirit. Each employee is also encouraged to read two books a year that they would not normally read, and to review them for colleagues. This is perceived to encourage 'freshness in employees' thinking and openness to new ideas' – one of the Project's key values (*ibid*: 107). Another practice is working by 'wine light': teams who are struggling with problems are encouraged to go out for dinner together and discuss the difficulties. Encouraging teams to spend time together outside work is also seen as helping to build closer relationships within the team. There is additionally a Members' Assembly (MA), which is a consultative group comprising elected representatives from all areas of Eden. Its aim is to represent all workers' views and give them a 'voice'.

Questions

1 What contextual factors might influence the approach to performance management in this organisation?

> 2   How would you carry out performance management in this organisation?

PERFORMANCE MANAGEMENT AS A STRATEGIC PROCESS

Performance management is frequently criticised as a rigid top-down system imposed by management, but at the operational and individual level performance management is better viewed as a process or continuous cycle that links various HR activities together. As Lowry (2002) asserts, conceptualised in this way, performance management can become a flexible, continuous and evolutionary process more suited to contemporary organisations (Lowry, 2002: 131).

This process involves a range of formal and informal interlinked performance management practices and processes, such as induction, job design, performance appraisal and feedback, training and development, coaching and mentoring, career development, talent management, competency frameworks, and reward. Arguably the process begins before an employee starts, with recruitment and selection, at which point individuals are selected who have the ability to perform well (the A in the AMO model) and fit with the organisational values. The main activity areas thereafter are outlined below, and explored in more depth in subsequent chapters of the book.

INDUCTION AND SOCIALISATION

The importance of induction and socialisation is frequently overlooked in both the performance management literature and in practice (Marchington and Wilkinson, 2012). However, if effectively managed, induction can provide the opportunity not only to welcome new recruits to the organisation but to help them become competent in their role as quickly as possible. Induction provides the chance to clarify the job and the expected standards of performance, explain how the role fits into the wider organisation, as well as assess individual learning and development needs. New recruits can be briefed about the organisation, its culture, the policies and procedures, and the 'way things are done around here'. In this way it is an important first step in building employee commitment, the psychological contract, motivation and performance, and is therefore a critical stage in the performance management process.

Induction also provides the benefits of socialisation by helping new recruits build up working relationships and begin to feel part of the team and wider organisation. Research shows that effective organisational socialisation results in positive outcomes such as enhanced job satisfaction, organisational commitment, improved person–organisation fit and lower intention to quit (Cooper-Thomas et al, 2012). Induction and socialisation can commence before new recruits have actually taken up their role (known as 'onboarding'), which avoids employees' being overloaded with new information at the start of their employment. The RSK Consultancy's online programme is available to staff before they formally join (Case Study 2.4). At Waitrose, graduates joining the retail management scheme are encouraged to set up their own Facebook groups to keep in touch with each other before and after starting their roles (IDS, 2011b). Nor should induction just be confined to newcomers. Existing employees can also benefit (as in the RSK Consultancy), particularly those transferring to a different part of the organisation or deployed in a merger or takeover.

CASE STUDY 2.4

ONLINE INDUCTION AT RSK ENVIRONMENT CONSULTANCY

In 2007/8, the Environment division of RSK, a consultancy group, experienced significant growth, expanding from 250 to 800 staff. In order to help integrate people, develop a cohesive culture, and improve retention, a new online interactive induction programme was developed.

Prior to implementation, voluntary turnover was around 18 per cent for employees with less than three years' service, but just 2.57 per cent for those with more than three years' service, suggesting that something was going wrong in the early years of service. One contributory factor was thought to be the induction process, which was predominantly a form-filling exercise and relied on the line manager to induct staff. Rapid growth in the business meant that line managers were often too busy to induct new staff properly and sessions were often cancelled.

The online programme, launched in December 2008, is mandatory for all new employees, can be used at home or at work, and is available to new employees before they start employment. Induction is no longer seen as a one-off event but as an on-going process. Existing employees have also been encouraged to complete the programme because it provides a wealth of information about the consultancy. It is designed to be visually exciting and attractive, and has a diverse approach to presenting information to suit the needs of all employees, including video clips, interactive graphics, photos and drawings.

There are 13 sections or modules to the programme, covering business principles, core activities, services, the business structure, internal services, and office administration, and it finishes with a survey questionnaire. The consultancy recognises that the 'human element' of induction is also critical, and there is still a first-day induction. A buddy scheme has also been introduced whereby existing employees volunteer to take on a mentoring role to help new recruits settle in. RSK also contacts new employees two months into their employment to see how they are getting on.

The online tool fits the company culture and growth of web-based technologies, and has all but halved voluntary labour turnover to 10 per cent, saving the organisation around £50,000 annually. In addition, employees are more engaged, corporate knowledge has improved and been translated into better cross-selling between divisions, and line managers are spending less time on induction activities.

Source: IRS *Employment Review*, Issue 935, 2009

Nine out of ten respondents to an IRS survey agreed that induction was the most crucial part of an employee's training (Wolff, 2010). Nevertheless, a quarter reported that induction has a very low priority in their organisation, and four out of ten believed induction needed a complete overhaul. Failure to support employees at this vital early stage can lead to employees' being ill-informed, confused and uncertain about their job role and the organisation's policies and practices. Feelings of low morale, alienation and insecurity are likely to result, individuals will take longer to reach their full potential, and productivity may be low. In the worst-case scenario employees may leave through either resignation or dismissal. Labour turnover data shows that employees are more likely to leave their job during the early months compared to any other time, and according to a CIPD survey, a fifth of new starters leave the organisation within the first six months (CIPD, 2009b).

REFLECTIVE ACTIVITY 2.3

1   What activities might you include in an induction programme?

2   Which would be core, and which optional?

PERFORMANCE PLANNING

Performance planning can begin at the induction phase but is an on-going process which involves informal and formal discussions between managers and employees to define and agree performance expectations. This includes behaviours that employees are expected to show and any outputs to be achieved. Such expectations must be linked to the organisation's values and objectives. More specifically, this part of the process includes:

- clarifying role expectations
- agreeing performance measures
- setting objectives
- formulating personal development plans.

According to Armstrong and Baron (2005), the starting point for performance and development planning is the role profile, which defines the results, knowledge, skills and behaviours required (Armstrong and Baron, 2005: 50). Thereafter, expectations can be defined as short- and medium-term objectives or targets. Measuring performance and setting objectives is considered in Chapter 5. On a formal basis, performance planning often follows on from the end-of-year review (see below), either at the same meeting or as a separate follow-on formal event. Formal personal development plans (PDPs) may be agreed which identify the development activities required to achieve individual objectives, how the development will be achieved, when the development will be achieved, and how the achievement will be measured (ACAS, 2010).

REVIEW AND FEEDBACK

Performance reviews provide the opportunity to discuss performance progress, clarify expectations, provide feedback, give recognition, assess performance and identify any development needs. Sometimes a rating of performance is given, particularly if performance is linked to reward. Receiving feedback, in particular, can be motivating and fulfils a basic need to be recognised and valued at work, and if positive may improve an individual's self-esteem. However, for feedback to be effective it must be a two-way communication process and the joint responsibility of managers and employees (Pulakos et al, 2008). The review is not a one-off event but should occur on a continuous basis through regular informal meetings, the annual appraisal, and sometimes formal interim reviews. Although normally undertaken by the line manager, it might also involve peers, subordinates, team colleagues, and the customer. For new recruits this process may formally begin with the probation review, at which new employees should be given an idea of how they are performing and, hopefully, have their position confirmed. Review and feedback is explored further in Chapter 6.

IDENTIFYING TRAINING, DEVELOPMENT AND REWARD OUTCOMES

The outcome of the formal review is the identification of training and development needs, and perhaps promotion or reward. Employee development is central to the process – and often seen as the *raison d'être* for performance management. However, reward and development often sit uneasily together, and where pay is involved it is recommended that it is addressed in a separate review. Chapters 7 and 8 discuss these issues in more depth.

COUNSELLING AND SUPPORT

Ideally, the process of on-going review and feedback should identify poor performance and enable problems to be resolved early on and so be 'nipped in the bud'. Where performance standards slip, counselling and support can be provided, and employees who consistently underperform may be placed on a performance improvement plan, or, in the worst-case scenario, a disciplinary procedure can be initiated. Poor performance may not always be attributable to capability issues, and may not necessarily be the fault of the individual. An employee may lack the necessary training or resources, may be unclear about what the job entails, may know what is required but not know how to achieve it, or lack influence over factors that would enable him or her to achieve higher levels of performance. Poor performance may also arise because of bullying or stress in the workplace. It can additionally be affected by factors outside the work environment, such as personal relationships and commitments. A CIPD absence survey (CIPD, 2009c) found that 43 per cent of respondents who were non-manual employees cited home and family responsibilities as a major reason for short-term absence, as did 39 per cent of respondents who were manual employees. Critical to managing under-performance is, therefore, a diagnosis of the problem: what is the nature of the problem, what are its causes, and how can it be resolved? Chapters 9 and 10 focus on managing under-performance.

FORMAL OR INFORMAL PROCESS

The degree to which formal and informal processes and practices are used varies between organisations. Formality provides clarity and structure, and endeavours to ensure consistency of treatment and fairness, and to minimise the potential for subjectivity and bias. Formal procedures and policies can be particularly important for inexperienced managers or those who lack confidence. There are, however, disadvantages. They can be cumbersome, complex and time-consuming to administer, difficult to adapt quickly, and can be viewed as constraining by managers. Informality, on the other hand, provides flexibility, can promote more personal communications between managers and employees, and may allow issues to be dealt with more quickly. Yet on the downside, it is difficult to ensure consistency of treatment and avoid subjectivity and bias. These issues are returned to in Chapters 4 and 9.

THE BENEFITS OF A STRATEGIC APPROACH TO PERFORMANCE MANAGEMENT

In summary, a strategic and integrated approach to performance management promises wide-ranging benefits (CIPD, 2009a; Pulakos, 2009; Fletcher, 2008; Aguinis, 2009; Biron *et al*, 2011). In particular, it seeks to:

- help the organisation achieve its strategic objectives
- enhance individual and group performance
- clarify organisational goals and create a 'line of sight' (Lawler, 1994) between what the individual does and what the organisation needs
- create a culture of performance and continuous improvement

- enhance motivation, commitment and engagement
- clarify individual responsibilities, expected standards of performance and behaviours
- develop employee capabilities
- help individuals develop a better understanding of themselves, their strengths and weaknesses, any development activities that are needed, and guide future career choices
- facilitate communication and involvement between managers and employees; managers and employees can work together to define expectations, review outcomes and agree development plans
- provide useful information for making HR-related decisions about reward, promotion and/or poor performance – these are sometimes referred to as the 'tactical' goals of performance management (eg Aguinis, 2009; Biron *et al*, 2011)
- help managers manage effectively – not only can it enable managers to gain an understanding of the people they manage, but through feedback and discussion it can increase managers' awareness of the impact of their own behaviour
- facilitate or support organisational change. In the UK public sector, for example, performance management has been used to bring about a change in culture and ethos. It can also be used to provide the motivation to change, and to train employees in the new skills required.

THE ROLE OF THE HR FUNCTION

Before concluding this chapter it is worth reflecting on the role and contribution of HR specialists. Although line managers are the enactors of performance management, there is a role for HR professionals. It includes designing and communicating a performance management strategy and its underpinning processes and policies, providing support and advice for managers and employees, and monitoring and evaluating schemes. It is HR's responsibility to ensure that performance management strategy and processes are aligned with the business strategy and take account of internal and external factors (such as the labour market), and that there is internal consistency within the policies and practices. Performance management policies and plans must be reviewed regularly to check for effectiveness and appropriateness in changing conditions. Chapter 1 noted that line managers frequently struggle in their role as managers of people, and HR must provide support in the implementation of these practices by means of training and development, clarifying role expectations, providing specialist advice and motivating line managers through reward and recognition. Marchington and Wilkinson (2012) also suggest that 'HR specialists need to be able to persuade line managers that procedures are valuable as tools rather than as millstones' (2012: 179) by, for example, laying the foundations of good practice, ensuring fairness and clarifying organisational objectives. More generally, the HR function has to provide a high-trust employment relations climate that stimulates discretionary behaviours and supports a positive psychological contract (Chapter 1). These issues are developed in Chapters 4, 8 and 12.

How this support is delivered very much depends on the structure and role of the HR function. This has been the subject of considerable on-going debate amongst practitioners and academics over the last decade, giving rise to many different HR role classifications (Legge, 1978; Tyson and Fell, 1986; Adams, 1991; Storey, 1992). One of the best known and mostly widely practised models is the 'three-legged stool' or business partnering model pioneered by Ulrich (1997). This is based on three elements: HR shared services, HR centres of excellence and the HR business partner.

- **HR shared services** handles all the routine 'transactional' services such as recruitment processing, payroll administration, absence and holiday records, and advice on straightforward HR-related issues. According to the CIPD (2012b), two distinctive features of HR shared service centres are: a) they offer a common service provision of routine HR administration and, sometimes, additional more complex HR services; and b) they are service-focused, enabling the customers of the shared service to specify the level and nature of the service.

- **Centres of excellence/expertise** comprise HR experts who have specialist knowledge and who develop HR policy for the organisation. They might, for instance, include pension specialists and employment lawyers.
- **HR business partners** are HR managers who are normally embedded in the business and who work closely with senior managers to influence and support strategy development and implementation.

DE&S, a section of the Ministry of Defence, has been operating this model since 2006 (see the case study below).

The model promises improved service efficiency and consistency, reduced costs, and an increased business focus and affords the HR function a more strategic role, thus enhancing its value. Despite its popularity, however, the model has been criticised for its idealism, and research is beginning to emerge which suggests that the anticipated benefits have not always materialised. Reduced quality of service, lack of clarity of HR ownership, lack of communication with HR, and a distancing of the relationship with HR, are some of the problems identified (Caldwell, 2003; Francis and Keegan, 2006).

REFLECTIVE ACTIVITY 2.4

What role might HR professionals undertake from each of the three areas in Ulrich's model (shared services, centres of expertise and business partners) in order to support a performance management strategy?

BUSINESS PARTNERING IN DE&S

CASE STUDY 2.5

Defence Equipment and Support (DE&S) is the procurement and support organisation within the UK Ministry of Defence (MoD), which was formed in April 2007 following the merger of the Defence Procurement Agency and the Defence Logistics Organisation. It operates as a single top-level budget within the Ministry of Defence with the mission *to equip and support our armed forces for operations now and in the future*. The organisation had a civilian and military workforce of around 24,500 in 2008, reduced to some 20,000 in 2012.

The way in which the HR function is structured and provides support has undergone radical change in recent years. HR was reformed from 2006 onwards in response to demands for cost-efficiency savings (the HR headcount was reduced by a third) and service quality improvement (consistency through standardisation), 'enabling and empowering line managers to manage their people'. Previously, the HR function had been organised along traditional lines – centrally run, but with personnel management advisers locally situated in the various operational departments who were responsible for day-to-day HR and case work. The new HR model accords with the Ulrich model (see Ulrich, 1997) of HR business partnering and has been shaped by local circumstances, specific to DE&S. It operates as follows:

- a shared services operation – a dedicated in-house agency called the

People, Pay and Pensions Agency (PPPA), which includes call-centre staff and expert back-office staff (subject matter experts) for complex cases

- operational HR is devolved to line managers
- in addition, there is a strategic HR team comprising business partners and a core Head Office strategic team.

Responsibility for operational HR now lies with line managers who are supported by the written information and guidance made available on the intranet, including the MoD's *Policy Rules and Guidance* for managing personnel, training and the PPPA shared service facility. The PPPA is a resource for employees and managers and provides information, advice and support on wide-ranging HR issues such as payroll, recruitment, absence management, discipline, and health and welfare. It is accessed via the website portal (the interface with the HR management system) that was substantially redesigned over 2009/10 to make it more intuitive and user-friendly.

At the local (departmental) level, HR business partners are present on the management board of the operating department to which they were assigned, and their role is to provide strategic advice and contribute to business planning. HR business partners are considered key agents in the management of change and encouraged to promote HR policy. In principle, they are not available to guide line managers on day-to-day HR delivery or performance management issues, although in practice in some areas HR business partners help line managers on transactional issues, because line managers tend to prefer to to seek support from a business partner rather than from the PPPA.

Source: Hutchinson and Tailby (2012)

CASE STUDY 2.6

THE JOHN LEWIS PARTNERSHIP

John Lewis Partnership (which comprises the two operating arms of the John Lewis department store and the Waitrose supermarket chain) is the country's largest example of co-ownership and one of the top UK retail businesses, employing some 81,000 'partners'. Its purpose is stated as 'the happiness of all our members, through their worthwhile and satisfying employment in a successful business'.

Over the last ten years John Lewis has embarked on an ambitious modernisation programme to achieve its aims of becoming a high-performing organisation, while maintaining its commitment to being an 'employer of distinction' and retaining its unique culture and ownership structure. An HR strategy has been developed to support the overall strategy and aims of the organisation which has, at its heart, a set of values described as 'powered by our principles' (PbOP). These principles (honesty, respect, recognition, common purpose) are embodied in six core work behaviours – 'about me', 'leading and developing', 'vision and creativity', 'team player', 'passionate retailer' and 'delivering results' – which form the basis of a competency and appraisal framework by which performance is measured. This is translated into a personal development folder that sets out job descriptions, performance measures and expected behaviours for individuals. It forms the basis of the annual appraisal with the line manager and provides clear examples of what is acceptable, what is unacceptable and what is outstanding behaviour, using the organisation's own language. For example: 'is enthusiastic and committed' is illustrated by a range of behaviours ranging from 'is moody or bad-tempered' (unacceptable) to 'spreads enthusiasm within their peer group' (outstanding). Annual pay increases and progression through the pay scales is dependent on the appraisal, and line managers have discretion to award increases within an affordable limit. Line managers also have discretion to reward partners in a more personal way through the 'One Step Beyond' Initiative by, for example, giving a bottle of champagne or allowing an unexpected Saturday off.

A new reward structure known as 'pay banding' was introduced which links these desired behaviours and performance directly to pay. There is also a bonus scheme based on annual profit. Benefits are considered generous – there is, for example, a non-contributory pension scheme which is unique in the sector.

In terms of voice, there is a democratic network of elected councils, committees and forums which give partners a say in the management of the business. Partners also have a voice through the 'Partner survey' and the internal monthly magazine *The Gazette*. Each store also has a Registrar who is independent of the branch and addresses issues of confidentiality.

Training and development needs are identified using the management of performance (MoP) toolkit, and a talent management programme is being developed.

Since this case study was written, the organisation has updated its values. Take a look at the organisation's website to see what they are.

Source: Hutchinson and Purcell, 2007

Questions

1   How does the John Lewis Partnership's HR strategy link to its values, aims and goals?

2   What changes would you make to the HR strategy to take account of the new set of values?

CONCLUSION

Performance management is a relatively new management concept, and this chapter has described its evolution from a very operational focus (eg performance appraisal) to a more sophisticated and strategically-oriented approach to managing people which emphasises the importance of integration. That means *vertical* integration, whereby performance management strategy, policies and practices are aligned with wider organisational objectives to support and deliver the organisation's aims and objectives. And there is also *horizontal* integration, which means that the different performance management practices must align with each other and reinforce the overarching strategy. This chapter has in addition argued that a strategic approach to managing performance should be a continuous process, incorporating both informal and informal activities; it must be flexible and, at the operational level, delivered by the line manager. There is a role for HR, but that is in the design of the strategy, providing guidance and advice, monitoring and review. The chapter has also made the point that context is all-important in performance management, and that any approach adopted has to fit the organisation's culture, its values, management style and the jobs that people do. Presented in this way makes performance management more relevant to the business, helps individuals understand what the organisation is about and its priorities, and how they can contribute to its success. It can be a powerful motivational tool, and a vehicle for building commitment and positive relationships between employees and their managers. It can be a tool for change, driving new behaviours and providing the motivation to change.

This, however, is of course the idealised view, and as attractive and essential as this model appears, there are real challenges in operationalising it. The chapter has considered some of these challenges, and subsequent chapters explore some of the difficulties in more depth.

EXPLORE FURTHER

Armstrong, M. and Baron, A. (2005) *Managing Performance: Performance management in action*. London: CIPD

Biron, M., Farndale, E. and Paauwe, J. (2011) 'Performance management effectiveness: lessons from world-leading firms', *International Journal of Human Resource Management*, Vol.22, No.6, March: 1294–1311

CIPD (2009) *Performance Management in Action: Current trends and practice*. Available online at: www.cipd.co.uk/binaries/ Performance_management_in_action.pdf

Den Hartog, D. N., Boselie, P. and Paauwe, J. (2004) 'Performance management: a model and research agenda', *Applied Psychology: An International Review*, Vol.53, No.4: 556–69

Haines, V. Y. and St-Onge, S. (2012) 'Performance management effectiveness: practices or context?', *International Journal of Human Resource Management*, Vol. 23, No.6, March: 1158–75

Hendry, C., Woodward, S. and Bradley, P. (2000) 'Performance and rewards: cleaning out the stables', *Human Resource Management Journal*, Vol.10, No.3: 46–62

IDS (2011) The performance management cycle. HR Studies 938, March

Kaplan, R. S. and Norton, D. P. (1996) *The Balanced Scorecard: Translating strategy into action*. Boston, MA: Harvard Business School Press

Truss, C., Mankin, D. and Kelliher, C. (2012) *Strategic Human Resource Management*, Chapters 3 and 4. Oxford: Oxford University Press

CHAPTER 3

Motivation at Work

SUE HUTCHINSON

LEARNING OUTCOMES

By the end of this chapter you should be able to

- understand the concept of motivation

- describe and critically evaluate key theories of motivation

- appreciate the contribution made by these theories to understanding workplace motivation and performance

- provide advice on the practical implications of these theories for effective performance management

- discuss the role of pay as a motivational tool.

INTRODUCTION

Motivation has always been a critical component of employee performance from a theoretical and management perspective. In the AMO theory of performance, as presented in Chapter 1, motivation is a contributor to positive discretionary effort. By understanding what motivates people at work, managers hope to be able to encourage people to work willingly and to their best ability – but how to elicit this effort is one of the most difficult challenges that managers face. We cannot actually see motivation: it is invisible and hard to measure directly. Motivation is also a very individual and personal thing, and whereas for some people money may be the most important motivator, others may want greater levels of responsibility and autonomy or a better work–life balance. Motivation levels can also fluctuate quite quickly, and even the most self-motivated individuals can experience a drop in motivation if they become frustrated or neglected. Although it is clear that people are usually motivated by something – even if it's trying hard to avoid work – there is no general consensus on what that something is.

Motivation is one of the most extensively researched topics in social sciences, with a long history spanning well over a century. As a result there is a huge but rather bewildering array of theories, all explaining motivation in slightly different ways. All are subject to varying degrees of criticism and empirical support. Many of the theories are old and their relevance to work in the twenty-first century has been questioned, and some were not designed with workplace motivation in mind in the first place. The research has tended to be 'careless' about how the concept of motivation is defined (Locke 2003), giving rise to a variety of definitions and methodological problems. There are also contradictory findings particularly concerning the capacity of money to motivate.

Nevertheless, despite their limitations these different theories have stimulated considerable debate, and all provide a valuable insight into workplace motivation to guide and inform performance management practice today.

This chapter begins by examining the concept of motivation, and goes on to consider some of the more significant theories, starting with some of the early approaches to motivation and then looking at two contrasting approaches: content- or needs-based theory (the 'what' of motivation) and process theories (the 'how' of motivation). The contribution these theories make to the practice of performance management is addressed throughout the chapter. The chapter concludes by considering the on-going and unresolved debate about the importance of pay as a motivator.

WHAT IS MOTIVATION?

Motivation is a very broad and abstract concept and one which is hard to assess directly in the workplace – as anyone will know who has tried to measure employee motivation. The term 'motivation' derives as an extension from a Latin word for 'motion' or 'movement' (*motus*) and is often used to refer to the effort or energy that an individual puts into an activity, but it is more complex than that. Locke and Latham (2004) describe motivation as the 'internal forces that impel action and the external factors that can act as inducements to action' (2004: 388) – in other words, the factors that push and pull us to behave in certain ways. External factors might include rewards and the nature of work performed, and internal factors are forces inherent in the person, such as individual needs and motives. There are three aspects of action that motivation can affect:

- direction or choice – what a person is trying to do
- effort or intensity – how hard a person is trying
- duration or persistence – how long a person goes on trying.

An essential feature of this definition is that motivation is an invisible, internal, hypothetical construct (Pinder, 1998) and this makes it difficult to measure and interpret. As Shields (2007) notes, the problem for management is that it is a state of mind, which cannot be observed directly but only inferred, normally after the event, from observed behaviour (Shields, 2007: 66). In a sports context, motivation seems fairly straightforward. If we were watching Rafael Nadal play a tennis match, it might be possible to assess how motivated he is by observing the effort, energy and determination he puts into his play, and the length of time he can sustain it for. His overarching goal will be to win, which will bring with it a substantial financial reward, recognition and advancement in global ranking. Other influences on his action will be his training, physical condition, skill, the playing conditions and perhaps the choice of racket. In a workplace setting, however, all this is much harder to assess.

Motivation, then, is not simply a behaviour and is not performance. It comes from inside a person and is the action and the forces that influence a person's choice of action. An important point emerging from this definition is that managers' ability to motivate employees is thus limited to influencing those factors that determine that action. Motivation cannot be altered at will by a manager. As Rollinson (2008: 196) points out:

> One of the enduring myths about motivation, however, is that managers 'motivate' their subordinates, and it is commonplace to hear them refer to it as some sort of medicine that can be dispensed in variable quantities to those who need it most. This is an impossibility ...

Another myth is that highly motivated employees always deliver better job performance. Performance does not depend on motivation alone, as suggested in the AMO model of performance (see Chapter 1). Skills and ability and having the opportunity to perform are other necessary ingredients.

EXTRINSIC AND INTRINSIC MOTIVATION

Motivation is often categorised under the broad headings of *extrinsic* and *intrinsic* motivation, which are closely related to the work of Herzberg and Maslow (discussed later in this chapter). Extrinsic motivation comes from an expectation of receiving extrinsic rewards, or tangible benefits which are external and provided by others, such as pay, promotion, careers, pensions, healthcare provision, and as such are partly beyond the control of individuals. Intrinsic motivation derives from the expectation of receiving intrinsic or 'psychological 'rewards, seen as the benefits which come from within the individual, such as feelings of self-esteem, respect, achievement and recognition, and often come from the nature of the work itself. The recognition that people are motivated by a combination of these factors has underpinned cafeteria-type reward packages, and more recently the concept of 'total reward', which emerged in the 1990s as a new way of thinking strategically about pay and benefits (see Case Study 3.1).

CASE STUDY 3.1

CASH AND NON-CASH REWARD SCHEMES

Increasingly, organisations are designing reward packages which recognise the individual nature of reward, and recognise that pay is not the only motivator. Two of the more popular approaches are flexible benefits and 'total reward'.

Flexible benefits

Flexible benefits – also known as cafeteria benefits – provide employees with a degree of choice among benefits to suit their personal requirements. Two main types of schemes exist. In the first, employees can retain their salary while varying the mix of benefits; in the second type, employees can adjust their salary by taking more or fewer benefits (CIPD, 2013a). Sometimes employers also offer a package of voluntary benefits which are products and services available for purchase by employees usually at a discount.

Subsea 7, an engineering and construction company, offers a flexible benefits scheme to its employees, which was introduced in 2007 as a means to differentiate the company from its competitors and aid recruitment and retention (Carty,

2009a). The company, which describes itself as 'international seabed-to-surface engineering, construction and services contractor to the offshore energy industry worldwide' (www.subsea7.com), employs in excess of 5,000 people from a diverse range of nationalities. The workforce comprises a mix of specialists in various disciplines covering marine work, development and construction on- and off-shore. Employees have a 'benefits allowance' and can select their preferred 'flex' options using the allowance on an annual basis. For example, employees can choose to:

- buy or sell five days' annual leave
- change life assurance (core cover is four times salary) to a maximum of six times salary or decrease to a minimum of twice salary
- opt out or decrease funding of personal accident insurance, and dental insurance, or add spouse/ partner at employee cost
- flex their own pension contribution

- increase childcare vouchers.

Other flexible benefits include travel insurance, cycle2work and payroll charitable giving.

Total reward

Total reward is a more holistic approach to reward which is designed to be strategic and includes a flexible mix of extrinsic and intrinsic rewards, including elements such as learning and development opportunities (CIPD, 2013b).

At KPMG, one of the UK's leading providers of professional services, total reward is designed to offer choice and flexibility based around a mix of rewards, and aims to deliver the firm's reward philosophy: 'To attract, develop, motivate and retain the best talent in the market, KPMG Europe is committed to a fair and flexible offering that sees us share our financial success through market-leading reward for market-leading performance' (IDS, 2008).

The total reward model is based around four key elements: 'total pay', 'individual growth', 'compelling future' and 'positive workplace'. Total pay, for example, comprises a basic salary, variable bonus, benefits and recognition. The bonus is assessed against a range of criteria based on individual and functional area performance, and includes demonstration of individual behaviours that support KPMG's values. These values are intended to promote the firm as a 'compelling place to work' and help build the organisation's reputation as a provider of high-quality services.

There is a flexible benefits option (Flextra), which is made up of basic salary plus funding for core benefits, and employees can choose to 'sell' certain core benefits or give up part of their basic salary to 'pay' for additional items. For example, a person can buy or sell up to five days' holiday a year as long as his or her annual allowance does not exceed 30 days or fall below 20 days.

The individual growth element includes training and development, and is supported by a network of people to give advice and guidance. This includes a mentor, a performance manager (who takes direct responsibility for the individual's development, helps set objectives, monitors performance and advises on problems) and a counselling partner who may be involved in monitoring the individual's long-term progress. The 'positive workplace' element is about creating a culture and environment in which employees are involved, and there is interesting work and open communications. This includes leadership role-models (such as people management leaders – see Chapter 4) and empowering staff to work flexibly. The firm offers an extensive range of flexible working arrangements including job-sharing, regular home-working, 'glide time' (in which staff can shift standard work hours to earlier or later in the day), annualised days (in which staff contract to work a set number of days each year) and unpaid career breaks.

Question

1   What are the advantages and disadvantages of these approaches for employers and employees?

Appelbaum *et al*'s (2000) study on high-performance working systems (HPWSs) (Chapter 1) differentiates between three types of motivation: financial or extrinsic motivation, intrinsic motivation, and motivation through the creation of a climate of mutual trust involving employees as stakeholders in the organisation. This third kind of motivation encourages employees to identify with the interests of the organisation and is influenced by a range of factors including line management behaviour and reward. For example, Appelbaum *et al* (2000) suggest that autocratic and capricious behaviour on the part of line managers, or 'in-your-face' status differentials such as separate car parking spaces or dining rooms for management, are unlikely to elicit feelings of trust or to encourage employees to see themselves as stakeholders (Appelbaum *et al*, 2000: 42). Some of these issues are developed further in Chapters 8 (reward) and 9 (under-performance).

 REFLECTIVE ACTIVITY 3.1

1   What motivates you at work to willingly exhibit 'positive discretionary behaviours'?

2   What is the relative importance of extrinsic and intrinsic rewards to you?

EARLY IDEAS ON MOTIVATION

Scientific management

Early ideas on work motivation can be traced back to Taylor's (1911) techniques for work organisation in industrial production in the early twentieth century which became known as 'scientific management'. Although not a theory on motivation, this approach contains some key assumptions about behaviour which have motivational implications – in particular, the use of (only) financial or economic incentives. Taylor's belief in 'economic man' assumed that employees make rational economic calculations and are driven by the desire to earn as much money as possible. A similar view is taken in McGregor's (1960) 'Theory X' proposition of human nature, developed later in the 1960s, which implied a 'carrot and stick' approach to motivation. Taylorism and scientific management principles have also been influential in the design and management of work processes and jobs – most notably, the belief that jobs should be simplified and organised in narrowly defined low-discretion tasks, with managers tightly controlling the work.

Although these principles were widely adopted in the 1920s and often significantly reduced costs and increased productivity, they have received strong criticism. The view of rational–economic man motivated purely by money ignores those intrinsic rewards that come from the experience of work, such as recognition, sense of achievement and personal development. Work under this regime was regarded as monotonous and boring and an attempt to de-skill and de-humanise work (Braverman, 1974). It was seen as a particularly direct form of management control and considered to foster worker compliance rather than commitment. Not surprisingly, it became associated with poor industrial relations, increased absenteeism and poor mental and physical health. Nevertheless, despite these strong criticisms, the underlying principles remain influential and still inform the design of workplaces processes, jobs and rewards schemes. The working methods of many call centres and fast-food chains, for example, retain strong similarities with Taylorism.

 REFLECTIVE ACTIVITY 3.2

Taylorism and call centre work

Call centres have frequently been referred to as the 'dark satanic mills' of the twentieth century

and accused of harbouring a contemporary form of Taylorism for white-collar workers (in Kinnie *et al*, 2000). Based on their research in four call centres in Scotland, Bain and colleagues (2002) provide examples of the dis-aggregation of employees' tasks by management, close supervision (eg call monitoring), and measurements to monitor, control and assess employee performance. In their article (Bain *et al*, 2002) they argue that the practice of target-setting to measure both the hard quantifiable aspects of employee tasks (eg number of calls answered, average call time) and the softer qualitative aspects of the role (eg rapport with the customer) are firmly rooted in Taylorist techniques. This has been facilitated by the nature of the work involved and computer/telephone technology.

Another study, however, by Kinnie *et al* (2000) portrays a slightly different picture. Based on research in two call centre operations, they reject the 'dark satanic mills' image and find that call centre staff have been managed through a mixture of control and commitment strategies. For example, at the RAC (one of the case studies), tightly-controlled heavily monitored and scripted work is combined with high-commitment practices such as close attention to recruitment and selection, extensive training and development, teamworking, incentives linked to performance, suggestion schemes, 'fun' incentives (eg spot prizes, themed fancy dress days, raffles) and social events. These practices, they suggest, are needed not only to provide high-quality service and to meet the pressure of the local labour market, but to ameliorate the tightly-controlled work environment (Kinnie *et al*, 2000: 982).

1   Discuss the view that it is possible to build employee motivation in circumstances where employees are tightly controlled.

The human relations movement

In the 1920s and 1930s a group of studies were carried out known as the Hawthorne Studies (Mayo, 1933; Roethlisberger and Dickson, 1939) which challenged the notion of 'economic man', replacing it with a picture of the 'social man'. This marked the beginning of what became known as the 'human relations movement', which emphasised the importance of social factors in the work environment. Although these studies have been criticised on methodological grounds and failure to take sufficient account of environmental factors, they have led to recognition that relationships at work, leadership and communication can influence motivation and performance.

The Hawthorne Studies

The Hawthorne Studies are often attributed to research by Elton Mayo, an industrial psychologist interested in finding the best working conditions for a group of employees at the General Electric Company in Chicago over the period 1924 to 1936. The studies examined the effect of different working conditions on productivity and found that variations in conditions such as changes to lighting, start and finish times, rest periods and payment schemes did not correlate with productivity, as hypothesised.

In the original study, designed to assess the effect of illumination on productivity for a section of female workers, one group was subject to changes in lighting and another – the control group – was not. However, the output for both groups increased each time the lighting changed (whether it was an increase or a decrease), suggesting that other factors were influencing productivity. This work was followed up by experiments including changes to start and finish times, rest periods, and length of lunchtimes. Productivity increased after every change. The conclusion was that higher productivity arose from worker satisfaction through being given special attention. For example, the researchers had allowed the workers certain privileges at work and taken a close interest in the group by studying them. The problem that individuals' behaviour was affected by the knowledge that they were being researched became known as the *Hawthorne effect*.

Subsequent studies led the researchers to discover that the need to belong to a group, team or organisation was of fundamental importance. They concluded that higher productivity arose from worker satisfaction through being given special attention, working as a close-knit group and being involved in decision-making. These findings can be contrasted with the work of Taylor, who assumed that high levels of pay and reward would be the only motivator required.

The assumptions inherent in the human relations movement have also influenced the development of subsequent theories on motivation. These are often separated into two groups which take different perspectives on the subject: content theories and process theories.

CONTENT THEORIES OF MOTIVATION

Essentially, content theories focus on what motivates people by considering the 'needs' that people are motivated to fulfil, such as maintaining an adequate standard of living, or security or achievement. In other words, they try to explain why an individual must act. Major theories include:

- Maslow's hierarchy of needs
- Alderfer's modified need hierarchy
- Herzberg's two-factor theory
- McClelland's theory of learned needs
- Hackman and Oldham's job characteristics model.

MASLOW: A HIERARCHY OF NEEDS

Maslow's 'hierarchy of needs' theory (1954), developed in the 1940s, contains some elements of the previous two theories but proposes an ascending hierarchy of needs rather than a single source of motivation. This hierarchy is usually displayed in the form of a pyramid with five types of need arranged in order of importance (Figure 3.1):

- physiological – the need for shelter, food, drink, warmth, sleep: these are basic survival needs related to the instinct for self-preservation
- safety – the need for protection from danger, security and stability
- social – the need to belong to a group or society, to love and be loved, to interact with others
- esteem – the need for self-esteem, self-respect, and the esteem, value and regard of others
- self-actualisation – the need for self-fulfilment, personal development and achievement, individually sometimes referred to as 'ego' needs.

Figure 3.1 Maslow's hierarchy of needs

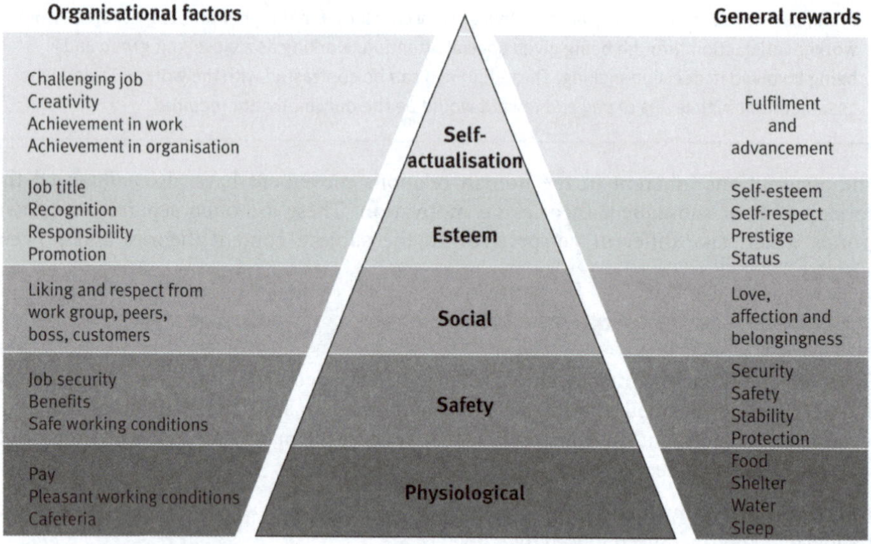

Source: adapted from Churchill, Ford and Walker (1976); Maslow (1954); Steers and Porter (1991)

Three assumptions underlie this theory. First, people are motivated by unsatisfied needs – satisfied needs are not motivators. Second, people's needs range from the most basic ('low-order') upwards to the more complex ('high-order') needs for self-fulfilment and growth. Third, individuals satisfy a lower-level need before moving upward and activating a new need. Thus, basic survival needs have to be fulfilled (food and drink and a home) before individuals consider their safety needs, and so on. Maslow believed that people have a strong desire to reach their full potential, represented as 'self-actualisation', although he recognised that few people ever reach this ultimate goal.

Maslow's work was based on general studies of human motivation, and as such was not directly related to the workplace, but has been adapted by others (eg Steers and Porter, 1991; Churchill *et al*, 1976) to apply to general rewards and the workplace, as shown in Figure 3.1. The model has some obvious implications for managing employees. Once an individual's basic needs are met through pay, job security and a supportive social environment (for example, by teamworking), motivation can be promoted through learning new skills, providing more responsibility and job enrichment. However, employees who are struggling to satisfy their own basic needs and those of their family are unlikely to be concerned about working as a team member or learning new skills.

Although this model clearly has an intuitive appeal, there are some strong criticisms. It has been interpreted variously by different people and there is some ambiguity defining the terms, particularly around the concept of 'self-actualisation'. The evidence to support it is limited (partly because of the different interpretations), raising questions about the basic assumptions underpinning Maslow's ideas. Studies have failed to support the need classification scheme and there is only partial support for the deprivation/dominance proposition (ie the higher the deficiency of a need, the higher its importance or desirability) (Wahba and Bridwell, 1976). Research has also largely rejected the gratification/activation hypothesis (ie once a need is satisfied, it no longer motivates, and the next need becomes important) (*ibid*). In reality, it seems plausible to argue that an individual may operate at more than one level at any one time. For example, more money and a more satisfying job may be equally motivating for a person.

Another argument raised, in common with nearly all content theories, is that the theory fails to account for individual differences, and like most other research on motivation, is based on US culture and values, raising questions about its universal applicability. For example, in some countries such as Japan and Greece, safety needs tend to be more important, whereas in Scandinavian countries social needs dominate (Adler *et al*, 1986). Chinese culture, which values collectivism and community activity, might predispose a different order of needs, as shown in the table produced by Huczynski and Buchanan (2007) – see Table 3.1.

Table 3.1 Social and cultural differences and the perception of needs

Maslow's hierarchy	Order	The hierarchy of needs in China
Self-actualisation	5	Safety (personal and national)
Esteem	4	Sense of belongingness
Love and affiliation	3	Esteem, family, tradition
Safety	2	Self-actualisation through fitting in
Physiological	1	Physiological

Source: adapted from Huczynski and Buchanan (2007)

REFLECTIVE ACTIVITY 3.3

Considering the variances between Maslow's (US) hierarchy and the hierarchy of needs in China, as shown in the table above, what implications might such a difference in culture have for managing performance in China?

A further difficulty is that in Maslow's theory satisfaction is the main motivation outcome of behaviour, but job satisfaction does not necessarily lead to improved employee performance, as discussed in Chapter 1.

Despite these criticisms, the work of Maslow has proved useful in generating ideas about motivation, and still seems to appeal to managers in the workplace today. A number of writers have modified and developed his work, including Alderfer.

ALDERFER'S MODIFIED NEED HIERARCHY

Alderfer (1972) proposed a theory based on three related needs in the organisational setting:

- **existence needs** which are concerned with basic survival and safety: pay and working conditions would fall into this group
- **relatedness needs** which are associated with love, belonging, affiliation and meaningful and positive interpersonal relationships: relationships with peers, supervisors and work colleagues are clearly relevant here
- **growth needs** which relate to the development of potential, and include self-esteem and the esteem of others, and self-actualisation.

Like Maslow, Alderfer proposed a hierarchical ordering (from existence to relatedness to growth) but suggested that these needs or levels are viewed more as a continuum than as discrete categories. He proposed that people could move around the hierarchy and that more than one need can be activated at any one time. He also argued that as well as progressing up the hierarchy, an individual might move down. This he termed the 'frustration regression' process, arguing that people's inability to grow in the ways in which they desired could lead to frustration. One of the implications of the theory is that if a person's needs are blocked at a particular level – for example, because the job does not offer sufficient opportunity for personnel development – managers should focus attention on interpersonal work relationships to satisfy relatedness needs. Although the theory has received little empirical testing, it is considered to make an important contribution to our understanding of motivation, particularly concerning a person's likely reaction when needs are not satisfied.

 CRITICAL REFLECTION 3.1

Frustration is generally considered to be a negative response to the blocking of a desired need and is often associated with defensive forms of behaviour such as aggression and withdrawal (Mullins, 2010). However, it is possible that some individuals could react in a more positive way by displaying constructive-type behaviours such as problem-solving to

remove the constraint, or, as suggested by Alderfer's model, restructure or compromise their needs.

1   What frustrations at work might lead to a) negative responses, and b) more positive responses, from individuals?

HERZBERG'S TWO-FACTOR THEORY

Herzberg's (1959) influential two-factor theory departs from the idea of a hierarchical order of needs and makes the distinction between extrinsic (hygiene) factors and intrinsic (motivating) factors. His initial study, based on interviews with US accountants and engineers, concluded that two different sets of factors affected motivation and satisfaction. Those giving rise to satisfaction he called 'motivators'; those giving rise to dissatisfaction he called 'hygiene' factors. The 'motivators' concern internal needs and are often to do with job content such as achievement, recognition, responsibility, personal growth and advancement, and the nature of the work itself. Interestingly, they have little to do with money or style of supervision. These intrinsic rewards are more akin to Maslow's higher-order needs, and lead to high levels of satisfaction, motivation and performance. Significantly, however, their absence does not lead to dissatisfaction, just no satisfaction.

'Hygiene' factors are features of the work environment such as the relationship with the supervisor, salary, job security, working conditions, company policy and administration and interpersonal relations. A lack of these factors leads to dissatisfaction but their presence just ensures a state of 'no satisfaction'. Significantly, they do not contribute to motivation or performance. Herzberg claimed that these factors were akin to 'removing happiness rather than making people happy', and should be so called because, like hygiene, the presence of them does not make you healthier but their absence can result in a deterioration of health.

The model has clear practical implications for the design of performance management and reward schemes. Managers who want to positively motivate staff must pay attention to intrinsic rewards, focusing on the job content, the opportunity for achievement, advancement and recognition. Furthermore, the theory suggests that pay and other extrinsic rewards rarely motivate people but could cause job dissatisfaction, leading to workplace conflict, absenteeism, labour turnover and low general morale. In that sense, pay is more powerful as a 'push factor' in employee turnover terms rather than as a 'pull factor' (Taylor, 2010). We return to the question of the potential of money to motivate at the end of the chapter.

Herzberg's theory is more applicable to the work situation compared to Maslow's approach, and has been highly influential in highlighting the importance of intrinsic rewards, particularly for professional workers. Nevertheless, the theory has been subject to criticism. It has not been well supported empirically and research has reported mixed results. The methodology has been questioned on the grounds of the reliability of procedures used, which were based on the critical incident technique (see Chapter 5) in which people were asked to relate incidents that had made them feel exceptionally good or bad about their jobs. The independent effects of hygiene factors and motivating factors are also open to question: critics have argued that these factors may be interlinked – the level and quality of supervision, for example (hygiene factor), may influence the nature of the work, level of responsibility or sense of achievement (motivating factors). Similarly, the hygiene factors are debatable, in particular pay, which other studies suggest can be a source of satisfaction. A replication study by Wernimont (1966) indicated that both motivators and hygiene factors are capable of leading to feelings of satisfaction or dissatisfaction, and there is considerable survey evidence that both intrinsic and extrinsic factors are important qualities that people seek in their work, as illustrated in Table 3.2. The relevance of the study to non-professional workers is also questioned – in particular, unskilled work which may be monotonous, uninteresting, repetitive and limited in scope. It could be argued that these are the jobs where motivation is particularly challenging for managers. Like Maslow's theory, the work can be criticised on the basis of its universal applicability. Not all individuals will be motivated by the identified factors: for example, some people do not like taking responsibility and are happy for others to do so; what are motivators for one culture could be hygiene factors in another (see Chapter 11 and *Activity* 3.3 above).

Table 3.2 Job attributes 'very important' to private and public sector employees in 2005

Described as 'very important' to them	Percentage in	
	Private sector (n=507)	Public sector (n=260)
A job that is useful to society	15	32
A job that enables someone to help other people	18	27
A job that enables someone to work independently	15	22
An interesting job	46	53
Job security	50	49
A job with good opportunity for advancement	24	21
A job that enables someone to decide their times and days of work	14	11
A high income	18	12

Source: British Social Attitudes Survey, 2008

Despite these criticisms, Herzberg's work remains highly influential and has drawn attention to the need to differentiate between intrinsic and extrinsic motivators and the importance of job design.

CASE STUDY 3.2

MOTIVATION AND JOB SATISFACTION AMONG HOTEL WORKERS IN BRAZIL

Brazil has the largest tourist industry in Latin America, the fifth largest population in the world and the ninth largest economy in the world. Its culture is almost the complete opposite of US culture in the Hofstede context (see Chapter 11), and seen to be high in power distance, collectivism, uncertainty avoidance and femininity, and displaying a moderate long-term orientation.

Sledge *et al*'s (2008) study of motivation and job satisfaction among hotel workers in Brazil found partial support for Herzberg's two-factor theory of motivation but also suggests that culture influences the degree of job satisfaction.

The results supported the use of Herzberg's motivators to promote job satisfaction among hotel employees and found that some hygiene factors did promote dissatisfaction, notably salary, security and policy administration. However, other hygiene factors such as supervision, working conditions, relationships with co-workers and status did not elicit strong dissatisfaction among employees.

Question

1   Read the article by Sledge *et al* (2008) and discuss what factors might explain these findings.

MCCLELLAND'S THEORY OF LEARNED NEEDS

The criticism that people have homogenous needs is partly addressed in McClelland's (1961) Achievement Needs theory, which suggests that individual motivations are influenced by three trait-like inner needs:

- achievement – the need to excel and achieve in areas that have significance for the individual
- power – the need to control or influence the behaviour of others
- affiliation – the need to develop close and meaningful interpersonal relationships.

McClelland argued that people develop a bias towards one of these needs, and suggested that these traits were based on experience and could be developed by, for example, education and training. He also maintained that needs vary according to the individual's position in the hierarchy – for instance, non-managerial employees are motivated mainly by the need for affiliation, junior and middle managers by the need for achievement, and senior managers by the need for power. Although the theory is generally accepted as having some validity, there are some criticisms. For example: his belief that individuals can be trained to have higher levels of needs for achievement is debatable since this could require a significant shift in personality. Like other context theories of motivation, there is the question of its applicability in different cultural settings. In collective cultures, for instance, the need for affiliation may be higher than the need for achievement and power.

REFLECTIVE ACTIVITY 3.4

Discuss the implications of McClelland's theory for performance management.

HACKMAN AND OLDHAM'S (1980) JOB CHARACTERISTICS MODEL

Hackman and Oldham's (1975, 1980) model builds on Herzberg's work, but like McClelland's theory it also recognises individual differences. The model proposes five specific job characteristics which can satisfy employees' intrinsic needs and promote motivation and performance:

- skill variety – the extent to which the job requires a diverse set of skills
- task identity – the extent to which a job produces a whole identifiable piece of work
- task significance – the extent to which the job has an impact on others, either at work or outside the organisation such as service/product users
- autonomy – the extent to which the job allows individuals to exercise choice and discretion in their work
- feedback – the extent to which the job itself provides information on how well the individual is performing.

These characteristics promote/trigger three 'critical psychological states' – experienced meaningfulness, experienced responsibility, and knowledge of results – which collectively influence motivation, job satisfaction and work performance. The first three job characteristics are believed to influence meaningfulness of the work, the fourth affects responsibility for work outcomes, and the fifth impacts on knowledge of results of work activities, as shown in Figure 3.2. The model also makes the point that the impact is moderated by the strength of an individual's growth needs (similar to Maslow's self-actualisation), satisfaction of hygiene factors and organisational culture (shown at the bottom of Figure 3.2). For example, the effects of these job characteristics are expected to be greater for individuals high on growth needs strength.

Figure 3.2 Hackman and Oldham's job characteristics model

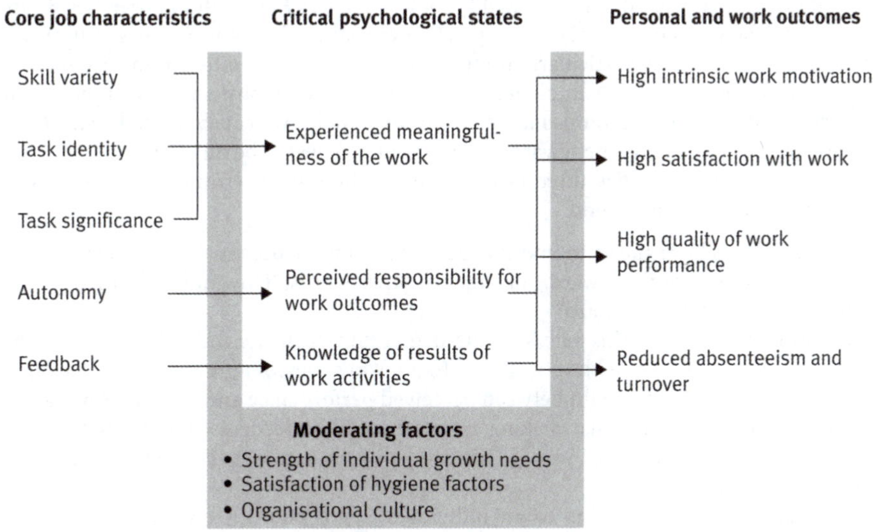

Source: based on Hackman and Oldham (1975, 1980)

Support for the theory can be found in Fried and Ferris's (1987) meta-analysis, which found that the five job characteristics are strongly positively related to internal job motivation and job satisfaction, although the relationships with job performance were weaker. There is less support, however, for the mediating effects of the critical psychological states. This model makes the case for job enrichment, and has further strong support in studies on HPWSs (Chapter 1). The model also makes the important point that job satisfaction and motivation are influenced not only by the design of jobs but by a range of other contextual factors.

PROCESS THEORIES OF MOTIVATION

Process theories help develop our understanding of motivation by seeking to explain the cognitive processes by which people make motivated decisions. As Chiang and Jang (2008: 314) explain:

> Process theories are, in effect, working models of the decision-making processes that individuals perform in order to determine whether they will be motivated to pursue certain activities and sustain a certain degree of productivity. Process theories help describe and explain how behaviour is directed, energised, sustained, or stopped.

Unlike most content theories, process theories acknowledge that what motivates one person to perform well may not be the same for others.

The key process theories for performance management include:

- expectancy theory
- goal-setting theory
- equity theory.

EXPECTANCY THEORY

Expectancy theory is not a single theory but a family of theories which examine how individuals are motivated by their expectations about outcomes at work. Pioneered by Vroom (1964) and subsequently refined by others such as Porter and Lawler (1968) and Chiang and Jang (2008) (see Case Study 3.3), expectancy theory is aimed specifically at work motivation and is particularly useful in offering insights into the management of performance and reward. In simple terms, expectancy theory posits that work behaviour is determined by the expectations individuals have of their own capabilities, the effort they are prepared to put in, and the rewards on offer or perceived to be on offer.

Vroom's model identifies three factors that combine to determine how much work effort an individual may expend:

- **valence** (V) – This is the value an individual places on the potential outcome/reward, or the attractiveness of the reward/outcome. In other words, 'How much do I really want this potential outcome/reward?'
- **instrumentality** (I) – This refers to the degree to which the individual believes that performing at the required level will lead to a positive outcome/reward. It is sometimes referred to as the 'line of sight between perceived performance and reward'. An example might be the probability that making extra sales will be recognised and result in extra pay or recognition. In other words, 'If I carry out the action, will I attain the required outcome/result?'
- **expectancy** (E) – This refers to an individual's perception of the probability that a specific effort will lead to the desired level of performance – for example, that making an extra effort, such as talking to the customer, will lead to extra sales. It will depend on the individual's skills and capabilities and the resources available. It will also require an evaluation of factors outside the control of the individual, such as the impact of other work colleagues or external constraints. In other words, 'If I try, can I carry out the action I am considering?'

The strength of the force to act (F), or motivation, can be expressed as an equation:

$$\text{Motivation (F)} = V \times I \times E$$

The implications are that individuals will expend most effort at work when they perceive that their efforts will result in a good performance leading to a desirable and valued outcome or reward. It also implies that if any of these components (V, I and E) is zero, overall motivation to pursue a particular course of action will also be zero. So if a person feels that an outcome is not attainable, he or she will have no motivation to act – regardless of ability or the potential reward. The theory emphasises the individual and complex nature of motivation. Valence is a subjective variable, and so, for example, whereas one individual may value pay as a reward, another may not. Although expectancy and instrumentality can be thought of as probabilities, these too are subject to individual evaluation. Vroom argued that people assess these two factors with reference to previous experiences, so if someone has been let down in the past (eg a promotion was not forthcoming), he or she is less likely to put in the extra effort in the future, and may become demotivated.

The theory offers practical insights into managing motivation in the workplace, highlights the importance of the management expectations, similar to the psychological contract (Chapter 1), and has clear practical implications for performance management and other HR policies and practices. For example:

- Set expectations during the selection and induction process so that employees do not begin a new job with over-inflated expectations.
- Design jobs and tasks so that expectations can be met. This includes making sure that roles and responsibilities are clearly defined, and that there are no conflicting role expectations.
- In order to perform well employees need to perceive they possess the necessary skills and abilities. This means ensuring that training, learning and support is available.
- Ensure that there is a clear, direct link between performance and rewards, and that employees understand that if they perform well, their efforts will be recognised and rewarded. Communication, empowerment and involvement policies clearly have an important role to play here.
- The rewards offered for performing well are valued by employees. Managers therefore need to discover and focus on the rewards that will incentivise individuals to improve performance – for example, is it pay or recognition or promotion? Nadler and Lawler (1979) stress that that the reward/outcome has to be significant, making the point that 'trivial rewards will result in trivial amounts of effort' (1979: 227). One of the problems with individual performance-related pay is that often the reward is too small to be of value. This is discussed in more detail in Chapter 8.
- Individuals will have different preferences for a particular outcome. This suggests designing and offering reward packages that are flexible and individualised – for example, through some form of cafeteria-style approach or total reward, as illustrated in the examples of Subsea 7 and KPMG (Case Study 3.1).
- There has to be a match between the rewards expected and those that are actually available. If promised rewards are not forthcoming, individuals are likely to become demotivated.
- Ensure that performance targets are achievable. The theory implies that if an employee believes a target is unobtainable – perhaps because the individual doesn't have the right information or the product is of poor quality – he or she will probably not try. Achievable targets must be set in the formal performance appraisal.

Vroom's theory has been extended by Porter and Lawler (1968), who go beyond motivational force and consider actual performance. They suggest that effort is mediated by an individual's abilities, traits (eg intelligence and personality) and perceptions of his or her role and opportunities. Rewards are introduced as an intervening variable, and job satisfaction is seen as a determinant of performance.

Figure 3.3 The Porter and Lawler motivation model

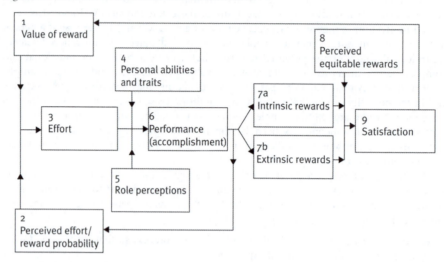

Source: Porter and Lawler (1968)

This is illustrated in Figure 3.3. How hard an individual tries, or the effort expended on a task (box numbered 3 in the figure), depends on the value of rewards (box 1) and an individual's expectations that those rewards are dependent on a given amount of effort (box 2). Effort, however, does not directly lead to performance (box 6) but is influenced by abilities and traits (box 4) and perceptions of the role (box 5). So, for example, if an individual lacks ability or does not have a clear perception of what is required in the role, effort can result in poor performance. Rewards (box 7a and 7b) are desirable outcomes. These combine with perceptions of equity (box 8) to influence satisfaction (box 9). Satisfaction also influences the perceived value of the reward (box 1) and thus has a feedback effect. This is one of the more significant features of the model.

Expectancy theory has an appealing logic, and there is some evidence to support it (Tien, 2000; Vansteenkiste *et al*, 2005). Nevertheless, the theory is subject to some criticism. It does not explain why people value or do not value a particular outcome, and this illustrates the theory's concentration on process rather than content. Moreover, the construct validity of the components remain little understood (Chiang and Jang, 2008). There are also difficulties in operationalising the theory. For example, there is an underlying assumption that behaviour is rational and premeditated and that we are conscious of our motives – but often behaviour at work can be unconscious or impulsive. Another major criticism of the theory is that the cognitive processes are complex and time-consuming, and can often exceed the working memory capacity (Lord *et al*, 2003).

CHIANG AND JANG'S MODIFIED EXPECTANCY THEORY

Chiang and Jang's (2008) study of expectancy theory in relation to US hotel employees confirmed the validity of expectancy theory, but suggested a modification to the theory so as to comprise five components:

- Expectancy
- Extrinsic instrumentality
- Intrinsic instrumentality
- Extrinsic valence
- Intrinsic valence.

Expectation led hotel employees to believe that their effort would lead to the desired performance. They thought that if they performed well in their job, they would have a sense of accomplishment and feel good about themselves (intrinsic instrumentality). However, the hotel employees did not think they would get better pay, monetary bonuses, pay increases or promotion (external instrumentality) even if they met their performance expectations. Valence was found to be an important attribute to motivation and the employees preferred intrinsic valences such as job responsibility, using their abilities and feelings of accomplishment, to extrinsic valences of good financial rewards and promotion.

These findings may seen surprising given that in the hotel sector employees receive low pay and pay is usually ranked as the top motivator in studies of hotel workers. Nonetheless, other studies also show that intrinsic outcomes may be more powerful motivators than extrinsic outcomes (eg Wahba and House, 1974). The results also highlight the importance of expectations and probability – employees may have had little expectation that financial rewards would be forthcoming.

Source: Chiang and Jang (2008)

GOAL-SETTING THEORY

Goal theory, pioneered by Locke (1976), is one of the most dominant theories on work motivation and has some similarities with the instrumentality and expectancy elements of expectancy theory. Very simply, this theory is based on the notion that a person's goals, defined as 'a level of performance proficiency that we wish to attain within a specified time period' (Latham and Locke, 2006: 332), determines their behaviour. The theory examines what types of goals are most successful in generating high levels of motivation, when these effects occur and why they occur. According to Locke and Latham (2002), there are a number of key conditions that make goals effective:

- Goals must be specific and challenging. Research shows that precisely-specified challenging goals produce better performance (if accepted) than easy or vague 'do-your-best'-type goals. Some organisations incorporate 'stretch goals' in individual performance objectives which are ambitious, highly targeted and designed to help employees reach their full potential.
- Goals must be capable of objective measurement so that performance can be evaluated.
- Goals must be attainable and time-bound. Goals that are too difficult are likely to demotivate and reduce performance. Deadlines and time-scales are needed to enable people to see how much effort is needed over a specified time.
- Prompt, precise feedback is required so that individuals know how they are performing.
- Goals must be 'owned' or accepted by employees to gain commitment. One way of achieving this is to have employees involved in the selection of goals.

- Employees must have knowledge, skills and resources, and believe they can accomplish the goals set (ie they must feel 'self-efficacy').

Goal-setting therefore has clear practical implications for performance management, which are developed in Chapters 5 and 6. The approach can be found in the development of SMART objectives which are commonly used in objective-setting.

Table 3.3 Ensuring that objectives are SMART

Specific	Outcomes need to be clearly defined, using a language that can be easily understood by employees and managers
Measurable	Outcomes should be capable of measurement on a quantitative and/or qualitative basis
Achievable	Although managers may set the objectives, they should be agreed with the employee as achievable, to ensure buy-in
Realistic	Targets should be set within the capabilities of the individual, but be challenging and offer the opportunity for development. They should also be in line with the job description and appropriate to the role
Time-bound	Target dates or time-scales should be set for the achievement of the objectives rather than be open-ended

Although strongly supported by research evidence (Locke *et al*, 1981), the ideas have attracted some criticism. For example, the model is not really a theory of motivation but a motivational tool, and simply accepts that goals are motivators, but fails to explain why they should have such a significant effect (Arnold *et al*, 1991). Goal-setting requires a certain 'tunnel vision' focus and may not be applicable in all situations, and indeed can be counterproductive for jobs that require creativity and improvisation. The premise that goals and responsibility for achieving them should be assigned to individuals runs counter to group work and teamworking. Too many goals can create confusion and ambiguity, and mean that performance towards one goal may be sacrificed to make way for another goal (Ambrose and Kulik, 1999). Providing effective feedback is also challenging and requires good communication skills if the process is to be constructive.

EQUITY THEORY

Equity theory (Adams, 1965) is based on exchange theory, concerns individuals' perceptions of fairness, and argues that people seek what they perceive to be equitable in return for their efforts. More specifically, the theory proposes that (Huseman *et al*, 1987):

- Individuals evaluate relationships by comparing their own input/output ratio with the equivalent ratio of others.
- People feel equally treated if they perceive that their input and output ratio is the same as others'. If these ratios are unequal, inequity exists.
- The greater the perception of inequity, the more distressed individuals feel. Inequity can occur when a person gets more (*over*-reward) or less (*under*-reward) than others.
- The greater the perceived distress, the stronger the motivation to act to restore equity. So, for example, a person who perceives they are underpaid or under-rewarded may reduce their amount of effort, resulting in poor performance, lack of co-operation,

absence or even conflict at work. Conversely, a person who thinks they are over-rewarded will work harder to restore equity.

An important point is that effort is perceived as a relative rather than an absolute term, and is subjective, so people doing the same work for the same pay may have different notions of 'felt-fairness', and one person may perceive their pay to be fair but another may not. This raises a fundamental question: 'Fairness in relation to what?' In other words, who are the comparator group? In a work environment, we would expect comparisons to be made with peers and other work colleagues, but other reference points could be a previous employer, other organisations, or even friends and partners. Interestingly, it is fair distribution between groups within the organisation (ie internal equity) which is used by the law to determine fairness in equal pay claims. Like most other theories on motivation, the theory has its origins in the USA, and Bolino and Turnley (2008) suggest that equity theory might be applied differently across the world. In collectivist cultures, for example (such as Pakistan or China), people are more likely to choose a group for comparison purposes (such as occupational group) whereas people in highly individualistic cultures (like the United States and the UK) are more likely to choose other individuals.

 HIGH PAY OR FAIR PAY?

CASE STUDY 3.4

When she founded BodyShop, Anita Roddick stated that at no point would her pay as CEO exceed ten times the bottom salary (although she subsequently changed that to twenty times the bottom salary), as she knew the demoralising and destabilising effect that wider differentials would have.

More recently (in 2010), the High Pay Commission took up the issues of pay differentials in a year-long inquiry into executive pay in UK companies. This independent body found that the pay gap between senior bosses and the average employee has grown substantially in the 30 years since the mid-1970s, and that the gap is now wider than at any time since Queen Victoria was on the throne. The Commission argued that this has had a 'corrosive' impact on society, is bad for the economy and has given rise to a growing sense of injustice. It also concluded that the argument that senior pay must rise in order to attract the best talent was a myth.

There has been a public backlash against high pay since the financial crisis of 2007, but the Commission's report (High Pay Commission, 2011) finds that the pay gap started to grow rapidly during the early 1980s. The average wage has risen by around 300 per cent since 1980, while the highest-paid company executives' 'stratospheric' pay increases have soared by more than 4,000 per cent over the same period. In 2011 (as economic growth slowed) executive pay in FTSE-100 companies grew by 49 per cent compared to just 2.7 per cent for the average employee.

The report cites the example of Barclays Bank, where top pay was 75 times that of the average worker. In 1979 it was 14.5 times. Over that period, the lead executive's annual pay in Barclays has risen by 4,899.4 per cent – from £87,323 to £4,365,636. At BP in 2011 the lead executive earned 63 times the amount of the average employee. In 1979 the multiple was 16.5.

The Commission recommends a 12-point plan to address this inequality, including a 'radical simplification' of executive pay and the placing of employees on remuneration committees, and that companies publish a ratio reflecting the difference between the top and the median wage. It also calls for the establishment of a new body to monitor high pay.

Source: High Pay Commission (2011)

Question

1   What are the arguments for and against the justification for such large pay differentials?

There is considerable research support for equity theory, which seems to work best in under-payment conditions and for hourly pay. Not surprisingly, the predictions of equity theory are less supported when people perceive they are over-rewarded. The theory also has other shortcomings. It does not predict which strategy a person will or should choose if they feel unfairly treated, for which there will always be a range of options with different consequences. Take the example of someone who has discovered that a work colleague is being paid more for the same job, but seemingly has been putting in no extra effort. The possible courses of action for reducing this perceived inequality include changing inputs (ie reduce work effort), changing outcomes (demand a pay increase or ask for the pay of the work colleague to be reduced), rationalising the inequality (perhaps the work colleague has better qualifications), making comparisons with someone else, or leaving the organisation. Only some of these have implications for effort and performance. Nor does the theory explain the choice of comparator group or person.

More recently, equity theory has been developed into theories of organisational justice (Rousseau, 1995) which focus on perceptions of fairness in the workplace. Three types of justice perceptions have been identified:

- **distributive justice**, which relates to employees' views about the fairness of decision-making outcomes such as rewards for work: this is very similar to equity theory
- **procedural justice**, which focuses on whether people believe the organisational procedures or the decision-making processes are fair
- **interactional justice**, which relates to people's perceptions about the fairness of the interpersonal treatment they receive, particularly from more senior figures.

All of these concepts are important in performance management. For instance, if someone feels they are paid poorly relative to people doing the same work, this is *distributive injustice*. If someone feels that judgements on performance are biased or the information used to assess performance is in some way inaccurate, they will perceive *procedural injustice*. A person who feels they were not given the chance to voice their views in the performance review process may perceive *interactional injustice*. Of significance for managers is the evidence that the three components of organisational justice interact, and the negative effect of one form of injustice can be partly mitigated if another is maintained (Cropanzano *et al*, 2007). The impact of an employee's being dissatisfied with his or her pay outcome in relation to others' (distributive injustice) will be lessened if at the same time he or she feels that the way this decision was arrived at was broadly fair (procedural justice). A key message from this, therefore, is that although it may not be possible to distribute rewards fairly according to everyone's satisfaction, it should be possible to minimise any negative outcome by distributing rewards using procedures which operate fairly and equitably, and maintaining good-quality relationships between line managers and employees.

Clearly, equity and organisation justice theories have major contributions to make to the design of performance management and reward schemes. In focusing on performance management, Paul Boselie proposes (2010: 180–1) that perceived procedural injustice by employees can be minimised when employees:

- participate in the development of the appraisal system
- understand the performance management system, the feedback process and the evaluation criteria
- agree with and accept the performance management system
- perceive that raters (supervisors, peers and subordinates) are well trained
- perceive a constructive and development-oriented performance management environment focused on rewards for good performance, and development opportunities in the case of poor performance
- get regular feedback, not just once a year
- have the opportunity to rate their performance (self-rating)
- have the opportunity to participate in the evaluation session.

DOES MONEY MOTIVATE?

Before concluding this chapter it is worth reflecting on the debate about the capacity of money to motivate employees. The American statistician Dr W. Edwards Deming's famous declaration in 1982 that 'Pay is not a motivator' may seem rather absurd to many people, particularly during an economic downturn. Money is, of course, important for what it can buy, but also because it can be symbolically important – as a status symbol or sign of recognition. Many organisations base their reward strategy on the assumption that money motivates, and there is evidence that money is the most important factor for people when deciding on a job (Barber and Bretz, 2000). But there are people who are motivated to work hard regardless of the financial reward – those, for example, who choose to work as volunteers for charitable institutions. And even if people are attracted by good pay, this does not mean that money is motivating. As Kohn (1993) points out, whereas it is plausible to assume that if someone's take-home pay was cut by half they would be demotivated enough to undermine performance, it does not necessarily follow that doubling someone's pay would result in better performance.

Peter Drucker (1974) once made the bold claim that 'there is not one shred of evidence for the alleged turning away from material rewards', and there is some theoretical support for the notion that money is a motivator. Taylor argued that people would only be motivated by financial incentives to work in an efficient and productive way. McGregor's (1960) Theory Y managers believe that employees can only be cajoled into working if offered financial incentives. Maslow (1943) claimed that pay would be a motivator, but only for those functioning at the lower levels of the hierarchy of needs. In expectancy theory pay is a motivator if it is desired by employees and they can identify the behaviours that will lead to higher payment – and they feel capable of delivering those behaviours. If money is a motivator, then equity and justice theory suggest that pay has to be fair in comparison to others' to be a motivational force. Locke and colleagues have also produced empirical and conceptual support for pay as a motivator (Locke *et al*, 1980).

Other theories, however, cast doubt on the value of money as a motivator. Herzberg argued that pay is not a motivator but is a 'hygiene' factor which can create or reduce dissatisfaction. According to him (Herzberg, 1987: 30):

> Managers do not motivate employees by giving them higher wages, more benefits or new status symbols. Rather, employees are motivated by their own inherent need to succeed at challenging tasks.

Lawler (1971), however, in reviewing the empirical evidence on pay, found that it was more highly rated than Herzberg suggested.

Others who reject the notion of money as a motivator include Deci and Ryan (1985), who argue that monetary reward undermines intrinsic motivation by focusing attention on extrinsic rewards. Moreover, large extrinsic rewards can actually decrease performance in tasks that require creativity and innovation. However, it seems that intrinsic motivation is only damaged if the person perceives extrinsic reward, such as pay, as an attempt to control their behaviour rather than provide information about it. This is highly relevant to performance-related pay and we return to this discussion in Chapter 8. Pfeffer (1998a) suggested that the idea that people work for money is a myth, arguing that there is a substantial body of research which demonstrates that external rewards undermine intrinsic motivation. Similar claims are made by Kohn (1993), who believes that extrinsic motivators do not alter the attitudes that underlie behaviours and do not elicit on-going commitment.

So what conclusions can be drawn? Clearly, the importance of pay as a motivator is not straightforward. For many people money is a motivator – but so are other issues, such as feeling recognised and valued, having responsibility and discretion, career opportunities, and getting a sense of achievement. Most people will not work without pay. However, its power to motivate will vary, depending upon individual circumstances and other factors internal and external to the work environment – as illustrated by a survey of teenagers and young adults (see Case Study 3.4). This issue is returned to in Chapter 8.

CASE STUDY 3.5

REWARD AMONG GENERATION Y: CASH IS KING

Until recently it was widely considered that Generation Y people (teenagers and young adults) valued flexible working, travel, and a good work–life balance above pay. However, a survey conducted by *Personnel Today* and Ipsos Mori in 2008 suggests that this may no longer be the case. The findings revealed that those aged between 18 and 28 considered money to be the most important benefit for Generation Y people. The most important employee benefits in five to ten years' time are felt likely to be:

- pay – 68 per cent
- learning and development – 10 per cent

- flexible working – 9 per cent
- other financial benefits – 6 per cent
- childcare benefits – 4 per cent
- holiday entitlement – 3 per cent.

Furthermore, 85 per cent of respondents said they would prefer their employer to offer cash as an incentive to boost performance. Heavy student debt, difficulties in getting on to the property ladder and rises in the cost of living are likely contributory factors.

Source: Berry (2008)

REFLECTIVE ACTIVITY 3.5

Teams and motivation

Theories on work motivation are premised on the assumption of workers as individual actors. It can be argued that group motivation to work is informed by individual motivation to do work. So if a person finds a job boring and demotivating, his/her perspective of that job will not change because he/she must now perform it with others. However, it could be argued that team members motivate and demotivate each other. Theory on collective efficacy (Bandura, 1986), which is based on the shared belief of team members that their team's capacity to perform is important, is relevant here. Theory on team social identity also provides useful insights into the motivation of teams. In a sports team setting, for example, in-group identity can be a powerful motivator for improving performance, particularly under strongly competitive conditions.

1   Do needs change because people work in groups?

2   What additional factors might influence motivation in a group setting at work?

Before answering these questions you may like to read the article by Theodore Lewis (2011) which critically examines the merits of two theories – social identity, and collective efficacy – as bases of group work motivation.

CONCLUSION

Motivation is a necessary contributor to performance (but not the only contributor) and managers have to understand why a person behaves in a certain way and the factors that may influence action. The problem, however, is that motivation is an invisible process and very individual in nature – what motivates one person may leave another completely unmotivated.

This chapter has considered some of the key theories on motivation and their relevance for performance management practice. Although there is no one universally accepted theory on motivation, there are an enormous number of established studies. All offer different perspectives and insights, and despite their shortcomings (and age) they remain highly influential. The chapter has considered what are called content theories, which try to explain the 'what' of motivation by focusing on needs that shape motivational action. Although each theory has its own view on which needs are most important, they can best be viewed as complementary. For example, Maslow and Alderfer's theories are closely related in viewing a hierarchical ordering of needs. Herzberg's hygiene factors are similar to Maslow's psychological, safety and affiliation needs, and Alderfer's existence and relatedness needs. Herzberg's motivators are broadly comparable with Maslow's higher-order needs, with growth in Alderfer's model, and power and achievement in McClelland's theory. One of the most important contributions these models make is to distinguish between extrinsic and intrinsic motivators. They also highlight the influence of the nature of the job and the importance of job design. However, these theories also share some shortcomings. They mostly adopt a universal perspective and assume that people have a common set of needs, ignoring individual differences and the impact of contextual factors such as national and organisational culture.

The chapter also considered the process theories which look at the cognitive processes to try to understand the 'why' of motivation. They are not grounded in the assumption of universality, and place emphasis on individual differences. In the main, the basic tenets of these theories remain unchallenged (Ambrose and Kulik, 1999: 278). They highlight the importance of managing expectations and fairness, similar to the psychological contract (Chapter 1). They acknowledge the importance of work and job context, and the need to establish clear links between reward and performance, to pay attention to feedback and goal-setting and the need for involvement. Effective performance management requires careful attention to all these issues, which are considered in more depth in subsequent chapters of this book.

EXPLORE FURTHER

Ambrose, M. L. and Kulik, C. T. (1999) 'Old friends, new faces: motivation research in the 1990s', *Journal of Management*, Vol.25: 213–92

Arnold, J. and Randall, R. (2010) *Work Psychology: Understanding human behaviour in the workplace*, 5th edition (Chapter 8). Harlow: FT/Prentice Hall

Herzberg, F. (1987 reprint) 'One more time: how do you motivate employees?', *Harvard Business Review*, Vol.65, No.5: 109–20

Latham, G. P. and Pinder, C. C. (2005) 'Work motivation theory and research at the dawn of the twenty-first century', *Annual Review of Psychology*, Vol.56: 485–516

Lewis, T. (2011) 'Assessing social identity and collective efficacy as theories of group motivation at work', *International Journal of Human Resource Management*, Vol.22, No.4: 963–80

Locke, E. A. and Latham, G. P. (2004) 'What should we do about motivation theory? Six recommendations for the twenty-first century', *Academy of Management Review*, Vol.29, No.3: 388–403

Pfeffer, J. (1998) 'Six dangerous myths about pay', *Harvard business Review*, Vol. 67, No.3, May–June: 109–19

Rollinson, D. (2008) *Organisational Behaviour and Analysis: An integrated approach*, 4th edition. Harlow: FT/Prentice Hall

Special issue of *Harvard Business Review*, 2003, 'Motivating people: how to get the most from your organization', Vol.81, No.1, January. This also includes five previously published articles including Herzberg's famous paper mentioned above

Wahba, M. A. and Bridwell, L. G. (1976) 'Maslow reconsidered: a review of research on the need hierarchy theory', *Organizational Behaviour and Human Performance*, Vol.15, No.2: 212–40

CHAPTER 4

The Role of Line Managers in Managing Performance

SUE HUTCHINSON

LEARNING OUTCOMES

By the end of this chapter you should be able to:

- explain how and why line management roles in managing and leading people have expanded

- understand the critical role that line managers play in managing performance

- appreciate the importance of effective leadership behaviour in people management

- critically evaluate the problems experienced by line managers in delivering their performance management responsibilities

- identify the ways in which the HR function and senior managers can support line managers in undertaking their performance management roles more effectively.

INTRODUCTION

Research shows that the key relationship in the workplace is between an individual employee and his or her immediate line manager, and that line managers have a significant impact on employee attitudes and performance-related behaviours. Line managers act as 'agents' of the organisation, and employees' views of the organisation can be shaped by the overall quality of their relationship with their line manager. In Chapter 1 it was shown how, as 'HR agents', line managers can influence employee attitudes and elicit discretionary behaviour by the way in which they interpret and apply people management practices and processes, or 'bring HR policies to life' (Hutchinson and Purcell, 2003) and show leadership. In doing so, they provide the vital link in the HR–performance chain. However, it is only recently that the significance of this body of managers has been understood, and public policy has now started to pay particular attention to this critical group of managers (see, for example, ACAS, 2009a; MacLeod and Clarke, 2009; UKCES, 2009). In 2009, the national review into employee engagement (MacLeod and Clarke, 2009: 80) stated:

> An engaging manager is at the heart of success in engaging the workforce. Accenture's internal research showed that 80 per cent of the variation in engagement levels was down to the line manager. As a result, employees' most

important relationship at work is with their line manager; people join organisations, but they leave managers.

Over the last few decades, the role of the line manager has changed significantly as much of the day-to-day responsibility for managing people has been transferred from the HR function to the line. In most organisations line managers are now expected to undertake operational responsibility for induction, set individual and team objectives, assess performance, provide feedback, identify training and development needs, act as coach and mentor, make reward decisions, provide career counselling, and handle under-performance. They are also increasingly expected to show leadership behaviours that motivate employees and encourage them to put in extra effort to 'go the extra mile' for the organisation. The demands on line managers are therefore considerable and require quite complex and subtle management skills. It is no surprise, then, that a growing body of research raises concerns about the effectiveness of line managers in their role as leaders and managers of people.

This chapter focuses on the role of line managers in performance management, and begins by exploring recent trends, before considering the theoretical and empirical evidence which suggests these managers play a critical role in leading and managing people. Although line managers operate at all levels of management, the focus of recent research has been on first and middle managers since it is these managers who are in regular and close contact with employees, tend to have the bigger teams to manage, and thus wield the potential to have the greatest impact on employees. The chapter then explores further their role in performance management, and the challenges and barriers they face in undertaking their performance management responsibilities, including issues of work overload, competing work priorities, and lack of skills and knowledge. The chapter concludes with a discussion on the support that organisations can provide to help line managers perform their role more effectively, paying particular attention to the role of the HR function and more senior managers.

INCREASED HRM RESPONSIBLITY TO THE LINE

The trend towards increasing devolution of HR activities to the line over the last few decades is now well documented (eg Renwick, 2003; Perry and Kulik, 2008; Hutchinson and Wood, 1995; Larsen and Brewster, 2003; Hutchinson and Purcell, 2007; IRS, 2008; Brandl *et al*, 2009). In an IRS survey of 121 organisations (IRS, 2008), four out of five organisations reported increased devolution of HR work to the line over the past three years, and two in three organisations predicted that line managers would take on greater HR activities in the next three years. In most organisations today (UK and globally), line managers are expected to routinely handle the operational aspects of recruitment and selection, performance appraisal, training, learning and development, reward, absenteeism, under-performance, and sometimes even the more specialist areas such as career management. These activities are either the sole responsibility of line managers or shared with the HR function, and managing performance is a key part of this role, as the results of another IRS survey show (see Table 4.1). This indicates that in 'Appraisals and performance management' and 'Coaching of direct reports', managers are more likely to take sole responsibility, whereas in other areas associated with performance management it is a shared responsibility with HR.

Table 4.1 Line manager responsibilities in performance management (percentages of organisations responding)

Area of HR work (n=123)	Shared responsibility %	Line manager sole responsibility %
Appraisals and performance management	28	69
Staff development	54	25
Absence management	56	38
Dealing with grievances	75	19
Disciplinary procedures	71	21
Coaching of direct reports	29	60
Pay decisions and/or communicating about pay	62	9

Source: Wolff (2010)

There is a clear rationale for locating performance management tasks within the line. It is, after all, the line manager who is in close and regular contact with employees, has direct responsibility for managing them on a day-to-day basis and is accountable for the performance of their business area. In discussing the front-line manager (FLM) role (team leaders and supervisors), ACAS (2009a: 3) considers that:

> FLMs are best placed to talk to employees, to listen to their concerns, to counsel and coach them, to check they meet their targets and to ensure they are committed to the business.

Advocates of devolution also argue that it saves costs, and that issues can be dealt with more speedily and reflect local conditions and business needs (Larsen and Brewster, 2003; Renwick, 2009; Brandl et al, 2009). Giving managers greater ownership should encourage greater commitment to performance management, and also, potentially, add variety to the line management role.

The emergence of the 'HRM model' over the last 20 or so years, and pressure for the HR function to make a more strategic contribution (Purcell et al, 2009; Reilly et al, 2007; Gilbert et al, 2011a) has undoubtedly influenced this trend. The model argues that because HR practice is critical to the core activities of the business, it is too important to be left to HR specialists alone, and that line managers should be closely involved as deliverers and drivers of HR policy (Storey, 2007). In operationalising the model it is line managers who put people management into practice or 'bring policies to life' (Hutchinson and Purcell, 2003), leaving the HR function free (in theory) to design the policies and focus on the more strategic aspects of their role. This is well illustrated in Ulrich's popular business partnering model (Ulrich, 1997), in which HR becomes a strategic business partner and centre of expertise, transferring the transactional HR work to the line, usually with the support of a shared service centre (see also Chapter 2). This has been facilitated by the growth in e-HR, such as the intranet which provides managers and employees access to HR policies, procedures and guidance.

Increased competitiveness and a much sharper focus on performance in organisations, individualisation of the employment relationship, decentralisation of decision-making, de-layering and the growth in teamworking have also contributed to devolution of HRM to the line (McGovern et al, 1997; Hales, 2005; Hutchinson and Purcell, 2010; Fenton-O'Creevy, 2001). More recently, the drive for cost efficiencies (eg the reduction in HR headcount) and improvements in service quality have also influenced this transition (Hutchinson and Tailby, 2012).

CRITICAL REFLECTION 4.1

Discuss the view that in devolving HR activities to the line, the HR function is distancing itself from employees and losing contact with the human side of its work.

You may like to read the journal articles by Francis and Keegan (2006) and Keegan and Francis (2010), who develop these points further in relation to the HR business partnering model.

THE LINE MANAGER'S CRITICAL ROLE IN MANAGING AND LEADING PEOPLE

Chapter 1 introduced the evidence that line management behaviour is fundamental to delivering the performance benefits of good HR policies. As 'HR agents' of the organisation, line managers can significantly influence employee job satisfaction, commitment and discretionary behaviour by the way in which they implement and enact HR policies and show leadership (Truss, 2001; Purcell *et al*, 2009). Indeed, 'poorly designed or inadequate HR policies can be "rescued" by good management behaviour in much the same way as "good" HR practices can be negated by poor front-line manager behaviour or weak leadership' (Purcell and Hutchinson, 2007: 4). Front-line managers, in particular (ie those at the lower levels of the management hierarchy), have the potential to have the greatest impact on employees since they tend to have the bigger teams to manage and because of their proximity and regular interaction with employees (Becker *et al*, 1996). The research undertaken by Purcell and others (Purcell *et al*, 2003; Hutchinson and Purcell, 2003) found that the key areas in which line managers have considerable involvement and make a difference to employee attitudes and performance include:

- performance appraisal
- training, coaching and guidance
- involvement and communication
- 'openness' or the ability to raise grievances and matters of concern
- work–life balance
- providing recognition and reward.

Further findings from this research are discussed below.

'UNLOCKING THE BLACK BOX' — THE VITAL ROLE OF LINE MANAGERS

The study by Purcell and colleagues, sponsored by the CIPD, sought to 'unlock the black box' and examine the link between people management and organisational performance. Based on case study research in 12 organisations, attitudinal data was collected from each organisation over a two-year period. Two surveys were conducted in each case study, 12 months apart, to track changes in attitudes against any organisational change.

In analysing the overall employee data set, the research team found that the way in which managers implemented HR practices and exercised leadership (by, for example, involving staff and responding to their suggestions, treating employees fairly and dealing with problems in the workplace) was strongly related to positive employee views on job satisfaction, job discretion, commitment and motivation (Hutchinson and Purcell, 2003: 14):

> The higher the employees rate FLMs [front-line managers] in terms of the way they manage people, the more committed and satisfied those employees will be, and the higher their levels of job discretion.

Managerial behaviour was also strongly linked to the way that the line managers were themselves managed and to the wider values and culture of the organisation.

Some of the case study organisations made significant changes to the roles and competence profiles of their line managers after the first-year survey. One of these was Selfridge's Trafford Park, Manchester, store. Following disappointing results on leadership behaviour and appraisal from the first-year employee attitude survey, the store invested in their team leader role. The role was redefined and all team leaders were required to reapply for this new position through a redesigned selection process which focused on behaviours as well as skill sets. Improvements were also made to the performance appraisal system for team leaders, linking it more to career opportunities and making it a core requirement to undertake staff appraisal and give emphasis to good leadership behaviour. The outcome, seen in the second-year employee survey results, suggested that these changes had very positive results. Employee attitudes improved, as seen in job satisfaction, commitment, and job influence, as did ratings of line management behaviour. The performance of the store also improved, and senior managers in the company attributed these improvements to changes made to the team leader role.

At the Royal United Hospital in Bath, similar results were found. Despite acute financial difficulties in the hospital, senior management changes and adverse national and local publicity, the department studied showed marked improvements in employee attitudes over the period of study. This was attributed to deliberate attempts to improve ward management skills and behaviours. It included a new recruitment and selection process which emphasised people management skills in addition to clinical skills, the implementation of a 360-degree appraisal scheme and greater support and training for ward managers. Employee job satisfaction, motivation and commitment improved markedly, and what once had been a retention blackspot ended the second year with no job vacancies (Purcell, Kinnie and Hutchinson, 2003; Hutchinson and Purcell, 2003).

RELATIONS-ORIENTED LEADERSHIP BEHAVIOUR

Similar findings are evidenced in a study of three service organisations in Belgium and Luxembourg (Gilbert *et al*, 2011a). Using the framework of social exchange theory (see Chapter 1), the research team investigated the impact of line managers and the HR department on employee affective commitment. Their findings showed that line managers can enhance employees' affective commitment by both effective enactment of HR practices and effective *relations-oriented leadership behaviour* (concern for human relations and providing friendly and supportive relationships with reports). They also found that high service quality by the HR function has a positive impact on employee affective commitment. Five specific relations-oriented leadership behaviours were found to be relevant to the line management role (based on the work of Yukl *et al*, 2002: 25):

- **supporting** – that is, acting considerately, showing sympathy and support when a person is upset or anxious, and providing encouragement and support for difficult and stressful tasks
- **developing** others, such as coaching and offering advice, providing opportunities for skill development and helping others learn how to improve their skills
- **recognition** – involving praise and recognition for effective performance, significant achievements, special contributions and performance improvement
- **consulting,** including conferring with people before making decisions that affect them, encouraging participation in decision-making and using the ideas and suggestion of others
- **empowering,** or giving employees substantial responsibility and discretion in their activities, and trusting people to solve problems and make decisions without getting prior approval.

Further evidence of the importance of line management behaviour can be found in research on leader–member exchange, perceived supervisor support and the psychological contract.

Leader–member exchange theory

Leader–member exchange theory (LMX) (Graen and Uhl-Bien, 1995; Uhl-Bien *et al*, 2000) examines the nature of the relationship between an employee ('member') and his or her immediate line manager ('leader'), arguing that the quality of this relationship will impact on employee outcomes and performance. The theory suggests that managers do not treat all employees the same but create 'in-groups' and 'out-groups'. Those in the 'in-group' have a high-quality LMX and receive more time, support and trust, compared to those in the 'out-group', who have a low-quality LMX. Furthermore, effectively developed relationships (ie those with high LMX) have been shown to have a positive impact on job performance, employee satisfaction, commitment and citizenship behaviours (Gerstner and Day, 1997). LMX theory is therefore useful in explaining why employees in the same team may have different experiences of HRM. For example, in-group members have been shown to receive higher performance ratings, more support and attention compared to out-group members even when they have performed at the same level (Varma and Stroh, 2001).

Supervisor support

Support from managers is also emphasised in research on perceived supervisor support (PSS) following organisational support theory. Organisational support theory suggests that employees develop general beliefs about the degree to which their organisation cares about their wellbeing and supports them (Eisenberger *et al*, 1986, 1997; Rhoades and Eisenberger, 2002). The theory argues that this belief arises from employees' experience of treatment by agents of the organisation, in particular their direct manager or supervisor. 'Because supervisors act as agents of the organisation, having responsibility for directing and evaluating subordinates' performance, employees view their supervisor's favourable or unfavourable orientation toward them as indicative of the organisation's support' (Rhoades and Eisenberger, 2002: 700). Acts of supervisory support include providing resources, training, work schedule flexibility and feedback (Byrne *et al*, 2012).

The psychological contract

In a study of 1,000 people in employment in Britain, Guest and Conway (2004: 19–23) found that effective supervisory leadership (rated on seven behaviours at work such as 'Motivating you to work effectively') was one of the strongest factors associated with a positive psychological contract (Chapter 1), organisational commitment, loyalty at work, satisfaction and loyalty to customers. In a smaller study of employees, supervisory support and mentor relationships have been shown to reduce the negative effects of psychological contract breach (Zagenczyk *et al*, 2009).

The conclusion from this body of research is clear. The quality of line managers is vital for individual and organisational performance and for performance management policies and practices to influence performance they must be successfully enacted by line managers. However, line managers are frequently cited as the weak link in the application of performance management policies (eg Hendry *et al*, 1997). Before this evidence is explored, line managers' involvement in performance management is considered.

LINE MANAGERS' INVOLVEMENT IN PERFORMANCE MANAGEMENT

Line managers act as the interface between the organisation and its workforce and as such are in a key position to translate and communicate the organisation's strategy, its values and its objectives – vital in any strategic approach to performance management (Chapter 2). As Marchington and Wilkinson (2012) note: 'They are in a position to strengthen, ignore, or even undermine the messages conveyed by the Big Idea'. Line managers are also critical sources of employees' perceptions of fairness and justice – for example, through performance appraisal, feedback and the allocation of rewards, which has implications for job performance, motivation and organisational citizenship behaviours (see also Chapters 1 and 3).

More specifically, they are involved in an extensive range of formal and informal performance management activities, which start as soon as an employee joins the organisation by way of induction and socialisation (see also Chapter 2). According to a CIPD survey (2007), induction was at that time a responsibility for line managers in 84 per cent of organisations. Specific responsibilities typically include providing information about the job and department, clarifying performance expectations, explaining policies and procedures (such as probation, leave, health and safety, the appraisal process, rules governing the use of the Internet and telephone calls), and more generally explaining 'the way things are done around here'. If there is a buddy or mentoring scheme, the line manager would normally be expected to allocate this role to an existing member of the team. The manager might also facilitate work shadowing or working alongside a member of staff to learn certain aspects of the role. A key part of the welcoming process involves socialising employees to make sure that new recruits feel part of the team, introducing them to work colleagues and any social networks, and perhaps providing a physical tour of the work site.

The line manager also plays a key role in the performance appraisal (PA) process, typically observing and assessing performance, conducting the formal review, providing regular feedback and support. By doing so, line managers have a critical role in determining employee perceptions of the effectiveness and usefulness of appraisals and, of course, the outcomes. PAs, however, are plagued by major problems (discussed further in Chapter 6), and there is growing evidence of variability in line management interpretation and delivery of performance appraisal policy (Hutchinson and Purcell, 2003; McGovern *et al*, 1997). Some of this concerns line managers' inability to make accurate and objective assessments. In examining supervisory strategies in performance management, Brown and Lim (2009) identify a range of situational and personal factors which contribute to the line manager's motivation to provide accurate assessments. Situational factors include organisational commitment, organisational climate, performance appraisal purpose, trust and confidence in the PA system, and accountability. For example, a participative climate can impact on line managers' motivation to provide accurate ratings and effective feedback (Tziner *et al*, 2001), whereas low levels of trust in the PA system will negatively impact on the managers' motivation to rate accurately. When the purpose of the PA system is evaluative (eg to allocate reward), managers tend to rate employees more leniently than when PAs are used for developmental purposes. Managers who feel accountable for assessments and are required to justify decisions made are more likely to provide accurate ratings. Personal factors include personality, self-efficacy, PA discomfort and goals (Brown and Lim, 2009). Highly conscientious managers, for example, are likely to give lower ratings, whereas supervisors high in agreeableness tend to give higher ratings (Bernardin *et al*, 2000). Managers with low levels of self efficacy may lack the motivation to undertake PAs (Tziner *et al*, 2005), although the research is less clear about the impact of those with high levels of self-efficacy. It is also well known that many managers feel uncomfortable with monitoring, rating and communicating feedback (eg Murphy and

Cleveland, 1995). Studies show that managers with high levels of discomfort tend to rate more leniently in order to avoid having a 'difficult conversation' and unpleasant consequences (Brown and Lim, 2009: 195). Managers also give different ratings depending on whether they facilitate the achievement of their own goals. Longenecker *et al* (1987) refer to the 'politics of performance appraisal', arguing that managers deliberately try to protect their own interests by manipulating ratings (see Chapter 6), and suggesting that managers inflate ratings to reflect favourably on themselves.

REFLECTIVE ACTIVITY 4.1

What can organisations do to improve the accuracy of line managers' assessments in performance appraisal?

Training, learning and development, which are at the heart of performance improvement (Chapter 7), are also key activities in which line managers have significant involvement, as confirmed by the CIPD learning and talent development survey, which in 2010 found that 81 per cent of respondents felt line managers had some responsibility for training, learning and development. Responsibilities are wide-ranging and include identifying, agreeing and planning training and development (usually done through the formal performance review and personnel development plans), delivering training, coaching and mentoring to develop work-related skills and abilities, and granting access to training in terms of approving attendance or of funding. Managers also have a facilitative role in providing support from trainers, peers and mentors and promoting knowledge-sharing (eg through team meetings or problem-solving work groups).

The potential benefits of line manager involvement in these activities has long been recognised (Gibb, 2003). It helps integrate the notion of learning and development into working life, can improve the quality of these activities, and can promote positive attitudes. Managerial coaching has been shown to be important for maximising employee engagement and performance and as a basis to facilitate change (Swart and Kinnie, 2010; Teague and Roche, 2012). Line managers can ensure that learning is directly linked to workplace activities and are ideally placed to evaluate the outcomes of learning, in relation to both the individual and the organisation (Purcell and Hutchinson, 2007b).

However, not all line managers may be motivated or skilled enough to carry out this role. In the 2007 CIPD survey roughly a quarter (23 per cent) of respondents (HR and training specialists) felt that line managers do not take their responsibility in learning and development seriously (CIPD, 2007), and a mere 4 per cent of respondents 'completely agreed' that line managers took their coaching role seriously, most citing issues of negative capability and consistency, as discussed later in this chapter.

Line managers also have a direct role to play in allocating or making recommendations about performance-related rewards (where they exist), as discussed further in Chapter 8. This includes using informal or 'unofficial' means to motivate and reward staff – something often ignored or underestimated in both the literature and in practice. This could involve giving access to training, secondments, flexible working, verbal praise and more intrinsic forms of reward, such as greater job discretion and responsibility or interesting project work. Although these can be powerful motivators, the very problem with these unofficial practices is that they rely on managers' discretion and are not subject to formal evaluation or monitoring.

Managing under-performance (eg lack of capability, sickness absence, poor attendance, inappropriate behaviour) also falls within the remit of the line manager, and is arguably one of the most challenging aspects of people management for any manager (see also Chapters 9 and 10). In an IRS survey, over 94 per cent of organisations reported that responsibility for managing under-performance lies principally with line managers, yet almost 60 per cent did not consider managers confident and competent in discharging this role (IRS, 2011). Surveys of line managers suggest they feel discomfort with this role because they lack the confidence and skills, because they dislike having 'difficult conversations' with staff, or because they do not want to deal with the potential consequences.

In practice managers appear to show a preference for informality in dealing with issues of conflict and discipline. This is partly due to an aversion to the time, cost and complexity of formal procedures, but also to a preference for reliance on 'gut feeling' and instinct, plus a lack of confidence in dealing with standardised procedures (Jones and Saundry, 2012). An informal approach also allows issues to be dealt with in a flexible and contingent manner, enabling managers to respond to individual circumstances and the work context. For example, managers might be more understanding of attendance issues if they know that an employee has caring responsibilities, or resist using formal procedures if they perceive it as counterproductive, leading, for example, to withdrawal of commitment or co-operation (*ibid*). However, as previously mentioned, informality raises concerns about consistency and fairness, and may undermine any well-designed performance management policies.

REFLECTIVE ACTIVITY 4.2

1   Consider an organisation you have worked for. Which performance management activities would you expect to have covered by formal written policies and procedures?

2   What organisational factors might influence the degree of formality?

DIFFICULTIES WITH LINE MANAGEMENT INVOLVEMENT IN PERFORMANCE MANAGEMENT

In devolving responsibility to the line there is an assumption that line managers implement policies as intended or as designed, but – as indicated previously – there is strong evidence of a gap between the formal intended HR practices and those experienced by the employee, with this difference explained by the variability in line management behaviour (Milsome, 2006; Hutchinson and Purcell, 2003; Renwick, 2003; Cunningham and Hyman, 1999; McGovern *et al*, 1997). This is evident in all activities associated with managing performance. For example, reporting on their research in seven leading-edge companies, McGovern *et al* (1997) found management implementation of performance appraisals uneven within organisations, and that the quality of the practice also varied (McGovern *et al*, 1997: 26). Further examples of differences between policy and practice were given in Table 1.1 in Chapter 1.

Although some line managers may consciously choose to behave inconsistently when applying HR practice because they want some flexibility in dealing with individual employees (Marchington and Wilkinson, 2012; Jones and Saundry, 2012), there is growing evidence that line managers face considerable difficulty in implementing their people management roles effectively. Table 4.2 indicates HR practitioners' assessment of line managers' ability to deal with HR work, and shows that in no case did a majority think that managers handled a particular activity well. Particular concerns were expressed with keeping personnel records, managing absence, team development, and on-going training.

Table 4.2 HR's assessment of line managers' ability to handle people management

Activity assessed	Handled well (%)	Handled badly (%)	Handled adequately (%)
Absence management	15.4	46.2	38.5
Appraisal and performance management	18.6	20.9	60.5
Discipline	20.0	20.0	60.0
Employee engagement	16.7	22.2	61.1
Flexible working	43.8	6.3	50.0
Grievances	—	16.7	83.3
Performance pay	16.7	20.8	62.5
Personnel records	33.3	50.0	16.7
Recognition of employee performance	9.1	30.3	60.6
Recruitment	33.3	16.7	50.0
Selection	34.6	15.4	50.0
Team briefing	25.7	18.8	55.4
Team development	21.3	34.4	44.3
Training – induction	47.4	10.5	42.1
Training – on-going	28.2	28.2	43.6
Employee welfare	12.5	12.5	75.0

Source: Milsome (2006)

Respondents to the e-reward survey on performance management in 2005 also expressed concerns about the ability of line managers:

- 89 per cent felt that line managers do not have the skills required
- 84 per cent felt that line managers do not discriminate sufficiently when assessing performance
- 75 per cent felt that line managers were not committed to performance management
- 76 per cent felt that line managers were reluctant to conduct performance reviews.

Whereas these surveys reflect the perspective of the HR practitioner, other studies confirm that line managers too recognise that they struggle to implement their people management responsibilities effectively (eg Hutchinson and Purcell, 2010; Nehles *et al*, 2006).

Researchers have identified a wide range of factors to explain why line management involvement is so problematic, and although some are specific to the role and organisational context, a number of common themes emerge. These themes overlap but can be categorised broadly under the following headings (Purcell *et al*, 2009; Perry and Kulik, 2008; Maxwell and Watson, 2006; Nehles *et al*, 2006):

- work overload and competing work priorities
- lack of lack of skills and knowledge
- lack of commitment

- inadequate organisational support.

These constraints are clearly evident in research on nurse managers in the NHS conducted on behalf of the Department of Health (see Case Study 4.1) and considered in more detail below.

WORK OVERLOAD AND COMPETING WORK PRIORITIES

For many managers, heavy workloads and increasing pressure prevent them from carrying out their performance management roles effectively. In studies of line managers in Hilton International hotels (Maxwell and Watson, 2006) and the NHS (Hutchinson and Purcell, 2010; Boaden et al, 2008), work overload was identified by managers as one of the biggest barriers to their involvement in HRM. This is particularly acute for front-line managers whose role has extended in recent years to include newer management responsibilities, such as people management and budgeting, without relinquishing any of their former roles (Hales, 2006; Hutchinson and Purcell, 2010). The workload is exacerbated when managers are under pressure to get work done quickly or when they find themselves taking on the work of others because they are managing a reduced workforce. The implications of these added work burdens are that HR work often gets squeezed, as suggested by this line manager in our recent research in a large public sector organisation (Hutchinson and Tailby, 2012):

> The role of the line manager (LM) has become progressively loaded over recent years, various specialist functions (most notably HR) becoming the responsibility of the LM with only the barest of training and backup. Most LMs now have a full-time 'day job' as well as their LM role, so at best we scrabble to find the time to do proper line management and often resort to managing on an exception basis.

Having multiple and competing responsibilities also creates tension and ambiguity within the role, and invariably means that managers are faced with having to prioritise their workload. This is evident in the study of nurse managers (see section below) who had to juggle the competing demands of service targets, costs and good practice HRM. When line managers were under pressure, priority was given to clinical work, and people management was afforded a low priority. Other studies confirm that line managers tend to focus on the short-term business priorities or the 'harder', more tangible outputs (eg monthly sales targets) rather than the 'softer' people management issues which do not produce an immediate return. McGovern et al note (McGovern et al, 1997: 26) how

> the short-term nature of managerial activity leads to a tendency to put a greater priority on the achievement of the numbers per se rather than the achievement of numbers through people.

REFLECTIVE ACTIVITY 4.3

The responsibilities of front-line managers

Characterised as 'mini-business managers' front-line managers have multiple responsibilities, including:

- day-to-day people management
- providing technical expertise
- work allocation and rota compilation
- monitoring work processes
- checking quality
- dealing with customers/clients/suppliers
- measuring operational performance
- managing operational costs.

1   How might these different responsibilities conflict with each other for a team leader in 2014?

Role ambiguity also occurs because of different expectations about the role. Hutchinson and Purcell's (2010) research in the NHS found a disparity between senior managers' expectations and perceptions of the role and line managers' experiences of their job. Senior managers considered that the clinical role dominated, but in practice line managers had much greater involvement in the non-clinical or management aspects of the role. As a consequence, much of the 'management' work, including HR duties, was covered on an overtime basis or simply did not get done. Wright *et al* (2001) also reported that senior managers and line managers have different views about what HR responsibilities are being devolved. Research in Hilton International UK Hotels by Maxwell and Watson (2006) also revealed perceptual differences, but this time between line managers and HR specialists. HR managers perceived line managers to have greater involvement in HR activities than did the line managers, particularly in discipline and grievance-handling and induction. Furthermore, they found that higher levels of agreement between the two different groups correlate with higher levels of hotel performance.

Gilbert *et al* (2011b) refer to this combination of role ambiguity and role overload as 'role stressors' which has far-reaching consequences, leading to negative work attitudes, less wellbeing and reduced overall individual performance – in addition to the damaging consequences for people management.

LACK OF SKILLS AND KNOWLEDGE

A consistent theme in the literature is that managers lack the skills and knowledge to perform their performance management role effectively: some of this evidence has been presented in the previous section (Harris *et al*, 2002; Nehles *et al*, 2006; Maxwell and Watson, 2006; Hutchinson and Purcell, 2010).

One reason for this is that key skills are not being sought in the recruitment and selection process. Many managers are still recruited or promoted on the basis of their technical or operational skills and job knowledge rather than the softer skills such as leadership, communication and interpersonal skills (Milsome, 2006). In the study of Hilton Hotels, managers felt that skills in time management, delegation, learning and communication were lacking. Lack of skills can translate into lack of confidence, and, when under pressure, it is no surprise that the people management side of the job often suffers as managers retreat into what they know best – the operational side of the job.

It is widely believed that one explanation for poor skills is lack of training and development. In a study of workplace conflict in Ireland, Teague and Roche (2012) found that although line managers were considered to play a significant role in the management of workplace conflict, they often lacked formal training or on-going assessment of their competence in this area. Hutchinson and Purcell's (2010) study of nurse managers found that although most had received some training in the previous 12 months, it was predominantly for clinical needs (see Case Study 4.1 below). Nevertheless, training does seem to be on offer in many organisations – 82 per cent of respondents to an IRS survey claimed to offer training for line managers to help them with their people management role, yet well over half (58 per cent) did not believe that line managers were adequately trained to manage people (Wolff, 2010). So why isn't this training producing the desired results? There are a number of plausible explanations. Firstly, managers may not be able to access the training because of funding constraints or lack of time. Heavy workloads and competing demands means that training is not a priority, as is confirmed by an IRS survey which reported that over half of the respondents felt that training is given a low priority in the overall business agenda. Secondly, some managers may be reluctant to train because they feel they don't need training – it may be that they feel that skills are best acquired by a mixture of 'learning by doing' and common sense (Cunningham and Hyman, 1995), and that they, as managers, intuitively know what is best for their staff – what motivates them, what pressures they face, and so on. The quality of training may also deter attendance. In a survey on line management training in people management 11 per cent of organisations felt the content of the training had let the organisation down (Wolff, 2010).

A third reason why training may not be effective relates to the frequency with which managers have to deal with people issues. No matter how much training a manager receives, it is of little use unless he or she can put it into practice, and there are likely to be some issues (such as disciplinaries, grievances and even recruitment) which managers only deal with occasionally, as this manager explains (Hutchinson and Tailby, 2012):

> Years can pass for a line manager without having to deal with HR issues like recruitment, grievance, inefficiency, disability, etc, so when you need to handle these issues it is unfamiliar territory and in the past we would turn to our HR colleagues in the organisation for advice. … If you are coming across issues for the first time, it can take a significant effort to get up to speed in order to manage the situation effectively.

To engage line managers in training, 78 per cent of HR respondents to an IRS survey (Wolff, 2010) believed that training should be compulsory if line managers are to perform more effectively, although few organisations appear to do this. Some have also argued that managers are less likely to develop others if they lack training and development themselves. Storey (1992) believes that 'managers who have themselves received little education and training are less likely to recognise or approve the need for investment in the training of their subordinates' (Storey, 1992: 213).

A lack of knowledge and understanding of HR policies and procedures may further constrain management practice (Nehles *et al*, 2006). Hutchinson and Purcell report that in their research some line managers were unclear about aspects of HR strategy and policy – for example, on the performance management process, particularly where there were links with pay. In the Hilton Hotels study, the researchers suggest that line managers' lack of understanding of the business and HR strategy may curtail their involvement in HR activities (Maxwell and Watson, 2006: 1162).

Managers may be applying policies wrongly but simply not be aware that they are breaking the rules. This 'management by omission' (Marchington and Wilkinson, 2008) is particularly problematic in the employee relations arena. Disciplinaries and grievances often go wrong because managers fail to follow the correct procedure in full. Examples include an employee who is not given the opportunity to respond to an allegation, an inadequate investigation, a warning not being sufficiently explicit, or a dismissal that occurs during the course of an argument. As already mentioned, managers appear to show a preference for informality, which allows them more discretion and flexibility in responding to individual problems and circumstances. All this highlights the need for HR specialists and the line to work more closely together, and for HR to consult line managers when designing policies, and to persuade them that procedures are 'valuable tools rather than millstones' (Marchington and Wilkinson, 2012: 179).

LACK OF MOTIVATION AND COMMITMENT TO UNDERTAKE PEOPLE MANAGEMENT

Many have questioned line managers' willingness and motivation to embrace HRM. Some have argued that line managers exhibit a 'disdain for HR work', viewing it as 'soft' management and 'pandering to the needs of the workforce' (Marchington and Wilkinson, 2012). Some line managers appear to show resentment, considering they have been 'dumped upon' and are doing the work of the HR function, and there can be little doubt that administrative work is frequently perceived as an unnecessary burden and can deter managers. However, some recent research suggests that line managers are increasingly accepting their involvement in HRM (Boaden *et al*, 2008; Hutchinson and Tailby, 2012). In a study of a large public sector organisation which had restructured the HR department to adopt the business partnering model, Hutchinson and Tailby found that most managers interviewed understood and were satisfied with their role in HR work, suggesting a willingness – or at worst, an acceptance – to undertake these activities. Nevertheless, it is well known that managers feel uncomfortable dealing with conflict and dislike holding those 'difficult conversations', which inevitably means a reluctance to undertake this type of work.

 REFLECTIVE ACTIVITY 4.4

Having 'difficult conversations'

Difficult conversations involve managing emotions and information in a sensitive way (ACAS, 2012a). Examples of 'difficult conversions' might include (Wilkes and Bates, 2010; ACAS, 2012a):

- delivering bad news (eg not having been selected for promotion)
- providing critical feedback on performance
- raising issues of misconduct
- raising issues of an employee's personal hygiene

- addressing conflict between colleagues
- investigating complaints
- providing feedback on someone more senior than yourself.

Provide some guidance for line managers on how to conduct a difficult conversation effectively. This should include the following areas:

- Preparation
- Communication
- Listening
- Action following the meeting.

It is true that HR work is often seen as discretionary compared to other requirements of the role, and relies on the manager's own sense of motivation and commitment for fulfilment (Purcell and Hutchinson, 2007a). According to McGovern *et al* (1997), the line manager's involvement in people management often lacks 'institutional reinforcement' through the organisation's policies because it does not appear in any formal or informal performance expectations. In other words, if 'people management' is not explicitly identified in policies or documentation (job and person descriptions, performance objectives, reward), it is easy to see how managers afford HR work a low priority or perceive it as a 'bolt-on' to the main activities of the role. This is supported by other research – for example, Boaden *et al*'s (2008) study found that only 37 per cent of line managers reported that they were appraised on their implementation of HR policies or people management skills.

Another impediment to commitment to people management may be lack of accountability. When managers lack authority (for example, to approve training or holiday requests or to determine the final outcome of performance-related pay), this can be a source of frustration and constraint. Similarly, if senior managers override the decisions of their more junior managers, this can lead to line managers' disengaging from the process.

LACK OF SUPPORT

How well line managers perceive they are supported in their performance management role will inevitably impact on the way they themselves manage, and their effectiveness in delivering HR work. Key is the relationship between line managers and the HR function, and to some extent the effectiveness of this relationship will partly depend on the structure, maturity and size of the HR function. The research reports mixed findings. Some report supportive relationships in which the HR function helps line managers implement HR policies (Boaden *et al*, 2008), but others find more negative experiences with line managers critical of HR support (Whittaker and Marchington, 2003; Hutchinson and Purcell, 2010). A common complaint expressed by line managers is that HR design policies which are out of touch with business realities and hard to operationalise, and in general there is certainly little evidence of line manager involvement in the design and development of HR policies. Other concerns include the lack of consistency in HR advice, poor training provision for line managers, lack of clarity in the procedures, and constraint of line managers' autonomy by HR, preventing the managers from making decisions. Some have also suggested that HR specialists may be unwilling to relinquish some of their operational responsibilities (Currie and Procter, 2001).

Senior management support has also been found to be lacking in terms of providing recognition, role clarity, time, realistic targets and role-modelling behaviour. In a CIPD survey 34 per cent of respondents felt that encouraging senior managers or leaders to act as role models or champions would encourage line manager buy-in to learning and development. A study of line management involvement in reward and training and learning and development (Hutchinson and Purcell, 2007) also found that positive role modelling of senior managers was of fundamental importance. Line managers can pick up signals from senior managers about how to behave and what to prioritise and bad habits as much as good ones are cloned – so if senior managers are not conducting appraisals, why should they? This was highlighted by one senior manager interviewed in the study, when asked about how line managers learned how to deliver their people management roles:

> Line managers receive very little specialty training to think about these elements. Most line managers copy their predecessor, in terms of what they do in this area, or their own manager – we call this 'clone syndrome'. If the job looks the same, then behave the same.

In the same study some line managers also complained of too much involvement by senior managers in the day-to-day management of their people. This was particularly evident in one unionised environment where some complained of 'too many backhand deals with unions' which interfered with their own management responsibilities. Currie and Procter's (2001) study found that first-line managers rarely saw their senior managers, leading to feelings of isolation and distance.

Research on the role of line managers in people management in the NHS – the UK's largest employer (and fifth largest employer in the world) – provides an example of many of the barriers faced by this body of managers (see Case Study 4.1 below).

MANAGERS' EXPERIENCES OF PEOPLE MANAGEMENT IN THE NHS

Research on front-line managers in the NHS uncovers some of the challenges these managers face in discharging their people management responsibilities. Hutchinson and Purcell (2010) studied the role of these junior managers, such as ward managers and paramedic supervisors, in seven NHS Trusts in England during the period 2005–2009. In health care the role of junior managers has changed significantly over the last few decades as policy-makers have sought to transform professionals into managers in a distinctive strategy intended to produce a more efficient and cost-effective service. In addition to clinical care work these managers were expected to undertake responsibility for the day-to-day running of a work area and its resources, including budget management, purchasing, management of the patient pathway, and people management.

As part of this study, line managers were interviewed about their interpretations and experiences of their role. The following key constraints to effective people management emerged:

- heavy workloads, pressure and stress
- role conflict and ambiguity
- lack of training in people management
- inadequate resources including finance and staff
- lack of support from HR and senior managers.

The research revealed that these managers had huge roles. In addition to the more traditional supervisory activities associated with the role (such as planning and scheduling of work, dealing with clinical work), managers had responsibility for performance issues, extensive communication (within the team, the Trust and externally), and newer responsibilities such as managing operational costs, and people management. Nearly all reported increasingly expansive HR duties and large spans of control. Selection, induction, appraisal, personnel development plans, training, providing recognition, communication and involvement, co-coordinating and maintaining effective teamwork, absence management, discipline and grievance-handling, and health and safety were undertaken by 90 per cent or more of respondents. A very slightly smaller percentage (80–89 per cent), and still a significant proportion, had responsibility for recruitment, maintaining staff records, activities associated with the 'improving working lives' initiative, and counselling (usually informal). The average team size was 26 staff, and just under a quarter (23 per cent) reported responsibility for 40 or more staff. In addition, over a third had responsibility for multiple teams. 93 per cent of managers 'agreed' or 'strongly agreed' that their job 'required them to work very hard'; 80 per cent felt their job was stressful; and over three quarters (79 per cent) felt they 'never seemed to have enough time to get their work done'. Nearly all (91 per cent) worked overtime on a regular basis, and well over half took work home regularly.

The multiplicity of roles these managers had to perform inevitably created problems of role conflict and ambiguity. Tensions were evident not only between maintaining high clinical standards and business targets but also within the management role itself, such as in balancing budgets while trying to maintain staff levels and improve staff morale. Differences between senior managers' expectations and perceptions of the role and the line managers' experiences of the job in terms of balancing workload commitments exacerbated this ambiguity. Compounding these problems were financial constraints and a general lack of resources (time, money and people).

Lack of appropriate skills and knowledge was another key constraint, partly because of inadequate training (formal and informal) to develop people management skills. Although nearly all (98 per cent) had received some form of training over the previous year, the majority of training was for clinical needs, and a significant proportion (37 per cent) claimed not to have received any management training. As one manager remarked: 'The limitations are that I am a clinician but also a manager – and I have never been trained in that.' There was a lack of any formalised approach to developing these skills, and even where training was available, financial and time constraints often prevented access to this type of training. 'Learning by doing' was the most common approach – but to be effective this required a blame-free performance culture in which staff could openly admit to mistakes: something that was notably lacking in some Trusts.

Line managers also felt generally unsupported and overlooked as a group. Active support was lacking from senior managers in terms of providing recognition, time and clarity to the role.

Senior managers also needed to act as good role models and adopt a more inclusive and open management style with better communication. More than half were dissatisfied with the support they received from the HR function, which was criticised for being 'too distanced from the workforce', producing mountains of policies that were impractical and difficult to implement, bureaucratic and often slow to respond' (Hutchinson and Purcell, 2010: 371).

Additionally, concerns about the management structure (for example, having to work with senior clinicians who were not subject to clear lines of hierarchical control), frequently changing Trust objectives and national priorities, the IT infrastructure and the mass of paperwork were other sources of constraint.

These obstacles meant that, in practice, managers gave priority to the clinical aspects of the role, and people management was afforded a low priority. HRM was perceived as discretionary by line managers and not contained in any performance expectations for the role such as job competencies. Paradoxically, however, allowing people management to take second place was likely to be counterproductive to the goal of achieving good patient care.

Source: adapted from Hutchinson and Purcell (2010)

SUPPORTING LINE MANAGERS IN PROVIDING EFFECTIVE PERFORMANCE MANAGEMENT

The research discussed thus far highlights the need for organisations to invest in line managers and for HR specialists and senior managers to work more closely with the line managers to help them in their role as managers of people.

The HR function can provide support in various ways (Gilbert *et al*, 2011b; Hutchinson and Purcell, 2007; 2010):

- by providing HR advice and support, particularly on specialist and more complex issues that involve the law, training and managing under-performers. In smaller firms this advice may be sought from ACAS, employer federations, solicitors and government departments (eg Business Link)

- by involving line managers in the development of performance management policies and procedures and providing clear guidelines on their implementation. Managers need policies and procedures that are easy to understand, relevant, straightforward to deliver and not overly bureaucratic and cumbersome. Ignoring managers in the design has been likened to 'designing a car without thinking about who is going to drive it' (Hutchinson and Purcell, 2007: 36), yet almost all organisations do it

- by careful recruitment and selection to ensure that line managers have the right skills for being good people managers. Typical competencies might include communication skills, team skills, leadership, and problem-solving, listening and coaching. This should be reflected in job descriptions and person specifications

- by clarifying job expectations and the relationship between HR and the line in terms of what activities line managers have sole responsibility for, which are shared and which are the responsibility of HR

- by providing training, learning and development so that managers have the appropriate skills and confidence to conduct effective performance appraisals, give feedback, support training and development, have 'difficult conversations' and demonstrate leadership. Consideration must be given to making training compulsory – but formal training on its own, such as management development programmes, is often not popular or effective. Other types of learning must be embedded in the workplace, such as on-the-job learning, coaching and mentoring, and informal training from managers and colleagues. The case studies below provides examples of different approaches used (see Case Study 4.2 and 4.4)

- by recognising that there may be particular HR policies and practices which managers respond to and which trigger positive discretionary behaviour, as suggested by the ideas of HR architecture (Lepak and Snell, 1999). The research undertaken by Purcell *et al* (2003) found that a particular mix of HR practices was necessary to support front-line managers:
  - ensuring good working relationships with their managers
  - providing career opportunities
  - supporting work–life balance
  - allowing managers to participate and feel involved in decisions
  - having an open culture which enables manager to discuss matters of concern
  - a sense of job security

- by motivating line managers to focus more on performance management tasks through establishing people management objectives in performance reviews, and providing incentives in the form of reward and recognition for good people management behaviour. As noted earlier, one of the reasons line managers fail to take people management issues seriously is that these duties are not prioritised in their own performance criteria. Upward appraisal and 360-degree feedback can help managers assess their progress and should reinforce the importance of carrying out performance activities well

- by developing the use of electronic HRM (e-HRM). Online systems can provide managers with access to HR policies, procedures and guidance, ease the completion of forms, provide personal records and other information, and help monitor processes.

However, although technology can facilitate, there is a danger that the monitoring and measurement of line management behaviour could be resented and perceived as another source of constraint. As McGovern *et al* (1997) argue: 'Rather than being empowered, managers would be caught up in an increasingly bureaucratic web of HR policies and procedures in which they not only implement policies but also have their own implementing of such policies monitored and evaluated' (McGovern *et al*, 1997: 27). These issues are examined in the final chapter.

Obviously, the ability of HR to provide such support depends on the structure and size of the HR function, and in the absence of an HR function, this support will be provided by senior managers and external bodies. This issue is also returned to in the final chapter.

CASE STUDY 4.2

DEVELOPING LINE MANAGERS' CAPABILITY: CASE STUDY EXAMPLES

Cheltenham Borough Council delivers a 'Crucial conversations' programme to help line managers handle difficult interactions (whether they are personal or work-related) and improve managers' skills and confidence (IDS, 2009a). Managers are encouraged to practise any crucial conversations firstly with a 'buddy' (a work colleague who has also attended the course) before they meet with the individual concerned. Buddies are expected to offer advice and explain how it feels to be on the receiving end of such feedback.

NEC Electronics provide online support for line managers to carry out performance appraisals (IDS, 2007). This is available on the intranet and includes details of the process, examples of behaviours and competencies, and tips on preparing for review meetings and how to give constructive feedback.

At Herbert Retail – a small organisation (employing around 180 people)

supplying products and services to the retail sector – line managers are expected to have sole responsibility for performance management, and take a very proactive role in this area (Suff, 2011c). A range of formal and informal training and development formats is offered to support managers in this role, including informal help from other managers and colleagues, external one-off conferences and seminars, in-house sessions and coaching from HR.

Network Rail have invested in a range of initiatives to train and develop line managers, which includes a leadership development programme, 'Stepping Stones', for those with leadership potential, a two-day role-playing module on performance management for all managers, and a coaching programme for managers which has created a pool of volunteer managers who are available to help other managers with particular problems (Wolff, 2010).

Regardless of the presence of an HR function, active support is needed from senior management (immediate managers and top managers) in setting and communicating the strategic direction of the organisation, its values and culture, and putting in place systems that provide a favourable 'climate' (Bowen and Ostroff, 2004). Senior managers also need to encourage a strong performance culture and one which is blame-free so that managers are not only rewarded for good people management behaviour but are also not afraid to admit to mistakes and shortcomings. They should provide role clarity so that managers (and employees) know what is expected from them, realistic targets and a balanced workload so that managers know what to prioritise and have the time to allocate to each task. Senior managers must also act as a positive role model by demonstrating the types of behaviours of a good people manager – for example, undertaking performance reviews, providing recognition, coaching and mentoring. On a more practical level, support can be provided such as administration, resources or mutual support groups. KPMG have introduced the role of 'people management leaders' to help develop staff (see Case Study 4.3 below). Selfridge's – one of the case study organisations in the study by Purcell and colleagues (Purcell *et al*, 2003) pertaining to line management performance in leading people – encouraged the development of a mutual support group so that managers could meet regularly to discuss areas of concern including how to have 'difficult conversations' and manage people.

CASE STUDY 4.3

PEOPLE MANAGEMENT LEADERS AT KPMG

KPMG, the large consultancy and accountancy firm, introduced the role of People Management Leaders (PMLs) across the business areas to help with developing staff. Staff feedback had revealed that managers did not have the capability (skills, time and attitude) to fulfil their role in developing staff, and that this was contributing to high turnover. Around 350 staff, typically at the senior management grade, were all identified as potentially great people managers and given the role of PML with full accountability for people management activities for a group of people in their department (between 20 and 100 people). KPMG has developed a support structure behind the PML network, including one-to-one coaching, annual conferences and development centres. This role has a high profile in the firm, regarded as career-enhancing for many, and ensures that the all staff are managed effectively and fairly in a way which brings out their full potential.

Source: MacLeod and Clarke (2009)

CASE STUDY 4.4

THE 'BELTS' APPROACH TO TRAINING AT THE BIG LOTTERY FUND

The BIG Lottery Fund is the largest lottery distributor and is responsible for handing out half of the money raised by the National Lottery to good causes. Its mission is to bring improvements to communities and the lives of people in need. It was formed in 2004 by the merger of the New Opportunities Fund and the Community Fund. Following the merger, the organisation launched a new performance management process to help unify the merged workforce which included a new competency framework aligned more closely with BLF's strategy (see also Chapter 2). On-going improvements have focused on training for line managers and consideration of paying for performance. Line managers play a key role in the performance management cycle, setting individual and team objectives, discussing desired behaviours (with reference to a competency framework), rating performance and producing an online performance development plan. In addition to the end-of-year review, there is a formal mid-year appraisal and managers are expected to undertake regular informal feedback throughout the year.

All line managers are provided with training and HR support on all aspects of the appraisal process, such as how to give feedback and help employees set realistic targets. Keen to reduce its reliance on formal training courses, the organisation is developing more experiential learning for managers, such as coaching, mentoring, project work, shadowing and on-the-job learning and online training. In response to feedback from an Investors in People (IiP) report, BIG is also introducing a talent-based leadership development initiative for line managers called 'Achieve', aimed at improving overall performance management and developing future leaders. Linked to this will be a 'belts' approach to training (based on using Six Sigma's black-belt phraseology) in performance management. Brown-belt training will be available to around 150 junior and middle managers, and around 100 more senior leaders will start on the black-belt programme. Managers who successfully obtain their brown belts by demonstrating the appropriate performance management skills and behaviours will be invited to become black belts. Security badges will show if someone is a brown or black belt manager.

BIG is also proposing to set up a network forum so that managers can collaborate with peers to share best practice in performance management. They also have a wiki where managers can share information and learning material, and the HR team have written a guidance document on 'Top Tips' to help managers carry out appraisals.

Source: IDS HR Studies 938, March 2011

Questions

1   Critically review BIG's initiatives for improving line managers' skills.

2   What would you include in the 'Top Tips' manual for line managers?

3   What other initiatives do you think BIG might introduce to help improve line management capability?

CONCLUSION

This chapter has focused on the role of line managers in managing and leading people, and shown that this body of managers holds a key position of influence as 'agents' of the organisation, being the primary means through which the organisation interacts with its employees. The quality of the relationship employees have with their manager, and employees' perceptions of their manager as a good manager and leader of people, can significantly impact on employee attitudes and performance-related behaviours. Positive experiences can evoke positive attitudes towards performance management practices and elicit positive discretionary behaviour. Negative experiences, however, can have damaging consequences for individual performance, even when performance management practices have been well designed.

The chapter has shown how, over the last few decades, the demands on line managers have grown. In many organisations line managers are now largely responsible for most aspects of performance management and expected to display a range of quite complex leadership behaviours and skills. However, research has consistently shown that line managers struggle to undertake these roles effectively. Given the critical role these managers play in influencing individual and organisational performance, it is vital, then, that organisations provide support. This chapter has explored how HR specialists and senior managers can help managers overcome the barriers of heavy workloads, role conflict, inadequate resources, and lack of competence, commitment and confidence. Perhaps above all, however, line managers have to understand and be persuaded of the implications of not taking performance management seriously, and the negative consequences this can have for employee attitudes, turnover, productivity, service quality and operational performance.

EXPLORE FURTHER

Gilbert, C., De Winne, S. and Sels, L. (2011) 'The influence of line managers and HR department on employees' affective commitment', *International Journal of Human Resource Management*, Vol.22, No.8: 1618–37

Hales, C. (2005) 'Rooted in supervision, branching into management: continuity and change in the role of first line manager', *Journal of Management Studies*, Vol. 42, No.3: 471–506

Hutchinson, S. and Purcell, J. (2007) *The Role of Line Managers in Reward, and Training, Learning and Development*. Research Report. London: CIPD

Hutchinson, S. and Purcell, J. (2010) 'Managing ward managers for roles in HRM in the NHS: overworked and under-resourced', *Human Resource Management Journal*, Vol.20, No.4: 357–74

McGovern, F., Gratton, L., Hope-Hailey, V., Stiles, P. and Truss, C. (1997) 'Human resource management on the line', *Human Resource Management Journal*, Vol.7, No.4: 12–29

Maxwell, G. A. and Watson, S. (2006) 'Perspectives on line managers in HRM: Hilton International's UK Hotels', *International Journal of Human Resource Management*, Vol.17, No.6: 1152–70

Perry, E. L. and Kulik, C. T. (2008) 'The devolution of HR to the line: implication of perceptions of people management effectiveness', *International Journal of Human Resource Management*, Vol.19, No.2: 262–73

Purcell, J. and Hutchinson, S. (2007) 'Front-line managers as agents in the HRM–performance causal chain: theory, analysis and evidence', *Human Resource Management Journal*, Vol.17, No.1: 3–20

Renwick, D. (2003) 'Line manager involvement in HRM: an inside view', *Employee Relations*, Vol.25, No.3: 262–80

CHAPTER 5

Defining and Measuring Individual Work Performance

SUE HUTCHINSON

LEARNING OUTCOMES

By the end of this chapter you should be able to:

- understand the meaning of 'work performance'

- identify and explain the key requirements for effective performance measurement

- understand the differences between an output-based approach and behavioural approaches

- describe and critique the main approaches to measuring performance

- advise management on the design and appropriateness of different measurement schemes.

INTRODUCTION

Defining and measuring work performance is generally considered a necessary and inevitable performance management activity, but one of the most difficult things to get right (Murphy, 2008). How do you know what to measure, what key activities make a difference, and whether you are measuring enough of the right things? Is it possible to measure all aspects of performance – such as creativity or inspiration? How do you take account of factors outside the control of the individual? And how can measures be designed which are sufficiently flexible to adapt to the increasingly turbulent environment that organisations have to respond to?

Organisations, their managers and employees need work measures for a variety of reasons. They provide the opportunity to identify good and poor performance, comprise a way to highlight any skills or knowledge gaps, and are the means by which performance improvements can be tracked. Although most managers probably think they are able to form an overall impression of an employee's performance, they need information to form evidence-based decisions about how individuals can best be deployed, developed and rewarded. Without this, judgements may be given undeservedly, they may be seen as evidence of favouritism or prejudice, and any attempt to manage performance can easily fall into disrepute. Performance indicators also help clarify the role, the expectations to be accomplished and create a 'line of sight' between what an individual does and what the organisation needs (Lawler, 1990) so that employees can make a specific and identifiable contribution.

But performance measurement is also contentious. Critics argue that performance measures are a new form of 'Taylorism', often perceived as forms of control which are 'inappropriately used to "police" performance' (Winstanley and Stuart-Smith, 1996: 66), which can add undue pressure and stress to working life. The use of forced distribution, or the 'rank-and-yank' approach to performance management (Redman, 2009), has also attracted considerable criticism, including accusations that it gives rise to a 'culture of fear'. In the finance sector over-reliance on hard quantifiable outputs linked to bonus payments has been blamed for the mis-selling of products and unnecessary risk-taking behaviour.

The chapter's main aim is to critically review some of the key approaches to measuring individual performance. First, the chapter begins by considering what is meant by 'work performance' and how it should be defined. Without some clear articulation or understanding of what performance is, it is impossible to assess what to measure and how to measure it. Is it simply what people produce – their outputs – or how they produce it – their behaviours? Or is it both (Armstrong, 2006: 102)? Second, the chapter presents the key criteria needed if measurements are to be meaningful, accurate and acceptable to both employees and managers. Third, the chapter considers how performance can be measured, differentiating between output-based approaches (what an employee achieves) and the behavioural approach (what an employee does), and their advantages and disadvantages. Finally, the chapter considers the ethics of measuring performance.

DEFINING WORK PERFORMANCE

An appropriate and logical starting point to measuring and managing performance is some clear conceptualisation of performance. According to Armstrong (2009), 'If you can't define it, you can't measure it' (Armstrong, 2009: 30). Latham *et al* (2007) believe that a clear articulation of performance is needed for the development of appropriate diagnostic tools, and is 'a prerequisite for the delivery of feedback and goal-setting' (Latham *et al*, 2007: 366). They argue that performance theory is needed which states:

- the relevant performance dimension
- the performance standards or expectations associated with alternative performance levels
- how situational constraints should be weighted – if at all
- the number of performance levels or gradients
- the extent to which performance should be based upon absolute versus relative comparison standards.

The concept of performance, however, is a complex one, and there are many different ways of interpreting it.

Performance is sometimes defined simply by outputs, such as achievement of pre-set objectives or units produced, and although this approach might be appropriate where there is a clear end product or output, it has limitations. In particular, it neglects the influence of factors outside the control of the individual, and does not explain the 'how' of performance. An alternative view is to focus on employee behaviours and/or actions. Aguinis (2009) maintains that 'performance is about behaviour, or what employees do, not about what employees produce or the outcomes of their work' (p78) (although he recognises that because it is not possible to observe all behaviours, measures of results may be necessary).

In the strategic view of performance management (Chapter 2), the starting point for any definition is the organisation's vision and strategy. Accordingly, a common conceptualisation of performance is behaviours or actions relevant to the attainment of the organisation's goals (Landy and Conte, 2010; Campbell *et al*, 1993). So if the organisation's aim is to increase market share, employee activities might be to increase sales by a certain amount. In their research on the people and performance link, Purcell *et al* (2003) report on how at Jaguar (now Jaguar Land Rover) the vision was 'quality' (see also Chapter 2). Employee and group activities were defined by quality metrics which had been developed 'to measure everything and identify appropriate actions' to underpin the organisation's 'big idea' (Purcell *et al*, 2003: 25).

Perhaps the most comprehensive and clear view of performance is to include both behaviours and results. In the words of Brumbach (1988: 389):

> Performance means both behaviours and results. Behaviours emanate from the performer and transform performance from abstraction to action. Not just the instruments for results, behaviours are also outcomes in their own right – the produce of mental and physical effort applied to tasks – and can be judged apart from results.

In the same vein, Armstrong (2006) considers performance to be about what people achieve (ie results or outputs) and how they achieve it (behaviours), concluding that when managing performance both inputs (knowledge, skills, competencies) and outputs (quantifiable results) ought to be considered.

Conceptualising performance as a behavioural phenomenon requires some understanding of what behaviours are. This is discussed below.

PERFORMANCE BEHAVIOURS

Behaviours are also complex and multidimensional. A common way of understanding behaviour is to break it down into two dimensions (Borman and Motowidlo, 1993) – namely, 'task performance' and 'contextual performance'. Task performance contributes to the technical core of the organisation (Motowidlo and Van Scotter, 1994: 476), and comprises job-specific behaviours (ie the core tasks normally contained in the job description) and non-specific tasks outside the core responsibility. A core task for a lecturer, for instance, would be to teach on courses; a non-specific task might be involvement in a special project on the development of online assessment. In contrast, contextual performance is defined as those behaviours that contribute to organisational effectiveness, such as volunteering to take on extra responsibilities that are not formally part of the role; endorsing, supporting and defending organisational decisions; helping and co-operating with others; following rules; and exerting extra effort on the job (Borman and Motowidlo, 1993). Conceptually, it is similar to organisational citizenship behaviour and positive discretionary behaviour (Chapter 1), and indirectly impacts on work climate, employee satisfaction and other employees' perceptions of support. Contextual performance is particularly important in certain contexts such as teamworking or where a high degree of flexibility is required. Aguinis (2009) gives the example of O$_2$'s call centre in Limerick in Ireland, where the performance management system includes task-related measures on productivity as well as context-related measures such as involvement in staff socialisation and contributions to team development. This approach is considered to have improved customer service and employee satisfaction.

 CRITICAL REFLECTION 5.1

Measuring and rewarding OCBs

There is a view that formally evaluating and rewarding OCBs may unintentionally inhibit this type of behaviour. Becton *et al* (2008) argue that the effects will differ depending on the motivation to exhibit OCB. For example, an employee who is intrinsically motivated to display OCB may perceive evaluation and reward for such behaviour as controlling, which may lower satisfaction derived from engaging in OCBs and thus inhibit this type of behaviour. In contrast, evaluating and rewarding employees who are extrinsically motivated to engage in OCB (eg for impression purposes) are likely to increase citizenship behaviours.

1   What are the advantages and disadvantages with formally assessing OCBs?

You may like to return to the discussion in Chapter 1 on OCBs.

These two types of behaviours, then, contribute independently to overall performance, and whereas task performance is role-specific, contextual performance is relevant to all roles regardless of function or hierarchical level. Another distinction is that they are triggered by different factors. Some commentators consider the primary antecedents for contextual behaviours to be personality measures, whereas for task behaviours it is ability and experience. Motowidlo and Van Scotter's (1994) research of US Air Force mechanics, for instance, found that experience explains more variance in task performance whereas personality explains more variance in contextual performance. This has some logic to it. Someone who is conscientious would be expected to go that 'extra mile' for their organisation, and the more experienced in the job, the more skilled. Nevertheless, the evidence is not conclusive. Organ and Ryan (1995) argue that conscientiousness is only moderately associated with contextual behaviour, and antecedents originating in the work context are seen as stronger predictors for this type of behaviour than personality traits (Organ *et al*, 2006). If this is the case, then, as Fuchs (2010) suggests, this is good news for organisations, in the sense that they can influence this type of behaviour whereas traits are not under their control. This is the assumption made in the model of the HR causal chain (Chapter 1).

Whereas this distinction is useful, there are practical challenges in applying it to the workplace. It may be possible, for example, to display good context-oriented performance but not necessarily good task performance, although of course poor task performance may be tolerated because someone displays high context-type behaviour. In practice, organisations seem to prefer to give emphasis to task performance and contextual performance is neglected, possibly because the former is easier to measure.

There are other ways of conceptualising work behaviours. Campbell *et al*'s (1993) model develops the definition by describing eight dimensions (although not all jobs may require all eight): job-specific proficiency, non-job-specific proficiency, written and oral communication, demonstration of effort, maintaining personal discipline, facilitating peer and team performance, supervision and leadership, and management and administration. Fuchs (2010) argues that work performance comprises functional (task and contextual work behaviours) and dysfunctional behaviours (counterproductive work behaviour and withdrawal of work behaviour). Chapter 9 considers the aspects of dysfunctional behaviour in more detail. Shields (2007) considers that there are three desirable behaviours: membership behaviour, task behaviour and organisational citizenship behaviour. Membership behaviour is demonstrated when an employee decides to join and remain in an organisation and manifests itself in low levels of absenteeism and low turnover.

REFLECTIVE ACTIVITY 5.1

Consider the following job roles:

- dentist
- bar tender
- journalist
- beach lifeguard

1   For each, how would you define performance in terms of task and contextual behaviours?

2   How would you measure this?

All of these insights make useful contributions to our understanding of performance, but common to all, and of fundamental importance to measuring and managing performance, is this distinction between prescribed and discretionary role behaviours.

KEY CRITERIA FOR PERFORMANCE MEASURES

Performance measures depend not only on how performance is defined but on the context within which the job is performed. As discussed in Chapter 1, performance does not happen in a vacuum, and a wide variety of factors (internal and external) can influence it. Although some of these may be under the control of the individual, many are not (eg technology, work climate and culture, the economic environment). Ideally, measurement should be free of contamination from influences outside the control of the individual (Latham *et al*, 2007), and one of the challenges is to determine how any constraints should be factored in when measuring performance.

To be effective, measures of performance must also aspire to the following requirements:

- validity
- reliability
- fairness
- practicability.

VALIDITY

Validity, in this context, essentially means the extent to which the performance criteria chosen measure that which they claim to measure. The higher the validity of performance measures, the more accurately they reflect what an employee is required to do. Shields (2007) identifies three dimensions to validity which are important for performance measurements:

- **construct validity** – This refers to the role-relevance of performance indicators. In other words, are the measurements the right things for the role?
- **content validity** – This concerns role representativeness. Do the performance measurements provide a representative and full coverage of all aspects of performance? Leaving out key aspects of the role would mean low content validity
- **criterion-related validity** – This is to do with the accuracy of performance measures in predicting the desired performance standards. Are you measuring what you say you are trying to measure? Using units produced to assess productivity would be invalid on this basis since it does not capture a time dimension or some other input.

 CRITICAL REFLECTION 5.2

Research by Michael West *et al* (2002) on the links between HR practices and performance in the NHS used a range of performance measures including mortality rates, waiting times, complaints and financial outcomes. Critics of this study suggest that the choice of mortality rates as an indicator of performance is invalid (low construct validity).

1   Do you agree with this view?

2   What measures might be used to improve the validity of the study?

RELIABILITY

Reliability concerns the accuracy of the measurements in terms of consistency and stability. Two types of reliability are particularly important in this context:

- test–retest reliability – whether the performance measurements are stable over time
- inter-rater reliability – the extent to which different raters agree on the performance of an individual.

High reliability, then, is achieved if a measurement repeatedly produces the same ratings for a specific level of performance, or assessors provide similar ratings of the same employee. Unreliability may occur when measurements are incomplete or inaccurate, and so it follows that if measurements are not valid, they will not be reliable. Reliability has been described as an 'elusive ideal' (Shields, 2007), and in practice performance assessments are notoriously unreliable largely because they are prone to intentional and unintentional bias or error. These issues are discussed further in Chapter 6.

FAIRNESS

The importance of fairness has a strong theoretical underpinning in theories of equity and justice, explored in Chapter 3. In this context, it means ensuring that measures are meaningful and accurate (validity and procedural fairness), are understood and accepted by employees (procedural fairness), and are applied fairly and consistently across the organisation and over time (reliability). Clearly, if measures are not valid or reliable, they will not be 'felt fair', and this will impact negatively on employee attitudes and behaviour, and raise doubts about the legitimacy of the performance management scheme.

PRACTICABILITY

The ease with which measurements can be gathered, the time involved in the design and capture of those measurements, and their cost-effectiveness are also important considerations. Practicability, however, can conflict with the other requirements. Sophisticated measurement schemes which are designed to improve reliability and validity (such as behaviourally based rating scales) can be costly and time-consuming to develop. Ensuring high content validity may necessitate an array of performance measures which are simply not practical to administer and manage.

   In sum, to meet these key criteria, organisations need to ensure that measurements (Shields, 2007: 128):

- accurately reflect current organisational and job priorities (ie have construct validity)
- measure enough of the right things (ie construct and content validity)
- use measures that accurately reflect performance on the chosen criteria (ie criterion-related validity)
- are applied consistently and accurately between raters and over time (ie reliability)
- relate to objectives or other performance standards that are realistic rather than too difficult or too easy (ie validity and procedural fairness, practicability)
- are understood and accepted by employees and managers (ie procedural fairness).

A considerable amount of research has been undertaken in the pursuit of these criteria, and a range of approaches developed, but there remains no ideal method. Each has its unique strengths and weaknesses in terms of validity, reliability, fairness and practicability – and these are considered below.

APPROACHES TO MEASURING PERFORMANCE

There are two main types of approach to measuring performance:

- the output- or outcome-based approach
- the behavioural approach.

An additional, but less popular approach is the traits-based approach in which raters evaluate traits such as cognitive abilities (eg intelligence) or personality (eg conscientiousness, integrity, dependability). According to Aguinis (2009), the approach is justified on the basis of a positive relationship between abilities and personality and desirable work-related behaviours, although, as discussed previously, the strength of that relationship may not be as strong as with other factors. However, other major problems with this approach are that traits are not under the control of individuals and generally remain stable over one's life-span, and there is a danger of cultural bias. Thus the development of traits for performance improvement purposes is not possible. Moreover, possessing certain 'desirable' traits (such as intelligence) does not mean that the person will perform better. Traits are also open to different interpretations, leaving them prone to bias and prejudice.

THE OUTPUT- OR OUTCOME-BASED APPROACH

The defining feature of this approach (also referred to as the results-based approach) is that tangible outcomes or results from work behaviours are measured quantifiably. Measurements are typically based on product or service quantity (eg the number of units produced), quality (eg the number of defects or customer complaints) or financial outcomes (eg the value of sales). If relevant, stakeholder attitudes and reactions can also be included, such as customer and supplier satisfaction, although this starts to introduce an element of subjectivity into what is an objective process. The author's first job as a fruit-picker on a Norfolk farm used a very simple payment-by-results scheme determined by quantity (number of punnets of blackberries) and quality (any damaged/bruised blackberries and the whole punnet was thrown away). A time dimension could have been added (eg per hour or per day) to measure productivity or efficiency. The method was straightforward, easy to understand and not open to dispute (although a little ruthless).

Technology has made it increasingly possible for organisations to obtain quantifiable performance data, as witnessed in call centre work, where a results-based approach is common, combining measures of quantity with quality. Typically, this might include (Kinnie, Hutchinson and Purcell, 2000):

- number of calls taken per hour (quantity)
- length of calls (quantity)
- length of time customer is waiting (quantity)
- customer satisfaction index (quality)
- adherence to call structure (quality).

Key performance indicators (KPIs) are often used as reference points for performance, against which targets can be set (see also the 'balanced scorecard' in Chapter 2). A KPI for a recruitment consultant might be 'new job orders filled', with a target of achieving £20,000 of sales each quarter.

OBJECTIVE-SETTING

A variation on this approach is management by objectives (MBO), a scientific approach popularised by Peter Drucker (1955), and often considered to be the antecedent of performance management. This approach stresses the quantification of objectives and seeks to systematically align organisational and individual objectives, focusing on future achievements rather than those of the past. MBO was adopted with some enthusiasm in the 1960s and 1970s for managers, but has since gone out of fashion and been replaced by goal-setting, informed by theory based on the work of Locke and colleagues (eg Locke, 1968; Latham and Locke, 2006), which was discussed in Chapter 3. The main difference is that in MBO, objectives are set unilaterally by management, whereas goal-setting advocates a more participative approach to setting objectives and reviewing performance, and in doing so encourages a degree of self-management (Shields, 2007). Potentially, a wider range of jobs can be covered by goal-setting, for although many jobs do not have specific quantifiable outputs, there are few for which some objectives cannot be set and worked towards for the forthcoming year. This is particularly helpful in the public sector where the impact of results is less tangible – see Case Study 5.1 on the Crown Prosecution Service below.

Like the CPS, many organisations adopt the SMART acronym (specific, measurable, attainable, realistic and time-bound), informed by goal-setting theory (see Chapter 3, and particularly Table 3.3), to establish some of the key requirements of objective-setting. A SMART objective for myself might be to lose half a stone (3.175 kilograms) by the time I go on holiday at the end of July. Proponents argue (in Pulakos and O'Leary, 2011) that SMART performance objectives can:

- encourage managers and employees to collaboratively identify performance objectives which are specific to an employee's job
- communicate and clarify what employees are accountable for delivering
- drive employees to achieve important results
- remove unfair subjectivity from the evaluation process.

 SETTING SMART OBJECTIVES IN THE CROWN PROSECUTION SERVICE

CASE STUDY 5.1

The Crown Prosecution Service (CPS) is the government department responsible for prosecuting criminal cases investigated by the police in England and Wales. Its work includes advising police on cases for possible prosecution, reviewing cases submitted by the police, determining charges, and preparing and presenting court cases. It employs prosecutors, case workers and administrators.

Performance management in the CPS is intended to be strategic, to be supportive and to help employees understand how their role contributes to the organisation's aims and goals. It is underpinned by a skills and values behaviours framework. At the beginning of the year corporate objectives are set which are translated into team and individual objectives.

Individuals have three different types of performance objective: 'standard performance objectives' which are focused on achieving the team performance and impact on daily work activities; 'improvement objectives' which address any gaps between actual and required skills and behaviours; and 'aspiration objectives' which concern an employee's career goals. Each employee agrees up to six goals in these areas with their line manager. In addition, employees are expected to set an equality and diversity objective, which is intended to promote a culture of inclusion and equality. Detailed guidance is available for employees and line managers to help set effective objectives, which are required to be SMART – that is:

- **S**pecific – involving a clearly defined final outcome
- **M**easurable – capable of consistent measurement so it is evident that the objective has been reached when it has
- **A**chievable – capable of achievement, and agreed to as such, but also challenging and offering development opportunities while also remaining compatible with other responsibilities and workload
- **R**ealistic – linked to the job description, but also to team priorities and organisational goals
- **T**ime-bound – with an established time-frame in which the objective is to be achieved.

The guide recommends that for each objective employees ask themselves 'Why am I doing this? What is going to be different? Will it help meet the organisation's objectives?' The use of positive language is encouraged in objective-setting to avoid terms that could lead to 'woolly' definitions – such as 'liaise with', 'develop a relationship with', or 'contribute to'.

Source: IDS HR Case Study 866, 2009a

Question

1   Can you think of an equality and diversity objective that is SMART and corresponds to the guidance provided?

BENEFITS AND PITFALLS

The appeal of the output-based approach is its simplicity and seeming objectivity, and as Shields (2007) notes, there is something inherently reassuring about results-based metrics that come up with a set of performance numbers (Shields, 2007: 126). For the employee there is clarity in what is required and the opportunity for immediate and continuous feedback on performance. Where objectives are set they can be linked to organisational goals to provide a 'line of sight' so that individuals can make an identifiable contribution, which can provide a real sense of achievement. Goal-setting, in particular, has been found to be a powerful motivator, encourages self-management, is participative in nature and, as such, complements a high-involvement culture (Chapter 2) (Shields, 2007; Fletcher, 2008). Results-based metrics are understandable, and in a language familiar to key stakeholders such as chief executives, finance directors, shareholders and customers. These benefits go some way to explaining why an output-oriented approach is so dominant. In the UK, 62 per cent of respondents to a CIPD survey in 2004 used 'objective-setting and review', and of these, 82 per cent rated the method as an effective performance management technique (CIPD, 2005a). In a later (but less comprehensive) survey, 75.3 per cent of respondents set objectives or targets (CIPD, 2009a). In the USA, organisations have historically been driven by a 'bottom-line' results focus (Pulakos *et al*, 2008) – no doubt partly driven by the litigious nature of US society and the desire to have an objective approach that cannot be challenged.

Nevertheless, output-based approaches have serious shortcomings. One of the problems is that 'what gets measured gets done'. It is also said that 'what is measured is what is easy to measure, not what is most important'. Mayo (2008) sums this up by quoting Albert Einstein: 'What counts can often not be counted, and what is counted often does not count.' Inappropriate performance indicators can result in unintended consequences or dysfunctional behaviour which can not only invalidate the conclusions on performance but negatively impact on performance. For example, assessing a bus service on punctuality might encourage bus drivers to drive straight past a few stops to make up time. Another example is using number of reported crimes and clear-up rates as indicators of crime reduction by police forces. This may result in some crimes not being recorded, or recorded only when they are solved, or 'wrongly' classified in some way. Government research suggests that the number of crimes that actually occur is about four times the number recorded (HMIC, 2000).

Of course, not all jobs can be measured in this way. The job of a surgeon, for instance, does not seem to lend itself to this type of approach (measuring the number of operations performed a day could be catastrophic!). Most jobs have some element of the work that is not amenable to hard measures, such as developing relationships, sharing information or supporting others.

Setting objectives in advance can also be very difficult for some jobs (Cascio, 1998; Levinson, 2005) – particularly those requiring a high degree of task flexibility or operating in a turbulent marketplace. The setting of SMART objectives, for example, has been crticised on the grounds that it is inflexible and assumes that organisations operate within stable environments. Rose (2000) suggests a more appropriate acronym for SMART targets is 'DUMB' – standing for Defective, Unrealistic, Misdirected and Bureaucratic. Writing good objectives and ensuring that they are fair and consistent for similar jobs can also be challenging for any manager, and requires training and regular review (Pulakos and O'Leary, 2011).

A results focus also fails to take account of contextual constraints which are outside the control of the individual. Referring again to the earlier example of a call centre, technological failure might result in an employee's receiving a low evaluation undeservedly. Sales of products as a performance indicator may ignore the state of the local/national economy. Work which requires a high degree of interdependence and teamwork can be adversely affected by working with unhelpful or difficult colleagues. Even the performance of a traffic warden – an obvious contender for a results-based approach (see Activity 5.2 below) – may be influenced by external constraints.

Latham et al (2007) also argue that the approach can encourage a 'results at all costs' mentality in which 'winning the game is perceived to be more important for one's own career than how one plays the game' (Latham et al, 2007: 367). This is evident in the risk-taking behaviour of financiers (see Chapter 8). Goal-setting has also been criticised for increasing stress, ignoring non-goal areas, and encouraging short-term thinking (Locke and Latham, 1984).

One of the key criticisms of this approach, however, is that it fails to explain the process or the means by which achievements are made, which is vital if we want to understand what and how performance improvements can be made. It is therefore counter to the development approaches of performance management.

Jobs that lend themselves best to this approach are those with relatively stable performance requirements and defined productivity measures, such as manufacturing jobs (Pulakos and O'Leary, 2011). Aguinis (2009) suggests that the approach is most appropriate when workers are skilled in the required behaviours, and results are not related and/or there are different ways to do the job well. There is strong evidence supporting goal-setting in certain contexts (Latham and Locke, 2006). Shields (2007), for example, reports that it has been found to be motivational in the public sector, particularly for managers, because of its transparency, ownership and objectivity (Shields, 2007: 132). Regular review of objectives to identify any external or personal changes that might impact on the achievement of outcomes can reduce some of the potential problems with this approach. Neverthelsss, a results focus does not work well where the nature of jobs is unpredictable and objectives change frequently, as in the case in R&D work where it is virtually impossible to predict when and what discoveries will be made. Pulakos et al (2008) note how objective-setting is difficult in economies dominated by knowledge and service sector jobs because work is more varied and subtle. It is also inappropriate when the output is heavily dependent on factors outside the employee's control.

REFLECTIVE ACTIVITY 5.2

Targeting traffic wardens

Many of us have no doubt felt that we have been given dubious tickets for parking offences, and made appeals on the basis of an unfair penalty, blaming it on over-zealous traffic wardens determined to reach their targets (which can be linked to non-financial reward – eg vouchers). At first glance, an output approach based on number of tickets issued seems an obvious choice for judging a traffic warden's performance, but consider the following facts:

● The objective of parking enforcement is to keep the traffic flowing, prevent accidents and ensure that there are no blockages for motorists.
● There will be lots of factors beyond the control of traffic wardens which impact on this aim (eg heavy volume of traffic, poor planning).

● The level of parking compliance may be high in an area (perhaps as a result of vigilant traffic wardens in the past), reducing the opportunity for issuing parking tickets.
● The time of day and the area the warden is assigned to mean that some will have greater opportunities to issue tickets than others.
● It ignores the quality of service – for example, poorly written tickets completed in haste. Tickets have to be discounted if they contain errors.

1 What other factors might influence the job of parking enforcement and are outside the control of the traffic warden?

2 What other types of measure could be used to achieve the overall aim of improving traffic flow?

BEHAVIOURAL APPROACHES

Partly in response to some of these difficulties organisations have moved towards a focus on assessing behaviours, reflecting the view that performance is actually behaviour rather than simply outputs. This process-oriented approach is arguably a more constructive and fairer way of measuring performance because it focuses on what a person actually does (or the 'how' of achievement), and recognises that there may be factors outside the control of the individual which influence performance, alleviating many of the difficulties associated with 'unequal opportunities to perform' (Pulakos *et al*, 2008). In contrast to the results-based approach, however, the measurement of behaviours is less easy to capture, and intrinsically judgemental, relying on human observation and assessment by others (eg managers, peers, subordinates and other stakeholders). It is therefore liable to bias and error – and herein lies the major problem with the approach. Although on the increase, the use of behavioural assessments is less common than a results approach, and reported to be used by 31 per cent in a CIPD survey (2005a), although just 39 per cent of those using it felt it to be effective. Competencies (performance inputs which comprise job knowledge, skills and abilities – see Chapter 7) are typically assessed by behaviourally based approaches.

There are a variety of approaches to measuring behaviours, and these are examined below.

NARRATIVES

Narratives are simply written statements summarising views about an individual's performance. When used for developmental purposes, narratives have the potential to provide meaningful information. They can convey what a person did in rich terms, be individually customised, and if specific examples are given, be valuable sources of feedback. However, without accompanying standards and detailed guidance (for example, asking for comments on particular behaviours), narrative descriptions can be highly unstructured, generalised and not very revealing. The approach is prone to distortion and can simply be a reflection of the manager's writing skills rather than of the performance of the individual being assessed. Narrative statements are probably most effective when combined with other approaches.

CRITICAL INCIDENTS

Critical incident technique was developed in the 1950s and is considered the foundation of most existing behavioural rating approaches (Shields, 2007: 161). Rather than making general judgements about different behaviours, the approach focuses attention on significant events that have occurred during the review period that provide examples of very good and very poor performance. An example of very effective behaviour for a lecturer might be 'Was solely responsible for designing a new core module for first-year students which received very positive student feedback on the content'. Complaints by students about poor time-keeping by the lecturer would be recorded as a negative critical incident.

Various techniques are employed to gather and record situations in which employees exhibit these critical behaviours, such as the use of critical incident forms. Employees can also undertake a self-assessment by, for example, keeping diaries of significant events. The main benefits of the approach are that it focuses on the job, analysis can identify areas for improvement, and it can be particularly useful for jobs which are difficult to quantify. Nevertheless, the approach is time-consuming and requires good observational skills and records of incidents, which can be intimidating for employees. Like narratives, it is also subject to bias through selective reporting of incidents, and it cannot be used for rating purposes.

PERFORMANCE RATINGS

The use of some form of rating scale to indicate the overall level of performance achieved is the most common and systematic way of assessing behaviours, and particularly helpful if the performance management scheme is used for decision-making purposes, such as informing pay decisions or developing talent. Scales can be defined numerically or alphabetically, and there is a wide choice of ways of presenting rating scales. Some of the main ones are illustrated in Figure 5.1 below. Typically, Likert-type scales are used to differentiate performance, usually covering the whole range from 'excellent' to 'very poor' (Example 1). Alternatively, the scale may record the frequency of behaviour (Example 2) or comparisons with others (Example 5). According to Armstrong (2006), an increasingly popular approach is to have scales which emphasise the positive and improvable nature of performance (Example 3). This avoids the use of an 'unacceptable' category, on the grounds that if someone's performance is totally unacceptable it should have been identified in the on-going process of performance management. This technique is helpful if the purpose of the assessment is developmental, and can encourage a culture of continuous improvement.

Figure 5.1 Examples of rating scales, by type

Example 1: Rating by means of verbally described (anchored) Likert scales

The employee's communication with the customer is:

1   Outstanding
2   Very good
3   Good
4   Fair
5   Less than adequate
6   Unsatisfactory

Example 2: Numerical ratings from best to worst, Likert scales (unanchored)

The person helps others who have heavy workloads

Always					Never
1	2	3	4	5	6

Example 3: Rating by positive definitions (Armstrong, 2006: 107)

Very effective: Meets all the objectives of the job. Exceeds required standards and consistently performs in a thoroughly proficient manner beyond normal expectations

Effective: Has achieved required objectives and standard of performance and meets the normal expectations of the role

Developing: A contribution that is stronger in some aspects of the job than others – most objectives are met but performance improvement should still take place

Basic: A contribution that indicates that there is considerable room for improvement in several definable areas

Example 4: Graphic rating scales detail the behaviours associated with the quality being rated

Communication with customer

Customers complain about communication style	Fails to listen and misunderstands customer needs	Expresses ideas clearly and directly	Conveys confidence when communicating	Communicates persuasively so as to produce positive results

Example 5: Comparative scales rate an individual on some quality relative to other individuals

In the area of co-operation this person:

Is one of the top performers
Performs better than most
Performs the same as most
Performs less well than most
Is one of the very poorest

Source: adapted from Woods and West (2010), and Fletcher (2008)

In practice, rating levels generally range from as few as three to as many as seven, and although arguments can be made for most levels of differentiation, meaningful distinctions are hard to make beyond seven categories (Fletcher, 2008), beyond which there is also greater potential for discrimination. In fact, there is no evidence that any one approach is better than the others. The norm is to use a five-level scale (two above-average levels, two less-than-average, and a satisfactory level), which is arguably more motivational than three points because the gap to the next level is more do-able on five points. On the other hand, five-point scales – or any odd number of scales – can tempt raters to over-use the middle category (sometimes referred to as the problem of 'central tendency' – see Chapter 6).

The advantages of using rating scales are that they are easy to understand, they convey clear messages to employees about how they are performing, they encourage a more analytical approach to assessment, and they force managers to be more accountable. They also facilitate comparisons between people, which, according to Fletcher (2008), is usually the *raison d'être* for using them (Fletcher, 2008: 17). It is also hard to have individual performance-related pay without rating scales since some form of categorisation of performance is needed, although in practice this is not the case. According to a CIPD e-reward survey in 2005, 23 per cent of those employers who pay for performance do not include ratings as part of the process.

Ratings, however, also have their shortcomings, and one of the key problems is that they are prone to bias and inconsistency between managers. The more unclearly the scales and behavioural criteria are defined, the more liable the method is to bias and unreliability. In example 1 there is no information provided on the categories, and it is highly unlikely that everyone will interpret 'good', 'very good', etc, in a similar way. What is 'good' leadership behaviour to one person may be very different for another. Similarly, in example 2 the levels of frequency may be applied differently by individuals. One way of reducing this is to use graphic rating scales (as in example 4) which provide descriptors to rate performance. Even with defined standards, however, managers may continue to use their own 'idiosyncratic rating standards', and interpret them from their own viewpoint (Pulakos and O'Leary, 2011).

Another difficulty is that raters are not good at using the full range of scales, causing problems of central tendency (by which nearly everyone is marked as average) and leniency (where raters are over-generous). These issues are considered further in Chapter 6. Schleicher *et al* (2009) report that 77 per cent of companies believe lenient appraisals threaten the validity of their appraisal scheme. There is also evidence that the purpose of the appraisal can affect the rating distribution (Greguras *et al*, 2003), and those used for decision-making purposes (eg pay or promotion) tend to be more lenient. Some have questioned whether it is necessary to use ratings when the performance management approach is purely developmental, arguing that employees become more concerned about their scores than understanding their development needs (Varma and Stroh, 2001).

There are also difficulties if an overall single rating of performance is needed – for example, should all criteria be weighted equally?

Many of these issues of reliability can be reduced through training, so that assessors are aware of their own biases, and the use of multiple reviewers, and monitoring (discussed in the following chapter). Fay and Latham (1982) found that rating errors are reduced significantly when raters receive rater error training. At Orange problems of leniency were addressed very simply by changing the titles of the grade descriptor (see Case Study 5.2). Behaviorally-based rating scales and forced distributions can also improve consistency and accuracy.

CASE STUDY 5.2

AVOIDING PROBLEMS OF LENIENCY AT ORANGE

In 2005, in the face of an increasingly tough marketplace, Orange reviewed its performance management system, which was linked to individual reward. As part of this the company reconsidered its five-point scale since, historically, people had been awarded exaggerated performance ratings. Orange believed this was because people struggled to accept that a rating of 3 meant they had 'met objectives and were doing a good job', and as a result managers were being over-generous with their ratings. To resolve this, the grading descriptor labels on the five-point scale were changed so that 1 became 'unacceptable', 2 was 'getting there', 3 (the mark of effective performance) became 'great stuff', 4 became 'excellent', and 5 was 'exceptional'.

Source: Johnson (2006)

BEHAVIOURALLY BASED RATING SCALES

Behaviourally based rating scales provide a series of performance dimensions linked to detailed behavioural descriptors, and attempt to minimise the scope for subjectivity in the assessment process. They are probably the most sophisticated approaches to measuring behaviour, and there are a number of methods, the most well known of which are behaviourally anchored rating scales (BARS) and behavioural observation scales (BOS).

BARS (Smith and Kendall, 1963), first introduced in the USA in the 1960s, provide descriptors of important job behaviours which are 'anchored' alongside a rating scale. The method seeks to improve inter-rater reliability and consistency by providing a frame of reference in the form of behavioural illustrations of what constitutes very poor, acceptable and outstanding behaviour (Latham *et al*, 2007: 367). The development of BARS involves the following stages:

- Job experts use a critical incident approach to provide examples of behaviours reflecting effective and ineffective job performance.
- The examples are grouped into a series of separate performance dimensions (eg excellent/good, average and poor/unsatisfactory performance).
- The second stage is repeated by another expert group to provide an independent check on the relevance of the behavioural examples to the dimensions, and thus check the validity of the process.
- For each dimension the examples are rated by the experts on a numerical scale. Any examples which are not rated similarly by different experts are deleted.
- The resulting continuum is assembled along a numerical rating scale to indicate a range from excellent to very poor – typically, the number of dimensions ranges from three (as in the example in Figure 5.2) to ten.

The thoroughness of the design process and use of job experts is intended to enhance the validity of behavioural assessments.

Figure 5.2 Example of a behaviourally anchored rating scale

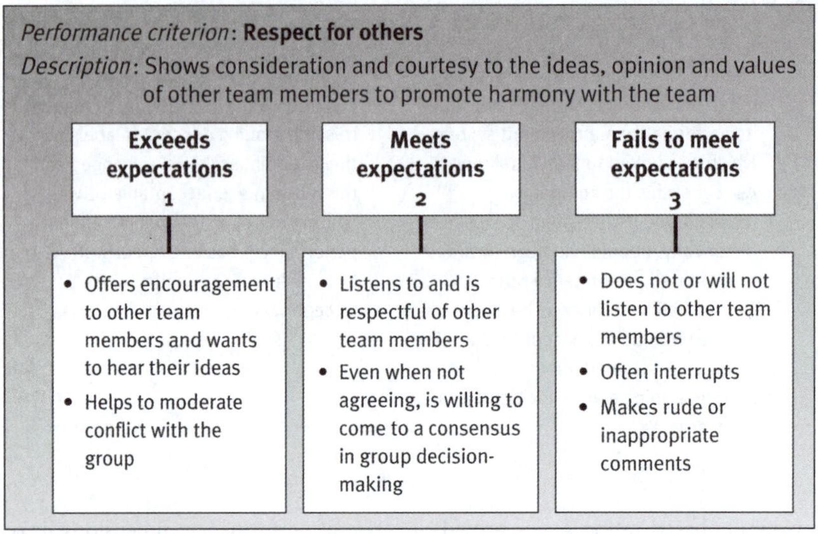

Performance criterion: **Respect for others**
Description: Shows consideration and courtesy to the ideas, opinion and values of other team members to promote harmony with the team

Exceeds expectations 1	**Meets expectations** 2	**Fails to meet expectations** 3
• Offers encouragement to other team members and wants to hear their ideas • Helps to moderate conflict with the group	• Listens to and is respectful of other team members • Even when not agreeing, is willing to come to a consensus in group decision-making	• Does not or will not listen to other team members • Often interrupts • Makes rude or inappropriate comments

BOS (Latham and Wexley, 1977) represent a variation on this approach in which the assessor makes a judgement about the frequency with which an employee demonstrates the behaviour. No significant differences have been found between BARS and BOS in terms of minimising rating errors or increasing inter-observer reliability (Latham *et al*, 2005).

Despite the considerable effort and cost involved to develop behaviourally based rating scales, research suggests that these techniques only produce results that are slightly better than well-constructed graphic rating scales, raising questions about whether developing a BARS approach is worthwhile. It is also possible that some behaviours may be overlooked, assessors may find it hard to match observed behaviours with the anchors used, and there may be conflations of behavioural criteria (Shields, 2007). As with all rating methods, the more elaborate the scales are, the harder is the differentiation between behaviours.

FORCED DISTRIBUTION

Forced distribution, popularised by Jack Welch, former CEO of General Electric, requires appraisers to fit evaluations to a particular distribution and use the full range of scales. The assumption is that the overall performance of employees conforms to a normally distributed curve (ie a bell curve, as in Figure 5.3) with a small percentage of people at the top and bottom of the curve and the majority in the middle. In the GE model 20 per cent of any group of managers were top performers, 70 per cent average and 10 per cent poor performers who were considered not worth retaining and removed in an approach that came to be known as 'ranking and yanking' (Redman, 2009).

Figure 5.3 GE model of the normal distribution bell curve for forced ranking

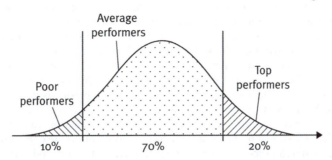

Advocates of this approach argue that it forces managers to differentiate between performers, thus avoiding problems of central tendency and leniency. It also enables organisations to identify the top performers who ought to be retained and developed and, if adopting the GE approach, to 'weed out the dead wood' (Welch and Welch, 2005). The idea, then, is one of continuous improvement with the performance bar continually being raised to help sustain a high-performance culture. Welch argued that this was motivating for top performers and believed that culling the bottom 10 per cent was 'good' for those employees who were removed, since it took them out of a situation which was not beneficial to them (in Lawler, 2003). The approach also aims to ensure greater consistency in marking between managers and, if linked to pay, can be an aid to budgetary control.

Nevertheless, the approach has been subject to huge criticism. The assumption that performance is normally distributed is highly questionable and has not been substantiated in the research (O'Boyle and Aguinis, 2012). By its very nature there will always be a bottom and a top percentage regardless of how well people perform, and managers can be forced into falsely identifying under- and over-performers to fill their quota. The poorer performers, for example, could well be performing at a perfectly acceptable level, and the top performers might not be doing all that much better. The approach is therefore clearly at odds with the principle that people should be evaluated on the basis of what they actually do. Lawler (2002) argues that it is punitive, inherently unfair and promotes a culture of 'survival of the fittest'. It can be demotivating for those not receiving an appropriate ranking, undermines teamworking since it discourages employees from engaging in collaborative-type behaviours ('The better my colleague does, the less chance I have to be rated at the top') and fosters unhealthy competition. It also penalises teams made up of mostly high performers. Moreover, it has the potential to place undue stress on employees, can lead to burn-out and promotes job insecurity. In their book *Hard Facts, Dangerous Half-Truths, and Total Nonsense*, Pfeffer and Sutton (2006) argue that there is no evidence that forced rankings improve performance, and that they couldn't find 'a shred of evidence that it is better to have just a few alpha dogs at the top and to treat everyone else as inferior'. Overall, the approach has the potential to breach the psychological contract, undermine trust and threaten any sense of distributive justice (Fletcher, 2008). For these reasons it is understandable that the benefits of forced ranking appear to be short-lived.

Despite this damning evidence, many high-profile organisations in the USA have used this approach (eg General Electric, Microsoft, Sun Microsystems, Ford and Hewlett Packard) and 20 per cent of Fortune-1000 companies are reported to use some form of forced distribution (Sears and McDermott, 2003). At GE the forced distribution system has been modified since its introduction because the company did not feel the approach conducive to fostering an innovative culture in which risk-taking and failure are part of the climate (Aguinis, 2009). Although the normal distribution is still referenced as a guideline, the 20/70/10 split has been removed so that work groups have more flexibility – eg more top performers or no bottom 10 per cent. Interestingly, the company has also begun to evaluate certain traits such as the ability to be innovative.

Not all organisations systematically remove the bottom performers, and not all use the 20/70/10 distribution (see Case Study 5.3 below). Although only about 4 per cent of UK organisations are believed to remove a fixed quota of staff each year, a survey of 562 UK managers found that 77 per cent felt that sacking a fixed amount of under-performing employees each year would boost financial performance and productivity (Arkin, 2007a).

In the UK the civil service uses a distribution curve to rank its senior civil servants into a top rank (top 25 per cent), a middle rank (65 per cent) and a bottom rank of 10 per cent. Each individual is assessed on his or her relative contribution to the organisation against peers in a moderation process. This use of a rating calibration or moderation process is quite common, particularly when reward is involved, and seeks to minimise some of the difficulties of distortion. Typically, managers meet after the initial assessments have taken place to try to ensure that ratings are applied consistently and that there is a appropriate spread of assessments across the scale. It also forces managers to be more accountable for their ratings. In some cases a separate group may do the calibration (eg more senior managers and an independent observer), although this runs the risk of disenfranchising immediate line managers from the process if their original decision is overturned (Hutchinson and Purcell, 2007).

 TRACKING PERFORMANCE AT NETWORK RAIL

CASE STUDY 5.3

Senior managers at Network Rail, the not-for-profit railway infrastructure company, rank professional and managerial staff according to guidelines which state that 10 per cent are expected to be 'A' performers, 20 per cent Bs, 50 per cent Cs and 20 per cent Ds, of whom a quarter are 'low Ds'. The groupings are linked to pay such that A-ranked performers receive larger increases than those in lower ranks. To avoid the problem of disadvantaging small teams or those made up mostly of high performers, Network Rail tries to achieve a broader distribution of performance by placing people in groups of about 150. The low Ds receive feedback about what they need to do to improve ... but some 'choose to leave'. Perhaps not surprisingly, there is a direct relationship between individuals'

rankings and their desire to stay in the organisation: turnover is much higher among the low Ds than among the A players, suggesting that this may be an effective way of motivating top performers.

However the organisation admits that it is hard on managers who have to implement it, and particularly difficult in an organisation with a long history of public sector values.

Source: Arkin (2007a)

Questions

1   Discuss the advantages and disadvantages of this approach.

2   Are there any changes you would make to this rating approach?

OTHER BEHAVIOURAL APPROACHES

Forced distributions are a form of ranking which allows some comparison to be made between individuals, but there are more basic approaches for assessing performance which involve ranking employees. In the *simple rank order* approach, employees are ranked from best to worst on the basis of comparative overall performance. *Alternation rank order* is similar except that comparisons are made by selecting the best and worst in relation to performance (or specific behavioural criteria), and placing their name at the top and bottom of the rank order. Then the second best and worst are chosen and so on until all employees have been ranked. An alternative, and slightly more reliable approach is by means of paired comparisons, in which each employee is compared with every other employee, one at a time, for each criterion (eg Mark is better than Rebecca at prioritising work). Each is then ranked according to the number of criteria for which he or she was judged to be the higher performer in each pairing. An example is given in Table 5.1.

Table 5.1 An example of paired comparisons

Jane is	Hilary is	Alan is	Nick is	
	not as good as	not as good as	not as good as	**Jane**
better than		not as good as	not as good as	**Hilary**
better than	better than		not as good as	**Alan**
better than	better than	better than		**Nick**
3	2	1	0	*Scores*

Source: adapted from Shields (2007)

The advantages of these techniques are that they are fairly easy to explain, and the potential for assessment errors such as leniency or central tendency is largely avoided. On the other hand, because of the absence of clear behavioural criteria they still remain highly subjective, and are generally considered unreliable with low validity. Moreover, these forms of ranking do not tell us the size of differences in performance, and assume that no individuals perform equally. Whereas the top and bottom may be easy to rank, the middle performers are less easy. Employees are often only compared using a single overall performance category rather than individual behaviours or competences, and so the resulting ranking are not specific enough to give detailed feedback. Also, to sum up the total performance of a person with a single rating seems a gross over-simplification of what may be a complex set of factors influencing that performance (Armstrong, 2006). The approaches are also impractical for larger numbers, and best suited to smaller organisations or small work groups.

COMPARATIVE VERSUS ABSOLUTE APPROACHES

Clearly, there is a wide choice of techniques for assessing behaviours, and all have their strengths and weaknesses. In terms of which to choose, a useful starting point is to categorise the choice of methods into two broad groups: comparative systems and absolute systems (Table 5.2), an approach favoured by both Aguinis (2009) and Shields (2007). Comparative methods seek to compare employees with each other by developing a ranking system on the basis of relative performance. Absolute systems seek to evaluate performance against a set of standard behavioural criteria, without direct reference to others. Essentially, the choice boils down to the aims of the performance management scheme and organisational context. Comparative methods are useful when there is a need to differentiate between individuals for decision-making purposes – eg pay or promotion – and are most appropriate for small workplaces or workgroups. They are also more cost-effective and can be monitored for unintentional error. Absolute methods have the potential to address validity and control for unintentional errors, but can also be more costly and time-consuming to design and implement. They are probably more useful in larger organisations, where there is a variety of jobs and the availability of multiple assessors.

Table 5.2 Comparative versus absolute methods of ranking

Comparative	Absolute
Simple rank order	Narratives/essays
Alternative rank order	Critical incidents
Paired comparisons	Graphic ratings scales
Forced distribution	Behavioural ratings

Before concluding this chapter it is worth returning to one of the debates about performance management as a means of control (Chapter 2), and other ethical concerns.

THE ETHICS OF PERFORMANCE MEASUREMENT

Radical critiques of performance management highlight ethical concerns that it is a means to control employees through the setting and monitoring of performance measurements to ensure that performance standards are met. This may be exacerbated by the use of multiple measures in the pursuit of more accurate and meaningful measures, which has unwittingly created a more onerous performance measurement regime. In their paper on the ethics of performance management, Winstanley and Stuart-Smith ask if performance management can become 'akin to a police state, where the control occurs through the collection of documentation and evidence, a dossier on an individual. Instead of standing over one's shoulder, supervision becomes a matter of spying through keyholes' (Winstanley and Stuart-Smith, 1996: 69). This is particularly noteworthy in certain sectors such as the call centre industry, where customer advisers are subject to high surveillance and monitoring.

There are also ethical issues concerning lack of fairness arising from subjectivity and bias, particularly problematic with the behavioural approach to assessment, involving implications for equal (or unequal) opportunities. To address these, and other problems, Winstanley and Stuart-Smith propose a more ethical approach to performance management building in respect for the individual, mutual respect, procedural fairness, transparency in decision-making and on-going dialogue. In terms of the design of performance measurements themselves, this means having measures that are transparent, agreed and applied fairly across the organisation. Appropriate training can also reduce the potential for distortions creeping into the assessment process. Hendry *et al* (2000) recommend that the amount of measurement should be limited, and that the focus should fall on a few key activities which make a difference. This can lessen perceptions of control. Issues of control are examined further in subsequent chapters.

CASE STUDY 5.4

TEACHERS' STANDARDS

As part of its modernisation agenda of public services, the UK's Labour government introduced performance-related pay (PRP) for teachers in England in 2000, although it had long been a feature in the USA. PRP was intended to enhance school leadership; improve teacher recruitment, retention and motivation; and deploy resources more flexibly (Farrell and Morris, 2009). The scheme was hugely controversial, but the principle of paying for performance has remained in force. A number of studies show that PRP works best where there are clearly measurable outcomes (Murnane and Cohen, 1986). A study of teachers in the USA found that most merit plans had been discontinued for a wide range of reasons including problems in judging teachers' performance and the failure to apply criteria fairly (Johnson, 1984).

In England new teachers' standards and regulations have been introduced which came into force in September 2012. Under these regulations:

- governing bodies and local authorities will have to have a written appraisal policy for their teachers
- governing bodies will have to appoint an external adviser to advise them with appraising the head teacher
- objectives will have to be set for each teacher which contribute to improving the education of pupils
- schools will have to have an annual appraisal process for teachers
- teachers will have to be given a written appraisal report which sets out:
  - an assessment of their performance
  - an assessment of their training and development needs
  - where relevant, a recommendation on pay progression.

Teaching standards

The performances of all teachers (except those who are qualified by virtue of their Qualified Teacher Learning and Skills (QTLS) status) are to be assessed against the teachers' standards. Government guidance outlines these as follows (Department for Education, 2012):

'Teachers make the education of their pupils their first concern, and are accountable for achieving the highest possible standards in work and conduct. Teachers act with honesty and integrity, have strong subject knowledge, keep their knowledge and skills as teachers up to date and are self-critical, forge positive professional relationships, and work with parents in the best interests of their pupils.'

The standards are in two parts: teaching standards, and standards relating to personal and professional conduct.

Teaching standards – A teacher must:

- set high expectations which inspire, motivate and challenge pupils
- promote good progress and outcomes by pupils
- demonstrate good subject and curriculum knowledge
- plan and teach well-structured lessons
- adapt teaching to respond to the strengths and needs of all pupils
- make accurate and productive use of assessment
- manage behaviour effectively to ensure a good and safe learning environment

- fulfil wider professional responsibilities.

Personal and professional conduct – Requirements are that teachers must uphold public trust in the profession and maintain high standards of ethics and behaviour, within and outside school. This includes treating pupils with dignity, building relationships rooted in mutual respect, having regard for the need to safeguard pupils' wellbeing, showing tolerance of and respect for the rights of others, not undermining fundamental British values, and tolerance of those with different faiths and beliefs. In addition, teachers must have regard for the ethos, policies and practices of the school in which they teach, and

maintain high standards in their own attendance and punctuality.

More information can be found on: www.education.gov.uk/publications/ eOrderingDownload/teachers %20standards.pdf

Question

1   Design a mix of objectives for teachers which meet some of the required teaching standards. The objectives set for each teacher have to be SMART (Specific, Measurable, Achievable, Realistic and Time-bound) and be appropriate to the teacher's role and level of experience.

CONCLUSION

In this chapter, performance has been shown to be a multi-dimensional concept, comprising two key dimensions of outputs and behaviours. A further distinction is made between prescribed and discretionary behaviours. This definition illustrates the complex set of interactions that contribute to our understanding of what performance is at the individual level, and starts to highlight some of the difficulties in deciding what to measure and how to measure it.

It should be apparent that no one method is likely to be consistently reliable, has perfect role validity, and is practical and cost-effective to deliver. Output-based approaches might be objective and quantifiable but do not take account of situational constraints outside the control of the individual, and are clearly not relevant for all roles, or all aspects of all roles. Nor do they capture what needs to be done to improve performance. Behavioural approaches focus on the 'how' of achievement and are helpful for developmental purposes, but rely on the judgements of others, are inherently subjective, and prone to error and bias. As Shields (2007) notes, they are difficult to do well and extremely easy to do badly.

In truth, performance measures are highly contextual and job-specific, and need to be constructed within the organisation's overall framework of values, strategy and goals. But even this may be limiting and not appropriate for all organisations, particularly those that have to respond to an increasingly volatile marketplace. Results-based approaches are more relevant for static jobs, and those with clearly defined outputs. Contemporary jobs in the service and knowledge sector are often far less stable, more varied and require behaviours (eg creativity and initiative) which are less amenable to an output-based form of assessment. Arguably, best practice is to include a mix of results (what has been achieved) and behaviours (how it has been achieved).

Performance management schemes must accurately reflect an individual's contribution, and this requires an accurate diagnosis of performance using some form of measurement. Without clear indicators of performance, performance management systems can fail. The challenge is to find measures that are meaningful, accurate and fair, but not overly cumbersome, costly or too controlling. No wonder the search for the ideal method has been likened to the unending quest for the Holy Grail.

EXPLORE FURTHER

Aguinis, H. (2009) *Performance Management*, 2nd edition (Chapters 4 and 5). Harlow: Pearson International

Armstrong, M. (2006) *Performance Management: Key strategies and practical guidelines* (Chapter 7). London: Kogan Page

Fuchs, S. (2010) 'Critical issues in people resourcing (1): reconceptualising employee performance', in Roper, I., Prouska, R. and U. C. Na Ayudhya (eds) *Critical Issues in Human Resource Management*. London: CIPD

Latham, G. P., Sulsky, L. M. and Macdonald, H. (2007) 'Performance management', in Boxall, P., Purcell, J. and Wright, P. (eds) *The Oxford Handbook of Human Resource Management*. Oxford: Oxford University Press

Motowidlo, S. J. and Van Scotter, J. R. (1994) 'Evidence that task performance should be distinguished from contextual performance', *Journal of Applied Psychology*, Vol.79, No.4: 475–80

Pulakos, E. D and O'Leary, R. S. (2011) 'Why is performance management broken?', *Industrial and Organisational Psychology*, Vol.4, No.2: 146–64

Shields, J. (2007) *Managing Employee Performance and Reward: Concepts, practice, strategies* (Chapters 5 and 6). Melbourne, Australia: Cambridge University Press

CHAPTER 6

Performance Appraisal and Feedback

SUE HUTCHINSON

LEARNING OUTCOMES

By the end of this chapter you should be able to:

- appreciate the meaning and the key elements of the performance appraisal process
- understand the potential benefits of performance appraisal
- evaluate the various approaches to reviewing individual performance
- critically analyse 360-degree feedback
- understand and explain the criticisms of the practice of appraisal
- provide advice on implementing an effective performance appraisal process.

INTRODUCTION

Performance appraisal or review has been described as a staple element of HRM, and a common mistake is to assume that performance appraisal is the same as performance management. But it is not. It is one element of performance management which involves a wide variety of HR activities, such as evaluating employee performance, providing feedback, setting goals or behavioural standards, assessing and determining training and development needs, and sometimes determining reward. It has been described as the central pillar of performance management, and today is a standard practice in most organisations. However, performance appraisal schemes are often complex and ambitious, and the design and practice of appraisal varies considerably. Although the potential benefits are great, the outcomes are often disappointing.

Performance appraisal has received considerable attention in the HRM and work psychology literature, and is one of the most heavily debated topics, dividing both academics and practitioners. On the one hand, there are those who dismiss it as a divisive form of management control, claiming that it is subject to rater bias, lacks consistency, and falls short of achieving the expected results. Grint (1993), for example, claims that 'There seems to be considerable, though not universal, dislike of and dissatisfaction with all performance appraisals to some degree' (Grint, 1993: 62), later adding that 'Rarely in the history of business can such a system have promised so much and delivered so little' (p64). On the other hand, there are those who see it as an essential management tool which offers considerable benefits to both employees and employers. In truth, experiences vary and although there are huge problems in operationalising performance appraisal, the practice is changing and developing as organisations try to respond to some of the difficulties.

The chapter begins by examining the meaning of appraisal, some trends and potential benefits. The discussion then moves on to consider different methods of appraisal in terms of sources of feedback, including newer approaches such as multi-source or 360-degree feedback. Other aspects of the appraisal process are considered elsewhere in this book (Chapters 5, 7 and 8), and Chapter 11 looks at appraisal from an international perspective and addresses the important influence of national culture. In the final section of this chapter we examine the criticisms of and difficulties with the practice of performance appraisal and consider how some of these issues may be addressed.

WHAT IS PERFORMANCE APPRAISAL?

Performance appraisal has been described (Brutus, Fletcher and Baldry, 2009: 1999) as:

> a dynamic process that requires a rater to observe and record the performance of others, to pose evaluative judgements as to the quality of that performance, to provide feedback to the individuals evaluated, and finally to outline the development opportunity to those same ratees.

It therefore encompasses a variety of activities and, as such, is an integral tool of performance management. Although this definition suggests a very formal process, most elements of appraisal should also be conducted informally – feedback, for example, should be done on a continuous, on-going process and not limited to a formal review (see Chapter 2).

The CIPD considers that there are five main elements of the formal appraisal process (CIPD, 2011a):

- **measurement** – assessing performance against agreed targets and objectives, and behaviour. This is discussed separately in Chapter 5
- **feedback** – providing individuals with information on their past performance and on what is required to perform well in the future
- **positive reinforcement** – emphasising what has been done well, making constructive comments about what might be improved, drawing out the importance of how the job is done and what is to be done, and ensuring that effort is directed at value-adding activities
- **an exchange of views** – an open exchange of views about what has happened, how appraisees can improve their performance, any support needed and future career apsirations
- **agreement** – all parties jointly coming to an understanding about what needs to be done to improve and sustain performance and to overcome any issues raised during the course of the discussion.

Performance appraisal schemes vary in terms of the degree and frequency of formality, the extent to which employees participate in the process, the sources of rating (such as line manager, peers, customers or colleagues), and the link to reward. To a great degree, the approach adopted will reflect the nature of the organisation, the managerial beliefs and preferences, the resources available, the types of jobs and the expertise the organisation possesses (Redman, 2009; Randell, 1994). Although the formal appraisal is typically conducted as a single one-off annual event, many organisations encourage additional interim reviews on a quarterly or half-yearly basis. In a high-technology business, for example, where the environment is changing rapidly, it may be necessary to hold reviews more frequently than once a year. New recruits, employees in new posts and those who are under-performing may also require more frequent reviews. The degree of formality in this event will also vary, partly depending on managers' preferences and style, and might take the form of a fairly free-flowing discussion between appraiser and appraisee or follow a more structured format. Formal appraisals may not necessarily be suitable for all organisations. In smaller companies, where employers are more likely to know their employees well, there may be no need to use a formal approach.

Frequently, distinctions are made in the literature between the evaluative and developmental objectives of performance appraisal. The more traditional evaluative approach focuses on assessing past performance against predetermined sets of performance criteria and is often associated with the top-down, more judgemental and 'harder' forms of performance management, and the allocation of reward (Redman, 2009). More recently, however, as indicated in Chapter 2, the purpose of appraisal has been extended to include a developmental orientation, often seen as the 'softer' approach, in which the emphasis is on communicating gaps in performance expectations, clarifying job objectives, and guiding training and development to improve skill and abilities (Chiang and Birtch, 2010). In practice it can be hard to achieve both sets of objectives, which are perceived to conflict, as discussed later in this chapter.

KEY TRENDS

The origins of appraisal have been traced back to third-century China (Grint, 1993), and in the UK early examples can be found in textile mills in the Industrial Revolution (Randell, 1989) where a 'silent monitor' board hung over each machine indicating daily performance by one of four colours. Its use is now widespread in Western and non-Western countries, and increasing, particularly for managers and professionals.

According the 2004 Workplace Employee Relations Survey (WERS), 78 per cent of British workplaces undertook performance appraisal, compared to 73 per cent in 1998 (Kersley *et al*, 2006). However, appraisals are not necessarily conducted on a regular basis or do not cover the whole workforce, and those who are covered may not have the same scheme. The WERS data finds that just under two thirds of workplaces (64 per cent) carried out regular appraisal for most (60 per cent or more) non-managerial employees. Preliminary findings from WERS 2011 suggest that this figure increased in 2011 (van Wanrooy *et al*, 2013). Appraisals were typically conducted annually – for example, 64 per cent of workplaces held annual reviews for non-managerial staff, and a further 16 per cent of workplaces conducted them half-yearly. In the vast majority of workplaces (96 per cent) appraisal resulted in an evaluation of employees' training needs, and in one third of workplaces (36 per cent) employees' pay was linked to the outcome (Kersley *et al*, 2006: 86–7). Appraisals are most commonly found in larger workplaces, workplaces that are part of larger organisations, those with a personnel specialist and a recognised union. (This last finding might seem surprising in view of the fact that one of the criticisms of performance appraisal is that it is a management tool to control employees.) Financial services, health and social work, education and public administration are most likely to use performance appraisal. Although historically the public sector has had little tradition in using performance appraisal, its use in this sector has grown significantly since the 1990s, partly in response to government attempts to introduce private sector 'best practice' into the civil service, local government, schools, universities and healthcare (Winchester and Bach, 1995).

The use of performance appraisal is least common in smaller workplaces, manufacturing, construction, and hotels and catering (Kersley *et al*, 2006). Very senior managers have also tended to be neglected in the performance appraisals process, although a recent code of practice has attempted to change this for board directors in the UK (see Reflective Activity 6.1).

REFLECTIVE ACTIVITY 6.1

Appraising board members

Performance evaluations of board directors are now a requirement of the UK Corporate Governance Code. The Code, which was updated in June 2010, recommends for the first time that the boards of large public companies undertake a 'formal and rigorous evaluation of their own performance' and that of its committees and individual directors. The annual report should state how this performance has been conducted. The rationale behind this is that it will help enhance the board's performance and improve awareness of its strengths and weaknesses. The Code also recommends that the chairman regularly reviews and agrees with each director their

training and development needs. In addition, the boards of FTSE-350 companies should have the performance reviews externally facilitated at least once every three years, and the senior independent chairman and the non-executive directors should meet regularly to review the chairman's performance. Research by the Law Debenture Governance Service in 2010 (Redmond, 2011) revealed that 34 per cent of the FTSE-100 companies carried out an external facilitated board evaluation (equating roughly to the three-year cycle), but that just 17 per cent of the FTSE-250 boards did so.

1   What are the advantages and disadvantages of evaluating the performance of board members?

THE BENEFITS OF PERFORMANCE APPRAISAL

At the core, performance appraisals are about motivating employees in order to improve performance, and the practice is grounded in theories of motivation, such as goal-setting, expectancy theory and equity theory (see Chapter 3).

Setting individual performance targets and objectives is a motivational device and can improve employee identification with, and commitment to, the organisation's goals and objectives. It also provides the opportunity to give direction to work efforts which will benefit the organisation.

Giving feedback is one of the most important parts of the performance appraisal process and, if handled in the right way, can be a very motivating experience and minimise any perceptions of procedural injustice. Feedback-seeking is seen as a proactive employee behaviour (Lam *et al*, 2007) and provides individuals with information on how well they are doing and how they can make improvements. It can be used to reinforce behaviour, give positive recognition, and enable an assessment of training and development needs and other forms of support. Studies show that giving feedback can enhance individual performance and increase the intrinsic motivation of employees (Kluger and DeNisi, 1996; Hackman and Oldham, 1975, 1980). Positive reinforcement has been shown to increase employees' 'self-efficacy beliefs', which in turn has been shown to increase performance (Bandura, 1993). Even feedback on weaknesses can increase performance, provided it is delivered effectively and the differences between self-ratings and ratings by others is not too great. Chen *et al* (2007) argue that negative feedback has a higher instrumental value than positive feedback, by giving employees a better idea of why they are under-performing and how to improve. They also found that the reaction to negative feedback can depend on the degree of trust between supervisors and subordinate. To be fully effective, feedback has to be given on a regular basis, not just in the formal review. Informal feedback can work particularly well in organisations with open and honest cultures, and be a particularly effective way of managing professional workers. At Microsoft (see Case Study 6.1) informal feedback is encouraged in addition to the formal development discussion and performance and merit reviews.

PROVIDING INFORMAL FEEDBACK AT MICROSOFT

CASE STUDY 6.1

In keeping with its culture of openness and honesty, Microsoft's approach to effective performance management relies on a system of regular informal one-to-one meetings of employees and their line managers. Although there are two formal reviews – one for performance and merit, and the other for development – employees are encouraged to meet with their manager to discuss personal performance issues outside the formal discussions. The frequency of these informal meetings varies: every employee is guaranteed time to talk with their manager on this basis and it is up to line managers to allocate their time appropriately.

The company also encourages employees to provide open and honest feedback for their own line managers using an online feedback tool which goes live in April and December of each year. Managers can request to extend this to 360-degree feedback for developmental purposes. The online tool can be accessed by every member of a manager's team, and employees outside the immediate team can also request to be included provided they have had contact with the manager.

Employees rate certain areas of a manager's performance against a five-point scale, and can also provide more detailed comments to questions such as 'What would you like your manager to do more of?' Although employees can choose to remain anonymous, the company feels that feedback is more useful if it comes from a named/known source, and this encourages employees to accept ownership of their comments. It is recommended that managers go back to employees to raise any issues that come out of this process and to clarify any comments they do not understand.

Source: IDS HR Case Study (2003)

Questions

1 What are the advantages and disadvantages of encouraging an informal approach?

2 The extent to which this process is actually formal is debatable. Discuss the view that rather than being an informal process, it is a question of formalising the informal.

Motivation can also be enhanced in other ways. The outcomes of performance appraisal – such as identifying training, learning and development needs, providing career counselling and making performance-related reward decisions – can be motivational if conducted in a fair and effective way. Under-performing employees can also be given encouragement, direction and support in the appraisal process. From the employers' perspective, the appraisal process also provides a basis on which to identify good performers with potential and suitability for promotion, which will assist with succession planning.

The performance appraisal process can facilitate communication between employee and manager and enhance employee involvement. Participation in appraisals has been found to be positively related with a range of positive employee reactions (eg Cawley *et al*, 1998). If employees make a contribution to the review, it can enhance their sense of control, it helps ensure that objectives are agreed which are relevant and achievable, and it improves employee buy-in to the process and any objectives set. When formalised, the process also helps develop consistency of treatment by ensuring that all managers meet their staff on a regular basis to discuss performance.

CRITICAL REFLECTION 6.1

Jackman and Strober (2003) suggest that some employees avoid feedback for fear that it will result in 'impossible demands' (Jackman and Strober, 2003: 101).

Provide some guidance for line managers on how to give constructive feedback and avoid making impossible demands that would increase workload and stress.

The benefits of appraisal are recognised in models of high-commitment HRM. Performance appraisal linked to compensation was one of the HR practices used in Huselid's study (1995), which established a link between HRM and performance. Similarly, appraisal was one of the practices studied in Guest *et al*'s research (2003) on the relationship between HRM and corporate performance. Research by Michael West and colleagues (2006) examining the HRM–performance link in the NHS suggested that a range of HRM policies including performance appraisal might contribute to high-quality healthcare (see also Chapter 2).

The potential benefits, then, of performance appraisal are wide-ranging. This was confirmed in an IRS survey of 154 organisations which in 2005 found that a large majority (90.9 per cent) of respondents felt that appraisals are an essential management tool which can improve individual and organisational performance (Wolff, 2005). Despite the good intentions behind performance appraisals, however, some have argued that they try to do too much, and the reality is that the practice is problematic and a 'high-risk activity' (Fletcher, 2008). In the IRS survey, 42 per cent believed appraisals were often badly conducted, suggesting that the practice does not match up to expectations. The reasons behind this are explored later in the chapter.

WHO DOES THE APPRAISING?

Choosing who does the appraising depends on what fits with the national and organisational culture, the aims of the performance management process, the group of employees to be appraised (eg managers or non-managers), the nature of the job and the resources available. The traditional approach has been for the immediate line manager to do the appraising, but increasingly organisations are adopting a more diversified approach partly because of concerns about objectivity and fairness, and the need to enhance the value of the process for employees. Sometimes organisations operate different arrangements for different groups of employees, and very occasionally employees are offered a choice of methods. The main approaches are:

- appraisal by the immediate line manager
- self-appraisal
- appraisal by peers
- appraisal by subordinates
- customer appraisal
- multi-level or 360-degree appraisal.

These alternatives are considered in more detail below. Particular attention is devoted to 360-degree appraisal because it provides the opportunity to compare the effects of feedback from different sources.

APPRAISAL BY IMMEDIATE LINE MANAGER

The traditional and most common form of review is appraisal by the immediate line manager, sometimes referred to as downward appraisal. In an IRS survey (Wolff, 2005), all respondent organisations reported using a scheme which involved a discussion with the line manager for at least some employee groups. On a formal basis, this normally involves a one-to-one meeting between the individual and his or her line manager, and often includes a self-assessment. A typical scenario might be the appraisee and appraiser completing identical appraisal forms, meeting to discuss these, and agreeing a report and/or plan on the basis of this discussion. The rationale behind this approach is that the line manager is normally in close and frequent contact with the employee, and thus best placed to assess the individual, and give guidance and support. The manager will be aware of the expectations of the role, of any factors that might influence an individual's performance such as individual and organisational constraints, and of the local business needs. This approach can also potentially strengthen the relationship between the manager and employee by facilitating discussion and, if combined with a self-assessment, offers the employee some control over the process and a greater say in his or her own development. In theory, at least, having two perspectives on performance rather than just one should also provide a more objective assessment. Nevertheless, this approach is not without its challenges, for above all it is prone to subjectivity and bias, as discussed later in this chapter, and relies on good line management skills. It also depends on having effectively developed relationships between the parties and the existence of mutual trust – otherwise disagreements may arise. Cultural differences must also be considered. For example, in collectivist cultures one-to-one reviews are unlikely to be acceptable and group-based evalutations are preferred (Chapter 11).

SELF-APPRAISAL

Self-appraisal relies on individuals' assessing their own performance, and is often incorporated within other methods – most notably, downward appraisal and 360-degree appraisal. Self-assessment has increased in popularity in recent years, and in a CIPD survey, 30 per cent of organisations reported that they used some form of self-assessment, and just over half (55 per cent) of them believed it to be effective (CIPD, 2005a). The advantages are that it forces individuals to reflect on their own performance and development needs, and, because it allows employees a voice in the process, it contributes to a sense of procedural justice and greater commitment. As a consequence, individuals are more likely to accept the outcome. Arguably, an individual is also in a better position to track their own performance compared to the line manager, who will have to monitor the performance of a number of employees and may only observe some aspects of an employee's work. In reality, however, individuals are not very good at rating their own performance in an objective way: generally, self-raters are overly lenient or too harsh on themselves. According to Jansen and Vloeberghs (1999), over-rating is more common than under-rating because people are usually more optimistic about their performance. Individual and personality characteristics, job pressures and past experience with feedback can influence self-ratings (Atwater, 1998). If rewards are linked to the appraisal, there will almost certainly be a tendency to over-inflate, and for this reason it is recommended that reward is not linked to the outcome of a self-appraisal. There may also be problems when discrepancies arise between self and others.

Self-assessment works best for jobs with high levels of discretion, when the work requires specialised skills or where the immediate manager does not have regular contact with the appraisee. It is also considered most appropriate when used for developmental purposes (when self-ratings tend to be less lenient) rather than evaluative. Fletcher (2008) advises that one of the most effective ways of using self-assessment is to ask the individual to assess performance against his or her own personal standards, rather than against other people's. Appraisees could, for example, be asked what they feel they have done best and least well in the last 12 months, rather than be required to make comparisons against others in the team. Employees must also have clear objectives, and fully understand the skills and competencies that are expected of the role if they are to self-assess.

UPWARD APPRAISAL

Upward appraisal is when direct reports comment on their manager's or superior's performance, usually anonymously. Although a relatively new practice in the UK, it has been adopted in a number of high-profile organisations such as BodyShop, WHSmith and British Airways over the last few decades, although it is still far from common practice (Redman, 2009). Like the other approaches, it is often a component of multi-level feedback, and can also be used alongside the more traditional downward appraisal. The rationale for this approach is that direct reports are better placed than other groups to provide meaningful feedback on certain management behaviours – in particular, leadership and people management. Also, because it involves multiple appraisers, the upward appraisal is, in theory, likely to be less prone to bias. By offering employees the opportunity to comment on their manager's performance, the approach is empowering for employees, should elicit greater commitment, and should encourage a more participative management style (Redman and Matthews, 1995). It can also be used to link managerial behaviour more closely with the values of the goals of the organisation.

Not surprisingly, the approach can be threatening and undermining for managers, who may perceived it as a tool to restrict management, and are thus likely to put up some resistance. This may be one reason for the low take-up in the UK. A frequently reported example is the Brazilian company Semco, in which managers are upwardly appraised every six months on a scale up to 100. Results are posted on a noticeboard and managers who consistently under-perform are edged out or simply 'fade away' (Redman and Matthews, 1995). As with the other approaches, there is also the potential for subjectivity and bias. Employees may rate their manager poorly in order to reek revenge, or be over-generous because they feel uncomfortable in giving an unfavourable rating or want to ingratiate themselves with their boss. Grint (1993) refers to the 'mutual supporters' club' effect of upward appraisal by which subordinates provide glowing references for their boss in return for subsequent favours, and argues that upward appraisal simply replaces 'the subjectivity of a single-author appraisal with the subjectivity of a collective appraisal' (Grint, 1993: 71). The approach also relies on direct reports' being in close and regular contact with their manager.

PEER APPRAISAL

This involves assessment by colleagues and is suited to team review or organisations with flatter structures. Like other methods, it often works best when combined with other approaches. Although there has been little research conducted on the validity and reliability of peer ratings, it is not unreasonable to assume that it is subject to some of the same types of bias attributed to upward and downward appraisals. Colleagues may be reluctant to be honest, and assessments can be influenced by jealousy or rivalry. In the US military – pioneers of this approach – it was termed 'screw your buddy' for obvious reasons.

CUSTOMER APPRAISALS

Increasingly in customer service environments such as retail, hospitality and financial services, employees are being assessed by the customer. There are a wide variety of techniques for gathering customer views, including customer surveys (eg telephone surveys at the end of a call), interviews and mystery shoppers. Mystery shopping typically involves staff from a specialist agency masquerading as real shoppers, observing and recording individual employees' interactions with the customers. Employees are normally made aware that a mystery shopper procedure is to be used, and sometimes even notified of the day of the visit.

Customer appraisals can rarely take into account all aspects of a person's performance and are normally used in addition to other approaches such as 360-degree feedback. This form of assessment, however, raises ethical questions about secret surveillance, and critics argue that it is a form of control and suggests a lack of management trust in employees. For this very reason it is often resented and resisted by employees, and there is evidence that employees consider the mystery shopper approach procedurally and distributively less fair than line manager assessment (Brender-Ilan and Shultz, 2005).

REFLECTIVE ACTIVITY 6.2

Customer feedback on HR professionals

Although feedback is clearly a good thing, many HR functions appear reluctant to find out what their own internal customers think about their performance. Previous research by the Institute for Employment Studies (IES) found that those HR functions which did gather customer feedback found it valuable and of direct use, particularly in clarifying the service priorities of their customers. Yet a significant minority of HR departments appear to shy away from asking for customer feedback. The fear of hearing bad news, raising expectations that cannot be met, and time and resource constraints are cited as reasons for this reluctance. There is also a view that in higher-value advisory work responses may be difficult to interpret. For example, if feedback suggests that the quality of advice was poor, is it because managers were given unwelcome advice, or because it was unhelpful or obstructive, or because it didn't address business concerns? With the more routine transactional work, metrics can be used (such as response-time to a query), but this will not capture all aspects of service quality such as whether the advice addressed the customer problem.

The research by IES identifies a number of ways of collecting this data, including focus groups, interviews, follow-up surveys on calls and mystery shopper methods.

Source: Reilly and Hirsh, 2012

1   What are the advantages and disadvantages of using internal customer feedback to assess a person who works in HR?

2   What sort of information might be captured in the feedback for a recruitment manager?

MULTI-SOURCE PERFORMANCE APPRAISALS

A more contemporary approach is feedback from a variety of different sources including peers, the line manager, subordinates, customers, suppliers and oneself (see Figure 6.1). More commonly referred to as multi-source or 360-degree appraisal (to reflect the all-encompassing direction of feedback), this approach has arisen partly in response to some of the problems with the more traditional methods and has proved a fertile ground for researchers to compare the effects of feedback from different sources.

Figure 6.1 Sources of feedback for 360-degree appraisal

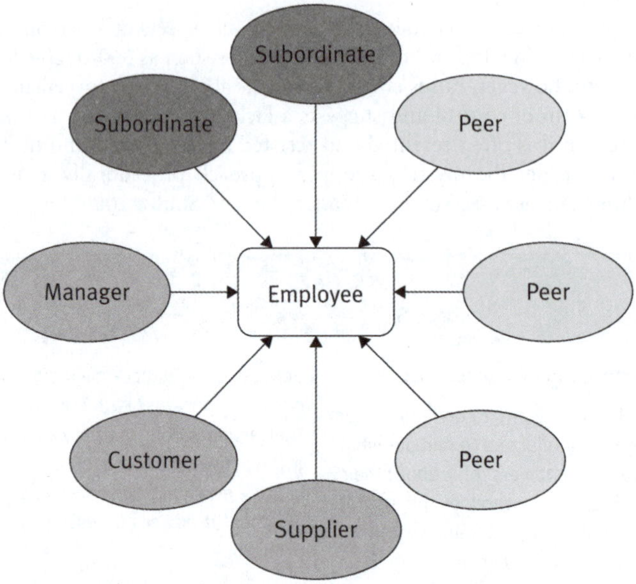

The origins of the approach can be traced back to the US Army in the 1970s, when researchers found that peers' opinions were a more accurate reflection of a soldier's performance than were those of superiors (Dugdill, 1994, reported in Redman, 2009). Today, the use of this approach appears to be widespread in the USA and is reported to be used by 90 per cent of the Fortune-1000 companies (see Dai *et al*, 2010). It was not until the mid-1990s, however, that the practice started to take root in the UK, although reports on its uptake are sketchy and varied. Fletcher, who has written and researched extensively on 360-degree feedback, reports on the 'enthusiastic and speedy' adoption of the approach (Fletcher, 2008). In contrast, Shields gives a more pessimistic account of 'a technique whose time has passed' (Shields, 2007: 149). A CIPD survey in 2004 reported that 14 per cent of organisations used this approach, compared to 11 per cent in 1997 (CIPD, 2005a), and in another survey, the IRS reported that 22.6 per cent of organisations used 360-degree appraisal for some employees (Wolff, 2005). On this basis it seems reasonable to conclude that it has been more than a just temporary fad, and is an approach which is here to stay, even if growth is slow. Take-up seems to be predominantly confined to larger employers and for the assessment of managers, and is increasingly being adopted for professionals such as medical consultants and other health professionals who work in multi-disciplinary teams (see Activity 6.6). Practice varies on whether the approach is mandatory or optional, and in some organisations it also varies depending on the group of employees – for example, it may be mandatory for top management and optional for lower levels of management.

Raters are usually anonymous, which can be particularly important for peers and subordinates who may feel uncomfortable or intimidated when rating their colleagues or boss. This also encourages assessors to be honest, and there is evidence that appraisers whose identity is known tend to give higher ratings than those who are anonymous (London and Smither, 1995; van der Heijden and Nijhoff, 2004). In some schemes the appraiser chooses whether to disclose his or her identity, and often the individual being assessed can nominate specific colleagues to appraise them (see the Group Aeroplan Case Study 6.2 below). The number of raters can range from as few as three to as many as 20, although if there are too few anonymity may be comprised. Hensel *et al* (2010) report that a minimum of three to five peer raters and one supervisor are needed for reliable feedback, and the CIPD suggests eight to ten assessors (CIPD, 2011b).

Typically, raters complete a feedback questionnaire which contains a range of questions or statements about the assessed individual's behaviour or competency, rated on a Likert-type scale (see Chapter 5). Additionally, there may be the opportunity to add free text comments which can be helpful for developmental purposes. Ratings are usually collated to provide an overall average score, and an average on each competency or behaviour. Depending on the number of raters, average scores may be broken down by rating groups (eg peers, subordinates, etc) so that differences in perspective can be explored. Overall feedback to appraisees is normally given by the person charged with collecting the information in the first place, which may be the HR manager, a consultant, a coach or the individual's manager. It is normally delivered on a one-to-one basis, although there are examples where feedback is discussed with some or all of the raters to allow a detailed discussion of the scores (Fletcher, 2008). What people do with feedback is critical, and there is clear evidence that working with a coach to review feedback, set development goals and discuss feedback with those who gave it leads to performance improvements (Smither *et al*, 2003; London and Smither, 1995). It is vital, then, that the person providing overall feedback is skilled and can interpret ratings from different (and sometimes contradictory) sources. Reports suggest an increased use of online 360-degree feedback which improves confidentiality and reduces time and effort (CIPD, 2011b), although the effectiveness of providing overall feedback in this impersonal way must be questioned, given the importance of feedback as a motivational device.

On the face of it, this approach seems to offer considerable benefits (Marchington and Wilkinson, 2012; Fletcher, 2008; Armstrong and Baron, 2005). The use of multiple reviewers means that a wide range of information can be gathered from different perspectives and a more balanced and accurate view of performance thus obtained. Different raters can report on the types of behaviours they are best placed to evaluate – work colleagues, for example, can evaluate the ability to engage in teamwork; customers can assess whether an employee communicates well with them, is polite, and so on. On this basis 360-degree appraisal offers greater reliability and validity compared to the alternatives, and is a procedurally fairer way of assessment which should ensure a higher chance of acceptance. It also offers the opportunity for improved self-awareness. Research suggests that greater self-awareness is linked to better performance by challenging individuals' perceptions of their own performance and providing the motivation to change. Any differences between the way individuals see themselves and how they are perceived by others can be identified, and over successive feedbacks individuals should become more realistic in their self-perceptions and any gap is reduced (Fletcher, 2008).

Multi-source feedback also offers subordinates and peers the opportunity to have a 'voice', commenting on the way they are supervised or on how work colleagues relate to them. As such it is an empowering mechanism, potentially offering employees some influence over the way they are managed and treated (Fletcher, 2008). A 360-degree questionnaire based on competences and their descriptors can also enhance the understanding across the organisation of appropriate performance-related behaviours.

The multi-source approach is particularly beneficial in certain contexts – for example, where a line manager does not fully understand all aspects of an individual's role, perhaps because the individual works in several different teams or works autonomously or semi-autonomously. It is also well suited to the service sector where customer feedback is important, or where teamworking is an important aspect of the role. It has also proved helpful for providing feedback for more senior managers who have historically tended to be neglected in the appraisal process, and where informal feedback on performance is harder to obtain on a day-to-day basis.

REFLECTIVE ACTIVITY 6.3

Cadburys has introduced a 720-degree feedback for their leadership development programme which includes input from a leader's family and friends *as well as* business colleagues and direct reports (Smedley, 2010).

1   What do you think are the advantages and disadvantages of using this multiple range of sources from inside and outside the organisation?

On the downside, however, there can be no doubt that the approach involves considerable effort on the part of a range of individuals (assessors, administrators, those giving the final feedback). It is time-consuming, particularly if run on an annual basis, costly to implement and administer, and the analysis of information can be complex.

There is also the problem of subjectivity. In principle, having multiple perspectives should create a more objective assessment, based on the assumption that 'subjectivity + subjectivity + subjectivity = objectivity' (van der Heijden and Nijhoff, 2004: 494). Sceptics argue, however, that if one person can be biased and unfair, so can another, and that with this approach 'We are just swapping one set of biased perceptions for a whole raft of them…' (Fletcher, 2008: 78). If assessment is linked to reward, there is the added risk that raters will not give honest feedback for fear of adversely affecting a person's pay, and for this very reason only a minority of UK organisations link 360-degree appraisal to reward. Allowing individuals to choose their own assessors is also likely to compromise objectivity – peers, for example, may be more generous in their ratings ('You scratch my back and I'll scratch yours'), and even if anonymity is promised, fears of being identified could mean that appraisers are more reluctant to give poor ratings. There is also evidence that 360-degree feedback is no more immune from ethnic bias than other forms of assessment (Fletcher, 2001).

In practice, it seems that organisations often have too few raters to improve the reliability and validity of assessments, and it is more common for organisations to use the rating of one supervisor and only two or three peer raters. Additional problems can arise if all raters are given the same indicators to assess against, rather than just evaluating those aspects they are best placed to judge. Different raters may also interpret performance behaviours differently – for example, a manager's conceptualisation of leadership skills may be different from the conceptualisation of peers. Differences between raters and oneself can also be problematic: if the difference between one's own ideas and others' is much greater than expected, it can be demotivating – especially if it relates to personal qualities (Brett and Atwater, 2001).

Making sense of the ratings is a further challenge. Averaging scores will hide dispersions or variances – for example, someone may come out as a middling performer when one group or individual has assessed them as excellent and another as poor. Variance in scores does not necessarily mean that someone has misjudged performance but simply reflects different perspectives and can be informative. This highlights the importance of having a skilled individual to interpret contradictory messages and provide follow-up feedback.

Research evidence on the effectiveness of 360-degree feedback is mixed, but on balance suggests modest improvements. Only 20 per cent of respondents to the aforementioned CIPD survey felt that 360-degree feedback was effective (CIPD, 2005a), and a meta-analysis of 24 longitudinal studies found only very small improvements in employee behaviour and attitudes following the introduction of 360-degree feedback (Smither *et al*, 2005). However, Fletcher and Baldry (1999) found that managers receiving this type of feedback were generally positive towards it and recognised its potential for improving performance, and Tyson and Ward (2004) report that senior managers' competency ratings significantly improved after feedback. One clear and consistent message from the research, however, is that 360-degree feedback is more likely to succeed if used for developmental purposes rather than as an evaluative or decision-making tool for, say, pay or promotion. Peer ratings, for example, have been shown to be less reliable, less valid and more generous when given for evaluation purposes than when used for development purposes (Pollack and Pollack, 1996), and the quality of subordinates' ratings is poorer when used for evaluative purposes (Greguras *et al*, 2003). Fletcher (2008) also suggests using 360-degree feedback on an occasional basis or as a one-off event rather than as an annual event. The feedback literature emphasises the need for the recipient to have trust in the source, so assessors should be credible to the recipient (DeNisi and Kluger, 2000; CIPD, 2011b). Assessors should not be forced to take part and should be given guidance about the information they are requested to put forward: they should, for example, be asking for specific examples of certain behaviours or only providing comments that can be supported with evidence.

To some extent the effectiveness of multi-source feedback depends on the culture and structure of the organisation and the jobs that people perform. It is best suited to organisational forms with flatter organisational hierarchies and a culture of openness and continuous improvement, and to organisations where customer feedback is important (Marchington and Wilkinson, 2012; Fletcher, 2008).

 ONLINE 360-DEGREE FEEDBACK AT GROUP AEROPLAN

CASE STUDY 6.2

At Group Aeroplan Europe a 360-degree appraisal is used to appraise all of its 250 employees in the UK. The Canadian-owned company operates the Nectar Loyalty programme through which customers of companies such as Sainsbury's, BP, American Express and EDF Energy collect points to redeem against a variety of goods and experiences.

Under the scheme employees agree with their line manager up to 11 people to rate their performance, which may include their line manager, colleagues, direct reports or external contacts, plus a self-assessment. The important point is to ensure a balanced view of performance, and there are a minimum of two raters from each category in order to preserve anonymity. These assessors are required to rate a range of core competency behaviours on a scale of 1 to 7 using an online tool. Employees who want more detailed feedback can also ask to be rated against further additional (set) behaviours, such as 'Treats everyone

fairly', or 'Makes a strong impression' or 'Maintains performance under pressure'. Each rater can also make additional comments to indicate what they feel the employee is particularly good at – or how they might become more effective.

The online system generates a detailed summary comparing the self-assessment with the feedback from reviewers. Additional reports can also be generated about the profile of raters, such as those who appear to be particularly lenient, busy or 'harried' when providing ratings (usually those providing feedback on a large number of employees) and the average length of time taken to complete a survey. It can also provide a breakdown of average scores by relationship with the ratee.

The 360-degree process is open for six weeks prior to the annual performance development review meeting. Results from the feedback are taken into account at the formal review with the line manager, who uses it to assess the employee against agreed objectives and competencies. The line manager awards an overall rating of performance which is used to determine the employee's annual bonus award and development needs. An important point is that this final rating may not necessarily equate to the average score obtained by the 360-degree feedback.

Final performance is awarded in line with a desired distribution curve over seven potential ratings, as shown listed alongside. A calibration process involving senior managers ensures that ratings conform with the desired distribution. The 'Superstar' ranking is rarely given and has to be approved by the company executive committee. Employees receiving a 1 or 2 rating are placed on a three-month performance development plan.

If there are concerns about an employee's performance, the company can also conduct a one-off 360-degree appraisal at any point in the year.

Desired distribution curve: performances and forced percentages

7	Superstar	(–)
6	Excellent performer	10 per cent
5	Very good performer	25 per cent
4	Good performer	50 per cent
3	Satisfactory performer	15 per cent
2	Under-performer	–
1	Non-performer	–

Source: IDS HR Study 866 (2009a)

Questions

1 What are the benefits and potential problems with this approach to reviewing performance?

2 What improvements would you recommend?

REFLECTIVE ACTIVITY 6.4

1 What form of appraisal assessment would be appropriate for

- a football coach?
- a lecturer?
- a musician in an orchestra?
- a postman or postwoman?

2 What advice would you give to enhance the effectiveness of each approach?

PROBLEMS WITH PERFORMANCE APPRAISALS

It will already be apparent that the practice of appraising performance is fraught with difficulties. As Boxall and Purcell (2011) note: 'The problem we must wrestle with is that good intentions in the PA area have often been associated with disappointing outcomes' (Boxall and Purcell, 2011: 217). In a review of 131 studies Kluger and DeNisi (1996) concluded that in more than one third of the cases performance feedback resulted in *decreased* performance. Employees often express dissatisfaction with both the decisions made as a result of performance assessment and the process of performance assessment (Milliman, Nason, Zhu and De Cieri, 2002), which may have longitudinal effects on overall job satisfaction and commitment (Blau, 1999). These views are shaped by perceptions of equity and organisational justice. For example, distributive injustice will be felt if reward allocations are thought to be unfair – that is, if the process is considered to be biased in some way, employees will feel procedural injustice.

The main problems can be categorised within the following areas:

- conflicting aims
- management behaviour
- subjectivity and bias
- control
- bureaucracy.

CONFLICTING AIMS

It was suggested early on in this chapter that there are two distinct objectives in performance appraisal – the evaluative and the developmental objectives – and that these are difficult to maintain in the same process and may conflict. Some of the research presented earlier on the effectiveness of feedback also found that feedback works best for developmental purposes. Evaluating performance requires raters to look backwards and make a judgement on past performance, whereas the developmental approach requires assessors to look forward and make suggestions for support. These approaches require quite different skills. Moreover, if evaluation is linked to reward, this can undermine the system since employees are likely to be reluctant to admit to any shortcomings or be open about their training needs when the outcome is going affect their pay. To overcome this, some organisations that reward performance keep the pay review separate from the development review.

MANAGEMENT BEHAVIOUR

There is a growing body of research which shows that it is the *quality* of the performance appraisal process which impacts on individual outcomes. Brown *et al*'s (2010) study of a large public sector organisation found that employees with low performance appraisal experiences were more likely to be dissatisfied with their job, to be less committed to the organisation and to be contemplating leaving the organisation. In Chapter 4 evidence was presented which showed that the quality of the appraisals is largely determined by the attitudes and behaviours of line managers, and that there can be considerable variability in line management behaviour in terms of how and (indeed) whether they carry out performance appraisals. Some commentators argue that managers are reluctant to undertake appraisals. For example, Heathfield (2007) notes that 'When surveyed about most disliked tasks, managers say they hate conducting appraisal second only to firing employees' (Heathfield, 2007: 6). Latham *et al* (1993) argue that managers fear the consequences of the process or feel the potential returns from their efforts are not worthwhile. It is well known that managers often struggle to give effective feedback, particularly to those who are under-performing and to the high performers, and dislike having 'difficult conversations' with poorer performers. Managers can also be resistant because they find it difficult to balance the conflicting roles of disciplinary 'judge' and helpful 'coach' and can be reluctant to 'play God' in evaluating their direct reports (Edwards *et al*, 1985; McGregor, 1957). It was also noted in Chapter 4 how problems of work overload, role conflict, inadequate resources and lack of competence and confidence can constrain line managers' ability, motivation and opportunity (AMO) to carry out performance appraisals effectively. All of these factors highlight the importance of training, resources, time and organisational support for managers.

The nature of the relationship between employee and manager has also been shown to be critical to the assessment of employee performance (in Brown and Lim, 2009). Research on leader–member exchange (LMX: see Chapter 4) tells us that the higher the quality of the relationship, the better a subordinate performs. In high LMX relationships, line managers provide the subordinate with more support and resources, which creates obligations for the subordinate to reciprocate by performing more effectively. The reaction to negative feedback can also depend on the degree of trust between supervisors and subordinate (Chen *et al*, 2007). Brown and Lim (2009) also point to research at the other end of the spectrum, on 'abusive supervision', which is the extent to which line managers engage in hostile verbal and non-verbal behaviours, excluding physical contact (Brown and Lim, 2009: 200–1). This can result in dysfunctional behaviour – eg acting as if one is too busy to undertake a task or acting as if one has forgotten to do something, which can be demonstrated in the performance review.

SUBJECTIVITY AND BIAS

The quality of appraisals is also influenced by the accuracy of the ratings or assessment. One of the major problems with all appraisals is the potential for distortion (intentional and unintentional) in the assessment of performance because of subjectivity and bias on the part of assessors. Inaccurate ratings increase employee mistrust in the performance appraisal system (Tziner and Murphy, 1999) by creating inequity and concerns over distributive justice and obviously make the assessment less useful for the organisation. The most common problem is the tendency for raters to promote higher evaluations than deserved (Brutus *et al*, 2009). Some of the most common distortions are outlined by Grint (1993) in his classic article critiquing performance appraisal:

- the **halo or horns effect**, by which one specific criterion or characteristic distorts the assessment of others – deciding that an employee is good in one area and giving them a similarly high marking in other aspects, regardless of performance, is demonstrating the halo effect. Alternatively, a serious mistake can mean that the appraiser gives a lower than expected rating in all other areas (the 'horns' effect)
- the **crony effect**, by which a distortion is caused by the closeness of the personal relationship between appraiser and appraised
- the **doppelgänger** effect, by which the rating reflects similarities (eg character, behaviour) between appraiser and appraisee
- the **Veblen effect**, or the problem of ranking everyone in the middle – named after Veblen's habit of awarding all students Cs irrespective of their quality. This occurs when appraisers are reluctant to rate individuals at the outer ends of the rating scale.

Other distortions that can occur (Furnham, 2004; Latham *et al*, 2007) include:

- the **recency effect**, by which only recent events influence the assessment either negatively or positively
- **confirmation bias**, by which the appraiser looks for information that confirms preconceived ideas about the employee
- **contrast error**, by which comparisons are made with other employees which distort assessments
- the **status effect**, by which those with higher-level positions are given more generous ratings.

Research has also shown that an individual's gender, age, ethnic origin and race may affect the appraisal. Males, for example, are usually rated as more effective than females (Latham *et al*, 2007). Chapter 4 discusses the evidence that a manager's personality can influence ratings.

Longenecker (1997) suggests there is a political dimension to assessments, arguing that managers deliberately try to protect their own interests and pursue their own agenda by manipulating ratings. This political activity represents a source of bias or inaccuracy in employee appraisal. 'No matter how well designed the appraisal system, no matter how effective the organisation's training programme, no matter how hard the issue of accuracy is stressed – when you turn managers loose in the real world, they consciously fudge the numbers' (Longenecker, 1997: 77). Managers may artificially deflate ratings in order to show who is boss or to scare better performance out of an employee or to punish a rebellious employee. Boxall and Purcell (2011) suggest that some managers use the appraisal system to exact revenge on their political rivals or 'hobble an individual's chances of advancement' (Boxall and Purcell, 2011: 218). On the other hand, managers may choose to inflate ratings because it reflects favourably on them as managers, or helps to promote a poor performer out of the department, or because they simply wish to avoid confrontation.

CRITICAL REFLECTION 6.2

The paradox of rating inflation

Although rating inflation can undermine the integrity of performance management and create feelings of inequity, it also has some positive benefits (Brutus *et al*, 2009). For example, it can improve a person's confidence and self-esteem and make him or her feel more positive, or it can help to avoid conflict with other employees.

1   Discuss the advantages and disadvantages of lenient ratings.

As described earlier, it is not just managers who are prone to subjectivity and bias, but all potential assessors. Nor are employees always the passive agents in performance appraisal (Brown and Lim, 2009). Those being assessed can distort ratings by engaging in 'impression management' and making the appraiser think they are better than they actually are (see Reflective Activity 6.5). It has also been found that when an employee overestimates his or her own performance, raters are more likely to give over-lenient ratings to protect the individual's self-esteem and the manager–employee relationship (Murphy and Cleveland, 1995).

To minimise bias and help achieve consistency in reporting standards, it is recommended that senior managers have the opportunity to comment upon and sign evaluations. Boxall and Purcell (2011) suggest that senior managers must improve accountability mechanisms around performance appraisal by, for example, requiring managers to justify evaluations, and by clarifying the purpose of appraisal. Managers could also keep running records of the performance of their employees and suitable training should be offered to all appraisers (ACAS, 2003). Raters can also be encouraged to provide accurate ratings by the quality of appraisal in their own job performance evaluation.

REFLECTIVE ACTIVITY 6.5

Impression management

Some employees are keen to present a favourable impression in performance appraisal settings, and Rosenfeld *et al* (2002) argue that some individuals are more motivated and skilled at engaging in 'impression management' than others.

Impression management refers to the process by which individuals try to influence the impression others have of them in order to create a desired image in the minds of others (Harris *et al*, 2007: 278). There are two types of impression management (IM): supervisor-focused and job-focused (Wayne and Linden,

1995). Research suggests that supervisor-focused IM can have a positive impact on performance assessments, so a manager who feels liked and admired by his or her employee is more likely to rate that person generously (Wayne and Linden, 1995). However, job-focused IM, which is designed to make employees appear more competent at their job, is less liked by supervisors: employees who adopt this approach tend to receive lower ratings from the supervisor (Ferris *et al*, 1994).

1   Thinking about your own experiences at work, provide examples of these different forms of IM

2   What can organisations do to alert managers to be aware of IM tactics and so be less susceptible to their effects?

CASE STUDY 6.3

ISSUES TO WATCH OUT FOR WHEN RATING PERFORMANCE: LUTON BOROUGH COUNCIL

Luton Borough Council employs around 4,000 employees and serves a population of over 184,000 in the town of Luton. In a revamped process, appraisals are held twice a year, although managers are also encouraged to provide staff with on-going feedback throughout the year. To help managers the HR function has produced guidelines highlighting the common problems that can arise when rating performance and advising on how to minimise these problems.

The halo and horns effect – In order to avoid one characteristic unduly influencing an assessment, the appraiser should judge all employees one after another on a single factor or trait before going on to judge them all again on the next factor. In this way, all employees are assessed relative to a consistent standard.

Variations in reporting standards – Consistency in marking is checked by senior managers who confirm line managers' assessments by comparing reporting standards and then counsel any managers who appear to be too lenient or too harsh.

Emphasis on the recent past – Because most appraisals report over a period of one year, it is recognised that some managers may find it difficult to recall and assess events that occurred in the earlier parts of the year. As a result, some managers may give undue emphasis to recent events, which can distort ratings. Managers are advised to keep notes on staff performance and gather evidence on performance over the year. This could include completed work by the employee, such as reports and projects, notes of previous one-to-ones, and third-party feedback (chosen by the employee to give a more balanced view of performance). Alternatively, managers should make informal records part-way through the year to help them be more objective later on.

The central tendency – Managers are warned of the tendency to lean towards the middle of the rating scale (particularly as the rating system has an odd number of rating points) and towards a reluctance to rate people at the outer ends of the rating scale. All managers who conduct appraisals have to be trained not only on the skills side – the 'how to do' it – but also on the reasons or the 'why we do it', so that they are aware of these problems and see how the process fits into the wider business strategy.

Source: adapted from IDS HR Study 938 (2011a)

CONTROL

Much of the critical literature on performance appraisal focuses on appraisal as a form of indirect control, and a means to elicit consent from employees for such control. This was discussed in Chapter 5 in relation to performance measurement. Bach (2005) and others apply the metaphor of the panopticon (Jeremy Bentham's late eighteenth-century model for prison construction involving control of the inmates by giving them to understand that they are under constant surveillance by monitors they cannot see) to the performance appraisal system, arguing that it is a 'form of disciplinary gaze' (Bach, 2005: 306). In discussing the introduction of appraisal in UK universities, Townley (1990) argues that the key driving force behind appraisal in the higher education sector is management's desire for control through attitudinal change, which leads to resentment and even resistance from employees (in Newton and Findlay, 1996). The potential for management control and increased surveillance is also evident in 360-degree appraisal, by which 'every customer, peer, subordinate and colleague is now a potential appraiser' (Redman, 2009: 180).

BUREAUCRACY

Managers and employees frequently complain of the prescriptive and overly detailed form-filling associated with performance management, and regard it is an administrative burden and too time-consuming (Stiles *et al*, 1997). Multi-rater systems in particular generate a lot of information which can be time-consuming to collate and analyse.

IMPROVING THE EFFECTIVENESS OF PERFORMANCE APPRAISAL

With the caveat that the organisational context will influence the design and operation of performance appraisal, it is worth summarising the ways in which organisations can improve the effectiveness of their appraisal schemes (ACAS, 2008; Fletcher, 2008; Boxall and Purcell, 2011):

- Appraisal schemes should be kept simple, clear and straightforward.
- Consultation should take place on the design and implementation of the scheme with the relevant parties, such as managers, employees and employee representatives.
- Senior managers should be committed to the idea of appraisals and ensure that time and resources are available to those conducting the appraisals.
- The objectives of the process must be clear, and if assessment is linked with reward, the assessment must be kept separate from the developmental review.
- All managers who carry out appraisals should receive appropriate skills training and other forms of organisational support (Chapter 4).
- Suitable training must be offered to all raters. This includes instruction on how to complete the necessary forms, on the reasons for performance appraisal, and on how it fits into the organisation's performance management strategy.
- Schemes should be monitored regularly to ensure that interviews take place and are carried out effectively and that all forms are completed. Schemes should be checked to see if they need modifying to meet the changing needs of the organisation.
- Performance criteria should be relevant to the job (as discussed further in Chapter 5).
- Clear definitions must be provided for performance criteria so that both managers and employees have a shared understanding of what is being assessed.
- Appraisal should take place frequently enough to avoid managers' having to rely too much on memory or impressions.
- It may be worth considering having more than one rater.
- Appraisers must be held accountable for their ratings.
- Senior managers should have the opportunity to comment upon and sign the appraisals.

● Managers should keep running records of the performance of their subordinates.

REFLECTIVE ACTIVITY 6.6

The Good Medical Practice Framework sets out the broad areas which should be covered in the appraisal of medical practitioners and on which recommendations to revalidate doctors are based. Revalidation is the process by which doctors demonstrate to the General Medical Council (GMC), normally every five years, that they are up to date and fit to practise. The Framework recommends six types of supporting information doctors must produce for their appraisal at least once in each five-year cycle. Such information must include evidence of:

● continuing professional development (CPD)
● improvement activity
● significant events and achievements
● feedback from colleagues
● feedback from patients
● a review of complaints and compliments.

Seeking feedback about a doctor's behaviour provides the opportunity for patients, non-medical co-workers (including professional managers and administrators) and medical colleagues (including trainees and juniors) to reflect on the professional skills and behaviour of a doctor.

1   Design two questionnaires to provide feedback on a doctor:

(a)   for use by patients

(b)   for use by colleagues.

2   What are the problems with gathering feedback in this way?

3   Should feedback be widened to include views from families and carers, suppliers and other customers?

The following website may be useful in answering these questions:

www.gmc-uk.org

CONCLUSION

This chapter has considered the theory and practice of performance appraisal, focusing on different methods of appraisal in terms of sources of feedback. In theory, performance appraisal is an 'objective, rational and systematic' way to manage performance (Chiang and Birtch, 2010) and, if managed well, a valuable tool. It is a process which is grounded in theories of motivation, commonly features in bundles of 'best-practice' HRM, and promises to improve individual performance and commitment. Although frequently portrayed as a management tool to control workers, performance appraisal has much to offer employees. They can receive feedback, access training and development, improve their career opportunities, have a greater 'voice', and possibly expect a reward for good performance. Beliefs in the positive power of appraisal are clearly evidenced by its widespread and growing use in organisations. Nevertheless, the reality is that too much is expected of appraisal, and the outcomes are often disappointing. Its usefulness and success largely depend on the accuracy of the ratings given, the behaviour and skill of managers, the degree to which it is a control tool for managers, and the involvement of employees. This is partly influenced by the nature of the organisation, management preferences and style, the resources available, and the types of employees and the jobs that they do. However, negative outcomes can be minimised by using performance appraisal as a developmental tool, taking a more diversified approach to feedback, involving employees, and training and supporting line managers and other assessors.

EXPLORE FURTHER

Armstrong, M. (2006) *Performance Management: Key strategies and practical guidelines*, 3rd edition (Chapters 2, 6, 7 and 12). London: Kogan Page

Atwater, L. E., Brett, J. F. and Charles, A. C. (2007) 'Multisource feedback: lessons learned and implications for practice', *Human Resource Management*, Vol.46, No.2, Summer: 285–307

Brown, M., Hyatt, D. and Benson, J. (2010) 'Consequences of the performance appraisal experience', *Personnel Review*, Vol.39, No.3: 375–96

Fletcher, C. (2008) *Appraisal, Feedback and Development: Making performance review work.* Abingdon: Routledge

Grint, K. (1993) 'What's wrong with performance appraisals? A critique and a suggestion', *Human Resource Management Journal*, Vol.3, No.3, Spring: 61–77

Kluger, A. N. and DeNisi, A. (1996) 'The effects of feedback intervention on performance: a historical review, a meta-analysis, and a preliminary feedback intervention theory', *Psychological Bulletin*, Vol.119, No.2: 254–84

Newton, T. and Findlay, P. (1996) 'Playing God? The performance of appraisal', *Human Resource Management Journal*, Vol.6, No.3: 42–58

Redman, T. and Wilkinson, A. (2009) *Contemporary Human Resource Management: Text and cases*, 3rd edition (Chapter 7). Harlow: FT/Prentice Hall

Shields, J. (2007) *Managing Employee Performance and Rewards: Concepts, practices, strategies* (Chapter 8). Cambridge/Melbourne: Cambridge University Press

Smither, J. W., London, M. L. and Reilly, R. R. (2005) 'Does performance improve following multi-source feedback? A theoretical model, meta-analysis, and review of empirical findings', *Personnel Psychology*, Vol.58: 33–66

CHAPTER 7

Integrating Learning and Performance

John Neugebauer

LEARNING OUTCOMES

By the end of this chapter you should be able to:

- understand the meaning of the terms 'training', 'learning', 'development' and 'competences'

- assess the link between training, learning and development (TLD) and organisational strategy and performance

- explain the importance of knowledge management and organisational learning in the success of the organisation and human capital development

- discuss how to analyse and evaluate training and development needs

- critically evaluate different approaches to delivering training, learning and development

- understand the importance of talent management as a performance management and human resource development tool.

INTRODUCTION

This chapter considers how training, learning and development (TLD) fits and works with performance management. Well-structured learning and development both complements and may be informed by performance management practices at individual, team, functional and organisational levels. Indeed, Brinkerhoff (2006: 307) observes that

> The performance improvement process has learning at its heart, but learning and performance are inseparable. Learning enables performance, and performance enables learning.

Similarly, it has been seen that the ability, motivation and opportunity (AMO) model (Appelbaum *et al*, 2000; Bailey *et al*, 2001) in Chapter 2 is a useful starting point to consider how HR policy and practice influence performance. TLD makes an important contribution to developing ability, and has an indirect influence on motivation and opportunity. For example, Meyer and Allen (1997) found that positive learning experiences were linked to commitment and work motivation. García (2005: 1704) also notes empirical support for TLD's providing such benefits as to motivate, to increase satisfaction at work, to enable a better understanding of the organisation's culture and aims, to increase employee participation, and to transfer and share new knowledge – with a resultant positive impact on organisational performance.

Even so, in an overview of research on how training is perceived within organisations, Giangreco, Sebastiano and Peccei (2009) observe that it can be seen in very polarised terms. For some organisations it may be seen as a panacea for all problems, whereas in others it is a cost in both time and money (p96). For the academic or the practising manager, it is important both to understand and position the investment in training and to see how this links with performance.

Performance management and TLD should be aligned with organisational goals. To illustrate this, look again at Chapter 2 and, for example, Hendry, Bradley and Perkins (1997) and Kaplan and Norton (1992). Similarly, Harrison (2009) positions performance management at the centre of the performance/training cycle. TLD must thus support organisational performance but also recognise the scarcity of resources within the organisation, so that these activities must compete with other organisational strategies and goals for investment.

Despite this García (2005: 1691) notes that 'the peculiarity of the staff function lies in the fact that it is less prepared than others to quantify its impact on the organisation's performance'. The challenge is to understand the causal link between learning and development activities, and their relationship to subsequent individual and organisational outcomes.

Performance management and TLD therefore combine both at the organisational level and at the individual level. Performance management contributes to the identification of TLD needs at the individual and organisation levels, to the successful transfer of learning within the workplace, and in the evaluation of the effectiveness of previously implemented training activities.

This chapter considers the general background to TLD in the organisation, including how we define 'training', 'learning' and 'development', and how all three concepts fit in with organisational strategy. It then considers in more detail how TLD needs within the workplace are analysed, met and evaluated. The chapter concludes with a review of talent management and a case study example which describes how a performance management and training system was designed and introduced into an engineering company.

DEFINING TRAINING, LEARNING, DEVELOPMENT (TLD) AND COMPETENCES

The terms 'training', 'learning' and 'development' are often used interchangeably, but it is helpful to recognise their more precise meanings in workplace practices.

Training may be defined as a process to enhance work performance and improve current or special personal knowledge, skills and attitudes so that a job is performed accurately and effectively, and ensures continuing improvement of work quality (Romanowska, 1993). Alternatively, Bramley (2003: 4) defines training as the process 'which is planned to facilitate learning so that people can become more effective in carrying out aspects of their work'.

Learning is regarded as the qualitative and relatively permanent change in how an individual sees, experiences or understands something in the real world (Marton and Ramsden, 1988). Learning may also be viewed as surface learning or deeper learning (see, for example, Biggs, 1991; Biggs and Collis, 1982; Marton and Säljö, 1976). In surface learning, an individual simply does enough to complete a task or pass an assessment – so surface learning is typically rote learning and memorising. However, in deep learning the learning is often cross-referred with other sources of learning, and a change of understanding of meaning or behaviour may take place.

Development tends to be used as a more wide-ranging longer-term concept. According to Nadler and Wiggs (1986), development relates to the preparation of employees for an uncertain future. It may include linking the organisation's business strategy to its retention strategy for employees, and linking careers with learning plans.

Examples of *training, learning* **and** *development* **in relation to a performance review**

Training leads to an improved ability to perform the role in the job (and is achieved, for example, via induction training, on-the-job training, attendance at a formal course or e-learning).

Learning: the performance review can be used to assess what the employee has learned and understood during the review period.

Development involves activities which support improvement in the employee's longer-term prospects – for example, temporary role responsibilities, job rotation, secondments, attachment to project teams, being assigned a mentor or coach.

If performance management objectives are important in describing *what* needs to be done in the coming review period, competences are important in defining *how* it is to be done – and so form part of the job or role specification, and the basis for selection, training and longer-term development.

A useful working definition (Whiddett and Hollyforde, 2003: 5–7) is that competences are:

> Behaviours that individuals demonstrate when undertaking job-relevant tasks effectively within an organisational context.

Woodruffe (1991 and 1993) distinguishes between 'competency' (measurable skills or behaviours of an individual employee) and 'competence' (as a more broadly-based concept that takes account of job functions and the employee attitudes and behaviours which underpin performance). Although there are many claimed antecedents to their use, dating back to the 1970s, the real impetus to engage with competence and competency frameworks on a widespread level came with the publication of Richard Boyatzis' book in 1982 on *The Competent Manager*.

Roberts (1997) categorised competences – which he called competencies – as:

- **natural competencies** – looking at personality factors such as being extravert/introvert, emotional stability, agreeableness, conscientiousness, and being open to variety of experience
- **acquired competencies** – knowledge and skill acquired at, or outside, work
- **adapting competencies** – how far an individual is able to adapt natural talents and skills to a new situation
- **performing competencies** – observable behaviours and outcomes.

By 2003, Rees noted a wide diversity of definitions of 'competence', although without an agreed working definition. For example, Chen and Naquin (2006: 266) include in their assessment of competences, 'the underlying individual work-related characteristics (eg skills, knowledge, attitudes, beliefs, motives and traits) that enable successful job performance … in keeping with the organisation's strategic functions (eg vision, mission, uniqueness, future orientation, success or survival)'. In the workplace, typical examples of competences would include factors such as teamworking, customer service orientation, problem-solving, delivering results, etc.

More detailed analysis on competences and performance remind us, however, that careful design and implementation are critical. Aside from the ease or the difficulty in using competence frameworks, there remains the question of the extent to which practising managers believe that the use of competences contributes to strategic performance. Here, Suff (2010) found strong, though not overwhelming, support in an IRS study based on 168 organisations: 75.4 per cent of organisations believed that competences played a vital role to support organisational mission and objectives, whereas

30 per cent reported problems in their use of competences. Furthermore, Suff (2010) found that the top three problems encountered with organisations were problems in ensuring that users knew how competences worked, buy-in and support issues, and resistance by line managers to their use. These results reinforce the suggestion made elsewhere in this chapter that problems with competence frameworks in the workplace are less about how they are designed, and more about how they are implemented and communicated to employees, and how well managers have been trained to undertake objective competence assessments. Furthermore, Caldwell (2008) found that using competences to select HR business partners was an effective use of competence frameworks; however, competence frameworks appeared to be less effective in developing HR business partners once they were appointed, failed to link HR strategic performance and business performance, and were thus poor predictors of HR business partner performance. These findings do not invalidate the use of competences in HR (or in any other occupational employment), since we have already seen in this and other chapters that system designs are not always followed through to successful implementation. But they do underline the critical importance of ensuring that competence frameworks are carefully designed within the organisation's overall vision, mission and goals; that they are successfully communicated; and that managers and employees take a joint stake in ensuring that they are properly used.

Having reviewed the building-blocks for TLD, the strategic perspective of these concepts is now considered below.

TLD AND THE ORGANISATION

TLD forms part of an organisation's human resource development (HRD) approach. Over the last 40 to 50 years, the term 'HRD' has evolved from what Nadler (1970) defined as organised activities undertaken within a specific time-frame in order to produce behavioural change, to a more strategic and integrated approach. Strategic human resource development (SHRD) can be seen as identifying the required skills and involving the active management of learning designed to support the long-term future and explicit corporate and business strategies (Hall, 1984). The emergence of SHRD has been linked to the resource-based view of the organisation (see Chapter 1), in which knowledge and skills within the organisation are important elements of competitive advantage (Hendry and Pettigrew, 1990). Furthermore, human capital theory (Lepak and Snell, 1999) sees investment in the development of employee competences and skills as important in the development and competitiveness of the organisation. Garavan (2007) argues that SHRD operates at many different levels within the organisation to connect new and existing knowledge and to enhance long-term organisational success.

Reflecting the interdependence of a strategic approach to understanding organisational performance, performance management and TLD requirements, the CIPD (2012c: 9) found that the top five priorities which are anticipated for the foreseeable future in the workplace are:

- greater integration of coaching, organisational development and performance management to drive organisational change
- greater responsibility devolved to learners and line managers
- the linking of learning and talent development with performance management and organisational development
- the closer integration of learning and development activity and business strategy
- more emphasis on monitoring, measuring and evaluating training effectiveness.

But as attractive and essential is the full integration of learning and development with overall organisation strategy, practical implementation may be challenging (see also Chapter 2).

The first challenge is at the strategy level of the organisation, where there may be gaps between clarity in or communication of organisational needs, and translating these into coherent TLD outcomes. In addition to a lack of quality in direction and a lack of learning, Beer and Eisenstat (2000) identified six 'silent killers' that doomed the delivery and implementation of organisational strategy as: a top-down or laissez-faire senior management style; an unclear strategy and conflict in priorities; an ineffective management team; poor vertical communication between levels of management and employees; poor co-ordination across businesses, functions or borders; and inadequate skills and under-development of leaders and managers at all levels of the organisation. These six 'silent killers' are, of course, as damaging to the alignment of performance management goals as they are to training and learning needs analysis.

Wider critical studies of organisational strategy also point to the difficulties an organisation may have in the successful design and implementation of strategy in complex and dynamic global markets (for example, Hamel, 2012). Organisational strategy clarity and aligned HRD plans may accordingly be difficult to integrate with the speed of changing competitor practices and organisational needs. However, Hamel (2012) translates the challenges of developing future organisational strategy as requiring a re-emphasis on developing the human capital of the organisation – and with it, a renewed emphasis on the value and importance of TLD.

The second challenge to the alignment of HRD with strategy is that performance gaps may not be gaps in the ability of the employee but shortcomings elsewhere within the organisation. It has already been noted that performance is an outcome of ability, motivation and opportunity. Other reasons for performance gaps are suggested in Table 7.1 below.

Table 7.1 Possible reasons for performance gaps

Learning and development reasons	Reasons not associated with learning and development
Weaknesses in: ● Selection ● Induction ● Setting performance standards ● Diagnosis/delivery/evaluation of training ● Managerial/supervisor support post-learning	Weaknesses in: ● Performance feedback ● Managerial behaviours leading to low motivation ● Equipment/IT support ● Job design ● Communication ● Work cultures ● Work relationships

Despite these practical and intellectual challenges in getting TLD as aligned as possible with organisational needs, knowledge and learning within the organisation are increasingly perceived as key to organisational success – and the background to this is explored below.

KNOWLEDGE MANAGEMENT AND ORGANISATIONAL LEARNING

This section explains how and why knowledge management is currently perceived as an important component – indeed, for some, a critical component – of an organisation's assets and competitive advantage. Drucker (1993) commented that knowledge was the only key to sustainable competitive advantage for an organisation. (Drucker was also credited, from 1954, with the introduction of the concept of management by objectives (MBO), the basis for linking individuals' goals with organisational aims.)

But an understanding of what knowledge is, and how it combines to add value for the organisation, is complex. Some of our 'knowledge' may be 'tacit' knowledge (Polanyi, 1966) – practical knowledge that we normally put into use more than we consciously express. Indeed, for Polanyi, if we can make our knowledge explicit, rather than tacit, that knowledge is 'information'. However, Nonaka and Takeuchi (1995) developed Polanyi's concept of tacit knowledge into a 'spiral of knowledge', in which tacit knowledge and explicit knowledge combined. The result was to regard knowledge as:

- **socialised knowledge** – individual tacit knowledge, then shared with others
- **externalised knowledge** – shared tacit knowledge which becomes individual explicit knowledge
- **combined knowledge** – individual explicit knowledge shared as explicit knowledge
- **internalised knowledge** – shared explicit knowledge which becomes individual tacit knowledge.

From their initial letters these steps are referred to as the SECI model (Nonaka and Takeuchi, 1995). However, that knowledge exists in an organisation is not the same as expecting that knowledge to be shared across the organisation. Pfeffer and Sutton (1999) have referred to this issue as 'the knowing–doing gap': the gap between knowing (what should be done), and doing (actually doing it).

A second concept which has to be taken into account in considering performance, knowledge, learning and organisational success is that of organisational learning, or the more theoretical concept of 'the learning organisation'. Both concepts recognise that organisations learn. Cyert and March (1963) argued that organisations respond to changes in the external environment and adapt their objectives and search routines, thereby achieving more effective alignment in their organisational strategy (cited in Shipton, 2006). For example, General Petraeus was reported as seeking to change army tactics in fighting terrorists by making the US Army a learning organisation (*Economist*, 2007). However, although the terms 'organisational learning' and 'the learning organisation' are sometimes – incorrectly – used synonymously, they are different. In this section, both terms are defined, and organisational learning is considered in the context of performance management.

Organisational learning has a long background in development as a concept – see, for example, Shipton's (2006) review of the typologies of organisation learning. A working definition of organisational learning (Swart *et al*, 2005: 46) is

> The process through which an entity (whether it be an individual, group of individuals that act on behalf of the organisation, or the organisation itself) employs enabling abilities to create permanent cognitive and behavioural change within a system. The changed behaviour of cognitive needs to be embedded in the fabric of the organisation will be evident in the organisational memory.

Both the concepts of organisational learning and the strategic perspective of performance management are therefore linked, in that both are seeking to acquire and deploy employee learning and development for the benefit of the organisation. But what does organisational learning look like in practice? One example, is how the Shell oil company became – or at least sought to present itself as – more environmentally aware following the public outcry in 1995 over the disposal of the redundant Brent Spar oil platform. Responding to Greenpeace and global public environmental concerns, Shell dismantled the platform rather than dump it in a deep-sea area as originally planned. Similarly, the response of the Metropolitan Police to the Macpherson Inquiry into the tragic death of

Stephen Lawrence, which summarised the police as 'institutionally racist' (Home Office, 1999, para 6.34), represented an attempt to change both individuals' attitudes and also the organisational culture and behaviour to become non-racist. In these two examples individual employees needed to learn – but so also did the organisation. Once organisation learning was adopted by the respective organisations, individuals' behaviour and actions could be deployed and monitored through performance management processes.

A contemporary example of organisational learning and knowledge exchange in the organisation of the Olympic Games is shown in Case Study 7.1.

CASE STUDY 7.1

ORGANISATIONAL LEARNING AND THE 2012 LONDON OLYMPICS

One of the knowledge management challenges for organisations is how to ensure that organisational learning is retained within the organisation and then shared (knowledge transfer). This organisational knowledge may be separated not just by individuals and role function but also by time and geography.

Consider the case of hosting an Olympic venue, in which the International Olympic Committee (IOC), which is ultimately responsible for the Olympic Games, shares organisational learning from venue to venue.

The IOC has set up knowledge management programmes since the Sydney 2002 Olympic Games, so that current hosts share their experience and know-how with the next host. The London Organising Committee (LOCOG) will therefore travel to Rio de Janeiro to pass on what was learned in London.

Source: *Economist* (2012)

In contrast to organisational learning, the concept of 'the learning organisation' involves more theoretical frameworks. Although there is not a single agreed definition of a learning organisation (Garvin, 1993), the two most prominent approaches are those of Senge (1990) and Pedler *et al* (1991).

Pedler *et al* (1991: 1) see the aim of the learning organisation as the 'facilitation of learning across all its members and [an organisation] which continuingly transforms itself'.

Senge (1990) proposed that for an organisation to be a learning organisation required five disciplines: systems thinking, personal mastery, mental models, shared vision, and team learning. Of all these elements, Senge stressed that systems thinking was of the greatest importance, so that the elements of the other four disciplines are successfully integrated. On the other hand, Pedler *et al*'s (1991) criteria were a learning approach to strategy, participative policy-making, the use of information technology to empower the workforce, flexibility in reward, and self-development for all.

Despite the apparent attractiveness and early popularity of the learning organisation concept, it has particular theoretical problems and idealistic assumptions. (For example, it fails to take account of power and politics in the organisation, and assumes that all employees want 'personal mastery'.)

This brief overview of organisational learning and the learning organisation has introduced the understanding that organisations can and do learn. And as they learn and adapt to the external environment, new work objectives and organisational values evolve and are codified into the organisation's objectives, and, in due course, into individual performance management objectives and individual learning plans. The section has also introduced some key ideas on the strategic background to how and why human resource development is so critical to the workplace. Knowledge and organisational learning further link performance management to HR policy and practice which integrate vertically and horizontally at the level of the individual and of the organisation so as to contribute to the longer-term success of the organisation.

The chapter now turns to consider how training is analysed, designed, delivered and evaluated within the organisation.

ANALYSING TRAINING NEEDS, TRAINING DELIVERY AND TRAINING EVALUATION

This section examines how training is analysed, designed, delivered and evaluated. An early approach to the management of training within the workplace was the systematic cycle of training – of planning, designing, implementing and evaluating training – which was adopted in the UK in the 1950s and 1960s, and defined by Boydell (1971). But although the cycle provides a useful overview of training as a process, it has been criticised for its simplicity. It fails to take full account of the wider pressures within the workplace, both internal and external, and suggests that each training cycle may have a clear start and end point, rather than the more dynamic and at times messy ways in which people learn. For example, it does not show the wider factors which are now regarded as essential – organisational goals determined by a review of organisational strategy, and individual needs determined through performance appraisal (as discussed earlier in this book). However, the Boydell model brings a focus to the design and implementation of training, and so the systematic training cycle is used as the main framework for this review.

ANALYSING TLD NEEDS AT ORGANISATIONAL, TEAM AND INDIVIDUAL LEVELS

Needs may be analysed at organisational, team/functional and individual levels, as demonstrated in Table 7.2.

Table 7.2 Analysing TLD needs at organisational, team/function and individual levels

Level	Typical needs	How identified
Organisational (Likely to be required for all or most of the employees in the organisation)	• Culture and values • Regulatory training (health and safety) • Diversity	• Review of key values, cultures or behaviours for all employees to follow, and which underpin the organisation's brand values and/or legal requirements
Team/functional (Applied to particular groups of employees)	• New processes (for example, introduction of customer relationship management system, or other new technology) • Training in care settings (perhaps for those who have direct contact with children or vulnerable adults) • Training for sales and service staff in new products • Team interaction and dynamics	• Organisational business plans, or as a response to external requirements, such as legislation changes • Performance appraisal and analysis of aggregated needs

Level	Typical needs	How identified
Individual	● Individual competence/skill gaps ● Individual development	● Role change ● Performance appraisal ● 360-degree feedback ● Assessment centres

Assessment centres (Chen and Naquin, 2006) may be used to gauge TLD needs, assessed on behaviour-based or work performance exercises. They may include work simulation exercises, group/team work with or without leaders, role-play, in-tray exercises and business games or simulations (Thornton and Mueller-Hanson, 2004). Assessment centres look at employee competences in a relatively controlled environment and are designed around standardised exercises. However, they also have a number of potential weaknesses in implementation: poor planning and design, inadequate job analysis, poorly defined work dimensions, poor exercises, lack of pilot evaluation, poor assessor training, poor behaviour documentation, misuses of results and inadequate candidate preparation (Caldwell *et al*, 2003).

In addition to manager or assessment centre methods, multi-rater/360-degree feedback assessment has also been used for competence assessment in much the same way as it may contribute to performance reviews. 360-degree feedback is gathered from a range of contributors (subordinates, peers, managers and customers: Chen and Naquin, 2006). In this way, employee feedback should remain relevant to the role but engage a wider range of stakeholders than does manager-alone assessment, and be more work-related and evidenced over a longer time-span than would be available for assessment centres. The CIPD (2012c) found that 22 per cent of organisations rated 360-degree feedback as effective for talent management (against only 3 per cent for assessment centres). Even so, a range of criticisms have been pointed towards 360-degree feedback (see also Chapter 6), including a lack of clarity on purpose, its use only to deal with under-performers, a lack of pilot testing, the breaching of confidentiality, a lack of measurement effectiveness, its being treated as an end in itself, not being part of a wider process and poor communication with those involved (Wimer and Nowack, 1998).

Once training needs have been identified and assessed, the next step is the design of TLD delivery.

DESIGNING TRAINING: JOB ANALYSIS AND HOW PEOPLE LEARN

JOB ANALYSIS

Job analysis is used to design what the organisation requires of a role, and helps to inform the job-holder about the responsibilities for the role, and the competences and skills required to perform it. (The resultant document is more generic than a simple list of performance management objectives, which set out what the employee is expected to achieve within a given time-frame.)

Much of the literature on job analysis tends to focus on defining what employees actually do. For example, Marchington and Wilkinson (2012) describe four approaches, involving job observation, work diaries, interviews, and work questionnaires and checklists. However, organisation design increasingly looks at top-down approaches, by which roles tend to be designed from the perspective of what employees should be doing to align with organisational goals.

HOW PEOPLE LEARN

An important consideration in delivering training is the importance of how individuals learn, and the differences in learning styles. There is no single agreed definition of learning style – indeed, according to Coffield *et al* (2004), there are 71 different learning style models which have been identified.

Despite the diversity in interpretations of learning styles which have been proposed, three of particular interest because of their widespread practical application are the Kolb (1984) cycle; Kolb, Osland and Rubin's learning cycle (1995) and Honey and Mumford's (1989) learning styles. Kolb's (1984) learning process was based on an earlier interpretation from Lewin's work and is described as a cycle from concrete action to testing new approaches; it is demonstrated in Figure 7.1.

Figure 7.1 Kolb's learning cycle

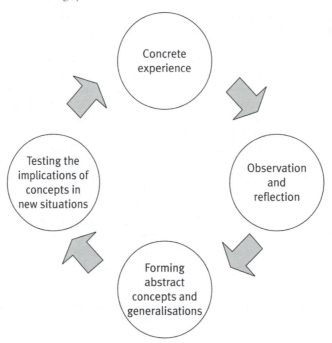

Source: Kolb, D. A. (1984) *Experiential Learning* (p21)

Honey and Mumford's (1989) learning styles look at individual styles from four different perspectives: **Activists** learn best by participating in actual work examples in the workplace or similar 'hands-on' activities in learning environments; **Reflectors** learn best when they have to observe, step back and review/reflect upon what has happened; **Pragmatists** prefer to see links between new information and real-life problems or issues; and **Theorists** prefer to learn through new concepts and theories, but while stepping back from real-life situations. We can appreciate the practical importance of some of the differences in learning styles when considering training delivery (see below). For example, on-the-job training remains a popular method of workplace training, and is likely to be of most interest to Activists and Pragmatists. On the other hand, other learners may prefer to go back to basic principles in a setting of formal classroom or e-learning (Theorists), and others will prefer to have time to think through new information (Reflectors). Most individuals have dominant and subsidiary learning styles, but developing a balanced approach to learning in all four styles enables learners to benefit from a wider range of learning opportunities.

REFLECTIVE ACTIVITY 7.1

Honey and Mumford's learning styles show the different ways in which people prefer to learn. Browse the web to find a copy of Honey and Mumford's learning style questionnaire/inventory, and consider what your own preferred style might be.

Try the same questionnaire with a range of other colleagues/students.

1   If you were to design training for that group of people, how would you adapt the training for the range of different styles you have found?

2   How would you now adapt learning design to adjust practice in doing a task, learning the theory of a task, or enabling learners to reflect on what they have learned or undertaken in the workplace?

Approaches to learning styles are important both to HRD specialists and to line managers. For HRD specialists a deep understanding of learning styles enables training solutions to take account of different preferences among learners (for example, in the design and delivery of formal training courses, balancing reading, practical work, reflection, coaching, etc). For line managers an understanding that team members will have different learning styles means that they know there will be different preferences in how the team members learn and develop work performance and how they change (whether through coaching, reflection learning techniques, on-the-job training, etc).

A thorough appreciation of the different learning styles therefore helps to inform good HRD design in delivering TLD solutions in the workplace.

METHODS AND APPROACHES IN DELIVERING TLD

Once needs have been identified, and the principles of learning styles have been taken into account, a broad range of approaches are available for delivering TLD solutions. This section considers the approaches most commonly used to deliver and review workplace learning (including on-the-job training, job rotation, and coaching and mentoring), face-to-face learning (including attendance at internal and external courses), e-learning and blended solutions.

The extent to which new skills, competences and knowledge may be transferred to the workplace is considered separately in the sections thereafter on the transfer of training and training evaluation.

ON-THE-JOB TRAINING

On-the-job training (OJT) refers to training which is undertaken in the workplace. Typically, OJT is carried out by a supervisor, manager or colleague who shows and/or explains to the employee what the job entails, and may include demonstrations and observed supervision of work. Training conducted this way may be formal and planned or informal and unplanned. Examples of this approach may range from demonstrations of work in a restaurant or on a production line, at-the-desk training in an office environment, to observed surgical operations, during which a senior surgeon monitors the work of a junior colleague. The benefits of OJT, as identified by Sisson (2001, cited in

Swart *et al*, 2005), relate to the practicality, informality, realism and hands-on nature of direct training in the workplace.

However, there are disadvantages too. Sisson (2001) identifies four possible problems with OJT:

- training has to fit around work – too much work to do means that training may not happen or is delayed
- training reflects the work actually to be done, so it may not cover the rarely encountered requirements for the job
- the colleague who provides the training usually only relies on experience, and may have little training expertise – furthermore, the colleague who provides the training may perpetuate non-orthodox, idiosyncratic or inappropriate ways of performing the role
- finally, the trainer may rely on show-and-tell to give instruction, and not take account of the wider range of learning styles.

Despite all the training and learning methods available in the workplace, OJT remains the third most popular method according to the CIPD (2012c), and reflects both formal – and often informal – training undertaken at the workplace by demonstration from a more senior or experienced employee, through job rotation or shadowing, or via observation and feedback.

FORMAL COURSES

For many, the idea of training, learning or development may first bring to mind attendance at an internal or external training course: this is reflected in the CIPD (2012c) survey that an internal formal course is still the most commonly reported method of accessing training.

The provision of TLD through this medium takes the learner out of the workplace and delivers learning which should, in principle, have clear objectives. Well-designed training courses also mean that consistent standards of learning may be achieved, in contrast to, say, OJT, where as we have seen barriers to learning may include the time taken to train and the risk of passing on 'wrong' ways to perform a role. However, as this section reveals, attendance on a formal training course is only one of a range of possible solutions. The earlier discussion on learning styles shows that formal courses may not be the ideal learning solution for all employees, and this section lists a wide range of alternative approaches that can be used.

Furthermore, research has demonstrated how important the perception of the trainer and the overall training experience is to the trainee in respect of the value of the learning, its potential usefulness in the workplace, and its value for individual longer-term development (Giangreco, Sebastiano and Peccei, 2009).

For the organisers of formal training courses, therefore, a range of research evidence points to the importance of such factors as the content/design of the training being delivered and the trainer's own performance (Kidder and Rouiller, 1997); the organisation of the training, including physical conditions and resources in the training area (Lee and Pershing, 2002); relevance to the workplace; and, by implication, performance management (Amietta, 2000) and training administration and delivery (North *et al*, 2000; Towler and Dipboye, 2001).

ACTION LEARNING

In contrast to the formality of training courses, Action Learning approaches owe their origin to work by Reg Revans, dating back to the late 1940s (Revans, 1980, 1982 and 1998). Action Learning has been defined as (Marquardt and Banks, 2010: 160):

a process and tool that enables individuals and groups to learn while solving problems and implementing actions.

Revans believed that learning only really took place in real-world experiences, and when individuals had co-learning support, acquired relevant knowledge, used creative problem-solving and inculcated experiential learning. The concept is expressed as the formula

$$L = P + Q$$

in which L is learning, P is programming and Q is questioning to develop deeper insight into what individuals experience.

Revans' ideas were later developed and adapted into a wide range of reflective learning techniques including Action Learning 'sets' (ALS), in which peer workers work in small teams to solve work problems while learning from each other's experience. Subsequent development and adaptation of the ALS approach has included running sets without a designated facilitator, therefore referred to as self-managed Action Learning (Bourner, O'Hara and Webber, 2002; O'Hara, Bourner and Webber, 2004), and using Action Learning in virtual learning communities (eg Shurville and Rospigliosi, 2009).

Marquardt and Banks (2010) evidence the application of Action Learning in complex problem-solving, leadership development and team-building, and cite a 2005 edition of *Business Week* which claimed that Action Learning was 'one of the key management development programmes of the past 125 years' (p159). Marquardt and Banks (2010: 159–60) also note that although Action Learning may be presented in a number of different forms, the underlying common principles of the approach are that it involves:

- **real work experience** – learning is acquired in the midst of action and focused on the task in hand
- **actual organisational experience and personal development** – participants work on problems aimed at organisational as well as personal development and at integration between them
- **peer learning** – learners work in peer learning teams to support *and challenge* each other
- **learning to learn** – users demonstrate learning-to-learn aptitude, entailing a search for fresh questions over expert knowledge.

Despite the relative simplicity of the Action Learning model, the approach has its critics. For instance, a number of writers, including Cho and Egan (2009), have criticised Action Learning for being all about 'action' while apparently having no method or structure to capture the learning from an event.

It has been claimed that Action Learning repays the cost of the learning by a factor of between 5 and 25 times the cost of the learning (eg Brenneman *et al*, 1998; Fulmer and Vicere, 1996; Raelin, 2008). Despite the continued widespread popularity of Action Learning, there is limited empirical evidence as to why it should be as successful as claimed. Nevertheless, Action Learning, with its close relationship to workplace issues and personal learning, may be seen to share close links with the aims and objectives of performance review and appraisal.

COACHING AND MENTORING

Coaching and mentoring provide an opportunity for the employee to learn from what happens in the workplace, to develop personal performance and increase work satisfaction, and may offer a chance to progress longer-term career plans. However, the two approaches are slightly different from each other.

At a practical level, the CIPD (2012d) found that the main uses for **coaching** were to assist performance management, to prepare and support people in leadership roles and to support learning and development. The key features of workplace coaching are (CIPD 2012d):

- It is usually non-directive.
- It focuses on improving performance and developing individuals' skills.
- Personal issues may be discussed but the emphasis is on performance at work.
- Coaching activities have both organisational and individual goals.
- It provides people with feedback on both their strengths and their weaknesses.
- It is a skilled activity, which should be delivered by people who are trained to do so. However, it can be carried out by line managers and others trained in basic coaching skills.

It may be undertaken within the organisation by a nominated coach or by the line manager or even a colleague, but a coach may also come from an external source. The CIPD (2012d) found that coaching was most likely to be undertaken by the line manager (46–53 per cent of the time over the previous four years, according to CIPD, 2012c), but this raises the question of whether managers are sufficiently well trained to do it, and whether coaching (which relies on a non-directional approach to employee learning and development) is actually appropriate in the light of the manager–subordinate power relationship. For example, Hersey and Blanchard (1969) noted even in the late 1960s that there were times when a line manager or leader would need to adopt different leadership styles based on 'tell/sell/participate/delegate' as part of his or her situational leadership. It may be necessary for the manager therefore to be very clear about when managerial direction is being given to the employee, and when instead the manager may be seeking to adopt a coaching style of employee feedback. But despite these potential limitations, coaching is often an integral part of the manager–employee relationship, and may occur informally or as part of more formal performance reviews. (See also Chapters 4 and 9.)

On the other hand, **mentoring** is likely to be a voluntary relationship, a longer-term process than coaching, involving a non-hierarchical relationship. Since line managers have a power relationship with the employee, line managers do not usually mentor direct reports but tend more often to mentor other employees within the organisation. The aim of mentoring is to help the employee where it is required, whether in work details or in more general organisational settings. An employee may have more than one mentor. The ideal mentor usually has more experience than the mentee, and, as consistent with the non-hierarchical relationship, should be able to discuss issues with the mentee in a non-judgemental fashion. Mentoring may be especially helpful at times of induction, as part of talent development programmes, or as positive action in helping to bring forward under-represented groups in the workforce as part of diversity programmes.

CONTINUING PROFESSIONAL DEVELOPMENT

Continuing professional development (CPD) was defined by the Construction Industry Council in 1986 (cited by Friedman, 2012: 8) as:

> The systematic maintenance, improvement and broadening of knowledge and skills, the development of personal qualities necessary for the execution of professional and technical duties throughout the individual's working life

Friedman (2012) goes on to say that of 102 professional bodies surveyed, 55 had their own definitions of CPD. It has been estimated that about 20 per cent of UK employees hold, or are working towards, professional qualifications (Gold and Smith, 2010). Many of these professional organisations (which include the Chartered Institute of Personnel and Development) require CPD as part of their members' role to ensure that professional workers remain up to date with learning and knowledge. An example, of the CPD requirement for dental workers is shown in Case Study 7.2.

EXAMPLE OF A CPD FRAMEWORK

The UK General Dental Council regulates dentistry professionals in the UK. All dentists, dental nurses, dental technicians, clinical dental technicians, dental hygienists, dental therapists and orthodontic therapists must be registered with the General Dental Council in order to work in the UK.

The standards to which dental practitioners are required to work are:

- putting patients' interests first, and acting to protect patients
- respecting patients' dignity and choices
- protecting the confidentiality of patients' information
- co-operating with other members of the dental team and other healthcare colleagues in the interests of patients
- maintaining one's own professional knowledge and competence
- being trustworthy.

Each of these standards is broken down into more detailed requirements.

The General Dental Council defines CPD as any activity which contributes to the professional development of dentists and dental care professionals, with the ultimate aim of benefiting their patients through up to date treatment and care.

Dental practitioners are therefore required to undertake 250 hours of CPD in each five-year cycle, and of this, 75 hours must be 'verifiable'. For these purposes, CPD may be defined as courses, lectures, distance learning, private study, journal reading, multimedia training, vocational training or general professional days, educational elements of professional and specialist society meetings, peer review and clinical audit, and/or background research. To maintain standards, CPD records must be submitted every five years to the GDC for review and approval of the CPD obligation.

The requirement for CPD is regarded as so fundamental to patient health and security that it has been incorporated into legislation under the Dentists Act 1984.

Source: derived from General Dental Council (2012); used with permission

The cycle for CPD is based on four stages – what and how I can learn, the action of learning, an evaluation of the learning including the benefits that the learning brings to individual work practices, and reflection on practice. These stages are represented in Figure 7.2 below.

Figure 7.2 The stages of CPD

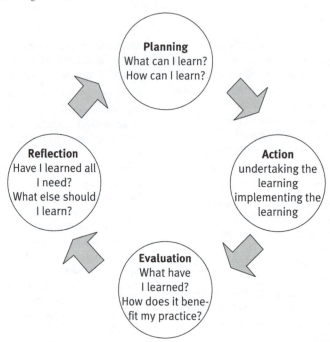

Source: based on Friedman (2012: 15)

Good CPD practice uses many of the learning approaches described in this chapter, with the aim of developing individuals' competences, knowledge and skills. Coaching and mentoring, reflective practice and Action Learning, as well as more conventional learning through formal courses, often form important components of CPD.

Despite the widespread use of CPD, Friedman (2012) points to some of the associated difficulties, particularly with the variety of stakeholders in CPD outcomes. For example, regulatory bodies may see CPD as a form of public protection, but one that is weak in comparison with other forms of regulation. On the other hand, organisations may prefer their own training approaches so as to develop and reinforce a particular organisational brand or culture, and may find professional CPD approaches at variance with those internal cultures. Furthermore, despite the widespread use and application of CPD, there are many different approaches to its practical application, many different standards, and many different degrees of engagement from those in the professional bodies themselves as to the usefulness of some CPD schemes (Friedman, 2012: 169ff).

In summary, CPD may not directly relate to an employee's current performance review or performance appraisal, but a well-executed CPD approach should certainly contribute to the employee's development and thus to longer-term competences, skills and the ability to perform.

E-LEARNING

The growth of appropriate communications technology (including fast broadband, Web 2.0, interactive media, virtual communities, blogs and social media platforms) has encouraged many organisations to adopt e-learning solutions for at least part of their training provision, their knowledge exchange and their development of organisational learning. Although there is no single definition of e-learning, it is considered to include instructional content or learning experiences delivered or enabled by electronic technology (Pantazis, 2002). The CIPD (2012e) defined e-learning as 'Learning that is delivered, enabled or mediated using electronic technology for the explicit purpose of training in organisations' (p1).

Much has been claimed of the potential benefits of e-learning. These benefits are held to include developing a global workforce, enabling shorter production cycles, supporting flatter organisations, greater flexibility for employees to access, support for a contingent/flexible workforce, help in retaining talent by providing access to wide learning resource support and accreditation; and support for productivity and profitability (Driscoll, 2002). Despite these claimed advantages as a training/learning solution, e-learning also has a number of barriers to its widespread adoption which are still to be overcome. For example, the CIPD (2011c) noted organisations' concerns about whether courses on e-learning were actually completed, and that e-learning is less suitable where individuals are less comfortable using IT.

In terms of the use of e-learning, the CIPD (2011c) found that 78 per cent of UK organisations used e-learning in at least some formats, particularly in large organisations employing over 5,000 staff (in which some 93 per cent used it) and in the public sector (also 93 per cent). The same survey found that e-learning use was growing as part of HRD provision, especially in relation to such training needs as compliance training (for example, health and safety, and hygiene) but that e-learning was perceived as more effective in its use when it was combined with other training and learning solutions – often referred to as 'blended learning' or 'integrated learning'.

INTEGRATING LEARNING APPROACHES

These approaches to HRD and TLD may be combined, deployed – and sometimes overlooked – in individual employee development, based on organisational culture and priorities for training and learning in the workplace. A timeline example of how they may typically be used and integrated with performance management is shown in Table 7.3.

Table 7.3 Sample training and learning timeline and performance management integration

Time in organisation	Typical learning need	Typical method(s) of delivery	Performance management/line manager role
Induction	● Introduction to the organisation ● Organisation values/culture ● Health and safety ● Diversity ● Key terms and conditions	● Face-to-face/e-learning	● Check training has been delivered ● Address any immediate issues/concerns ● May allocate mentor/buddy to help settling-in process

Time in organisation	Typical learning need	Typical method(s) of delivery	Performance management/line manager role
Job familiarisation	• Role introduction • Key duties	• On-the-job training • Manager/supervisor instruction • E-learning • Face-to-face in classroom (especially for large-scale recruitment and process-related work – for example, call centres)	• Support transfer of learning • Check training delivered • Reinforce key training messages • Review work performance and learning gaps over time
Enhancing job competences and skills	• Increasing role effectiveness • Addressing performance gaps	• Often a continuation of job familiarisation (above), adapted for individual's progress	• Informally via line manager or mentor • More formal review via the performance review or probationary review process • More experienced employees may also be involved with mentoring or coaching less experienced employees
Longer-term development	• Longer and deeper preparation of competences and skills in current role, or preparation for new role	• Individual reflective learning • Continuing professional development (CPD) • Coaching/mentoring • Assessment centres • 360-degree feedback • May include inclusion in talent management programme	• Formally and informally via line manager feedback and performance reviews

PREFERENCES FOR LEARNING APPROACHES

Despite the investments made in designing and delivering TLD solutions, CIPD surveys consistently suggest that practitioners believe that learning closest to the workplace is the most effective. Most popular in terms of perceived effectiveness are in-house development programmes (52 per cent), coaching by line managers (46 per cent) and on-the-job training (29 per cent). Job rotation, job shadowing and secondments (23 per cent) are consistently rated the most effective, whereas other forms of TLD, such as audio and video tapes (2 per cent), e-learning (11 per cent), external conferences and workshops (14 per cent), and formal education and courses (12 per cent) are rated among the least effective (CIPD, 2012c). Other learning methods such as non-managerial coaching, mentoring, Action Learning sets and internal knowledge-sharing events fall within the mid-range of perceived effectiveness (CIPD, 2012c).

TRANSFER FROM THE PLACE OF LEARNING TO WORK PRACTICES

Once TLD interventions have been delivered, how sure may we be that the new skills, competences, knowledge and technical skills learned are actually applied within the workplace? We have already noted the importance of the Ability–Motivation–Opportunity (AMO) model in workplace performance (see Chapter 1). On the subject of the transfer of learning, a key consideration is whether the employee will have the *opportunity* to apply the new learning. The alternative is that the training will be ignored, and the employee will instead be encouraged or allowed by other employees, or even by the line manager, to use other work practices. Brinkerhoff (2006) found in a study of a marketing programme in a Fortune-100 organisation that only 17 per cent of training participants actually used the skills in the workplace that they had learned on a training programme.

This is the great issue of the transfer of learning. Baldwin and Ford (1988) specifically describe the transfer of learning as the generalisation of learning, trained skills and behaviours from the training environment to the work environment, as well as the maintenance of trained skills and behaviours or the length of time that trained material is used on the job following a training intervention. Saks and Burke (2012: 119) observe that failure to transfer learning from the training area to the workplace leads directly to a failure to achieve performance improvement, also effectively signalling the failure of costly training programmes.

In the transfer of learning, as has been seen elsewhere in this book, the role of the line manager is significant, especially when linked to the review of learning during performance reviews. Even so, the evidence from the CIPD (2011b) is that such linking by the line manager is normally done 'informally', and only discussed in performance reviews about half the time. Van den Bossche *et al* (2010) and Velada *et al* (2007) underlined the value of both formal and informal performance feedback to a positive perspective of the transfer of learning. Similarly, Brinkerhoff (2006: 304) found that '80 per cent or more of the eventual impact of training is determined by performance system factors, while the remaining 20 per cent or so is driven by variations in the quality of the training intervention itself and the characteristics of the learner, such as inherent ability and motivational values'.

THE EVALUATION OF TLD

Whether training, learning or development is seen as an investment or a cost, it consumes the financial and time resources of the organisation. So resources allocated to training must be prioritised against other scarce needs within the organisation, such as investment in marketing, machinery, property or IT. Both to understand what the return on that cost to the organisation may be, and to understand the effectiveness of the training intervention itself, it follows that TLD interventions should be open to the same evaluation scrutiny as other forms of organisational activity.

Despite this García (2005: 1691) notes that the staff function seems less prepared than others to quantify its impact on organisational performance. The challenge is therefore to understand the causal link between learning and development actions, and their relationship to subsequent organisational outcome. For example, we may deliver a training intervention against an assessed need, but to what extent can subsequent outcomes be linked to the training? A car sales executive may be given highly-rated sales training, but it may be difficult to show a clear link to subsequent car sales. After all, rising sales volumes may be due to other internal variables such as improved manufacture or logistics, or external variables such as better car design or the increased availability of car finance.

Training evaluation has been defined as systematic process of collecting data in an effort to determine the effectiveness and/or efficiency of training programmes and to make decisions about training (eg Brown and Gerhardt, 2002; Brown and Sitzmann, 2011). However, other perspectives suggest that it may include less formalised evaluations of learning (eg Hamblin, 1974).

Easterby-Smith (1994) identifies four reasons for evaluation:

- proving – demonstrating that an outcome has justified the cost of training
- improving – to understand how training interventions may be improved and further developed
- learning – so that learners can review what has been learned and what they may use in the workplace
- controlling – to monitor the quality and consistency of training provision, which of course tends to be the managerial focus of the training department.

Of the many approaches to training evaluation that are available, perhaps the most commonly cited is that of Kirkpatrick (for example, 1967, 1994). This uses a four-stage approach to evaluation of learning at the reaction level (commonly used at the end of courses); at the intermediate level, to assess or test how far training objectives have been achieved; at the intermediate level, which assesses the extent to which training has impacted on job performance in the workplace (this is also referred to as transfer of training, as considered above); and at the ultimate level, evaluating how training has impacted upon functional, team, departmental or organisational performance. Since Kirkpatrick's original work, a fifth level of evaluation has been added – return on investment, which aims to link the costs of training to organisational performance benefits.

The costs of training extend well beyond the cost of training course attendance. Cascio (1991) identified the 'hidden costs of learning' to include training and job analysis time, design time, all training material costs, trainer and trainee time, as well as lost production. And even when these costs have been identified, insufficient resources and interest may be given to actually measuring them and attempting to link them to a training intervention. Furthermore, it is recognised that evaluation of training and learning should be undertaken before, during and after the event itself. To accommodate this broader view, Warr, Bird and Rackham (1970) and Hamblin (1974) developed the CIRO evaluation model which incorporates Context, Inputs (including costs, as listed above), Reactions and Outcomes.

In these ways, performance management can be seen as one of the interactive processes necessary to conduct training evaluation: it potentially provides both formal and informal settings for the intermediate level of training evaluation, and, to the extent that performance management outcomes may be aggregated by the organisation, may also contribute to Kirkpatrick's ultimate-level evaluation. In practice, however, both Kirkpatrick's training evaluation methodology as well as organisational practices in the application of formal training evaluation are heavily criticised.

Giangreco, Sebastiano and Peccei (2009) point to the 'interesting dichotomy' that whereas academics emphasise the importance of studying all four of Kirkpatrick's evaluation levels, such concerns rarely apply in organisations' training evaluation. This lack of concern may be either because the organisations are not interested in this deeper evaluation or – as suggested by Plant and Ryan (1992) and Mann and Robertson (1996) – because they find it difficult to undertake full training evaluation. Other evaluation models which attempt to build on the perceived gaps in the Kirkpatrick model include Brinkerhoff's (2006), which seeks to adopt a holistic approach to understanding all the components of training and learning outcomes (including the role of trainers, systems, senior leaders and line managers), recognising that 'no single party alone can assure success, nor can [any] alone take the credit' (p306).

A further issue in evaluation is to recognise that not all training and learning, and not all evaluation, are undertaken in a formal setting such as a performance review. To illustrate this, consider Table 7.4. Here, TLD is recognised as either formal (for which there should be clear training or learning objectives identified beforehand, such as planned attendance on a course, following identification of a learning need arising from a performance appraisal) or informal (when there may have been no training or learning objectives in advance, such as experience within a job role, leading to further reflection or learning by the individual). Evaluation of informal learning is difficult because of the difficulty in measuring what has been learned, and consequently in measuring how much use has been made of the learning.

Table 7.4 Evaluation of formal and informal learning

	Formal learning	Informal learning ('learning by doing')
General comments	Formal learning is a key focus for evaluation and usually undertaken by training evaluations, interviews and observations.	Informal learning is altogether a grey area since it does not usually have clear objectives at the outset, so making evaluation very difficult. Nonetheless, informal learning may be included in post-training evaluation and involve the observation of on-the-job performance.
Residual grey area	Reflection on activities during a formal training event.	Reflection on activities while receiving informal learning.

Source: adapted from Swart, Mann, Brown and Price (2005: 331)

The CIPD's (2012c) Annual Survey of UK learning and development found that 85–93 per cent of organisations employing over 250 staff had specific training budgets, and even among smaller organisations the proportion was 62–77 per cent. Actual figures on the full costs of training per head of staff is more difficult to calculate and (see the comments above from Cascio, 1991) may fail to take account of all training (such as on-the-job training) and thus the costs involved. The CIPD (2012c) estimated from its survey that the median spend on training was £276. Even so, in an earlier survey, the CIPD (2008) found that 82 per cent of employees surveyed had received some form of training in the previous year, and of those, 92 per cent believed that the training had been successful. Further underlining the important role of the line manager, 68 per cent of what was useful in the follow-up of the course was attributed to the line manager, whereas HR and training departments accounted for 22 per cent (CIPD, 2008).

REFLECTIVE ACTIVITY 7.2

This chapter has underlined how important it is that HRD may be used to align individual behaviours with strategic organisational needs, to enhance employee skills and behaviours, and to achieve, maintain and develop professional standards.

If you are in, or plan to be in, a professional body, it is suggested that you find the CPD framework for that profession.

1   How would you assess your own competences against that framework?

2   What advice might a third party give you towards developing your competences within that framework? (Do you have a coach or mentor with whom to discuss this?)

3   What actions will you now take to develop your competences?

The chapter now turns to consider two further dimensions that illustrate how HRD and performance management interact in practice. The first examines talent management, and the second (in the form of a case study) looks at the practical implementation of a performance management process in an engineering company.

TALENT MANAGEMENT AND LEARNING

An overview of talent management is included in this chapter to demonstrate how talent management takes account of the current performance, the future potential (often identified through competences) and the future learning needs of that part of the workforce considered to be 'talent'. Good talent management programmes therefore bring together the benefits of performance management, competence frameworks and HRD

Talent management considers longer-term succession planning and linked TLD requirements for the organisation. In this way, talent management uses current performance management approaches and an assessment of future potential to sustain and develop longer-term performance for the organisation and the individual, and to identify training, learning and development requirements. Approaches to talent management are first explained below, then critically assessed.

Talent and talent management are concepts that cover a broad range of interpretations. In their definition of talent management, Marchington and Wilkinson (2012) described both the individual and the strategic HRM imperatives by defining talent management as identifying, nurturing, progressing, rewarding and retaining key individuals for the development of future organisational sustainability (p201). Blass (2007) described the interdependencies between talent management and performance management, and also noted that performance management systems were, at least in principle, a good basis for talent management systems. In this way, talent management links organisation strategy, employee performance and potential, and supports aligning HRD with organisational goals.

The need for a more methodical approach to managing and developing future workforce requirements was highlighted by Charan (2010), who noted the paradox by which the care organisations took great pains in managing their finances but adopted a 'scant approach' (p2) to identifying and developing their leaders. Charan therefore urges organisations to review their people strategy as regularly as their operations, business performance strategy and budgets.

Talent management approaches such as those advocated by Charan *et al* (2011) depend on a systematic review of employees' performance management outcomes, and their assessed potential. Performance results may be assessed from current and/or historical performance management results, and potential assessed from a methodical review of employee competences. Competences may be measured from a number of perspectives, including assessment centres (see above), line manager observation and competence assessments from workplace observations.

Once people are identified as 'talent', programmes for developing them may include promotions, project work, management training schemes, pursuit of qualifications, mentoring, secondments, transfers and job shadowing (Blass, 2007). Performance may be monitored through regular performance management reviews, and future potential assessed though competence assessment. Talent management programmes should be a dynamic process, and the progress and suitability of those in the talent pool should be kept under regular review.

Despite the activities in developing talent, questions remain as to its effectiveness in providing identifiable organisational benefits. At the strategic level, Guthridge *et al* (2006) in a survey of 50 senior executives found that there was a strategic failure to link talent management strategies to business strategy. Blass (2007: 3) noted that talent management processes varied across organisations, and that although alignment with business strategy was considered critical, 'in practice they are too often developed in isolation'. Furthermore, at the individual level Blass (2007) found that only 31 per cent of managers had any real confidence that their organisational performance management systems could identify high potential talent.

At a practical level, the CIPD (2012c) found that only 6 per cent of organisations regarded their talent management activities as 'very effective', 50 per cent as 'fairly effective', but 15 per cent as 'fairly ineffective' or 'very ineffective'. The CIPD (2012c) suggested a slight fall in organisations adopting active talent management development programmes – down to 54 per cent in 2012 from 61 per cent the previous year. Approximately 73 per cent of organisations concentrated talent management activities on high-potential employees, followed by senior managers (62 per cent), graduates (51 per cent) and 'all staff' (44 per cent) (CIPD, 2012c).

Overall, therefore, talent management uses a specific application of the performance–potential–development–succession planning link in organisational development. It provides a basis for organisations to identify, develop and plan for key future people requirements. However, its success in achieving these aims depends critically on how effectively it is implemented and managed within the organisation, and how the combined elements of performance management, potential and development can be both managed at individual levels and aligned with realistic longer-term organisational needs.

THE DESIGN AND IMPLEMENTATION OF A PERFORMANCE MANAGEMENT PROCESS

The case study below provides a real-life example of how a performance management process was designed and implemented for an engineering company. After reading the case study, you are invited to respond to the Questions at the end.

CASE STUDY 7.3

PERFORMANCE MANAGEMENT AND LEARNING PROCESS IN AN ENGINEERING COMPANY

SPACE Engineering is a medium-sized organisation that provides national refrigeration services for retailers across the UK. Customer requirements are for a fast and efficient service. Stock must be managed without damage to customer service or sales. Most employees are located in one geographical centre, but a significant number – mainly engineers – are based in remote sites nationally. Although this brings the engineers closer to the national customer base, it presents a challenge to ensure that all staff across the country work to standards consistent with SPACE's customer service and organisational goals.

The aims of the system as set up were to:

- give feedback to all staff, including those working remotely
- integrate performance objectives with organisational priorities, especially in relation to major national contracts
- identify training needs at functional and individual levels
- utilise a process that was user-friendly
- review the effectiveness of previous training
- use competence and skills analysis to identify future talent for further development
- facilitate record-keeping by means of IT applications.

At the introduction of the new performance management process, a new performance appraisal process was also brought in, which included background training for line managers within SPACE.

Performance management objectives are identified at:

- organisational level (reflecting, for instance, organisation service values)
- functional level (to ensure consistent objectives in delivering contractual service requirements)
- individual level (addressing more personal performance goals).

To align with organisational business needs, the key competences were identified as:

- business awareness
- communication
- customer focus
- personal development
- problem-solving
- team commitment
- being results-driven
- health and safety/environmental awareness.

Each of these competences was defined in more detail, listed against examples of behaviours mapped to SPACE requirements.

Employees are rated under each key competence as:

1   Requires improvement, or

2   Is suitable for the current role, or

3   Is suitable for a more senior role.

Identifying training needs

The performance management scheme, as monitored on screen, enables managers to consider HRD at the same time as each employee's work objectives and performance. Managers and employees have the opportunity to enter and review technical skill achievements and development requirements. On the SPACE Performance Appraisal program, separate screens are available for performance objectives, performance appraisal and achievement, training needs, and the manager's and the employee's comment. With an online-based application, performance appraisals may thus be undertaken locally, then centrally analysed for key HRD requirements and evaluation of previous training.

Questions

1   What are the strengths and weaknesses in the design of the performance management process?

2   What steps would you take to review the overall implementation of the performance management system within SPACE?

3   The case study mentions that field engineers are geographically scattered. What additional challenges does this present for line managers? How could such challenges be addressed?

4   The performance review process enables managers to identify individual training needs. What other sources of training requirements should be considered?

CONCLUSION

At the start of this chapter, Brinkerhoff's (2006) observation on the interdependence of performance and training was noted: performance improvement has learning at its heart, and learning and performance are inseparable. Learning, development, and knowledge are perceived as critical to the overall success of the organisation, and the interaction between performance management and HRD go hand in hand in achieving this aim.

The chapter has critically examined some of the concepts and processes behind these assertions. It has considered HRD from the strategic perspective of the organisation, and its contribution to human capital development. Organisational learning shows how organisations are also capable of learning as individual entities.

TLD needs analysis has been discussed at organisational, functional and individual levels, and the chapter has considered how plans are implemented and evaluated accordingly.

Designing and delivering training have been examined. Courses and on-the-job training remain popular, although other methods such as Action Learning, coaching and mentoring are important and effective at an individual level. E-learning solutions have also been discussed, and despite widespread evidence of their adoption, e-learning appears to be most useful when it is part of blended solutions to learning.

The chapter has reinforced the importance of effective transfer of learning from the learning intervention to successful implementation within the workplace. It has also considered the importance of evaluating learning interventions: we have seen that HRD must compete for time, resources and finance with other investment decisions within the workplace. But despite this, training evaluation approaches are too often left to reactions to a course, rather than a longer-term analysis of individual and organisational impact.

At a practical level, the chapter has also examined talent management as an integration of performance and development, and described a typical performance management/training needs analysis process designed and implemented for an engineering company.

In summary, HRD has been examined in the context of both organisational and individual perspectives. Successful HRD requires considerable input from HRD professionals in the organisational and individual assessment of needs and design, delivery and evaluation of learning solutions. However, the chapter again underlines the importance of the performance management process as integral to its success. Once again, it has also underlined the role of the line manager (see Chapters 1 and 4), working within the performance management framework to identify needs, to ensure successful transfer of learning back into the workplace, to provide feedback and evaluation, and to pass on informal workplace learning.

EXPLORE FURTHER

Garavan, T. N. (2007) 'A strategic perspective on human resource development', *Advances in Developing Human Resources*, Vol.9, No.1, February: 11–30

Gibb, S. (2008) *Human Resource Development: Processes, practices and perspectives*, 2nd edition. Basingstoke: Palgrave Macmillan

Gold, J., Holden, R., Iles, P., Stewart, J. and Beardwell, J. (2010) *Human Resource Development: Theory and practice*. Basingstoke: Palgrave Macmillan

Harrison, R. (2009) *Learning and Development*, 5th edition. London: CIPD

Hislop, D. (2009) 'Knowledge management and human resource management', in Redman, T. and Wilkinson, A. (eds) *Contemporary Human Resource Management: Text and cases*, 2nd/3rd edition. Harlow: Pearson

Marchington, M. and Wilkinson, A. (2012) *Human Resource Management at Work: People management and development*, 5th edition. London: CIPD

Reid, M. A., Barrington, B. and Brown, M. (2007) *Human Resource Development: Beyond training interventions*, 7th edition. London: CIPD

Stewart, J. and Rigg, C. (2011) *Learning and Talent Development*. London: CIPD

Swart, J., Mann, C., Brown, S. and Price, A. (2005) *Human Resource Development: Strategy and tactics* (especially Chapters 1–2). London: Elsevier/Butterworth-Heinemann

CHAPTER 8

Performance-related Rewards

SUE HUTCHINSON

LEARNING OUTCOMES

By the end of this chapter you should be able to:

- explain and understand the concept of performance-related reward and recent trends

- outline the general arguments for and against the introduction of performance-related rewards

- understand the different approaches that link reward to individual, team and organisational performance

- critically evaluate individual performance-related pay

- advise on the implications of performance-related reward for HR practice.

INTRODUCTION

The idea of 'a fair day's pay for a fair day's work', or the effort–reward deal which underpins the design of all reward schemes, implies that all forms of reward – even base pay – have performance standards or expectations attached to them. However, schemes vary in how explicit this relationship is. 'Performance-related reward' is the umbrella term used for remuneration schemes in which all or some of reward is dependent on some measure of performance or contribution (objective or subjective), and this implies that the reward will vary according to that performance. Sometimes referred to as 'contingent reward' or 'variable reward', this type of approach encompasses a diverse range of reward practices, ranging from piecework to individual performance-related pay (merit pay) to stock options for senior executives. It can also include the more intrinsic or 'psychological' rewards, and can reward individual or collective behaviour. These different forms of reward vary in their power to bring about the desired outcomes (Prendergast, 1999), and ultimately the choice of scheme (if there is to be one) depends on the circumstances of the organisation, the type of roles and the required effects.

The nature and use of performance-based rewards has changed significantly in the UK, particularly over the last three decades. Nevertheless, the principle of relating reward to performance seems to be firmly established in most UK organisations, based on the belief that it will elicit greater work effort, improve recruitment and retention and include an element of fairness within the reward package. However, opinion is hugely divided over whether it works in practice, and there has been particularly strong criticism of the notion of linking pay and other extrinsic rewards to performance (eg Kohn, 1993; Pfeffer, 1998b). The subject was raised in Chapter 3, in relation to the question of whether pay really does motivate.

This chapter explores the different forms of performance-related rewards and their advantages and disadvantages, and uses the terms 'variable pay', 'contingent pay' and 'incentive pay' to also cover the concept of performance-related reward. As an introduction, the chapter begins by exploring the main categories and types of performance-related reward, the key trends and some of the general reasons for adopting such schemes, as well as some general criticisms. The chapter then examines one of the most popular forms of performance-related reward – individual performance-related pay – and the evidence for and against utilising such schemes. The rest of the chapter considers other types of schemes and their consequences.

WHAT IS PERFORMANCE-RELATED REWARD?

The defining feature of this type of reward is that some or all of employee remuneration is dependent on some assessment of performance (Bryson et al, 2009), whether that be individual, team/group or organisational performance. When designing a performance-based reward scheme there are four key questions to consider (Shields, 2007; Perkins and White, 2011). These are:

- What is being assessed?
- Whose performance is being assessed?
- Over what period of time is the performance being assessed?
- What form does the contingent reward take?

The first issue concerns the criteria for assessing performance: should it be based on behaviours or results, or on a combination of the two? Results-based approaches – such as piecework, commission, bonuses and stock options – are generally more straightforward to measure than behaviours, and are more appropriate where performance outcomes can be accurately specified, quantified and measured, such as in a sales environment. Behavioural measurements are more qualitative in nature and more likely to be found where outputs are less tangible, such as in the public sector and in research and development environments. Chapter 5 considered these alternative forms of measurement in more detail.

As for whose performance is measured, it might be an individual, team, work group, workplace or organisation. Generally, research suggests that the closer the performance unit is to the employee, the more effective the outcome (Heywood and Jirjahn, 2006; Prendergast, 1999). An individual payment-by-results (PBR) scheme, involving a direct link between individual performance and pay, is likely to have the strongest incentive effects, whereas reward schemes linked to organisation-wide criteria tend to have the weakest incentive effects (Bryson et al, 2012). Systems linked to some form of collective performance are also vulnerable to 'free-rider effects' whereby less effective individuals take advantage of better-performing colleagues, or to 'the Ringelmann effect', named after Maximilien Ringelmann, who found that having group members work together on a task actually results in significantly less effort than when individual members work alone (Ringelmann, 1913). Group-wide schemes are also likely to have more 'noise' compared to individual-based schemes in that they will be more influenced by factors outside the control of the individual (Bryson et al, 2009). On the other hand, collective-based rewards can encourage collaborative and co-operative behaviours, and enhance employee identity with the organisation, whereas individual-based schemes can give rise to dysfunctional effects such as manipulation of output, conflict and the pursuit of goals contrary to the organisational objective. This is particularly evident for piecework and executive stock options, as discussed later in the chapter.

Historically, the emphasis has been on individual rewards, although there is increasing interest in collective incentives – in particular, organisation-wide schemes such as save as you earn (SAYE) schemes and share incentive plans (SIPs). It is of course possible to operate a combination of levels – for example, an individual might receive a personal bonus plus an organisation-wide bonus.

The time-frame is important because it may influence the motivational impact of the reward, and there is some evidence that the reward will only be effective in behavioural terms if it is awarded close to the time in which the performance is achieved. Some individual results-based schemes (eg piecework) have a very short time period (eg a shift, a day, or a week) in contrast to organisation-based schemes (eg share options) which normally require longer time-frames (a year or more).

The final issue concerns the form of the reward, such as cash, company shares, or non-financial benefits (for example, holidays, recognition, learning and development opportunities and greater responsibility). The most common form is cash, based on the assumption that money is a key motivator, although many challenge this assumption (see Chapter 3), and there is no doubt that non-financial rewards can also incentivise. Non-financial rewards are also a fairly cost-effective way of improving performance, and can say a lot about the culture and values of the organisation, as in the case of Nationwide (see Case Study 8.1 below). Arguably, the use of this form of reward is under-developed, although the growth in the practice of 'total reward' policies which encompasses the tangible and intangible elements of reward suggests that employers are starting to recognise that pay is not the only motivator.

 REWARDING STAFF AT NATIONWIDE BUILDING SOCIETY

CASE STUDY 8.1

At Nationwide, recognition is one of the preferred ways of motivating staff, in keeping with the values of the Society. In the branches a team bonus is based on performance targets and takes the form of reward vouchers rather than cash. This is not only cost-effective but a popular way of rewarding staff. High-performance league competitions are run under the title of the 'Diamond Club' scheme, rewarding top-performing branches, areas and individuals on a monthly and annual basis. Branches compete within the same grade (based on a branches grading model) and winners receive a visit from the executive or divisional director, who presents a team plaque or individual award certificate and pin badge. The annual award-winning team also receive some money to pay for a team event of their choosing, while individual winners receive small rewards such as a weekend or theatre trip.

Source: Purcell *et al* (2003)

THE USE OF PERFORMANCE-RELATED REWARDS

The principle of relating reward to performance is not new: piecework and various forms of bonus plans based on levels of output or production have been around for hundreds of years. Since the 1980s there has been a significant increase in the use of contingent pay in the UK. According to the 2004 Workplace Employee Relations Survey (WERS), the incidence of all forms of contingent pay grew in the economy between 1984 and 1990, from 41 per cent to 56 per cent, but showed a slight fall to 55 per cent up to 2004 (Bryson *et al*, 2009: 9). First findings from the 2011 WERS (van Wanrooy *et al*, 2013) indicate that the proportion of workplaces using these types of pay schemes has remained broadly constant since 2004. The decline of collective bargaining, the rise of 'HRM' and other approaches to the management process, increased product market competition, the globalisation of production, and changes in the political landscape over the last quarter-century are likely contributors to this initial growth (Bryson *et al*, 2009: 3).

However, the nature and use of this type of approach has changed significantly in the UK. One of the most significant developments has been the growth in performance-related pay. Analysis of the 1998–2004 WIRS/WERS panel dataset shows that the use of performance-related pay (merit pay and payment by results) rose from 20 per cent to 32 per cent over this period in continuing workplaces (ie those that appear in both the 1998 and 2004 listings) (Kersley *et al*, 2006). Overall, some two fifths of workplaces (40 per cent) had some form of performance-related pay; 9 per cent used merit pay alone; 23 per cent used payment by results (PBR); and a further 7 per cent used both payment by results and merit pay. Where incentive payments were made, employees in sales and customer-service roles were most likely to receive them. The CIPD reward management survey (2012) of 455 respondents shows a much higher incidence of performance-related pay schemes, just under two thirds of organisations surveyed operating some form of performance-related reward, incentive and recognition schemes. These were most common in the private sector (78 per cent), very large organisations (92 per cent) and divisions of internationally-owned organisations (80 per cent). They were least common in the voluntary, community and not-for-profit sector (38 per cent), and small and medium-sized organisations (59 per cent). The differences between the WERS and CIPD datasets may be due to sample size, composition of respondents and different definitions.

The most common forms of individual performance-related reward schemes (Table 8.1) involved individual bonuses and merit pay rises, followed by combination schemes (a mix of individuals, group and/or organisational performance). Piece-rates are the least common form of performance-related reward, followed by *ad hoc* project-based schemes, group non-monetary incentives and gain-sharing. This pattern is broadly true across all sectors. Goal-sharing and profit share are the most common forms of collective reward, with a few exceptions: in the public sector group-based monetary awards dominate and profit share is the least-used type of reward.

In terms of who is covered, the same survey shows that managers and professionals were more likely to be covered than other types of employees.

Table 8.1 Types of performance-related reward and recognition (by percentage of respondents)

	All sectors	Manufacturing and production sector	Private sector	Public sector	Voluntary, community and not-for-profit
Individual performance-related reward					
Individual bonuses	67	78	62	82	62
Merit pay rises	57	64	52	49	62
Combination schemes	40	53	45	8	14
Sales commission	37	32	51	5	14
Individual non-monetary recognition awards	34	34	31	33	38
Other individual cash-based incentives	26	17	33	15	5

	All sectors	Manufacturing and production sector	Private sector	Public sector	Voluntary, community and not-for-profit
Ad hoc/project-based schemes	18	17	19	18	5
Piece-rates	2	3	2	0	0
Group performance-related reward					
Goal-sharing	48	46	51	39	50
Profit sharing	38	39	42	0	40
Group- or team-based non-monetary recognition	27	18	22	62	40
Gain-sharing	22	27	21	15	0
Group- or team-based non-monetary incentives	19	9	20	15	30

Source: CIPD (2012f)

Looking across countries, there is huge diversity in the use of performance-related reward, mainly due to differences in national culture, legislation and institutional arrangements such as fiscal incentives (eg reduced taxation for variable elements of pay). Chapter 11 contains a fuller discussion on these influences. Bryson *et al*'s (2012) detailed analysis of performance pay schemes in Europe and the USA shows that the share of workers receiving any form of incentive pay (eg individual, profit-/gain-sharing and share ownership) varies considerably between countries, ranging from 10 per cent to 15 per cent in some European countries to over 40 per cent in Scandinavian countries and the USA (2012: 17). They also find that individual pay schemes and financial participation are on the increase in Europe, although their incidence remains much lower than in the USA. The Cranet-E survey (Chapter 11) and EPOC survey also provide details of company pay practices in Europe and other countries.

MOTIVES FOR INTRODUCING PERFORMANCE-RELATED REWARD

The overarching rationale for using performance-related rewards is to improve employee performance or productivity and thus organisational performance. The key arguments in favour of this approach (Kessler and Purcell, 1992; Bryson *et al*, 2009; ACAS, 2005) are:

- to elicit greater work effort from employees
- to enhance job satisfaction and employee commitment to the organisation
- to help attract and retain employees, particularly high performers and when the labour market is tight
- to implement a fairer reward system by rewarding those who perform most effectively
- to facilitate a change in organisational culture and values. Kessler and Purcell (1992) argue that it can send out a message about 'what sort of company we are', and can facilitate a change in culture. They give the example of how the introduction of performance-related pay (PRP) for senior managers in a public sector organisation to be privatised was done because it was deemed 'appropriate' for private sector organisations

and generated a 'performance-oriented' culture. In the Post Office, individual PRP was designed to break down the ideology of corporate paternalism and centralisation

- to enable greater employee involvement by encouraging employees' buy-in to the organisation's success
- to communicate information about the objectives and performance expectations of the organisation
- to give greater responsibility to line managers
- to exercise a degree of financial control – targeting pay where it is most effective
- to act as a substitute for direct monitoring of employee performance.

The fundamental aim of improving performance is based on the underlying assumption that reward linked to performance will increase the work motivation to perform. The most relevant theories underpinning this are expectancy theory, goal-setting theory and equity theory (see Chapter 3). All differ in emphasis. Briefly, expectancy theory suggests that employees will respond to an incentive or reward on offer if they value it, if they believe good performance will be instrumental in bringing about the desired reward, and if they expect that their efforts will achieve the desired performance. The most motivating schemes then will be those with clear links between performance and the rewards that people really want and employees feel they can deliver. Goal-setting theory places less emphasis on rewards and more on the need to have specific, challenging goals which are attainable, together with feedback that is timely. Equity and justice theories imply that organisations should seek to influence employees' perceptions of equity by fairly allocating rewards. Linking reward to performance in some way is an attempt to ensure a sense of 'felt-fairness' by reflecting differential performance.

Support for linking reward to performance can be found among many proponents of the 'best practice' model of HRM, although the particular form this takes varies (see Table 8.2). Pfeffer (1998a, b), for example, advocates the use of profit sharing and other organisationally based incentives but condemns individual-based pay as dangerous and destructive .

Table 8.2 Studies on HRM and performance containing performance-related reward

Study	Reward method in the HR system
Betcherman *et al* (1994)	Variable pay
Ichniowski *et al* (1997)	Profit sharing, incentives with quality bonus
Kalleberg *et al* (1996)	Bonuses for performance, profit sharing or stock options
Patterson *et al* (1997)	Incentive pay as individual item
Delery and Doty (1996)	Performance-based compensation
Youndt *et al* (1996)	Group-based incentives
Huselid (1995)	Profit share and gain-sharing plans
Becker and Huselid (1998)	Merit or incentive pay based on performance appraisal and profit sharing and/or gain-sharing plans
MacDuffie (1995)	Contingent pay
Guest and Hoque (1994)	Merit pay
Pfeffer (1998a)	High pay contingent on organisational performance

Source: adapted from Wood (1999)

ARGUMENTS AGAINST PERFORMANCE-BASED REWARD

Not everyone, however, is enthusiastic about contingent reward schemes. Many of the disadvantages of using extrinsic reward for performance are summed up by Kohn (1993: 57–60) in his much-cited article in the *Harvard Business Review* on 'Why incentive plans cannot work'. His main points are:

- Pay is not a motivator. Kohn dismisses the idea that pay motivates, citing survey evidence to support Herzberg's claim that pay is a hygiene factor which can demotivate rather than positively motivate.
- Rewards punish. Kohn argues that by making rewards contingent on certain behaviours, managers are manipulating their employees, which will have a punitive effect over time. Also, not receiving an expected reward is indistinguishable from being punished. Anyone who has tried to bribe their children ('Do this and you'll get that') may sympathise with this view, which can lead to cries that parents are being too controlling, and feelings of resentment and defiance.
- Rewards rupture relationships. Rewarding individuals encourages competitiveness and undermines teamwork and co-operative work relationships, particularly when there is a fixed amount of reward to distribute. 'For each person who wins, there are many others who carry with them the feeling of having lost. And the more these awards are publicised through the use of memos, newsletters and awards banquets, the more detrimental their impact can be' (Kohn, 1993: 58).
- Rewards deter managers from addressing the underlying reasons for poor performance, such as asking if employees are adequately prepared for the demands of the job. In this way it discourages managers from concentrating on effective management behaviour – for example, giving feedback and support, and providing meaningful work.
- Rewards inhibit risk-taking and creativity by encouraging a focus on specific behaviours.
- Extrinsic rewards undermine intrinsic interest in the job. Kohn and many others (eg Deci, 1971; Pfeffer, 1998b; Deci *et al*, 2001) believe that performance-contingent rewards significantly undermine intrinsic motivation and performance, and there is evidence that employees who do not receive any special reward may outperform those who do. Kohn argues that financial rewards are perceived as a 'bribe', and if people have to be bribed to do something, it must be something they do not want to do. However, the extent to which intrinsic motivation is adversely affected by rewards is contested by others (see the Critical Reflection below). For a more detailed discussion, see Guthrie (2007), Cameron (2001), and Fang and Gerhart (2012).

Others have further argued that the real problem is that rewards work too well (Pfeffer and Sutton 2006; Beer and Cannon, 2004). 'Specifically, they motivate employees to focus excessively on doing what they need to do to gain rewards, sometimes at the expense of doing things that would help the organisation' (Beer and Cannon, 2004: 4). The result can be dsyfunctional behaviour or unintended consequences (see also Chapter 5). Pfeffer and Sutton (2006) give the example of garbage truck drivers on an incentive system, which meant that if they finished early they could go home and still receive full pay for their shift. The aim was to reduce overtime payments – but the result was that those who received incentive pay went to landfill sites in trucks way over the weight limit, resulting in more traffic accidents, or drivers who missed picking up rubbish en route.

Furthermore, there are difficulties in setting appropriate performance measures (Chapter 5). Incentive schemes only work if people have enough information to work effectively and performance is under the control of the individuals who are set the incentives. Also, rewarding performance may not be appropriate for all organisational cultures. For example, Beer and Cannon's study of Hewlett-Packard in the mid-1990s suggests that the implementation costs and risks of performance pay systems may be greater in high-commitment cultures where trust and employee commitment are crucial to the long-term success of the business.

CRITICAL REFLECTION 8.1

Does pay for performance diminish intrinsic interest?

There is considerable debate in the literature concerning the question whether performance-related reward decreases intrinsic motivation and satisfaction, with counterproductive effects on performance. Such claims are primarily based on the application of cognitive evaluation theory (CET) and on research in non-

workplace settings, like educational settings. For example, if students are rewarded for doing an interesting task, the claim is that they will come to like the task less, and engage in it less once the rewards are no longer forthcoming (Cameron, 2001: 29).

1   Can you think of examples from your own experiences (work or non-work) to support or contest this theory?

INDIVIDUALISED PERFORMANCE-RELATED PAY

Individualised performance-related pay (IPRP) is one of the most common, and controversial, forms of performance-related reward. The term is generally used to describe pay progression through a grade or band, and situations in which advancement is dependent on some evaluation of an individual's performance, usually linked to the formal performance appraisal/review. This 'classic' form of IPRP is also referred to as 'merit pay' or 'appraisal-related pay' (ACAS, 1990). Typically the review process may provide for:

- *either* pay progression entirely on the basis of individual performance appraisal ratings (known as 'all-merit' awards): this is the approach adopted by CABI (see Case Study 8.2 below)
- *or* a general pay rise for employees in addition to an element that is linked to individual performance ('basic-plus-merit' awards).

According to an IRS survey (2011), the second option is the more popular. These pay increases awarded through PRP are normally consolidated into basic pay. IPRP can also operate as an annual one-off merit bonus that does not relate to pay progression and is not consolidated into base pay, but in this section we examine the classic form. One-off bonus payments are considered later in the chapter.

IPRP has increased in popularity in the both the UK and globally. Even in Asian countries, where research suggests that IPRP may not be an appropriate cultural fit, organisations are using individual performance-related pay, including Japan and (South) Korea which have traditionally emphasised seniority-based pay (Chang and Hahn, 2006; Merriman, 2010). The cultural dimension is discussed further in Chapter 11. UK estimates of the coverage of IPRP vary, partly as a result of differing definitions adopted by researchers (CIPD, 2012g). However, some general trends can be identified (CIPD, 2012g; IRS, 2011; Cranet, 2011):

- Individual PRP is more common in the private sector, and in large organisations. It is virtually the norm in some sectors, such as financial services.
- Although much less commonly used in the public sector, its use has increased since the 1980s (for example, local government, the NHS, the Civil Service and teachers).
- Merit pay most commonly covers managerial and professional staff, and is least common for manual or lower-grade employees.

- There are differences in coverage internationally – for example, the use of IPRP for manual workers is extensive in the USA and Germany but hardly used at all for manual workers in France and Sweden.

 CABI

CASE STUDY 8.2

CABI is a not-for-profit science-based development and information organisation which provides information and scientific knowledge in answer to problems in agriculture and the environment, such as improving crop yields or undertaking pest control. It does this through a range of services including publishing, development projects and research. It is owned by 45 member countries, and was established by statutory instrument with the UK government. Although its work is mainly focused on developing countries, in 2009/2010 it helped eradicate the invasive Japanese knotweed from the Olympic site in London. It employs a staff of 200 in Oxford and Surrey, around two thirds of whom are highly qualified scientists. In 2009 it changed its reward strategy (for employees below senior management level) from an incremental system to progression based on performance. This allowed staff who were stuck at the top of the incremental scales some flexibility to progress.

There are seven grades in the pay structure (excluding senior managers), and pay progression is determined by a pay range matrix depending on the performance rating given through the appraisal process. There is a five-point rating scale ('distinguished', 'superior', 'successful', 'needs improvement' and 'unacceptable'), and a moderation process by which HR and line managers meet to try to ensure consistency in ratings. Pay ranges for each grade are centred on a target rate, which represents the market median and is equivalent to 100 points. Each range spans from 'position in range' (PIR) 85 to PIR 115. The target pay rates are reviewed regularly and based on Hay Group data for the region. The main aims of the reward strategy are to get good performers to the market median as quickly as possible, and to allow employees to progress beyond this point if they continue to perform well. The largest proportion of funds are directed to the highest performers on the lowest PIR, as indicated in the example below.

Performance rating	Percentage increase for PIR 85-94	Percentage increase for PIR 95-104	Percentage increase for PIR 105-115
Distinguished	8	6	4
Superior	6	5	3
Successful	5	3	2
Needs improvement	2	1	0
Unacceptable	0	0	0

Each year the organisation specifies the total pot available for wage increases based on market competiveness, business performance and affordability, and the distribution of this pot is negotiated with the recognised trade union (Prospect). No separate increase is given for cost-of-living rises. To move up to the next pay range, employees have to demonstrate that they are operating at that level (eg by changing jobs or as a result of job growth) but are not allowed to progress on the basis of acquiring new skills or qualifications.

Source: IDS HR Study 929 (2010a)

Questions

1   Identify and discuss the advantages and disadvantages of the scheme.

2   Are there are improvements to this approach that you would recommend?

Despite the growth in IPRP, opinion among both academics and practitioners is hugely divided over whether it works in practice. Table 8.3 summarises the main benefits and problems with IPRP, some of which have been covered earlier in the chapter and elsewhere (eg Chapter 5).

Table 8.3 Arguments for and against individualised performance-related pay

For	Against
– Motivates staff	– Does not motivate staff
– Improves individual performance	– Decreases intrinsic motivation
– Improves organisational performance	– Pay awards are too low
– Is a fair and equitable way of rewarding individuals	– Measuring performance is difficult
– Aids recruitment and retention	– Implementation is problematic – eg subjective judgements by managers
– Facilitates flexibility in rewarding employees	– Undermines teamworking
– Rewards exceptional performance	– Fails to reinforce organisational objectives
– Is thought by employees to be good in principle	– Creates tension between pay and training and development
– Focuses on key objectives	– Employees perceive lack of transparency
– Controls pay costs	– Financial constraints mean funds may not be available
	– Is not appropriate for all cultures

The specific arguments in favour of IPRP (Lawler, 2003; Kessler and Purcell, 1992; ACAS, 2005; Armstrong, 2009; IRS, 2011) are that it provides a clear line of sight between the behaviour of individuals and their rewards, thus providing a strong motivational effect, as suggested by expectancy theory. Because it allows individuals to be rewarded in line with their contribution, it is a fair and equitable system of reward. It offers flexibility to recruit and retain valuable employees by targeting the higher performers, who could be expected to have an above-average market value in the external labour market. Conversely, it can help remove poor performers because their pay will fall relative to the external market and they will not be able to afford to remain employees. It also delivers the message that performance is important, helps embed a high-performance culture and allows better control over pay costs.

Although IPRP is invariably introduced as a management initiative, employees seem to think in principle it is a good practice. In one of the early studies of IPRP in the public sector, a survey of 2,000 Inland Revenue staff revealed that 57 per cent felt that performance pay was good in principle, and 58 per cent disagreed with the statement 'The idea of performance pay is fundamentally unfair' (Marsden and Richardson, 1994). In a

CIPD survey on employee pay attitudes (2010a) 60 per cent of private sector employees said they would like to be paid according to 'how well I perform'.

Nevertheless, the criticisms are wide-ranging and suggest a more complex picture. As previously noted, the view that pay is a motivator has been challenged by many (eg Kohn, 1993; Pfeffer, 1998b). According to Isaac (2001), the longer PRP schemes operate for, the more ineffective they become as a motivator. It was clear in the study of Inland Revenue staff (which assessed pay motivation using 16 statements) that relatively few staff felt that IPRP provided them with the motivation to change their work behaviour, and thus 'it was hard to see how it could have enhanced employee performance' (Marsden and Richardson, 1994: 1). The study concluded that this was because the scheme was judged to operate unfairly: staff believed that a quota system was in operation for markings, that there was favouritism, and that the markings took insufficient account of job allocation. The problems of setting accurate and appropriate performance measures and the distorting effects of subjectivity have been taken up in earlier chapters, but are key problems identified with the IPRP process. Additionally, IPRP places huge responsibility on the line manager, who is expected to make decisions about individual performance, and defend and justify those decisions (Kessler and Purcell, 1992). The problems with line management behaviour have also been previously noted.

Other arguments against the use of IPRP are that pay can decrease intrinsic motivation, it undermines teamworking by emphasising individual success sometimes at the expense of peers, and encourages a short-term focus on performance. Danford *et al*'s study (2005) of the aeronautical manufacturing industry found that 85 per cent of those surveyed thought performance-related pay damaged team spirit. There are some who argue that by making pay contingent on performance, management is signalling that they are in control, reducing trust and increasing conflict at work.

There is also a potential tension between pay and training (see Chapter 6). Linking pay to appraisal turns the review into a backward-looking event, and employees may become defensive and be less receptive to training, development and counselling. Furthermore, the PRP element of pay is often relatively small, and may not be of sufficient value to be desired by all employees (Hendry *et al*, 2000). Kauhanen and Piekkola (2006) suggest that 5 per cent of total salary is the minimum pay needed to achieve a motivational effect. Others have suggested that increases in the order of 10 per cent to 15 per cent are required to have an impact on performance. Heading the list of problems in an IRS survey (2011) on PRP was the fact that the pay awards were too low to motivate staff, although 54 per cent admitted that their pay award had been affected by the recession. Linked to this is the fact that the financial constraints under which such schemes operate can present difficulties, particularly in recessionary times when funds may not be available and schemes have to be abandoned or suspended.

Heery argues that IPRP is unethical (Heery, 2000) because it threatens employment security by putting people's income at risk, thus undermining employee commitment; is potentially unjust in terms of both procedural and distributive justice leading to claims of discrimination; and is undemocratic in that it undermines collective bargaining.

Many have questioned successive governments' belief in the merits of performance-related pay for public sector employees, claiming that they ignore the evidence that it has limited impact on employee motivation, can damage teamworking and may be divisive in the workplace. There are a number of distinct issues that arise when introducing PRP into a public sector setting. Multiple targets and multiple stakeholders make measurement problematic, and many public sector employees work in teams – eg teachers – in which individual contribution is difficult to isolate. Moreover, many public sector workers are driven by intrinsic motivation – eg nurses – and arguably motivated by a public service ethos that could actually be undermined by some forms of PRP. Also, the financial incentives delivered are relatively small. However, Dowling and Richardson's (1997) study of senior managers in the NHS suggests that PRP can work, but it is contingent on the way in which work objectives are set, and on perceptions of the appropriateness or attractiveness of the rewards in the public sector. More recently, David Marsden (2004) has revisited his earlier research on IPRP in the public sector, and suggests he is more positive about the possible benefits (see Case Study 8.3 below).

CASE STUDY 8.3

MERIT PAY CAN IMPROVE PERFORMANCE DESPITE FAILING TO MOTIVATE STAFF

In a discussion paper about incentive pay in the public sector, David Marsden (2004) considers the paradox of performance-related pay systems and asks 'Why does performance-related pay continue to be widely used despite the evidence that it fails to motivate employees?' In this paper he details the way successive governments have sought to press ahead with PRP despite the widespread evidence that such schemes are divisive and very unpopular with staff. Marsden points to previous research which shows that the anticipated consequence of introducing PRP – the improvement of motivation – has proved elusive. However, there is evidence that it does bring about improved performance by the way in which it links to appraisal and forces line managers to set clear goals for staff. Furthermore, when goal-setting is consensual and the outcome of negotiation between individual employees and their managers (ie when it is not a 'top-down' process), positive results can be realised. For example, performance-based pay for schoolteachers in 2000 was initially thought to be inappropriate for their kind of work, despite the fact that this was introduced partly to recruit and motivate staff. Over the years, however, some schools have found positive results through integrating teacher classroom activity better with school goals and priorities, and thus achieving better pupil test results. In conclusion Marsden notes that 'The unintended consequence of the long road travelled by performance-related pay and performance management in the public sector has been the emergence of a new channel for employee voice, this time at the individual rather than at the collective level.'

The UK Coalition Government appears keen to pursue the agenda for IPRP in the public sector, and in March 2011 the Hutton Review (Hutton, 2011), examining senior public pay, recommended that there 'needs to be a better balance between rewards and penalties in performance pay schemes'. In 2012 the House of Commons Education Committee recommended further changes to performance-related pay for teachers.

What can we conclude about IPRP? Clearly, it is not 'a silver bullet' (CIPD, 2012g), not appropriate for all organisations, and is extremely difficult to manage well. The evidence is mixed (for a detailed discussion, see Perkins and White, 2011: 193). Most of the support for improved employee performance comes from US studies. For example, Huselid's (1995) study of HR practices found a correlation between organisations that had appraisal-related pay and those that had higher annual sales per employee. Heneman's (1992) review of 42 studies concluded that performance increased when pay was linked to performance. Gerhart and Rynes (2003), in their review of merit pay conclude that 'Despite considerable scepticism about merit pay, the actual evidence on merit pay is primarily positive' (Gerhart and Rynes, 2003: 189). However, in the UK a lot of the research has been critical, although much of it has related to the public sector. There is evidence, nonetheless, that the design and implementation of PRP schemes is critical for their success – in particular, the ability to measure performance and the quality of appraisal (eg Kessler, 1994; Marsden *et al*, 2001). Belfield and Marsden (2003) find that the workplace context is important, arguing that monitoring environments in which employee performance can be cheaply and easily measured are better suited to PRP. Yet there is very telling evidence from an IRS survey (IRS, 2011) which revealed that although the majority of organisations had clear objectives for their performance-related pay schemes, the vast majority – over three quarters (76.3 per cent) – did not evaluate the effectiveness of their scheme in meeting its objectives. This is surprising in view of the fact that the main aim, as given by an overwhelming 91 per cent of respondents, was to improve individual performance, and there is considerable investment of effort in operating such schemes.

REFLECTIVE ACTIVITY 8.1

What advice would you give to an organisation that is seeking to introduce IPRP in order to maximise success?

OTHER FORMS OF REWARD

INDIVIDUAL PAYMENT BY RESULTS

Payment by results (PBR), the most traditional form of reward for performance, is where pay 'is determined objectively by the amount of work done or its value' (Kersley *et al*, 2006: 190). Such schemes aim to increase individual output by establishing a clear 'line of sight' between results and rewards, and so, in theory, have a stronger motivational impact compared to other approaches Historically, however, they have been associated with encouraging 'wages drift' and conflict, and earnings may fluctuate through no fault of the individual. Employees can relate all of a person's pay or just part of the overall package to output and the main types of schemes are piecework, work-measured schemes, commission and results-based individual bonuses.

According to WERS 2004, just over a third of private sector workplaces (with five or more employees) use some form of individual PBR, covering some 43 per cent of employees. However, in manufacturing, where such schemes have long been a feature, just 21 per cent of organisations used such schemes – a significant decline from 36 per cent in 1990. In a study of the decline in incentive pay in British manufacturing, Arrowsmith and Marginson (2010) found that companies were rejecting individual PBR in favour of aggregate bonus schemes linked to establishment or enterprise results. This decline, they suggest, is due to 'modernisation' of manufacturing workplace practices and the growth in high-performance work systems such as teamworking, flexibility, employee involvement and quality initiatives, plus a more sophisticated use of technology.

Piecework is one of the oldest forms of performance-based pay and has a long tradition in British manufacturing, particularly in engineering, printing and textiles although now largely confined to the low-paid and often hidden economy, such as home-workers in clothing and agriculture (Perkins and White, 2011). The aim of piecework was to increase productivity by linking a rate of pay to each 'piece' of work or unit of output produced – for example, £1 for every unit produced. Its attraction is that it establishes a clear link between output with pay, is simple to understand and requires little supervision because the reward system itself encourages employees to be self-managed in terms of work effort. Many studies have shown that piecework can improve productivity. For example, Bryson *et al* (2012) report on window-screen fitters in the company Safelite where productivity rose by 44 per cent when the company switched to piece-rate payments.

Despite these positive reports, piecework pay has been on the decline, partly because of the potential for control that can be exerted on the system. Employees can regulate their work to restrict output, and employers can cut the rate of the job if production rises. Piecework also encourages employees to focus exclusively on those activities which trigger payments, and may compromise quality and safety. In reviewing the demise of piecework in two manufacturing companies, Arrowsmith and Marginson (2010) cite problems of administration, equity (because some product lines involved more difficult jobs than others and some employees were required to move between jobs), identifying individual contribution, and the need to focus on quality and reduce re-work costs as reasons for the withdrawal of these schemes in favour of collective-based approaches.

Work-measured schemes came to replace traditional piecework in the twentieth century, but these too have declined in use. This is where a 'standard time' or 'standard output level' is set, using work study methods, and incentive payments are linked to output achieved relative to the standard set or time saved in performing the task (ACAS, 2006). Although successful in some contexts (eg short-cycle repetitive work), these schemes are often complex and time-consuming to develop, are subject to manipulation by employees and employers, and are consequently often associated with conflict and dispute.

SALES COMMISSION

Commission on sales is also one of the oldest forms of reward for performance and is still widely used in retail, finance and insurance. An example of a successful sales commission scheme is illustrated in the example of Artizan hairdressers (see Case Study 8.4 below), operating in a sector in which this approach is quite common. In the 2012 CIPD Reward Management survey, 37.3 per cent of organisations used this form of payment (Table 8.1). Some jobs are rewarded entirely on commission (although pay must meet the minimum wage), but it is more common for commission to be paid on top of a basic salary – for example, 10 per cent of base pay for every item sold. Its attraction lies in its power to motivate, its simplicity, the ability to give instant feedback, and the reduced need for direct supervision (which is particularly important for sales staff operating in the field). Like other forms of PBR, however, it can create uncertainty in earnings and ignores aspects of demand which are outside the control of employees. When commission accounts for a high proportion of total earnings, such schemes can also result in aggressive and even negligent behaviour, as witnessed by the mis-selling of pensions in the 1990s by financial services sales staff. It can also create unnecessary competition and neglects other aspects of the job such as quality of service.

CASE STUDY 8.4

COMMISSION-BASED PAY AT ARTIZAN HAIR SALON

Founded in 1986, Artizan is a highly successful hair salon in Bath. All staff are paid on a commission basis (which is normal practice in the industry), depending on their status, and this is seen as strong motivational tool and an aid to recruitment and retention. Staff who work in the salon are either employed or self-employed (there is approximately a 50/50 split) and set weekly targets based on sales, which are reviewed every three months. Employees are paid a weekly salary plus a commission rate when they exceed their target. These salary increments are based on hitting the main weekly target, averaged over a three-month period. So, for example, an employee with a target of £450 per week who brings in, on average £600 per week, would receive 20 per cent of the additional amount (ie £30 per week).

Once employees have proved they have a good, loyal client base (eg they are generating a regular income of over £1,200 per week), they can opt for self-employment. Self-employed hairdressers receive a fixed percentage of their weekly turnover, normally around half of their weekly client takings. So someone bringing in £1,200 per week would receive £600 commission. The majority of hairdressers want to become self-employed because potential earnings are higher and they have greater flexibility in terms of the hours they work. From the company's perspective, overall responsibility for performance is transferred to the stylist, who still represents the brand and is involved in the business.

Performance is very visible in this environment, and a stylist's client base is based on repeat business and recommendations. The approach is perceived as fair, straightforward and transparent, and allows the business to keep control of margins. The salon is considered an excellent place to work. Staff turnover and absence is very low, and some stylists have been there for between 15 and 20 years.

INDIVIDUAL BONUSES

Individual results-based bonuses are becoming more popular and were used by over two thirds of respondent organisations to the CIPD 2012 Reward Management survey (Table 8.1). The approach is normally associated with managers, particularly senior managers, and certain professional occupations, and is widespread in the financial sector, where annual bonuses can be multiples of the basic salary. The advantages are that employees can focus their efforts on certain objectives, and since the bonus is not normally consolidated into basic pay, there is no permanent increase in the wages bill. It can also aid recruitment and retention, a frequent claim used to justify the high bonuses paid in the financial sector (see Case Study 8.5 below).

CASE STUDY 8.5

BONUS PAYMENTS TO CEOs AND BANKERS

The bonuses paid to bankers and CEOs have sparked huge controversy in both the UK and the USA over the last few years. This is because, firstly, the payment of large bonuses to bankers created a culture which promoted risk-taking for individual gain, which is considered to have contributed to the 2008 banking crisis. Secondly, bankers have continued to be paid significant bonuses and proved resistant to any reduction in their bonus payments, using the argument that they risk losing top staff to overseas financial institutions which are more lightly regulated. Thirdly, for banks who had been bailed out by the taxpayer in 2008, such as the Royal Bank of Scotland and Northern Rock, this has led to criticisms that bankers (including their CEOs) are being rewarded for failure (Brockett, 2009). In 2012 the scale of opposition to a £1 million bonus payment to the Chief Executive (CE) of the Royal Bank of Scotland (82 per cent owned by the taxpayer) led to Stephen Hester's eventually waiving his bonus. Towards the end of the same year the Aviva boss resigned after his pay and bonus were criticised on the basis that 'there should be no payment for failure'. In the USA, President Barack Obama imposed fixed limits on executive pay and bonus curbs for all banks receiving state aid, and critics called for similar direct government intervention in the UK.

In 2011 the Committee of European Banking Supervisors (CEBS) announced restrictions on the bonuses that banks can pay their staff. The recommendations required that banks:

- appoint an independent remuneration committee
- defer 40 per cent–60 per cent of bonuses for three to five years, and pay 50 per cent of bonuses in shares (rather than in cash)
- set a maximum bonus level as a percentage of an individual's basic pay
- exclude any 'award for failure' from severance pay packages
- publish pay details for 'senior management and risk-takers'.

The rules mean that bankers receive only 20 per cent–30 per cent of their bonuses in immediate cash. The guidelines took effect from 1 January 2012. The European Commission is planning further changes.

CRITICAL REFLECTION 8.2

Hendry *et al* (2000: 9) ask 'Does an executive bonus function as an incentive or as a historic reward for what has been achieved, or is it even purely symbolic [of status]?'

Discuss this question.

TEAM-BASED REWARDS

Under these schemes the reward is allocated between team or group members. Although team-based rewards have been around a long time for manual employees, it was not until the 1990s that organisations started to link team performance to some form of reward for non-manual employees. Parts of the UK civil service (the Employment Service, the Benefits Agency, HM Customs & Excise and the Inland Revenue) experimented with team-based rewards for non-managerial staff following the publication of the Makinson Report, *Incentives for Change*, for the Government's Public Service Productivity Panel in 2000, although with mixed success. The Report argued that team-based performance should prove easier to measure than the process of isolating individual contributions in an environment where collective targets were more important than individual ones.

The main rationale for this approach is that it reinforces behaviours associated with effective teamworking such as collaboration, knowledge-sharing, flexibility and communication, and encourages team members to work together (Perkins and White, 2011; Reilly *et al*, 2005). Indeed, this was the thinking behind an experiment with team-based pay in the UK's NHS (Reilly *et al*, 2005), detailed in Case Study 8.6 below. It also serves to reinforce group or team objectives and can encourage weaker team members to improve performance. The approach is not without its problems, however. Such schemes fail to distinguish individual contributions and are vulnerable to 'free-riders' who do not pull their weight in the team, as described previously. It can be demotivating for employees who want to be rewarded for their individual effort or who resent the fact that pay is dependent upon the performance of others. It can also encourage harmful competition between teams, leading to inter-team rivalry and conflict. Pressure on individual team members to perform and heightened peer surveillance can potentially create conflict within groups. It can also inhibit movement between teams as employees tend to seek to belong to the high-achieving teams.

 TRIALLING TEAM-BASED PAY IN THE NHS

CASE STUDY 8.6

In their article 'Team-based pay in the United Kingdom', Reilly and colleagues report on a two-year experiment on team-based pay in the NHS. The experiment selected 17 teams in a range of NHS Trusts, and offered two different types of reward for the achievement of targets – one was a cash bonus for lower-paid ancillary staff, and the other offered mixed rewards (cash and money to put into an 'improvement fund' to spend on staff facilities and development). The trial produced mixed results. On the positive side, many of the targets were met, such as improved recording of patient records, better inter-disciplinary working, improved links with community services, better absence management, and quicker responses from some support staff (portering and security). Many staff involved in the trials also felt positive about their experiences, particularly where targets had been met, and felt that team pay helped improve services.

However, not all sites met their targets, and some participants were less than positive about the benefits from the scheme. A significant minority of staff felt that it was wrong to receive incentives for their performance, claiming that they were motivated by their vocation at work and did the best they could for patients regardless of any incentives. Some even felt it was insulting to be offered cash to improve performance.

The pilot study concluded that although there were many issues specific to the NHS and to the public sector more widely, there were some clear conditions for success that would be more widely applicable. For example, such schemes must have a clear purpose in terms of what they are trying to achieve, and this has to be understood by all participants. Up-front leadership was also important, in terms of commitment to the schemes and demonstrating the importance of targets and their value to the organisations. Staff also had to have trust in that leadership. Communication at all stages of the implementation was highlighted, and first-line supervision and middle managers had to be well briefed on its aims and operation. Good-quality project management and data management was also important, and targets had to be clear and simple. The researchers also believed that team-based pay would only be successful for a limited period, partly because of employees' concerns that the performance bar would be continually raised, resulting in 'employee burn-out'.

Source: Reilly *et al* (2005)

Designing appropriately based team measures and rewards can also be challenging. Teams come in all shapes and sizes, and any incentive has to fit the architecture of the team. For project-based teams, for example, it seems appropriate to reward all equally, since this type of work often requires collaborative working and the sharing of knowledge between people with often quite different specialisms. Reward would be on a project-by-project basis against predetermined targets or goals. Team-based reward appears to work best in small teams (Burgess *et al*, 2004), where teams are easily defined and well established (Armstrong, 2000), and where a team has considerable control over what it does.

Shields (2007) identifies four main approaches for distributing team reward (Shields, 2007: 441):

- Each member of the team receives the same cash sum.
- Reward is in the form of non-cash recognition – eg formal recognition for top-performing teams perhaps by way of a certificate at an annual award ceremony, an all-expenses-paid social event or a holiday.
- Team bonuses are paid as a percentage of individual base pay.
- Individual awards are based on individual appraisal ratings.

The first two methods appear to be the fairest in that rewards are the same for each group or team member. One such cash-based approach is used by Fenner Dunlop, the conveyor-belt manufacturers (see Case Study 8.7 below). Non-financial treats are given to successful teams in Alan Sugar's *The Apprentice* TV show each week, such as a visit to a health spa or a five-star meal – although this is clearly secondary to the final prize of £250,000 investment to the winner to start his or her own business! The last two approaches allow for differentiation between team members based on either individual pay or individual performance, and are likely to militate against team cohesion.

 TEAM-LEVEL BONUSES AT FENNER DUNLOP

CASE STUDY 8.7

Despite the fact that teamworking skills and behaviours are increasingly demanded by employers, team-based reward remains a marginal reward practice (Carty, 2009b). One reason for the low take-up is that it is difficult to put into practice, involving problems of setting and communicating objectives and targets, understanding the mechanics of the scheme, putting the team together, and getting buy-in from team members. Consider the following example.

Fenner Dunlop, manufacturers of conveyor belts for the international mining and industrial markets, introduced a new team-based bonus scheme in 2006, replacing its former two-tier incentive scheme which had rewarded both individual and team performance (Carty, 2009b). Under the new bonus scheme, only work group productivity and performance is rewarded (the old individual bonus element was consolidated into basic pay), and is linked to key performance indicators (KPIs) across the company's departments. Departments are measured on either the weight of the conveyor belt they produce or the length of the belt, set against all paid hours worked to achieve the results. Initially, paid sickness absences and training hours were included in the KPI bonus hours, but following a review long-term absence (defined as four weeks or more) and off-the-job training was removed from the calculation (the inclusion of these training hours was seen as a disincentive to development). On-the-job training (eg induction training) was left in because previously there had been a tendency to take time over induction training, which meant that people did not get up to speed in

the job as quickly as possible. A norm is set for KPI bonus levels (initially £15 per person per week) and bonuses increase by increments of £1 per individual per week for each percentage point of productivity output achieved above the set norm. There is no ceiling on payments made. If targets are not achieved, however, bonus payments are reduced by 2 per cent for each percentage point below the norm. This means that employees lose bonus payments quicker than they can increase them, and is seen as a way of encouraging employees to, at a minimum, maintain productivity levels.

Question

1   What are the advantages and disadvantages of this approach?

ORGANISATION-BASED REWARDS

Collective rewards linked to organisation-wide criteria are fundamentally different from individual-based rewards. They are generally considered to have weaker incentive effects because employees have less power to influence the outcomes, and some have doubted whether they have any incentive effects at all, especially in large organisations (Oyer, 2004; Prendergast, 1999). Nevertheless, the use of collective forms of reward has increased markedly over the last 30 years. Like team-based rewards, they can encourage collaborative and co-operative behaviours, but can also strengthen identification with organisational objectives and are more likely to elicit organisational citizenship behaviours than are individual-based schemes (Shields, 2007). They are therefore more appropriate in organisations where work is interdependent and organised on a cross-functional basis, where the nature of work or occupations means that individual performance is difficult to measure and usually more amenable to trade unions, since they do not preclude individual wage bargaining taking place. As noted earlier, Arrowsmith and Marginson (2010) attribute the decline of individual payment by results and the growth of profit share bonuses in manufacturing to changes in the organisation of work and to growth in high-performance work systems.

These types of schemes are normally categorised as short-term, to be delivered within a year or less, or as longer-term over more than 12 months. Short-term collective rewards come in two forms: profit sharing (cash or stock schemes) and gain-sharing. Profit share typically involves making bonus payments (additional to base pay) based on a formula which links bonus to profit. An alternative is the stock option, whereby profits are paid as shares in the company. Clearly, this type of scheme is only applicable to private sector organisations. It may apply to all employees, although there may be a minimum service requirement. According to WERS 2004, 30 per cent of workplaces had some employees in receipt of profit-related payments, and two thirds of schemes covered non-managerial employees – only a minority limited membership to management. One of the obvious problems with profit share is that external factors such as interest rates, bad debts and taxation can influence profitability – and these are factors outside the control of the individual.

Gain-sharing differs from profit sharing in that it seeks to share the financial benefits of any improvements in productivity performance with employees. The advantage of gain-sharing is that employees see their contribution to the total effort of the enterprise, and the research evidence suggests positive outcomes (Shields, 2007). Those external factors that can influence profits are therefore ignored and performance is likely to be more closely linked to employees' ability to affect outcomes. According to Katz and Kahn (1996), for gain-sharing to work employees must be given the opportunity to participate in the solution of production and other organisational problems, any gains must be tied to the success of the entire firm, implementation of any changes must be participative, and there must be a genuine partnership between employees and employer. Gain-sharing, however, remains a minority practice in the UK but is well established in the USA. For more detail on gain-sharing and a case study example read the article by Gardner (2011).

Employee share ownership schemes (ESOPs) are longer-term collective rewards which grew in popularity in the 1990s partly because of the tax incentives offered to make them attractive. Employees are either given shares in the company or employees purchase shares over time from their own funds or through a fund established by the company. In the UK there are four types of scheme:

- share incentive plans
- savings-related schemes (also known as Save-as-You-Earn, or SAYE)
- enterprise management schemes
- company share option plans.

According to WERS 2004 (Kersley et al, 2006), 21 per cent of workplaces had some form of employee share ownership scheme, and the most common type was SAYE (13 per cent of workplaces), followed by share incentive plans (8 per cent) and company share option plans (6 per cent). In just over three quarters of organisations (76 per cent) in which such schemes operated, all categories of staff were eligible to participate. The fundamental key difference between these type of schemes and short-term collective rewards is that employees have a stake in the ownership of the company. Because they do, it is a form of financial participation and thus a mechanism to strengthen employee commitment, loyalty and motivation. Employees should have a better understanding of the company's performance, and there is evidence that organisations in which employees have a financial stake perform better (Bryson and Freeman, 2006). In 2012, the UK Coalition Government showed support for ESOPs and launched two proposals to promote their use. The disadvantage is that employees are financially dependent on the business and more at risk if the business collapses. A widely quoted example is that of Marconi, where employees facing redundancy in 2002 found the value of their shares fall by 97 per cent over the previous 12 months. Critics also argue that the link between reward and effort is so distant that such schemes serve no real incentive value (Perkins and White, 2011). In practice, it appears that the value of shares owned by employees does not tend to be high, nor are they retained for long periods (Hyman, 2000). Research (Pendleton et al, 1998) suggests that employee commitment only increased where significant portions of equity were transferred to employees and some control over the business was transferred to employee representatives. Research on Eircom – the Republic of Ireland's former national communications company – shows mixed results on ESOPs. For example, despite the substantial employee shareholding, the majority of employees felt that their influence had actually decreased in the decade since the ESOP was first introduced in 1998 (McCarthy and Palcic, 2012).

CASE STUDY 8.8

ARE LONG-TERM INCENTIVES AN EFFECTIVE WAY OF MOTIVATING SENIOR EXECUTIVES?

The Greenbury Report published in 1995 recommended that UK companies adopt performance-related long-term incentive plans (LTIPs) for senior executives, in preference to traditional share options. According to the Report, stock options had a number of shortcomings in that they were led by windfall gains as a result of stock market movements and did not encourage directors to build significant shareholding in their employing companies. In theory, LTIPs work by aligning the interest of executives and shareholders and minimising agency risk and cost. They also aim to improve recruitment, retention and motivation of senior executives to maximise efforts and give high performance.

Since that time LTIPs have become a major component of senior executive reward systems in UK listed companies, and in 2009 LTIPs comprised around 38 per cent of total earnings of executives in the FTSE-100 companies, and 33 per cent in the FTSE-mid-250 (2010b). However, based on an empirical study of FTSE-350 senior executives, research by Pepper, Gore and Crossman (2012) concludes that LTIPs are generally not efficient or effective in meeting their objectives.

Source: Pepper, Gore and Crossman (2012)

OTHER FORMS OF RECOGNITION

Recognition awards can be a powerful motivator but are often overlooked in the literature. Typically found in service and customer-facing organisations, these awards are normally associated with rewarding above-average or outstanding performance. They are generally more affordable than, say, merit-based pay and can take the form of cash or non-cash, apply to individuals or teams, and be contained in the formal reward policy or be more informal and left to the discretion of line managers. Recognition can be as straightforward as a verbal or written 'thank you', and the key attraction is that this form of reward represents a flexible, simple, cost-effective and often immediate way to acknowledge good performance (Shields, 2007). As one respondent to CIPD research on line managers and reward (Hutchinson and Purcell, 2003) indicated: 'If someone comes down and says you are doing a good job or you handled that well, it is worth more than a good pay rise.' Recognition can also be a more personalised and exciting way to show appreciation, and fun to have. Nelson (1994) notes that 'If you can reward a person and have fun in the process, you will satisfy two important desires of most employees: to be appreciated for the work they do and to enjoy their jobs in the workplace' (Nelson, 1994: 73). This form of reward is often highly visible, and, if non-financial can be more enduring and have a 'trophy value' that serves to remind the recipient of recognition given (Shields, 2007). Non-financial awards also meet needs-based theories of motivation – in particular, Maslow's needs for social affiliation, esteem and self-actualisation, and Herzberg's 'motivators' (Chapter 3).

Financial awards normally take the form of a lump sum discretionary bonus, but non-financial recognition can take a variety of forms. Examples include (McAdams, 1999; Hutchinson and Purcell, 2007; CIPD, 2013c):

- a personal thank you or praise (verbal or written)

- retail vouchers
- tickets for activities/special events such as meals out, hotel spa accommodation/ treatments or hot-air ballooning trips
- travel – such as an all-expenses-paid trip for individuals, the family or the team
- a symbolic award such as a personal letter from the CEO, merchandise (flowers, bottle of wine, watches, iPod) or certificate, or badge
- publicity in the in-house journal
- learning and development opportunities
- time off with pay
- access to flexible working.

On the downside, however, such rewards can lack credibility, be potentially divisive by creating winners and losers, lead to claims of favouritism, and might be regarded as 'tokenism' and patronising. Arguably, they also do little to motivate the poorer performers.

REFLECTIVE ACTIVITY 8.2

Greenpeace's mission is: *We defend the natural world and promote peace by investigating, exposing and confronting environmental abuse, and championing environmentally responsible solutions* (www.greenpeace.co.uk).

1   What might be the contents of a performance-based reward package for

Greenpeace, in which volunteers are not paid?

2   What are the advantages and disadvantages of such an approach?

CONCLUSION

This chapter has covered the different forms of performance-based reward, the financial and the non-financial, addressed the motives behind the adoption of these practices and examined critiques of such practices. A complex picture emerges of how remuneration affects performance and the process involved. Decisions have to be made about what is being assessed, whose performance is being measured and how people are to be rewarded. Different approaches have different consequences, which means that organisations have to be clear about the desired outcomes of any scheme. For example, some research suggests that collective forms are less likely to have a direct motivational impact on individuals but may promote positive attitudes and behaviours such as greater commitment to the organisation, and more co-operative relationships.

On the face of it, the principle of linking reward to performance is sound. Performance-based reward has the power to motivate and meet a basic human need for achievement, and is, potentially, a fair way of treating people. Indeed, employees seem to accept the principle of rewarding performance. However, opinions are divided on the effectiveness of such schemes, and the evidence is mixed. Many of these types of schemes are founded on the belief that money is a motivator – but as we saw in Chapter 3, money is not the sole motivational force and, indeed, some believe that a focus on extrinsic contingent reward can have a negative impact on intrinsic motivation and performance. Yet on balance it seems fair to conclude that these schemes have the potential for positive outcomes, but their design and implementation are critical to acceptance and success. As Armstrong (2000) wisely comments on performance pay: 'The problem with contingent pay is not that the principle is faulty but that the practice is flawed' (Armstrong, 2000: 106). It can be hard to get right, and easy to get it wrong. What works in one environment or for one section of the workforce may not work for others. Schemes need to fit the type of work, culture, expectations and values of employees. They must be administered in a procedurally fair way, performance criteria must to be valid and applied in an objective and consistent way, and careful consideration has to be given to the reward distribution. Employees need to feel some control over their performance, and rewards should be of value to their recipients, and commensurate with the performance measured. Financial *and* non-financial rewards must be considered. Employees should be involved in the design and implementation of such schemes, which must be monitored and evaluated to ensure that they fulfil the desired objectives.

EXPLORE FURTHER

Arrowsmith, J. and Marginson, P. (2010) 'The decline of incentive pay in British manufacturing', *Industrial Relations Journal*, Vol.41, No.4: 289–311

Bryson, A., Pendleton, A. and Whitfield, K. (2009) 'The changing use of contingent pay at the modern British workplace', National Institute of Economic and Social Research Discussion Paper No.319

Bryson, A., Freeman, R., Lucifora, C., Pellizzari, M. and Perotin, V. (2012) 'Paying for performance: incentive pay schemes and employees' financial participation', Centre for Economic Performance Discussion Paper No.1112, London School of Economics

CIPD (2012) *Reward Management*. Annual Survey Report. London: CIPD

Kessler, I. and Purcell, J. (1992) 'Performance-related pay: objectives and applications', *Human Resource Management Journal*, Vol.2, No.3: 34–59

Kohn, A. (1993) 'Why incentive plans cannot work', *Harvard Business Review*, Vol. 71, No.5, Sept–Oct: 54–63

Marsden, D. (2004) 'The role of performance-related pay in renegotiating the "effort bargain": the case of the British public service', *Industrial and Labor Relations Review*, Vol.57, No.3: 350–70

Marsden, D. (2009) 'The paradox of performance-related pay systems: why do we keep adopting them in the face of evidence that they fail to motivate?', Centre for Economic Performance Discussion Paper No.946, London School of Economics

Perkins, S. and White, G. (2011) *Reward Management*. London: CIPD

Sharp, R. (2011) 'Performance-related pay: the 2011 XpertHR survey', *IRS Employment Review*, 2 September

CHAPTER 9

Managing Under-Performance

GRAEME MATHER

LEARNING OUTCOMES

By the end of the chapter you should be able to:

- understand how under-performance is conceptualised
- comment on the scope of under-performance in the UK
- critically assess the different explanations for under-performance
- explain how under-performance is managed with reference to both informal and formal techniques.

INTRODUCTION

> Once they enter the workplace, the British are among the worst idlers in the world. … We work among the lowest hours, we retire early, and our productivity is poor.

So say a group of Conservative MPs in a recent book, *Britannia Unchained* (Kwarteng *et al*, 2012: 61), which is highly critical of UK economic performance. They argue that Britain must work much harder to catch up with the more successful economies of Brazil and Canada, for example. They also express concern about the relatively poor performance of British workers, and castigate them for their poor work ethic and lack of effort. Although these views have attracted much media attention, there is nothing new here. Similar debates have been had since the onset of the Industrial Revolution. However, an examination of the empirical evidence reveals a more nuanced picture of productivity and performance. Data recently published by the Office for National Statistics (ONS) indicated that in 2011 UK output *per hour* grew faster than in Germany and the United States, but output *per worker* remained relatively flat during the same period (Office for National Statistics, 2012a: 1) Discussions on the causes of under-performance have attracted less attention. These are just as important because they enable us to move beyond the level of common sense and anecdote in order to understand why some workers under-perform, and provide us with insights into managing under-performance.

This chapter begins by suggesting critical insights into how under-performance is variously conceptualised. Definitions and the meaning of individual performance have been examined in previous chapters (Chapters 1 and 5). In this chapter under-performance is construed as dysfunctional behaviour from a management perspective, but also explained in terms of its rationality from the point of view of the worker. The scope of under-performance in the UK is then assessed with reference to the available empirical survey data. These findings reveal that line managers do not feel confident about managing under-performance, and it continues to be an enduring concern for a majority of respondents. The causes of under-performance are investigated from a variety of different perspectives, ranging from explanations based on individual difference through to structural accounts that examine under-performance in the context of capitalist political economy. Finally, the chapter explores the various techniques and underlying philosophies used to manage under-performance. These include informal techniques such as regular feedback, coaching and mentoring, and the more formal techniques associated with (in)capability and discipline. Although absence is increasingly managed in the context of under-performance, it is not discussed here because it is explored it its own right in Chapter 10.

CONCEPTUALISING UNDER-PERFORMANCE

Definitions elsewhere in this book (eg Chapter 5) variously acknowledge performance as a multi-dimensional construct comprising the two key dimensions of outputs and behaviours. Conceptualising performance in this way has clear implications for how it is measured and managed. For example, performance can be measured in terms of the average speed of responding to an enquiry in a call centre, the number of students recruited to and retained on a particular educational course, or the extent to which individual workers demonstrate which core organisational (behavioural) values inform their job performance.

Fuchs (2010) maintains that it is possible to conceptualise workplace performance in terms of organisational goal-directed behaviours that can be either task- or context-oriented. For example, task-oriented behaviour is a manifestation of those general and specific tasks relating to particular jobs or roles. Context-oriented behaviour manifests as discretionary behaviour and can be summed up by the term 'corporate citizenship'. As discussed in Chapter 1, this is the sort of behaviour we would expect to observe in the 'high-performance workplace', and is associated with the AMO model of performance (Appelbaum *et al*, 2000). Fuchs observes that behaviour directed towards achieving organisational goals is best described as functional. In other words, it has a positive purpose in ensuring the survival and sustainability of the organisation. However, as he goes on to acknowledge, worker behaviour can also be dysfunctional and negative (from the point of view of the organisation), and therefore, in such circumstances, is associated with 'counterproductive work (CPW)' and 'withdrawal work behaviour (WWB)' (Fuchs, 2010: 154).

Both CPW and WWB manifest themselves at individual, group and organisational levels. The former is argued to be behaviour which is deemed to be harmful both to employees and to the organisation as a whole (Griffin *et al*, 1998). The latter may be understood in terms of behaviours which are directed towards distancing oneself psychologically and physically from the organisation (Colquitt *et al*, 2009).

Conceptualising under-performance as dysfunctional worker behaviour provides a useful starting point for examining both the potential manifestations and possible causes of under-performance. However, by applying an alternative perspective, it becomes clear that some aspects of the same behaviour may be seen as entirely rational (or completely functional) from a worker point of view. For example, the findings of the bank wiring observation room stage of the 'Hawthorne experiments' (Mayo, 1933) revealed that workers restricted their output in response to the introduction of a piece-rate payment system. Although evidently an example of workers' 'under-performance', it was concluded that these workers appeared to be behaving in a rational and logical way to maximise their own economic interests (Roethlisberger and Dickson, 1939). Similarly, Roy (1952; 1954) and Lupton (1963) found that workers on piecework rates 'made out' by employing a variety of strategies including 'quota restrictions' and 'goldbricking' to restrict their output while still managing to earn a bonus.

REFLECTIVE ACTIVITY 9.1

Think of examples of workplace behaviour that managers may define as 'dysfunctional' but that may be defined by workers as 'rational'.

THE SCOPE OF UNDER-PERFORMANCE

Assessing the extent of under-performance in the UK is problematic for several reasons. First, there are the difficulties associated with collecting sufficient empirical data from a large enough sample of organisations to render generalisations meaningful. Second, how performance and, more importantly, under-performance is defined will determine what is measured and how measurements are taken. Third, and for the reasons already rehearsed here, instances of under-performance really depend on who is asked for the opinion. However, this has not deterred some from attempting to calculate the cost of under-performance to the UK economy. For example, *Personnel Today*'s 'Tough Love' survey (Tasker, 2006) estimated that poorly performing staff cost employers up to £32 million per year. It is worth bearing in mind that this figure was arrived at by extrapolating the responses of 800 HR professionals who reported that, on average, 16 % of their employees were under-performing.

Perhaps more important was the emphasis that the same survey placed on under-performance as an area of real concern for contemporary organisations. The survey reported that 23 respondents regarded under-performance to be a 'major problem' in their organisations, while 768 respondents felt that under-performance was an 'organisational issue'. This general picture also emerged in an IRS survey conducted in the same year (Suff, 2006) and was based on data collected on the scope of under-performance from a total of 107 organisations in both the public and private sectors employing over 142,000 workers. In this survey, 16 per cent of the respondents reported that under-performance was an issue 'to a considerable extent', and more than 74 per cent noted that under-performance was an issue 'to some extent' in their organisations. Only 8 per cent of respondents reported that, for them, under-performance was not an issue. A larger survey on managing under-performance conducted in 2011 (Suff, 2011a), and based on a sample of 165 organisations employing over 500,000 workers, revealed that 5.8 per cent of the respondents believed that under-performance was an issue 'to a considerable extent', while 81 per cent believed that under-performance was an issue 'to some extent'. Again only a minority of respondents – in this case 11.7 per cent – reported that under-performance was not an issue.

Care should be exercised when drawing comparisons between the survey data on the scope of under-performance. Taken at face value we may conclude that the severity of individual under-performance has diminished slightly in the intervening period between the surveys, but that employers increasingly regard under-performance as an issue worthy of management interventions. However, such comparisons should be tempered by the fact that we are not necessarily comparing like with like. For example, organisations may have different ways of defining and measuring under-performance, and these may change over time within individual organisations as performance management architectures are periodically reviewed and reinvented. Large-scale longitudinal surveys that take these factors into account may go some way to providing us with more valid and reliable data from which to draw comparisons.

Empirical survey data (Suff, 2006; 2009; 2011a) also provide an insight into how workplace under-performance is identified and categorised. Respondents were asked to identify the most common manifestations of individual worker under-performance in their organisations. The following list summarises their responses:

- absence
- (in)capability
- inappropriate attitudes and behaviours towards colleagues and customers
- a poor standard of work
- failing to meet objectives
- bad time-keeping
- failing to meet deadlines
- disregarding workplace norms and rules
- insubordination
- low output.

CRITICAL REFLECTION 9.1

1   What are the key challenges faced by managers in their attempts to accurately measure under-performance in the workplace?

2   What steps can be taken to provide them with the data that would assist them in this process?

Although this list provides us with an insight into how under-performance manifests itself in the workplace, it tells us little of the potential causes. Common sense or anecdotal explanations fail to identify or capture the complex interaction of variables that contribute to our understanding of under-performance. Some of these are discussed below.

EXPLAINING UNDER-PERFORMANCE AS AN 'INDIVIDUAL WORKER PROBLEM'

Reports concerning the under-performance of workers are nothing new. A reading of numerous historical accounts reveals owners and managers bewailing the fact that workers consistently under-perform in their work. For example, Josiah Wedgwood was known to have commented on the slothful nature of his workforce (in Storey, 1983). In 1901 a series of articles published in *The Times* newspaper criticised British workers for doing as little as possible for as much as possible at a time when UK industry was faced with relatively high production costs and the threat of foreign competition. Managers were reported as saying that their employees cared more about drinking and football than work (in Nichols, 1986). Similarly, Taylor (1947) concluded from his observations of US workers that without close supervision they would 'soldier' – in other words, would take it easy and do very little. Indeed, much of these analyses of workers have also been captured by a range of early motivation theories, such as McGregor's (1960) (motivation) Theory X, which characterises managers as believing that workers are inherently disinterested and lazy (see Chapter 3). However, neo-humanist explanations of motivation, including McGregor's, have been criticised for being overly simplistic, of little substance and underpinned by pseudo-scientific jargon … but which are, nevertheless, highly marketable (Watson, 1980).

Many contemporary explanations focus on the psychology of individual differences to explain how personality traits can account for workers' under-performance. Fox and Spector (1999) argue that traits such as anger and anxiety are correlated with dysfunctional behaviour (characterised by CWB and WWB), as are the traits associated with Type B personality (Chamorro-Premuzic, 2007). Personality traits may predispose one to behave in a particular way in a given situation. For example, those with high anxiety or anger personality scores may have a predisposition to act in a dysfunctional manner given a particular set of organisational/situational conditions such as a routine, repetitive or uninteresting work environment that fails to offer adequate levels of job satisfaction. Similarly, those with Type B personalities may be predisposed to exhibit relatively lower levels of commitment and loyalty and are more likely to be negligent than Type A personalities (Fuchs, 2010).

Such accounts neglect the influence of factors other than personality traits. Previous chapters have discussed some of the other individual and organisational factors that can influence performance, such as organisational climate, HR policies and practices, work practices and work relationships, age and tenure. It is also the case that effort and fatigue impact on levels of individual worker performance. Baldamus (1961: 29–30) defines effort as 'The sum total of physical and mental exertion, tedium, fatigue, or any other disagreeable aspect of work. … Effort defies rigorous definition and is certainly immeasurable.' However, as Nichols (1986) points out, effort has a psychological as well as a physiological dimension; he asserts (p44) that 'Effort … much like attitudes may prove [a] poor predictor of behaviour; [thus likewise proving to] be a poor predictor of productivity and performance.'

TRUST, MOTIVATION AND COMMITMENT

Chapter 1 drew out some of the links between various concepts such as the psychological contract, trust, motivation, employee commitment and employee performance. Some accounts (Heavey et al, 2011; Gould-Williams and Davis, 2005; Guest and Conway, 2002) suggest that high levels of employee performance are predicated on high levels of trust and motivation, which are both inextricably linked to levels of employee commitment. Where trust, motivation and commitment are weak we might expect to see dysfunctional behaviour that delivers low levels of performance. Theories of motivation and the psychological contract are dealt with elsewhere (see Chapters 1 and 3), so for the purposes of this chapter we concentrate on the relationship between motivation, trust and commitment, and the implications this relationship has for performance and under-performance.

A review of the literature demonstrates a clear link between trust and commitment (Achrol, 1991; Morgan and Hunt, 1994). Moreover, Heavey et al (2011) found a strong positive correlation between the two, and together they appear to contribute to organisational 'efficiency, effectiveness and productivity' (Morgan and Hunt, 1994: 22). In Chapter 1 commitment is defined as 'the relative strength of an individual's identification with and involvement in an organisation' (Mowday et al, 1979: 226). Although multifaceted, the general consensus is that commitment can be understood in terms of identifying with the vision and goals of the organisation, discretionary effort and a willingness to remain in the organisation (Porter et al, 1974).

Trust is also a multifaceted concept. However, those investigating the nature of trust rather than identifying its antecedents have identified two broad components – namely, cognitive and emotional (Young and Daniel, 2003). The cognitive component of trust is characterised by rational, calculating, co-operative decision-making and was identified by Deutsch (1958) in a series of experiments based on the prisoner's dilemma scenario. The emotional component has been described variously as vulnerability (Kramer, 1999), acceptance (Bonoma, 1976), respect (Jackson, 1985) and security (Zand, 1978).

In the context of the workplace, trust manifests itself at both an interpersonal and an organisational level. At an interpersonal level, trust is conceptualised as an attitude (Skinner and Searle, 2011) and as such comprises the following components:

- affective (a set of feelings and beliefs)
- cognitive (the knowledge we have of the object of the attitude)
- behavioural (overt behaviour, which in the context of the workplace includes performance or under-performance).

The affective and cognitive components are shaped in part by the attributions we vicariously make of the actions of those in whom we place our trust (Whitener *et al*, 1998). The behavioural component is the external manifestation of one's attitudes and beliefs, and this is tempered by situational constraints. In other words, depending on the attributions made, we may develop a set of internal beliefs and schemata equating to trust that are demonstrated in our workplace behaviour. We may, however, mistrust the actions of others and demonstrate this either overtly or mask our behaviour if it is expedient to do so.

Similarly, interpersonal trustworthiness is based on our attributions of others and, according to Mayer *et al* (1995), comprises the following three components:

- ability (attributions made about skill and competence)
- benevolence (attributions made about the motives of others to act in a way that benefits us)
- integrity (attributions about principled behaviour).

Thus, in the context of the workplace, the extent to which trust develops depends on the perceptions and attributions that are made about the behaviour of those in whom we wish to place our trust. This will be between worker and manager, between tiers of management, and between workers. Mistrust leads to low levels of motivation and commitment (Carnevale and Wechsler, 1992). Empirical evidence on trust between managers and workers based on the WERS 2004 findings (Kersley *et al*, 2006) presents a mixed picture. Trust was measured on three dimensions:

- the extent to which managers or worker representatives honoured commitments made
- the extent to which each genuinely tried to understand the other's perspective
- the extent to which each acted with honesty and integrity.

Levels of mutual trust were lower in the context of a unionised workplace environment, 31 per cent of respondents reporting that mutual trust existed, 13 per cent of trade union representatives reporting that they trusted the management, and 31 per cent of managers reporting that they trusted trade union representatives. In the context of non-union environments, 64 per cent of respondents reported that mutual trust existed, 17 per cent of employee representatives reported that they trusted the management, and 12 per cent of managers reported that they trusted the employee representatives. More recent empirical evidence revealed that only 50 per cent of respondents reported mutual trust between themselves and their line manager, while 10 per cent reported that they had no trust in their line manager and that their line manager had no trust in them (Worrall and Cooper, 2012). These findings do not appear to represent the type of 'high-trust' working relationships that are argued to underpin high levels of performance, and indeed the concept of the high-performance work environment (Appelbaum *et al*, 2000).

Aside from working relationships, trust can also be conceptualised in systems terms. 'Systems trust' is a term used to describe how organisational structures and systems – including policies, procedures, strategic vision and goals – shape trust between the individual worker and the organisation (Skinner and Searle, 2011). In this context, trust is presented as a form of social exchange characterised by the organisation valuing and caring for its employees (Eisenberger *et al*, 1990) and employees' reciprocating by developing positive attitudes towards, and commitment to, the organisation (Aryee *et al*, 2002). The key point with regard to under-performance is the espoused link between trust, motivation and worker performance. Individuals are more likely to believe the organisation to be trustworthy if they perceive clear and unambiguous links between organisational systems and structure and organisational behaviour. In other words, trust between the individual and the organisation is more likely to develop when employees' expectations of being managed fairly and consistently are met and are embedded in organisational behaviour. This has obvious implications for the design, management and perceived legitimacy of an organisation's formal performance management scheme.

Closely related to the concept of trust are employees' perceptions of fairness and organisational justice (Chapter 3), which have clear implications for performance and under-performance. Perceptions of managerial fairness, for example, can be correlated with job satisfaction, commitment and decisions to remain or leave the organisation (Tekleab *et al*, 2005). Similarly, Jawahar (2007) maintains that employees' perceptions of fairness in the context of performance appraisals in general, and appraiser feedback in particular, shape attitudes towards the credibility and value of appraisal. Moreover, as Lawler (1994) points out, the perceived fairness of appraisal can impact either positively or negatively on employee motivation and attitudes held about the organisation. How justice is judged in such circumstances is variable. As outlined in Chapter 3, distinctions have been made between 'distributive justice' (Greenberg, 1988), 'procedural justice' (Thibaut and Walker, 1975) and 'interactional justice' (Bies and Moag, 1986). In the context of managing under-performance, Jawahar (2007: 738) says:

> [The] literature has clearly established that people care about fairness of their outcomes (distributive justice), the procedures to which they are subjected (procedural justice) and fairness of the interpersonal treatment and communication that they receive (interactional justice).

Thus far we have examined trust at an interpersonal level, at the level of the organisation and as a form of social exchange. By examining it in the context of the employment relationship, characterised here as a form of economic exchange, further insights into the nature of trust, or lack of trust, are obtainable. Viewed in this way, we see that trust is tempered by workplace power relations, job regulation, the amount of discretion afforded to workers and the dialectics of control and resistance (Fox, 1974). Further insights are to be had by examining the development of trust *between* workers, expressed in terms of solidarity and collectivism, which represents a challenge to the managerial prerogative (Mather, 2011).

We can now sum up the relationship between trust, commitment, motivation and performance. Trust is an antecedent to organisational commitment, so we can expect low commitment in the context of low trust and the converse in the context of high trust. Trust is associated with motivation and motivation is a key factor in performance. So, as Heavey *et al* (2011) posit, trust must also be a key determinant of performance. Thus we can speculate that in the context of a low-commitment, low-trust organisational environment we might expect to find low levels of motivation and poor or under-performance.

 CRITICAL REFLECTION 9.2

What steps can line managers take to build trust between themselves and those who they manage?

By viewing under-performance as a structural, rather than an individual, phenomenon it can be understood as part of a wider set of unwanted or undesired labour problems that are 'generated by the defects and maladjustments in the employment relationship' (Kaufman, 1993: 5). These can manifest themselves *inter alia* in collective worker resistance to technological change and job restructuring (Cutler, 1992) and relatively low production levels and job insecurity (Kaufman, 1993). The general 'labour problem' has been cast as a power struggle for control over production between the forces of capital and of labour (Kaufman, 1993). This concept challenges the basic tenets of *laissez-faire* capitalism that are underpinned by classic economic theory. To put it simply, we should not assume that the interests of employees and employers coalesce in the context of a free market economy. Although workers are 'free' to sell their labour power in the marketplace and employers are free to buy it, the relationship between the two parties is characterised by a power imbalance biased towards employers. As Kahn-Freund (cited in Wedderburn, 1986: 5) reminds us, in its inception

> it is an act of submission; in its operation it is a condition of subordination, however much the subordination may be concealed.

The cash nexus between employers and employees is complex. What employers actually buy is the capacity to labour and not actual labour. Employers are therefore tasked with extracting value from labour. To achieve this, labour has to be managed at the point of production to ensure that the capacity to work is translated into actual work. However, as Cressey and Macinnes (1980: 14) point out:

> capital must surrender the means of production to the control of the worker for their actual use in the production process ... the workers themselves actually control the detail of the performance of their tasks ... it is precisely because capital must surrender the use of its means of production that capital must to some degree seek a co-operative relationship with it.

The relationship between capital and labour is explored in more detail in the context of the employment contract by Edwards (1986). He maintains that the vagaries of the employment contract in determining how much effort is required, combined with management strategies intended to realise worker performance, provide the context to an employment relationship between manager and employee that is both contradictory and antagonistic. He argues that it is contradictory in the sense that managers pursue the twin objectives of job control and promoting worker creativity, and antagonistic in the sense that managers deploy labour power in ways that maximise the extraction of value from it. Empirical evidence to support this assertion is found in Danford *et al*'s (2004) study of high-performance workplaces. For example, they found that team work was organised to maximise 'labour utilisation' rather than 'employee empowerment'.

The relationship between capital and labour is characterised not only by a cash nexus but in political and ideological terms as well. For example, successive UK governments have to varying degrees accommodated or opposed the demands of collective labour. The Conservative Government of the 1980s attempted to resolve the labour problem by weakening the collective power of labour and promoting managements' right to manage. Cutler (1992: 162) explains:

> Thus, a plethora of legislative measures restricted the powers of trade unions and narrowed the scope of individual employment rights. Further, at least the tolerance of mass unemployment was seen as having the effect of helping management to

assert its prerogatives: to ... control the allocation of labour and demand a more 'reasonable' level of effort.

What we see here is a raft of political initiatives designed to legitimise management's right to manage worker effort or performance, and implicit within this is the right to manage under-performance. The efficacy of the managerial prerogative depends on the extent to which it is perceived as legitimate by those to whom it is directed. Legitimacy may be achieved through direct action or oppression, as was the case in the early stages of the Industrial Revolution where factory supervisors would physically punish relatively minor misdoings (Storey, 1983). However, as Rousseau (1947) asserts, we are more likely to accept the legitimacy of authority if we feel a sense of commitment rather than coercion. This returns us to the logics and the allure of employee commitment and high-trust working relations already discussed in this chapter. Attempts to transform coercion into commitment in the context of the employment relationship are underpinned by an ideological assimilation of the managerial prerogative that is buttressed by a persuasive management discourse. This means that employees are exposed to a set of ideas and beliefs that are designed to legitimise the managerial prerogative. Management ideology can thus be seen as 'all ideas which are espoused by, or for, those who exercise authority ... and which seek to explain and justify that authority' (Bendix, 1956: 2). And as 'a set of beliefs which management seeks to propagate in order to inspire acceptance and approval of managerial autonomy by the general public and by specific groups of workers' (McGivering et al, 1969: 91).

However, the extent to which workers assimilate management ideology depends on how well management discourse is received and accommodated. Acceptance or resistance depends largely on the collective or individual mind-set or perspective of the workers. For example, they are more likely to accept the legitimacy of management ideology in the context of a highly developed sense of moral obligation to the overarching rules and regulations that govern the workplace employment relationship, or 'social organisation', as Fox (1985) terms it. A low level of moral obligation or involvement is characterised by indifference and a lack of commitment to the organisation. Thus, as Fox (1985: 13–14) points out:

> At one extreme [they will] work indifferently, regulate their own behaviour in ways which obstruct management purposes, quietly subvert authority or openly challenge it ... At the other extreme, their responses may be such as to prompt them to work keenly and conscientiously, offer willing co-operation with management's leadership [and] submit readily to its command ...

Clearly, there are some useful insights here into explanations of performance and under-performance that acknowledge the role of different perspectives on the employment relationship. Both management and employee expectations of commitment, effort and acceptable levels of performance are shaped by perspectives held either collectively or individually.

The beliefs and values of management ideology are summarised by the unitary perspective. As the term implies, there is only once source of legitimate authority: the management prerogative, or 'right to manage'. The team 'analogy' is often used to describe the management–employee relationship, with its emphasis on common goals and a shared vision of how to achieve them. The 'team coach' is often on hand to motivate team players to achieve their corporate aspirations. This sense of shared corporate identity is reinforced by labelling employees as 'partners' or 'colleagues', buttressed by claims that these employees are the organisation's most valuable asset. From this perspective managers are seen as a source of inspirational leadership, 'promoting harmony of purpose ... building up loyalty and *esprit de corps*' (Fox, 1966: 370). More importantly, the assumption is that managers are accepted by the employees as the legitimate decision-makers within an organisation, based on the view that all will benefit from the decisions made.

If this is the case, we would expect employees to accept the legitimacy of managerial definitions of performance and under-performance, and to acknowledge the legitimacy of the various interventions designed to manage individual under-performance. From the unitary perspective, logically, we must conclude that under-performance is attributable to individual rather than the structural causes associated with the contested nature of the employment relationship (discussed earlier in this chapter). If managers and employees share the same values and beliefs about how best to manage the employment relationship, there is no basis for contestation and therefore no conflict between the two parties. As was also highlighted earlier in the chapter, there are clear differences between employer and employee expectations of what constitutes 'good' performance. Elsewhere in this book we also note that absenteeism is problematic and there remain manifestations of individual and collective conflict in UK employee relations (Kersley *et al*, 2006). The evidence therefore suggests that workplace conflict clearly does exist and must be managed.

Prescriptions for how best to resolve such conflict depend upon the prevailing perspective. From a unitary perspective, conflict is largely regarded as arising from an incongruity between employee and organisational values, thus placing the problem firmly on the shoulders of the individual employee. In such circumstances, conflict resolution is initially predicated on more effective communication, but it may also result in worker discipline and dismissal. Fox (1966) questions the validity of the unitary perspective when arguing that it simply does not represent the lived reality of the workplace. He argues that the workplace represents a microcosm of society and is characterised by competing interest groups with some evidence of shared decision-making. These ideas are summed up by the pluralist perspective, defined by Fox (1985: 26) as 'a coalition of interest groups presided over by a top management which serves the long-term needs of the organisation as a whole …'.

The pluralist perspective acknowledges the inevitability of workplace conflict as each interest group pursues its particular workplace agenda. From this perspective, conflict is best managed by joint decision-making. Historically, in the UK this has been achieved through the mechanism of collective bargaining. The implication here is that employees have a legitimate right to workplace decision-making, either indirectly via trade unions or directly via works councils, for example. Such mechanisms represent a challenge to the management prerogative, and may be resisted by managers, depending on how they perceive the relative strength of labour. Managers are thus more likely to engage with mechanisms which allow worker participation when (Newton and Findlay, 1996: 46):

> they are facing significant challenges, when organised labour has considerable bargaining power or when the costs of, or limitations to, more overt control methods are felt to be prohibitive.

Although the management prerogative is weakened in such circumstances, employees are more likely to accept and commit to terms and conditions when the outcomes are based on a set of negotiated voluntary agreements. The implications for managing performance and under-performance are clear. Where policies and procedures have been jointly agreed and voluntarily accepted, employees are likely to have a stronger obligation to them than if they had been unilaterally imposed.

The radical perspective focuses on the power imbalance between capital and labour and has been discussed elsewhere in this chapter in the context of the labour problem and the contested nature of the employment relationship. Fox (1985) argues that from this perspective employees are relatively powerless, and are encouraged to accept the legitimacy of the managerial prerogative. However, he maintains (Fox, 1985: 34) that:

their subordinate and inferior position precludes them from participating in [the organisation] with enthusiasm and commitment ... Cynicism and distrust of 'them' [management] may not be far below the surface.

From a radical perspective, performance management is viewed in the context of the asymmetrical nature of workplace power relationships (see also Chapter 6). Thus the strategies designed to manage under-performance reinforce the managerial prerogative and are buttressed by a persuasive management discourse emphasising that the individual employee must take ownership of, and be responsible for, his or her own performance. Performance surveillance techniques (Newton and Findlay, 1996; Ball, 2003) provide managers with constant feedback that is then used to make decisions about whether to reward or punish individual employees. In this context, managers may secure employee compliance, but they are unlikely to cultivate employee engagement with the performance management process.

REFLECTIVE ACTIVITY 9.2

Use the perspectives outlined above to explain why some employees consistently under-perform in their work.

MANAGING UNDER-PERFORMANCE

The techniques used to manage under-performance are generally based on either of two broad sets of assumptions – namely, that individuals do not possess the skills and abilities to perform to an acceptable level, or that they are unwilling to do so.

Looking at some of the early attempts to manage workplace performance, including those based on 'scientific management' (Taylor, 1947) and the human relations school (Mayo, 1933), we can see that the commonly held belief was that employees inherently under-performed. There was thus a need to devise management interventions aimed at motivating employees to work more efficiently and to be more productive.

Taylor (1947) maintained that worker efficiency and high productivity levels could be achieved only by applying the principles of scientific management (see Chapter 3). The role of management was to discover the 'one best way' to do the job and to recruit the most suitable workers to perform the task. The successful application of scientific management depended on the ability of managers to acquire a thorough knowledge of the job through a systematic study of its constituent parts, so, as Taylor noted (pp51–2):

Under scientific management absolutely every element ... becomes the subject of exact, precise, scientific investigation and knowledge to replace the old 'I guess so'. Every motion, every small fact, becomes the subject of careful, scientific investigation.

Managers thus become responsible for work planning (task conception) and employees have no role other than to follow precisely the instructions given to them (task execution). Maximum productivity and efficiency (good performance) are maintained through incentivised pay schemes to overcome worker resistance to the scientific management's integral elements of close supervision and the monotonous nature of such work.

Similarly, the human relations school was concerned with managing under-performance. The Hawthorne Studies appeared to demonstrate that work-group norms functioned to restrict output (Mayo, 1933). Mayo's interpretation was that workers act in non-logical or irrational ways in their response to workplace situations, whereas managers respond logically. He therefore stressed the importance of leadership, particularly at the level of supervisor (or first level of management) in motivating workers to perform. The role of managers in motivating workers to perform more effectively and efficiently is explored more fully in the neo-human relations literature. Motivation, as discussed in Chapter 3, is an elusive concept, compounded by the fact that it 'is tremendously complex, and what is unravelled with any degree of assurance is small indeed' (Herzberg, 1987: 109).

However, as explained in Chapter 3, it comprises three components: direction (what an individual attempts to achieve), effort (how hard he or she tries), and persistence (the amount of time spent trying). An interesting point here in the context of managing under-performance is the extent to which we would allow individual discretion in direction, effort and persistence, or the extent to which these components should be managed.

Elements of scientific management, human relations and neo-human relations traditions represent some of the key antecedents to HRM. HRM practice is broadly classified as either 'hard' or 'soft' (Storey, 1989). These practices have clear implications for the management of under-performance. For example, the hard approach 'emphasises the quantitative, calculative, and business strategic aspects of managing headcount resource in a rational way as for any other economic factor' (Legge, 1995: 66). Such an approach places an emphasis on minimising unit labour costs through procedural rule-based mechanisms of worker control (Gould-Williams and Davies, 2005). This inevitably leads to formal approaches to managing under-performance, including the use of capability and disciplinary procedures. Soft HRM practices, on the other hand, employ strategies to secure worker engagement and commitment through the rhetoric of trust, empowerment and a shared vision (Legge, 1995). A premium is then placed on training and developing employees, and on teamworking to maximise creative potential. Following the logic of this general approach, under-performance is managed by (re)communicating organisational expectations, combined with developmental interventions which are underpinned by coaching and mentoring.

Chapter 4 reviewed the literature which suggests that HRM responsibilities have increasingly been devolved to line managers, and that line managers face considerable constraint in discharging their HRM responsibilities, which can impact negatively on employee performance. The empirical evidence suggests that line managers feel less confident in managing under-performance (Jones and Saundry, 2012). For example, an IRS survey (Suff, 2006) revealed that nearly 69 per cent of respondents disagreed with the statement that 'Managers in the organisation are confident and competent in managing under-performance'. The findings also reveal that although managers are often trained in

- appraisal skills
- general management abilities
- handling capability and discipline
- interviewing skills
- performance management procedures,

they are less well versed in the 'softer 'skills of

- training and coaching
- conflict management
- managing 'difficult conversations'
- negotiating.

More recent empirical evidence (Suff, 2011) provides an insight into the most and least effective strategies that are used to manage under-performance. Respondents were asked for their opinion on the efficacy of the techniques used to manage under-performance in their organisations. The findings are summarised in Table 9.1.

Table 9.1 The efficacy of techniques used to manage performance

Technique	% of employers who believed the technique	
	was effective/was productive	was not effective/was counterproductive
Regular informal feedback and guidance	99	1
Formal performance reviews	95	5
Employee development and training	98	2
Maintaining employee motivation	87	13
Capability procedure	89	11
Disciplinary procedure	84	16
Coaching	95	5
Soft skills performance indicators/measures	85	15
Counselling	82	18
Financial performance indicators/measures	64	36
Employee assistance programme	59	41

Source: adapted from Suff (2011a)

Care must be taken when analysing these responses, because we have no way of knowing how each organisation conceptualises and measures 'effectiveness', nor can we assume that each technique is applied consistently within or between the organisations sampled. Moreover, some techniques may be more effective than others, depending on individual employee predispositions. For example, informal approaches may work better for those who demonstrate commitment than for those who withdraw either psychologically or physically from the organisation. To summarise: the data provides an insight into employers' perceptions of what they believe works best for managing under-performance in their organisations.

INFORMAL TECHNIQUES FOR MANAGING UNDER-PERFORMANCE

The evidence suggests that one of the most effective informal ways to manage under-performance relies on line managers' providing regular, informal feedback to employees. For this approach to work effectively, managers must be able to assimilate evidence about employee performance from a variety of sources on an on-going basis. The basic premise is that this acts to alert line managers to the early stages of any under-performance and thereby enables them to adopt a more proactive approach, so that employees can be 'steered' towards acceptable levels of performance (see Case Study 9.1 below). It also requires that line managers are adept in using the so-called 'soft skills' in their interactions with employees – already identified in this and other chapters as being an area in which line managers often feel less well-versed. Moreover, the preparatory work needed to give on-going feedback can be time-consuming, and other pressing demands associated with the role of line management may take priority (Hutchinson and Purcell, 2010; Marchington and Wilkinson, 2012). These demands on line managers are also underlined in a recent large-scale survey of UK managers (Worrall and Cooper, 2012). The same survey also reported that only 42 per cent of employees received regular feedback on their performance, compared to 45 per cent in 2009. This would suggest that arguably one of the most effective informal ways of managing under-performance is being squeezed out by the demands of the line manager role itself.

INFORMA

Informa is a global concern providing specialist information and services for a variety of businesses. Its UK operation employs around 4,000 staff. In 2005 a new performance management scheme was implemented, largely in response to staff feedback which criticised the perceived lack of career development.

The new scheme was designed to give employees much more responsibility for assessing their own performance and development needs. In addition, they were also given the responsibility for setting their own targets mapped against overall business goals.

Informa takes a proactive approach to managing under-performance. The performance of employees new to the organisation is closely monitored and reviewed over a six-month probationary period. If employees fail to meet Informa's performance expectations by the end of the probationary period, their contact is terminated. For established employees under-performance is dealt with informally by the line manager as soon as it arises. This is done by reviewing current objectives and setting new ones that are then closely monitored. If there is insufficient improvement within a specified time-frame, formal procedures are instigated. Employees are given further opportunities to improve; however, if they continue to under-perform, they face dismissal after a series of written warnings.

Source: IDS (2007) *Performance Management*. HR Study 839: 27–31

Of growing importance are those techniques for managing under-performance that focus on facilitating individual employee skill, knowledge, attitudes and development. These are often used in the context of coaching and mentoring (see also Chapter 7). According to Aguinis (2009: 227–8):

> Coaching involves directing, motivating and rewarding employee behaviour … It is a day-to-day function that involves observing performance, complimenting good work, and helping to correct and improve any performance that does not meet expectations and standards.

Moreover, it aims to facilitate an organisational culture which is accepted by employees, and which enables managers not only to genuinely inspire individual employee performance, but to manage under-performance with interventions designed to develop appropriate skills, abilities and attitudes (Suff, 2009). Coaching can take many forms. For example, Armstrong (2009) asserts that it is based on a set of interpersonal interactions that utilise 'enabling' rather than didactic learning strategies, which provide feedback on progress and which draw on experience to provide learning opportunities. Aguinis (2007) identifies four general principles for successful coaching outcomes:

- establishing and maintaining a trusting relationship (key elements include active listening skills, empathy, compassion and a collaborative rather than top-down approach to coaching)
- acknowledging that change is driven by the individual (based on the premise that change comes from within and is the responsibility of the individual)
- adopting an ideographic approach to understanding individual differences (an acceptance that the individual is unique and that there are qualitative differences

between people, rather than an assumption that differences exist as a matter of degree conceptualised by the nomothetic approach to understanding individual differences)

- the coach is to facilitate change but does not control the learning process (the coach will guide the individual towards meeting developmental goals).

Clearly, successful coaching interventions will rely heavily on the skills, attributes and qualities of the coach. Those who aspire to the role must therefore have a clear understanding of, and a genuine commitment to, the principles set out above. Organisations that are committed to coaching employees invest in the training of managers to equip them with both theoretical and practical coaching skills. The Britannia Group, for example, requires its in-house coaches to have gained the Institute of Leadership and Management (ILM) Level 7 Certificate in Executive Coaching and Mentoring as a prerequisite to coaching employees (IDS, 2009b: 6).

Empirical evidence reveals that coaching is increasingly used to manage under-performance. For example, a recent CIPD survey (2011d) reported that 43 per cent of respondents used coaching to address under-performance, compared to 20 per cent in 2009. The findings also illustrated the dual role played by coaching, noting that 48 per cent of respondents used it as a technique to build on good performance, compared to 20 per cent in 2009.

The terms 'coaching' and 'mentoring' are often used synonymously. Indeed, some organisations do not distinguish between the two (Suff, 2009). Although coaching and mentoring skills may be similar, the two interventions have different purposes. In the context of managing under-performance, mentoring is a proactive intervention underpinned by a more informal long-term relationship between mentor and mentee. As Armstrong (2009) points out, coaching complements the acquisition and development of the skills, abilities and behaviours necessary to perform at an acceptable level. The mentoring relationship is, therefore, qualitatively different, in that a more experienced member of the organisation will support a new or less experienced employee through the socialisation processes involved in meeting the challenges of promotion, or those faced by an individual who is new to the organisation.

Although coaching and mentoring are relatively cost-effective interventions for managing under-performance, the measurement of their success is more problematic. Some organisations are unable to undertake any formal assessment of such interventions owing to the confidential nature of the coaching relationship. However, we may be able to infer the benefits of coaching and mentoring by measuring staff attitudes and commitment (Suff, 2009). Formal measures taken usually rely on reports written by coaches detailing what they have achieved (Suff, 2009).

A key factor in the success of coaching and mentoring interventions is how well the coach or mentor performs his or her role. To effect qualitative changes in skills, ability, knowledge and behaviour, mentors must act with integrity, trust and benevolence. Moreover, these characteristics should be reflected in the way managers go about the business of coaching and mentoring. A recent survey of managers reported that 52 per cent of junior managers thought that the overall management style in their organisations was bureaucratic, and only 10 per cent believed it to be empowering (Worrall and Cooper, 2012). These findings are hardly conducive to successful enabling cultures associated with coaching and mentoring initiatives. Moreover, when managers were asked who should be responsible for employee wellbeing, 63 per cent agreed that HR should take responsibility and 33 per cent agreed that it should be the responsibility of individual employees. Although care should be taken in generalising these findings, they do highlight some potential barriers to successful coaching and mentoring interventions, particularly when these activities are conducted by line managers.

CRITICAL REFLECTION 9.3

What are the challenges faced by line managers when they use informal techniques to address under-performance? You may find it useful to revisit Chapter 4, which discusses the role of line managers in more depth.

FORMAL TECHNIQUES FOR MANAGING UNDER-PERFORMANCE

Formal techniques for managing under-performance rely on the use of specific policies designed to manage employee (in)capability or absence, or to discipline behaviour defined as unacceptable by the organisation. It is generally regarded as best practice to address under-performance in the first instance with informal interventions buttressed by line manager feedback. This can include having 'the difficult conversation' with an under-performing employee (ACAS, 2010). Formal measures are employed to manage under-performance if the employee fails to respond adequately to the informal interventions. Policies on managing (in)capability and discipline may stipulate the use of informal measures to address under-performance before formal steps are taken to address the problem.

A key difference between informal and formal measures is that the latter must operate within legal guidelines on (in)capability, disability and unfair dismissal, and be undertaken mindful of employees' recourse to representation, in-house grievance procedures and employment tribunals (ACAS, 2010). They are reactive rather than proactive interventions to manage under-performance. In other words, they are designed to correct under-performance once it has occurred, rather than attempts to ensure that it does not occur.

MANAGING UNDER-PERFORMANCE USING CAPABILITY PROCEDURES

A broad spectrum of measures is taken into consideration when managing under-performance using capability procedures (procedures intended to deal with an employee's apparent incapability), including:

- skill
- aptitude
- ability
- competence
- knowledge
- attitudes
- behaviour.

In assessing the causes of under-performance in the context of capability procedures, care must be taken to ensure that issues related to disability or absence due to long-term illness are dealt with using alternative policies and procedures. The underlying logic of the approach is that efforts should be made to enable the employee to reach an acceptable level of performance, supported by individual performance improvement plans, and supported by the informal techniques already discussed. If these interventions fail to deliver the required performance improvements within agreed time-scales, formal capability measures usually follow.

In the context of formal capability procedures, performance concerns will be discussed and an opportunity be afforded the individual to give an account of why he or she is under-performing. If concerns still remain, a written warning may be issued detailing the performance improvements required, including the steps needed to achieve them within a specified time-scale (see Case Study 9.2 below). If the individual continues to under-perform, he or she may receive a final written warning, reiterating what needs to be done to improve within a given time-scale. If at the end of the period no further improvement is evidenced, the decision can be taken to dismiss the employee on the grounds of lack of capability. The procedure must be seen to be fair and transparent, and should include provisions for employees to be accompanied at formal meetings and they should have the right to appeal against decisions made against them (ACAS, 2009b).

 ANGLIAN WATER

CASE STUDY 9.2

Anglian Water has around 6 million customers and employs nearly 3,500 employees. A new performance management scheme was developed in 2005. The project was led by the 'People Performance team', who regularly met with a steering group made up of 'influential people from each business unit … that were truly representative of their business area' (IDS, 2007: 20). The new scheme was designed to clarify expectations of job roles, provide more accurate guidance on setting objectives and on how they could be achieved, place more emphasis on employee development, and give line managers more discretion over rewarding individual performance.

The company acknowledged the important role line managers play in managing performance. With this in mind, line managers were given training in all aspects of the new performance management scheme. The training programmes included techniques that could be used to manage under-performance, such as giving constructive feedback, having 'difficult conversations' with employees, and coaching.

In terms of how individual performance is rated at the end of each performance cycle, the company uses the following scale:

● Does not meet expectations
● Almost meets expectations
● Meets expectations
● Exceeds expectations.

Employees who are rated as almost meeting or failing to meet expectations are identified as under-performing in their job. As such they are subject to the company's formal capability procedures. Initially, they are given support by their line manager who will coach them to meet new targets set out in a performance improvement plan. If employees fail to make satisfactory progress in their performance within a set deadline, the formal capability procedure is instigated. This is designed to manage specific aspects of under-performance – namely, deficiencies in:

● knowledge
● skill
● ability.

The company manages (in)capability using three formal stages:

Stage one – A formal meeting is convened to discuss performance concerns. The employee may be given the opportunity to follow an additional improvement plan, reasonable adjustments to the job may be made, retraining or redeployment may be recommended. Alternatively, the employee may be dismissed at this stage.

Stage two – The alternatives to dismissal are reviewed at this stage with a set time-scale for improvement.

Stage three – A formal meeting is convened if there is insufficient evidence of performance improvement.

The employee can be dismissed at this stage. Employees have the right to appeal against this decision.

Under-performance on the grounds of 'unacceptable behaviour' or 'lack of effort' is dealt with formally using the company's disciplinary procedure.

Source: IDS (2007) *Performance Management*. HR Study 839: 20–6

MANAGING UNDER-PERFORMANCE USING DISCIPLINARY PROCEDURES

Discipline represents an alternative way of managing under-performance. Although the procedures used are similar to those of capability, in that informal means are exhausted before formal disciplinary measures are invoked, the scope of disciplinary procedures is much broader, covering many aspects of employee conduct. This is reflected in some key differences, including evidence-gathering, possible suspension from duties, and a formal disciplinary hearing (ACAS, 2009b). According to the CIPD (2012h), the disciplinary procedure functions to:

- communicate the organisation's expectations of acceptable standards of performance and conduct, and the consequences of failing to meet these
- reveal the potential barriers to acceptable levels of performance and conduct, and direct employees accordingly
- enable employees to improve levels of performance or conduct using agreed time-bound improvement plans
- redress issues of performance and conduct without recourse to employment tribunals.

If we examine the nature of workplace discipline more closely, we see that it may be used to buttress the management prerogative through the enforcement of rules and procedures. As Harbison and Myers (1959: 47–8) point out:

> The logic of industrialisation impels the employer to covet the role of rule-maker ... [It] requires that workers take orders from management. The prerogative of management is to prescribe duties, assign tasks and get satisfactory performance. To do this it must maintain discipline.

For discipline to be effective, employees should accept or even internalise the rules and procedures. As Clancy and Seifert (2000) point out, workplace rules can be either unilaterally imposed or jointly agreed by the process of collective bargaining. Viewing the unilateral imposition of rules through a critical lens, and noting the problems associated with unilateral rule imposition already discussed in this chapter, we observe that it may afford managers with further opportunities to control performance and conduct. As Storey (1983: 129) asserts:

> the essential point to note about discipline relates to the strategic attempts socially to construct a dominant definition of reality whereby acts of challenge, recalcitrance and resistance routinely attract a label of culpable transgression. Managers as agents ... mandated to define and treat individual acts of deviance are thereby put in possession of a potentially potent control device.

From this perspective discipline is seen as a social construct. Within this context, behaviour that transcends workplace disciplinary rules is defined as deviant or maladjusted by those with the power to do so. If an employee is labelled 'deviant', 'troublemaker', 'a member of the awkward squad', or other soubriquets, his or her subsequent behaviour may be viewed through the same lens, and with potentially damaging consequences for the employee.

Historically, workplace discipline was used in a punitive way. Harsh arbitrary penalties including beatings, fines and instant dismissal were commonplace in nineteenth-century factories. Gradually, more enlightened approaches to discipline were introduced, based on corrective measures and underpinned by notions of education and reform. Discipline now had a moral dimension and was seen as a vehicle for transmitting middle-class moral values to the working classes (Storey, 1983). Thus the values of hard work, obeying the orders of those in authority and an acceptance of the legitimacy of rules and regulations were embedded within workplace discipline. Best employment practice favours the corrective approach (Edwards and Whitston, 1994), but punitive measures are commonly used (Rollinson *et al*, 1997). Distinguishing between the two is problematic, not least because each term is open to interpretation and each may be used to a greater or lesser extent, depending on management assumptions about the potential causes of under-performance and unacceptable conduct. If we place the underpinning philosophies of each approach on a continuum, with retribution at one end, rehabilitation at the other and deterrence at the centre, we see that punitive approaches are influenced by notions of guilt and sanctions, whereas the correctional approach is characterised by training, development and precise communication of what the employee needs to do. This returns us to the benefits of informal approaches to managing under-performance already rehearsed in this chapter. Deterrence acts as a warning to all of the consequences of failing to meet acceptable levels of conduct or performance. Both the punitive and correctional approaches to discipline inevitably involve sanctions. How they are applied differentiates the two approaches (Rollinson *et al*, 1997).

Although it is beyond the scope of this chapter to discuss the UK legal framework applying to the management of under-performance, it is worth noting that some recent developments have brought the issue of under-performance into sharp focus. For example, the current Coalition Government has implemented some of the recommendations of the Beecroft Report (2011), including the extension from one to two years in the qualifying period for unfair dismissal.

In his report, Beecroft further recommended (p4) that the grounds for unfair dismissal (for reasons other than discrimination) should be amended to allow employers to dismiss employees:

> if the employer simply states that he [*sic*] is not happy with the employee's performance and then consults, gives notice and pays a defined level of compensation.

Although the Coalition Government has not implemented this particular recommendation, it has signalled to employers that, 'As long as you act fairly and reasonably ... you are entitled to ... dismiss an employee for poor performance' (Department for Business Innovation and Skills, 2012: 2).

SUMMARY OF MANAGING UNDER-PERFORMANCE

A key feature of performance management is regular informal feedback on performance given to employees by their line managers. In addition to this we would also expect formal feedback to comprise an essential part of the performance appraisal process. Line managers are thus best placed to identify issues of under-performance as they arise. Decisions on how best to manage it will largely depend on the management style, any constraints managers face, and the apparent causes. In the first instance, managers may be able to address the problem by having 'the difficult conversation', pointing out the nature of the problem and the steps necessary to reach acceptable levels of performance – although, as discussed in Chapter 4, managers frequently feel uncomfortable having to do this. Other informal techniques can also be implemented, including coaching and mentoring, that focus on helping the employee to develop the necessary skills, abilities and behaviours within a prescribed time-frame. If the employee fails to respond to the informal interventions, formal procedures may be evoked, including capability and disciplinary procedures. These should be used in accordance with the ACAS guidelines (2009b) because employers must be mindful of their legal obligations, particularly when a decision is made to dismiss an employee. However, as noted above, the Coalition Government appears to be giving clear signals about dismissal on the grounds of poor performance that may well serve to embolden employers in this matter. The formal procedures may be used in a punitive way to punish under-performance, in a corrective way to facilitate better performance, or in a deterrent way to serve as a warning to all employees of the potential dangers of under-performance.

CRITICAL REFLECTION 9.4

What measures should to be taken to deliver fairness, transparency and consistency when managing under-performance using formal techniques?

 WESTCOLL

CASE STUDY 9.3

Westcoll is a general college of further education located in the west of England.

The college recruited 15,000 students this academic year, the majority of which are 16- to 19-year-old full-time students. The college currently has 12,000 part-time adult learners and 700 14- to 16-year-olds who are either recruited to apprenticeship programmes or who study at the college in collaboration with some of the local schools.

The Principal (Chief Executive) and the Board of Governors have decided that the college should be more business-focused, and the college's strategic plan is being reworked to assimilate this idea. Although the college is currently operating at a surplus, it is expected to face budget cuts of £6 million over the next four years. A restructuring exercise has recently been implemented and some curriculum areas are being merged. It is anticipated that there will be a staff reduction of 8 per cent across all levels.

The college currently has 700 staff including 50 employees on part-time contracts. There are an additional 30 people employed on fixed-term contracts. The average annual staff turnover is 16 per cent, and staff absences are currently running at a rate of 7.5 per cent (the sector benchmark is 4 per cent).

The college recognises three trade unions:

- ACM, representing college managers (density 20 per cent)
- UNISON, representing administrative staff (density 40 per cent)
- UCU, representing the lecturing staff (density 60 per cent).

A longstanding joint consultative committee (JCC) exists with 'single-table' bargaining arrangements. The union representatives and members of the senior management team (SMT), including the HR director, meet at regular intervals throughout the academic year. Although there are no formal information and consultation arrangements in place, the JCC is regarded as the most appropriate forum for such matters to be discussed. A recent SMT strategy has been to inform and consult rather than negotiate, and the unions now feel that they are being marginalised from some key areas of decision-making.

The college has recently appointed a new HR director who previously worked in both the manufacturing and service sectors. She is currently developing a three-year HR strategy that she believes will help Westcoll achieve its aspiration to provide outstanding educational provision for its customers.

She wishes to introduce alternative employee voice mechanisms because she feels that these will be more representative and inclusive. To this end, a revamped staff survey was drawn up and rolled out across the college. The response rate was low, and worryingly, the analysis revealed low levels of trust, staff morale and engagement.

So far she has identified several key areas for development in the college, including the current performance management scheme.

This scheme was introduced some years ago as part of a two-year pay deal, and was the subject of lengthy negotiations with the recognised trade unions. The HR director has noted some weaknesses in the way that performance is managed in the college, including:

- There is limited staff buy-in to the principles of performance management.

- An inconsistent approach to managing excellent and poor performance has become evident.
- Some line managers appear over-zealous, whereas others seem to lack the confidence to manage poorly performing staff.
- There is little evidence of a coherent training programme in the 'soft' HR skills of giving feedback, coaching and mentoring.
- The outcomes of several capability/disciplinary procedures have been successfully challenged by the trade union representatives.

The HR director is keen to develop and roll out a new performance management scheme that will address all of these problems.

Questions

1   What advice would you give to the HR director to help her manage under-performance in the short term while the new scheme is being developed?

2   What elements should be included in the new scheme to manage under-performance effectively in the long term?

3   Who should be involved in the design and implementation of the new performance management scheme, and why? (What are the possible implications for managing under-performance?)

CONCLUSION

The chapter has discussed the competing, and contradictory explanations that contribute to our understanding of employee performance and under-performance. When making sense of under-performance it is easy to rely on anecdotes and 'common sense' about both the causes and the solutions. However, what has been noted here is that there is a complex array of variables that may variously impact on under-performance: trust (or mistrust) between managers and managed; commitment and motivation; and individual employee predispositions to respond in particular, and sometimes negative, ways to a range of organisational stimuli. All of these variables potentially enter into the mix that may contribute to under-performance. In addition, there are structural explanations that offer alternative insights into the debates about under-performance. These debates are discussed here in the context of the labour problem – they illustrate both the complex nature of the employment relationship and the challenges that this complexity presents when contemplating the management of under-performance.

It is widely acknowledged that line managers play a key role in managing under-performance. This chapter, like Chapter 4, has sought to highlight some of the real challenges they face when tasked with performing this aspect of their job. Notwithstanding the issue of managers' accepting their human resource management responsibilities and devoting adequate time to discharging them, the evidence presented in this chapter suggests that they would benefit from more training in the 'softer' skills of people management. Moreover, the informal techniques currently used to manage under-performance, including coaching and mentoring, are underpinned by a set of unitary assumptions. To be effective they require employees to accept the legitimacy of such interventions as well as a commitment to the wider organisational goals and organisational culture.

Reliance on the formal techniques of capability and disciplinary procedures for managing under-performance also presents their particular set of challenges, not least the absolute need to ensure that the process is fair and transparent, that employees are fully informed of the nature of the problem, and that they have the right to be accompanied at formal meetings, and to appeal against any decisions made against them. With respect to using discipline to manage under-performance, this chapter has observed that it can be used to punish, to correct behaviour, or to serve as a deterrent to others in relation to the dangers of under-performing. The current ACAS guidelines on managing discipline (2009b) recommend that when employers introduce workplace procedures, they should consider consultation with employees rather than going down the route of unilateral imposition.

Such a position reflects the general debates raised within this chapter as to the perceived legitimacy of rules and decision-making in the workplace – it has been noted that the right to manage *per se*, and within this, the right to impose rules, does not of itself secure the levels of employee commitment and buy-in required of employees in a high-performance workplace.

EXPLORE FURTHER

Fox, A. (1985) *Man Mismanagement*, 2nd edition. London: Hutchinson

Fuchs, S. (2010) 'Critical issues in people resourcing (1): reconceptualising employee performance', in Roper, I., Prouska, R. and Na Ayudhya, U. C. (eds) *Critical Issues in Human Resource Management*. London: CIPD

Gould-Williams, J. and Davies, F. (2005) 'Using social exchange theory to predict the effects of HRM practice on employee outcomes: an analysis of public sector workers', *Public Management Review*, Vol.7, No.1: 1–24

Heavey, C., Halliday, S. V., Gilbert, D. and Murphy, E. (2011) 'Enhancing performance: bringing trust, commitment and motivation together in organisations', *Journal of General Management*, Vol.36, No.3: 1–18

Storey, J. (1983) *Management Prerogative and the Question of Control*. London: Routledge & Kegan Paul

Worrall, L. and Cooper C. (2012) *The Quality of Working Life 2012: Managers' wellbeing, motivation and productivity*. London: Chartered Management Institute

CHAPTER 10

Absence Management

JANE MOORE

LEARNING OUTCOMES

By the end of this chapter you should be able to:

- understand current trends in levels of absence and the current public policy context

- appreciate the complex nature of causes of absence and the difficulties this complexity poses for its management

- identify and critically evaluate a range of absence management strategies

- appreciate the impact of absence management strategies on individual employees and on organisational performance.

INTRODUCTION

The topic of absence management – or attendance management, as more proactive approaches tend to be labelled – has risen up the management agenda in recent years. There is a growing recognition that it is possible to control and therefore reduce absence, leading to potential cost savings and improved organisational performance: 76 per cent of respondents to a recent CIPD survey (CIPD, 2012i) believe it is possible to further reduce absence levels. This is an attractive proposition, particularly for organisations operating in fiercely competitive markets or under strict financial constraints. It is also against a backdrop of growing interest in wellbeing and healthier lifestyles generally, promoted by the government and public service bodies and taken up by many organisations.

However, the management of absence is not a new concern for employers, and has long been recognised as an unpopular activity for managers and one that they are not perceived to be good at (eg Wolff, 2011; James *et al*, 2002). By its very nature, tackling absence presents a number of dilemmas. There is frequently ambiguity over the aims of absence management policies and the level of attendance they seek to achieve. Consistency of approach is more problematic than with other performance management processes, due to the varied nature of illness, from chronic conditions to temporary injuries. In addition, this can be clouded by uncertainty over whether absence is due to genuine illness or not. Finally, managers often feel uncomfortable holding difficult conversations with employees about absence for fear of straying into potentially sensitive health or personal issues.

This chapter considers absence as a form of under-performance which has the potential to be reduced through effective management. 'Absence' in this chapter refers to absence attributed to sickness and does not include other types of authorised or unauthorised absence. The chapter starts by considering the current interest in absence management and wellbeing generally, and then reviews recent trends in levels of absence. It moves on to an exploration of causes of absence before considering different strategies for managing absence. It concludes with a review of the implications of some of these strategies for organisational performance.

THE CONTEXT FOR WELLNESS AT WORK

In March 2007 the government commissioned Dame Carol Black to undertake a wide-ranging review of the health of Britain's working-age population. This led to the publication a year later of the influential report *Working for a Healthier Tomorrow*, which called for urgent and comprehensive reform and a new approach to health and work in Britain (Black, 2008). Some of the key findings from the report were that:

- Work is good for people in terms of both long-term health and family wellbeing.
- Ill health costs the country over £100 billion per annum – more than the annual budget for the NHS.
- The importance of physical and mental health is insufficiently recognised within society.
- GPs often feel ill-equipped to advise patients on remaining in or returning to work, and the current sickness certification process focuses on what people cannot do and promotes the view that being in work when not 100 per cent fit could impede recovery.
- The scale of the numbers on incapacity benefit represents a failure of healthcare and employment support systems.
- Occupational health services are detached from mainstream healthcare, which undermines a holistic approach to patient care.

Following the report the well-publicised 'fit note' (Statement of Fitness to Work) was introduced in April 2010, replacing the former 'sick note', with the aim of encouraging doctors to consider whether people could return to work on a phased basis or with changes to working hours or duties. Shortly afterwards it was announced that the 1.5 million people receiving the state incapacity benefit would be re-assessed with a view to helping more claimants back into work. A further independent review into sickness absence was commissioned by the government in February 2011, with the aim of exploring radical new ways of changing the current sickness absence system to help more people stay in work and reduce costs (Department for Work and Pensions, 2011). These moves represent a clear challenge to the perception that it is necessary to be 100 per cent fit in order to work.

One of the main drivers behind these initiatives is clearly one of cost-saving, but they have also contributed to greater awareness of health issues within the workplace and the development of a culture of wellness rather than sickness, involving more proactive approaches to health promotion and wellbeing. Absence management processes are now frequently part of broader wellbeing strategies (IDS, 2011c). CIPD survey data (CIPD, 2012i) indicates that over half of respondents have an employee wellbeing strategy in place. The content of these varies considerably, but common benefits are access to counselling services, employee assistance schemes, stop-smoking support and advice on healthy eating. IDS (2011c) data identifies gym membership, health checks, walking and running clubs, physiotherapy, stress counselling and complementary therapies as benefits offered by some organisations.

The impact of some of these developments on the level and nature of absence is considered below.

CRITICAL REFLECTION 10.1

1 To what extent is government promotion of a wellness agenda likely to influence levels of workplace absence? What other factors might also be relevant?

2 What impact could 'fit notes' have on absence management? Can you foresee any difficulties that might arise involving them?

LEVELS AND COSTS OF ABSENCE

Most data shows a gradual but steady decrease in absence levels in recent years compared to the record highs of the late 1980s and early 1990s. The CBI (2011) reports that levels of absence have dropped by more than a quarter from an average of more than eight days per annum per employee in the late 1980s to 6½ days per employee in 2010. ONS data shows a fall of 26 per cent between 1993 and 2012 (Office for National Statistics, 2012b). Other surveys report similar findings (see Table 10.1).

Table 10.1 Average number of days of absence per employee per year 2012–2006

	2012	2011	2010	2009	2008	2007	2006
CIPD	6.8	7.7	7.7	7.4	8.0	7.6	8
CBI	–	–	6.5	6.4	–	6.7	–
IRS*	–	–	6.5	6.8	7.1	7.4	8

* IRS data shows median number
Sources: CIPD (2012i); CBI (2011); Suff, R. (2011)

Surveys also reveal consistent findings on variations in absence levels between sectors, the public sector and the not-for-profit sector recording higher levels than private sector services – 7.9, 8.2 and 5.7 days per employee respectively, according to the CIPD (2012i) survey. There are also consistent findings of large variations in absence within sectors with the CBI survey, revealing, for example, that absence in the best-performing quartile stood at an average of 2.2 days compared to the lowest-performing quartile in which the average was 10.7 days. (CBI, 2011).

A number of absence trends have been noted over the years:

● Large organisations have higher levels of absence than smaller organisations. CBI data reveals that organisations with over 5,000 employees have average absence rates of 8.2 days per employee compared with small organisations (less than 50 employees), which show absence rates of only 4.5 days (CBI, 2011).
● Manual workers have higher levels of absence than non-manual workers (although recent data shows this gap to be narrowing).
● Females have higher absence levels than males. ONS (2012b) data shows that females are absent 2.3 days per year on average compared to 1.5 days for males.
● Older employees have higher absence levels than younger employees: the 50–64 age range shows the highest absence rate at 2.5 per cent, compared with the 16–34 age group at 1.5 per cent, according to recent ONS data (2012b).

The costs of absence, although notoriously difficult to calculate with much accuracy (Pilbeam and Corbridge, 2010), provide a compelling case for action. The Department for Work and Pensions estimates that absence costs employers £9 billion and costs the state £13 billion (Black and Frost, 2011). The CBI places direct costs of absence for employers at £17 billion (CBI, 2011). Estimated costs per employee vary from £553 per annum per absent employee (Suff, 2011) to £760 (CBI, 2011), and these do not take into account less tangible costs such as loss of productivity, quality or continuity of service, additional pressures on remaining employees, and the impact on job satisfaction and morale.

Although the steady decrease in absence levels could be a cause for optimism about the success of recent more vigorous absence management initiatives, it is not altogether surprising that absence should reach its lowest level during periods of slow economic growth and recession. These years have also witnessed widespread redundancies, and the public sector in particular has faced unprecedented financial cuts and reorganisation as the government tackles the fiscal deficit. 47 per cent of organisations in the CIPD 2012 survey reported using employee absence records as part of their criteria for redundancy selection, and 30 per cent of organisations reported an increase in the number of people coming to work ill during during the previous 12 months (CIPD, 2012i). This has led to concerns that true levels of absence are masked by 'presenteeism', a concept that has recently attracted heightened attention, and refers to attendance at work when unwell. Presenteeism raises concerns about under-performance, productivity and, in some contexts, workplace safety, and is examined in more detail in the final section of this chapter.

THE CAUSES OF ABSENCE

A logical starting point when considering why employees are absent would seem to be the reasons given by employees themselves to explain their absence. Survey data shows reasonably consistent findings on the main causes of employee absence, although the incidence of stress and mental ill-health-related absence has risen considerably in recent years.

Table 10.2 Reasons given by employees for absence

Manual workers	Non-manual workers
Top five reasons for short-term absence:	*Top five reasons for short-term absence:*
• Minor illnesses (eg colds/flu, stomach upsets, headaches and migraines) • Musculoskeletal injuries (eg neck strains and repetitive strain injury) • Back pain • Stress • Recurring medical conditions (eg asthma, angina)	• Minor illnesses (eg colds/flu, stomach upsets, headaches and migraines) • Stress • Musculoskeletal injuries (eg neck strains and repetitive strain injury) • Back pain • Recurring medical conditions (eg asthma, angina)
Top five reasons for long-term absence (four weeks or more):	*Top five reasons for long-term absence (four weeks or more):*
• Acute medical conditions (eg stroke, heart attack, cancer) • Stress • Musculoskeletal injuries • Back pain • Mental ill health (eg clinical depression, anxiety)	• Stress • Acute medical conditions (eg stroke, heart attack, cancer) • Mental ill health (eg clinical depression, anxiety) • Musculoskeletal injuries • Back pain

Source: CIPD Absence Management Survey (2012i)

However, it is likely that the reasons given by employees provide only a partial explanation of the real causes of absence. As noted by Torrington *et al* (2011), employees are likely only to offer explanations for absence which they perceive their organisation to view as legitimate. The uneven spread of absence across sectors and organisations would suggest that factors other than genuine ill health come into play. The CIPD survey (2011e) reports, for example, that absence levels between UK call centres can vary from 4 per cent to 48 per cent, a variation which is unlikely to be solely related to differing levels of ill health.

There is frequent reference in the media to 'pulling a sickie' (taking time off work when fit) and, although accurate statistics on this are hard to obtain, a PricewaterhouseCoopers poll conducted in 2011 (PricewaterhouseCoopers, 2011) found that 34 per cent of respondents admitted lying to take time off work, commonly cited reasons being:

- boredom and depression at work (61 per cent)
- hangovers (18 per cent)
- good weather (11 per cent)
- romance (5 per cent).

 CRITICAL REFLECTION 10.2

How could you find out whether employees are absent due to 'boredom and depression' – and what could you do about this?

It has long been recognised that the underlying causes of absence from work are complex and multi-faceted, which has led to a considerable body of research in this area. Some of the early studies attempted to identify a single factor to explain absence which might then be the focus of appropriate interventions. The link between job dissatisfaction and absence was a key theme in early studies, but attempts to find empirical evidence to support a robust causal link were fruitless (Nicholson, 1977). Moreover, no explanation could be found through these theories for the significant variations in absence levels between individual employees (Evans and Palmer, 1997), and attention moved towards considering multiple factors which could influence absence in different contexts.

One of the most influential early approaches is that of Steers and Rhodes (1978), who produced a 'process model of employee attendance'. This aimed to identify the major sets of variables that influence absence behaviour and their interrelationship, by attempting to fit together 'the array of piecemeal findings on the subject' from a review of over 100 previous studies of absence (Steers and Rhodes, 1978: 392).

This model importantly noted that attendance is largely a function of two variables – *motivation to attend* and *ability to attend* – which represent two broad groupings of influences. **Motivation to attend** is influenced by factors associated with satisfaction with the job situation and internal and external pressures to attend work. Based on fairly modest findings from previous research studies, Steers and Rhodes (1978) include job scope, job level, role stress, work-group size, leader style, co-worker relations and opportunity for advancement under the heading of 'job situation'. A second set of influences are described as 'employee values and job expectations', and these are thought to exert an influence on job satisfaction and also to be influenced by a number of personal characteristics (education, tenure, age, sex, family size). The second main set of influences on motivation to attend relate to pressures to attend, which include market and economic conditions, incentive and reward systems, work-group norms, the personal work ethic and organisational commitment.

The model also recognises that even when someone has high motivation to attend there are instances when attendance is not possible, and lists a number of barriers to attendance (illness or accidents, family responsibilities, transportation difficulties) under the heading of **Ability to attend**. The model therefore presents a wide range of influences on the decision to attend work and the ability to attend work, relating both to individuals themselves and to the environment within which they work. Some of them are under the control of the employees whereas others are not. The model also emphasises the interactional nature of the variables. For example, employees' expectations of their job and the degree to which these are met are likely to impact upon their overall satisfaction with the job. In turn, employee expectations might be influenced by personal characteristics such as level of education. Steers and Rhodes (1978) also acknowledge that different variables may exert varying levels of influence on different employees, thus suggesting that understanding the causes of absence is far from straightforward.

A simplified 'diagnostic' model was subsequently produced to help managers understand absence within their organisations. This model still focuses on the individual employee's decision to attend but pays greater attention to 'organisational practices' and 'absence culture' as factors influencing motivation to attend and perceived ability to attend (Rhodes and Steers, 1990).

Figure 10.1 The Rhodes and Steers diagnostic model

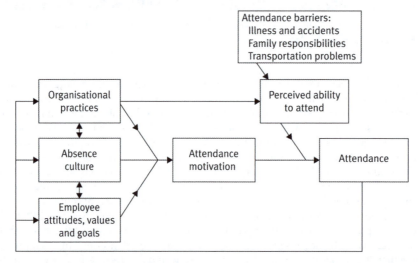

Source: Rhodes and Steers (1990)

REFLECTIVE ACTIVITY 10.1

Consider the Rhodes and Steers models in relation to your experience of absence behaviour in the workplace, or to times when you have been absent from work or studies.

1   How helpful are these models in explaining causes of absence?

2   What implications do they have for the management of absence?

Although Steers and Rhodes' work has attracted criticism due to the lack of precision of some of the definitions, leading to difficulties with empirical testing (Brooke, 1986), it remains one of the most influential and frequently cited models in the absenteeism literature (Burton *et al*, 2002) and has been the foundation for much subsequent research, some of which is considered below.

A basic premise of Steers and Rhodes' work and much of the research which followed is that absence is at least partly a voluntary behaviour. The influences upon this behaviour can be explored further by grouping them under the broad headings of 'individual characteristics and attitudes' and 'organisational influences'.

INDIVIDUAL CHARACTERISTICS AND ATTITUDES

As noted above, there is evidence of consistent trends in absence behaviour relating to personal characteristics such as gender and age. The increase in absence related to older age is likely to be due to the greater susceptibility to illness at older ages rather than to lower attendance motivation. However, the position regarding gender-related absence might be less straightforward. Several commentators have observed that although there is evidence that females make greater use generally of health services than males (Scambler, 2008), higher levels of female absence could also be related to childcare responsibilities or other family demands (Brooke and Price, 1989). Warr and Yearta (1995) in a large-scale study found that women between the ages of 20 and 29 had particularly high absence levels, which they speculated was due to childcare demands.

There is clear evidence that previous absence behaviour is a reliable predictor of future absence (Breaugh, 1981; Kelly 1983), particularly where frequency of absence (ie number of episodes rather than number of days) is concerned, suggesting that certain individuals may be more 'absence-prone' than others. Although this could in a minority of cases be due to frequent spells of ill health, the role of personality could also be influential. A study carried out by Judge *et al* (1997) sought to find a relationship between personality, based on the five-factor model, and absence. They found links between 'extraversion' and 'conscientiousness' and absence, and concluded that 'carefree, excitement-seeking and hedonistic' extraverts were more likely to be absent than other employees, speculating that extraverts might view work as dull and routine or an obstacle to involvement in more exciting leisure activities – and therefore take time off. Conversely, they found that conscientiousness was related to low levels of absence possibly due to the dutifulness and self-discipline associated with this trait, which leads to less absence-prone behaviour.

CRITICAL REFLECTION 10.3

1   What are the implications of the findings on personal characteristics and absence for organisations?

2   What difficulties do these present for an organisation that wishes to prevent absence?

The notion and importance of discretionary behaviour was examined in Chapter 1. Defined as 'the sort of everyday behaviour that the employer wants but has to rely on the employee to deliver' (Purcell *et al*, 2003: 5), there is also a recognition that discretionary behaviour can be withdrawn. Absence can be a form of withdrawal of discretionary behaviour or, as described by Fuchs (2010), work withdrawal behaviour (WWB). This is the type of dysfunctional behaviour that results when an employee is disengaged from his or her job and psychologically or physically withdraws from the organisation (see also Chapter 9). WWB can be evident through a range of different behaviours, including leaving the organisation altogether, voicing complaints, lateness or absence. At an individual level a number of factors can lead to absence as a form of WWB. Iverson and Deery (2001) noted the importance of low job satisfaction, which they found to have a negative impact on a range of withdrawal behaviours, including lateness, leaving early and absence. They also found that individuals who showed 'positive affectivity' or feelings of enthusiasm, positive emotions and active engagement were less likely to be absent. These traits could also be linked to extraversion, adding further support to the findings of Judge *et al* (1997), cited above.

There are also a number of organisational influences on WWB and absence that are discussed below.

ORGANISATIONAL INFLUENCES

The job situation

Rhodes and Steers' process model (1978) recognises satisfaction with the job situation as one of the main influences on motivation to attend. This is a broad category but is likely to include characteristics of the job itself and the work environment. As noted by Huczynski and Fitzpatrick (1989), if employees enjoy their work situation and the tasks associated with their job they will be more likely to want to come to work. Much of the research into the link between job satisfaction and absence has however produced mixed findings or only tenuous links between the two. A six-year study by Rentsch and Steel (1998) did find a positive link between some aspects of job design frequently associated with job satisfaction and absence, notably skill variety, task identity and autonomy. This suggests that employees who have varied jobs with clear task identity and some degree of control are less likely to be absent. Huczynski and Fitzpatrick (1989) also found support for the view that high levels of task repetitiveness led to low job satisfaction and in turn high absence. It is also clear that employee perceptions of these aspects of their jobs are likely to vary, making it impossible to design universally satisfying jobs.

Some of the literature on the causes of stress-related absence has pointed to factors associated with the job or the work environment as leading to stress, and therefore, in many cases, absence. These are well summarised by Arnold and Randall (2010) and include:

- long hours
- work overload
- pressure to meet tight deadlines
- work which is too difficult
- lack of clear sense of purpose
- repetitive routines, boring or under-stimulating work
- emotional labour.

The physical work environment itself has also been associated with absenteeism generally and also with stress and employee wellbeing. Huczynski and Fitzpatrick (1989) cite a number of surveys showing a link between poor working conditions, poorly maintained equipment and machinery, problems with temperature and lighting, and absence or stress. The nature of this link is a little unclear but it is possible that poor working conditions may influence motivation to attend as well as ability to attend through accidents or injuries. More recent research carried out by Taylor *et al* (2003) into occupational ill health within a Scottish call centre found that as well as the impact of workplace and ergonomic factors (eg temperature problems and poor workspace design), the distinctive characteristics of the call-handling process and the target-driven environment had a significant impact on absence and ill health, which was exacerbated by the punitive approach to absence management adopted by the call centre management. Arnold and

Randall (2010) note that there has been a long association between poor physical surroundings and mental and physical health, and that it can vary considerably between occupations. Some of these problems can be minimised by involving employees in workplace design.

Absence cultures

While acknowledging the research into the wide range of factors relating to individual characteristics and attitudes towards jobs, the limitations of regarding absence solely as a 'private' behaviour independent of its social context have been identified by a number of commentators (eg Martocchio, 1994; Nicholson and Johns, 1985). Strikingly different levels of absence are frequently observed between departments or teams within the same organisation or between different areas of a business. One possible explanation for this could be the operation of different sets of workplace norms leading to different absence cultures. Described as 'the set of shared understandings about absence legitimacy … and the established custom and practice of employee absence behaviour and its control' (Johns and Nicholson, 1982, cited in Nicholson and Johns, 1985: 136), an absence culture derives from the norms relating to levels and patterns of absence behaviour and expectations about the sanctions used in response to absence. Absence cultures can be negative or positive, signalling, for example, that absence is a legitimate response to dissatisfaction leading to potentially high levels of absence or, conversely, consisting of norms relating to good attendance. The absence culture of the organisation or of a subgroup is assimilated by employees in the same way as other cultural influences as part of the process of socialisation. Norms arise from both the formal rules established by management and the informal rules established by work groups. If, for example, an organisation has an absence management procedure that is rarely used by managers and odd days of absence are mostly ignored, it is likely that employees will soon form expectations that this type of absence is condoned and possibly even an entitlement (around one fifth of employers in a 2011 CBI survey thought absence was viewed as an entitlement by their employees).

 CRITICAL REFLECTION 10.4

Consider the workplace norms relating to absence in your organisation or in organisations you have worked for.

1   How have these norms developed?

2   What does the culture encourage – absence or attendance?

Another form of pressure on attendance is through the influence of strong, cohesive work groups or teams. Where teams are highly interdependent and absence is likely to disrupt performance, there can be strong peer pressure to attend (Grinyer and Singleton, 2000; Dunn and Wilkinson, 2002). Baker-McClearn *et al* (2010: 322) in a study of nine UK organisations found that employees in the public sector in particular had strong loyalties both to the general public and to their teams and were reluctant to take time off when ill, leading to a form of 'personally mediated presenteeism'. Recognition of the influence exerted by peer or team pressure has led to some interest in team-based incentives and rewards relating to attendance. For example, HBOS introduced team-based days out as a reward for good attendance, and Contact 24 – an outsourced contact centre provider, part of the MM Group – displayed attendance league tables showing the attendance records of each team (IDS, 2005).

The way absence is managed has a significant impact on the development of absence cultures and, as in Case Study 10.1 below, many organisations are now adopting more robust and proactive approaches towards absence management in an attempt to change the culture from one of absence to one of attendance.

CASE STUDY 10.1

CHANGING AN ABSENCE CULTURE AT THE DRIVER AND VEHICLE LICENSING AGENCY (DVLA)

The DVLA used to have one of the highest rates of sickness absence within the public sector but managed to reduce this by almost 50 per cent, from an average of 14 days per employee in 2005 to 7.2 days in 2010. Spurred on by a National Audit Office report, which criticised the DVLA for its high levels of absence and the perception among employees that it was 'soft' on absence, the DVLA decided to overhaul its approach to absence management. It aimed to move from a reactive and largely ineffective approach towards an approach which integrated absence management into a wider strategy designed to promote employee health and wellbeing. One of the particular challenges for the DVLA was the need to address attitudes towards sickness absence which were embedded within a culture where taking sick leave was viewed as a way of life and often supplemented annual leave.

To develop the new approach, the recently appointed HR director set up a steering group consisting of key stakeholders, including trade union representatives and occupational health specialists, to ensure that the initiative, although driven by senior management, would also have the support of other interested parties. Aspects introduced included:

- the setting of new and more challenging absence targets
- speedier referrals to occupational health specialists, with immediate referrals for stress-related illness and musculoskeletal disorders, which were the main causes of absence
- training for line managers to support them in applying the policies and managing absence more effectively
- health interventions – for example, access to psychology and occupational therapy specialists, health education programmes – and more lighthearted events to encourage healthier lifestyles
- stress management support and a new employee assistance programme
- the appointment of 'attendance managers' to assist in absence 'hot spots'.

Attention was also paid to reviewing the quality of working life in some of its more routinised areas, and to addressing problems within the contact centre where employees could not take leave at short notice and therefore resorted to sickness absence.

Source: adapted from IDS (2011c) HR Studies 936

APPROACHES TO THE MANAGEMENT OF ABSENCE

Approaches towards the management of absence can be grouped under two broad headings: punitive approaches, and preventative approaches. In punitive approaches the emphasis is primarily on deterring employees from being absent through the use of stringent absence management policies, including the use of sanctions for excessive absence. Preventative approaches seek to encourage better levels of general health and wellbeing among the workforce and sometimes attempt to address the causes of absence. In practice, these approaches are rarely mutually exclusive, most organisations adopting elements of both. They can therefore be better described as representing shifts of emphasis rather than discrete approaches. In addition, a third approach, which offers a 'carrot' instead of, or as well as, the 'stick' of the punitive approach, is the use of attendance incentives. Common to all approaches are questions of who takes the main responsibility for the management of absence and how is it measured and reported.

RESPONSIBILITY FOR ABSENCE MANAGEMENT

The trend towards the devolution of HR activities to line managers over the past few decades was discussed in Chapter 4, and absence management is no exception. Responsibility for absence in most organisations rests primarily with line managers, often supported by HR, Occupational Health departments and sometimes external absence management specialists (IDS, 2011c). The Black Report (2008) *Working for a Healthier Tomorrow* recognised that line managers have a direct impact on the health, safety and overall wellbeing of their staff through their behaviours, and that they had to have the necessary competencies and skills to be effective. CIPD survey data (2012i) found that in 70 per cent of organisations line managers took the main responsibility for absence management. This role frequently involves completing sickness forms, re-allocating the absentee's workload, carrying out return-to-work interviews and on-going monitoring. As noted in Chapter 4, line managers are often not considered to be confident or competent in carrying out activities associated with managing under-performance, including absence. Table 4.2 (Milsome, 2006) in Chapter 4 indicates that HR managers thought only 15.4 per cent of line managers handled cases of absence well, and 46.2 per cent handled them badly. Difficulties with the line manager role are discussed in detail in Chapter 4, but some specific problems have been identified that relate to the management of absence.

Research carried out by McHugh (2002) within local government organisations in Northern Ireland found that there were varying levels of awareness of absence management policies among line managers. Dunn and Wilkinson (2002) found that managers within the private sector often did not welcome the devolution of responsibility for absence management, and came up with evidence of 'passing the baton' between the line and HR. They found varying levels of line manager ownership and interest in absence management. Inconsistencies in the implementation of absence management policy, both within and between organisations, were observed by both authors, and these mostly occurred where line managers exercised discretion in dealing with individual cases (McHugh, 2002). Most managers showed a preference for informal approaches to absence management rather than applying disciplinary procedures. Problems of lack of time to deal with absence and a lack of training – as well as reluctance on the part of managers to attend training – were also highlighted. This led to managers' feeling embarrassed about conducting interviews with staff and being uncomfortable with investigating reasons behind absences (Dunn and Wilkinson, 2002). Similar findings were reached by James *et al* (2002) in their study into the management of long-term absence. Around two thirds of the HR managers interviewed reported that line managers failed to follow guidelines relating to maintaining contact with absent employees and exploring ways of helping them to return to work. This was attributed to lack of time and lack of awareness of organisational procedures stemming from lack of training, and an underlying unwillingness on the part of managers to deal with issues of sickness. Case Study 10.2 below describes Kent County Council's attempts to address this.

CASE STUDY 10.2

BUILDING LINE MANAGER CONFIDENCE AT KENT COUNTY COUNCIL

Kent County Council's (KCC) attempt to develop a positive attendance culture was based upon the belief that 'the management role in managing attendance was central', and a core aim was to build line manager confidence and competence in managing people with health or disability issues.

A wide range of training courses are offered to managers to encourage them to engage in more robust discussions with employees about attendance. These include courses on coaching skills, managing difficult conversations well, stress management and living skills, positive management of mental health and managing change. In addition, 'speed surgeries' are available to managers to 'myth-bust' around what they can and cannot do in managing attendance.

A number of other improvements to the wider management of attendance were introduced at the same time, and significant improvements in attendance have been reported. As a result of the support and guidance provided, line managers are now considered to be 'much more confident and empowered to have conversations about absence and health issues'.

Source: adapted from CIPD (2011e: 31)

In an attempt to encourage managers to address absence management and apply company procedures, some organisations have introduced incentives, such as bonuses for achieving absence targets, or have included absence management targets within performance management processes (IDS, 2011c).

MEASURING AND MONITORING ABSENCE

Absence measurement and reporting is the cornerstone for most attempts to manage absence, and it is common for organisations to review their methods of collecting and recording absence data when designing absence management strategies. The CIPD reported that revised or new monitoring procedures were the most frequent change made to absence management in 2012 (CIPD, 2012i). This data is usually derived from self-certificate forms completed by employees or 'fit notes' provided by GPs, and its accuracy is therefore contingent upon reliable reporting and completion of the forms. Although such monitoring is now very widely used, Dunn and Wilkinson (2002) found from their research into seven UK organisations that the value placed on absence monitoring reports by line managers varies widely.

There are a number of different ways of defining and measuring absence but the following measures are typically used. **The overall absence rate** shows the amount of time lost due to absence as a percentage of total working time, and can be expressed as a percentage or an average number of days per employee.

$$\text{The overall absence rate } = \frac{\text{Number of days/shifts lost to absence}}{\text{Total number of days/shifts}} \times 100$$

This measure is frequently used in survey and benchmarking data but only provides an overview of sickness levels: it does not show length or frequency of absences or help identify 'hot spots' of absence.

The frequency rate highlights the number of episodes of absence taken by employees by showing the average number of absences per employee, expressed as a percentage. This measure, however, does not take into account the length of each spell.

$$\text{The absence frequency rate} = \frac{\text{Number of spells of absence}}{\text{Number of employees}} \times 100$$

Although these two measures provide useful information on the extent and incidence of absence and are helpful for benchmarking and comparison, it is likely that managers will also need more detailed individual data showing total absence, number of spells, nature and pattern of absence in order to address absence problems.

In many organisations the most disruptive type of absence is that consisting of a series of short spells of absence, and where this is the main target of absence management policies, a measurement technique known as **the Bradford factor** (due to a supposed link with Bradford University) is sometimes used. This technique gives a high weighting to short spells of absence thus enabling easy identification of individuals showing this pattern of absence.

The Bradford factor calculation is as follows (IDS, 2011c):

$$\text{The Bradford point score} = S \times S \times D$$

where S is the number of spells of absence over the last year, and D is the number of days of absence in the last year.

So, for example, in respect of employees with 14 days' absence in one rolling year, the Bradford score can vary enormously depending on the number of occasions involved:

> One absence of 14 days $= 14$ points (ie $1 \times 1 \times 14$)
> Seven absences of two days each $= 686$ points (ie $7 \times 7 \times 14$)
> 14 absences of one day each $= 2,744$ points (ie $14 \times 14 \times 14$)

This form of measurement is often used as a 'trigger' to instigate a review of the absence of individuals who reach a specified number of points. The trigger figure can vary widely, IDS data (2011c) identifying scores of between 27 per 13-week period to 350 per year, although a typical trigger score is 50 points. In many organisations, high Bradford point scores lead to an escalation of the absence management process.

Although effective in highlighting individuals with high numbers of spells of absence, the Bradford factor approach has attracted some criticism. Unless the calculation itself is visible and well communicated to employees, action taken as a result of a high Bradford point score could be perceived as inconsistent or unfair. This would be particularly problematic when absence levels contribute to decisions on reward. To mitigate this, some organisations exempt certain employees from Bradford factor calculations (eg pregnant women and staff with disabilities).

The use of trigger points generally to instigate action on absence has shown a steady increase in recent years. The CIPD (2012i) reports that 21 per cent of organisations introduced some kind of trigger point system in the previous 12 months, and Milsome (2010) found that 87 per cent of organisations used one or more triggers – 91 per cent regarding them as successful. Dunn and Wilkinson (2002) found that some managers welcomed the clarity of approach provided by the communication of trigger points whereas others viewed them as unhelpful in that they encouraged employees to view time off up to the trigger point as acceptable.

PUNITIVE APPROACHES

Much has been written about the role and impact of organisational control policies within the wider employee relations literature (eg Edwards and Whitston, 1989), and this has been discussed in relation to performance management in Chapter 9. Approaches to absence management which aim to exert pressure on employees to attend work through the enforcement of stringent policies and procedures are an example of this type of control. Typically, such approaches contain elements of the following (IDS, 2011c; CIPD, 2012i):

- clear and well-communicated absence or attendance management policies
- the provision of regular absence management information for managers
- attendance targets
- well-defined absence notification procedures
- trigger points specifying a level of absence that will instigate investigation
- return-to-work interviews
- early referrals to Occupational Health services
- the use of sanctions for persistent absentees
- links to disciplinary or capability procedures
- training for managers in the operation of absence management procedures.

Although the detailed implementation of punitive absence policies varies considerably, some trends have emerged in recent years. Arrangements for **the notification of absence** have been tightened up in many organisations, supplemented by the requirement for managers in some organisations to keep in regular contact with absent employees, even those on short-term absence (IDS, 2011c). Some organisations now require employees to report absence to an external supplier, often a nurse-led telephone service, as in the example in Case Study 10.3 below, where immediate medical advice is provided and the line manager is notified of the absence. The aim of such schemes is to help employees back to work as soon as possible, and to streamline the reporting process. Although this may be seen as part of an initiative to promote greater wellbeing and speedier return to work, there is undoubtedly also an underlying objective to deter those who may not wish to discuss the reason for their absence with a health professional.

NURSE-LED REPORTING SYSTEM AT FIRST GROUP

CASE STUDY 10.3

In response to problems of under-recording of absence and the disruption caused to bus services by unpredictable absence, First Group introduced a system whereby absent employees were required to contact a call centre run by Active Health Partners (AHP) and to speak initially to a nurse who would provide immediate medical advice and log details of the absence. AHP also provide an online database which records trends and can generate online return-to-work forms for managers to complete. During the initial six-month pilot scheme, a 20 per cent fall in absence was achieved, and a survey conducted by the company reported that 76 per cent of employees believed the new system to be very helpful.

Source: Pollitt (2008)

Return-to-work (RTW) interviews are very widely used and are recommended as good practice by bodies such as ACAS and the CIPD. The CIPD reports that such interviews are used by 90 per cent of all organisations and are consistently rated by managers as the most effective tool for managing absence (CIPD, 2012i). Many organisations view them as 'central to their absence management strategies' (IDS, 2011c: 7) and expect line managers to carry them out as soon as possible after every absence. Training is provided for managers in many organisations on how to conduct these interviews (Wolff, 2011). RTW interviews can have a dual purpose in both identifying health or other problems and enabling appropriate action or support to be implemented, while at the same time acting as a reminder that absence has been noted and further action, including sanctions, could follow. They potentially provide opportunities for managers to (IDS, 2011c: 8):

- welcome the employee back to work and show concern for his or her welfare
- make sure that the employee is fully recovered and fit to return to work
- discuss the reasons for the employee's absence
- review the employee's overall absence record and discuss any worrying patterns, such as frequent short-term absences
- remind the employee of the impact of absence both on colleagues and on the business as a whole
- set targets for improvements and explain the consequences of further absences.

Baker-McClearn *et al* (2010), from their research with 123 managers and employees within nine UK case study organisations, found that RTW interviews were frequently perceived as 'organisational tools' with a punitive rather than a welfare focus, designed to get people back to work rather than show concern for their wellbeing. Employees reported feeling as if they had been 'told off' rather than offered support, and this led to anxiety about these interviews. Dunn and Wilkinson (2002), in their research among managers, encountered more mixed responses, some managers finding the interviews useful in helping to uncover underlying reasons for absence and for increasing employees' awareness of pressures to attend work. One HR manager commented (Dunn and Wilkinson, 2002: 237):

> We have found that return-to-work interviews can be one of the best deterrents to would be malingerers … We've seen a steady fall in absence since their introduction.

They also found that many interviews did not take place due to time pressures or were not perceived necessary by managers, particularly where there were close relationships between managers and staff. Another manager commented (Dunn and Wilkinson, 2002: 237):

> In our business, people know their staff very well. A return-to-work interview would become faintly artificial and counterproductive. Here at headquarters we've got highly professional people who work weekends and till 10 o'clock at night. It would be a bit 'naff' really.

These findings suggest that there can be a significant gap between employee and employer perceptions of the purpose of RTW interviews, which could be exacerbated by other problems within the organisation, such as low employee morale and lack of trust between management and employees (McHugh, 2002).

A range of **sanctions** can be used as part of a punitive approach, particularly in relation to short-term absence. These include the use of warnings and ultimately, in some cases, dismissal through disciplinary or capability procedures, withholding of sick pay and reductions in bonuses or annual leave entitlement (CIPD, 2012i; Dunn and Wilkinson, 2002). In many cases attendance records are considered part of wider performance management and can affect appraisal ratings, with subsequent effects on pay, promotion or job security. CIPD (2012i) survey data suggests that managers consider the use of disciplinary action for unacceptable absence and the restriction of sick pay to be 'effective' methods of absence control. Dunn and Wilkinson (2002), however, found that managers were inconsistent in their application of sanctions and showed preference for an informal approach to managing absence rather than applying disciplinary rules. Interestingly, Harvey and Nicholson (1993: 854) in their research into employee perceptions of incentives and penalties in the Civil Service, found that two thirds of employees in the study endorsed the use of penalties as long as they were not used to penalise genuine absence. They found that employees had a 'powerful sense of what is fair and unfair in terms of attendance and absence' with clear implications for the on-going psychological contract and employee commitment. Case Study 10.4 below illustrates the incorporation of sanctions into a wider absence management process.

 THE TESCO SCHEME TO REDUCE UNPLANNED ABSENCE

CASE STUDY 10.4

In 2004 Tesco piloted a scheme aimed at reducing short-term unplanned absence. Staff in new stores were given three extra days holiday per year but sick pay was removed for the first three days of absence, irrespective of whether they related to genuine illness or not. A Tesco spokeswoman explained that the aim was to 'encourage people to plan absences. We do not want to penalise people who are genuinely ill, but we do want to discourage people from taking the odd day off.' Absence for longer than three days would continue to be paid.

At the same time incentives, in the form of shopping vouchers, were introduced for those with no absence in a twelve-month period.

Prior to this a 'Supporting your Attendance' scheme had been

introduced the year before involving 'welcome back' meetings following unplanned absence, along with training for managers emphasising the importance of coaching and treating employees as individuals. Absence management also became part of managers' performance reviews.

Source: adapted from Pollitt (2004) and CIPD (2005b)

Questions

1   How effective do you think the Tesco approach might be?

2   What conditions would have to be in place for this to operate successfully?

PREVENTATIVE APPROACHES

It can be argued that control-focused and punitive forms of absence management address the symptoms of absence rather than the causes (McHugh, 2002). In contrast, preventative approaches are generally more holistic and aim to create an environment in which absence is less likely and, in some cases, attempt to directly address the root causes of absence. In response to changing social attitudes and increasing employee expectations it is now relatively common to find absence management forming part of broader employee wellbeing strategies which aim to improve the overall health of the workforce and encourage a culture of wellness (Pilbeam and Corbridge, 2010). Such approaches are consistent with the recent government initiatives to reduce ill health and worklessness discussed earlier in the chapter. The CIPD (2012i) has observed a steady increase in the number of organisations that have an employee wellbeing strategy in place, this being more likely in the public than the private sector. There is considerable variety in the types of benefits offered, but the most common are access to employee assistance or counselling services, followed by stop-smoking support and subsidised gym membership (CIPD, 2012i). The CBI (2011) also notes increased interest in employee wellbeing schemes, 74 per cent of organisations in a recent survey citing employee wellbeing as a priority over the next 12 months. Planned areas for action are listed in Table 10.3.

Table 10.3 Employee wellbeing – planned areas for action (%)

Action	All	Public sector	Private sector
Occupational health advice	74	89	68
Praise for a job well done	61	58	62
Honest feedback from supervisors	57	58	57
Access to mental wellbeing and stress support	55	68	50
Development opportunities	51	55	50
Personal counselling	51	68	44
Work–life balance advice/support	49	71	41
Health diet advice	46	61	40
Stop-smoking support	36	45	33
Subsidised gym membership/sporting opportunities	36	34	37
Employer-funded medical checkups	28	16	33
Support in dealing with drink and substance abuse	25	32	22
Immunisation – eg flu vaccination	24	18	27
Other	9	5	10

Source: CBI (2011)

Many of these initiatives aim to improve the health of the workforce generally by encouraging and supporting employees to become fitter and healthier, and are not directly linked to causes of absence. A more targeted approach is adopted in some cases. The Health and Safety Executive (HSE), for example, reports on a range of organisations who have directly addressed high rates of absence due to musculoskeletal disorders (MSDs) by making ergonomic changes to the workplace. Other organisations have supplemented this by introducing on-site physiotherapy services and paid time off for doctor's visits in a more proactive approach towards MSDs (PricewaterhouseCoopers, 2008).

Research carried out by Pricewaterhouse Coopers (2008) for the government's Health, Work and Wellbeing partnership sought to make a business case for the adoption of wellness programmes. From a review of 55 case study organisations they found positive results for the impact of such programmes against a number of indicators, including sickness absence, turnover, accidents and injuries and employee satisfaction. The impact on sickness absence was particularly marked, 45 out of 55 companies reporting reductions in absence ranging from 10 per cent to 97 per cent, with an average of 30 to 40 per cent.

From their research for the Health, Work and Wellbeing partnership, PricewaterhouseCoopers developed a conceptual model representing a 'holistic approach to wellness' incorporating three main types of intervention:

- **health- and safety-related initiatives** based on statutory regulation and government requirements
- **managing ill health initiatives** involving occupational health, absence and disability management

- **prevention and promotion initiatives** involving health promotion, work–life balance and stress management, career and personal development, and primary care.

Research also points to factors associated with the organisational context which influence absence and should therefore be included in preventative approaches. McHugh (2002: 723) likens absence to a 'viral infection which adversely affects, and is affected by, the overall health of the organisational system'. From her research into district councils within Northern Ireland she found that high levels of absence were accompanied by a number of other problems including low morale, feelings of being undervalued, low levels of trust between management and staff, and 'them and us' attitudes. These other problems associated with poor organisational health generally were thought to be the root of much of the absence, and she concluded that organisations should acknowledge the interdependence of wider organisational issues, including culture, employee commitment and adaptation to change, and absence, if longer-term solutions to absence are to be achieved. The more recent financial pressures on the public sector and local government in particular make these findings even more pertinent.

More recently, Irvine (2011) has investigated the influence of contextual factors other than ill health on employee absence, against the backdrop of the recent government policy initiatives aimed at reducing workplace absence and promoting the view that work is good for you. She notes that the initiatives which followed the Black Report (2008) have acknowledged the interrelatedness of health and work but have not so far taken into account the role of individual employment conditions in influencing absence behaviour. Based upon a study of people who had recent experience of managing mental health and employment across a range of organisations and geographical regions, she found that individual decisions on whether or not to attend work were not solely based on employee perceptions of their state of health but were also influenced by such factors as the availability of sick pay, perceived job security and flexibility and job control. Employees with generous sick pay arrangements and where absence was not perceived to place at risk their future employment were mostly to be found in large organisations and, not surprisingly, felt able to take time off with greater peace of mind than those working in less secure employment with limited or no sick pay entitlement. Within the context of mental health conditions, flexible working arrangements enabled employees to manage their work around times when they were feeling less well and thus take less absence. This is an encouraging finding for organisations whose wellness strategies include flexible working arrangements, although Irvine (2011) cautions that it can also lead to presenteeism in the form of employees appearing to be working while being unproductive due to ill health.

This research suggests that wellness strategies aimed at preventing absence due to ill health could be undermined if account is not taken of wider contextual factors including management practices, employment conditions and the organisation of work.

REFLECTIVE ACTIVITY 10.2

Approaches to managing absence

Reflect upon your experience of absence management strategies.

1   Have these approaches been perceived as primarily punitive or preventative?

2   Which elements of the overall approach have had the greatest impact on absence?

INCENTIVES FOR ATTENDANCE

A more contentious approach to absence management is the provision of attendance incentives. Although not widely used – by only 13 per cent of organisations overall, according to CIPD data (2012i) – their use is more prevalent in manufacturing and production environments and less likely in the public sector (20 per cent and 5 per cent respectively, according to the CIPD, 2012i). The types of rewards offered are varied and may include financial bonuses, entry into prize draws, additional leave or flexi-time, vouchers, or letters of recognition. Organisational responses to incentive schemes linked to attendance are ambivalent (Huczynski and Fitzpatrick, 1989), many employers expressing the view that employees should not be rewarded twice for attending work. Huczynski and Fitzpatrick (1989) concluded from their review of research that although some organisations reported short-term decreases in absence, there were a number of potential disadvantages including:

- incentives tend to be more effective in motivating those who already have good attendance records
- if an employee is absent and loses the reward, there is little motivation for continued good attendance – which can have the perverse effect of increasing absence
- often schemes are not cost-effective
- short-term reductions in absence are often not sustained (although this is difficult to substantiate due to the short-term nature of many incentive schemes).

In their research into employee attitudes towards penalties and incentives within a Civil Service department, Harvey and Nicholson (1993: 854) found support for the view that 'employment entails a commitment to attend and therefore additional incentives would be inappropriate'. They found that just over half of the employees surveyed supported some kind of incentive – a cash bonus being the most popular, followed by written or verbal recognition for good attendance. Several respondents were proud of their good attendance record but felt it was not recognised by their managers. These employees, however, were not currently receiving attendance incentives, which are rare within this context, and these findings might not be replicated in a manufacturing environment where such incentives are more common. Dunn and Wilkinson (2002) found that managers working with blue-collar and clerical workers were sceptical of attendance bonuses and the idea of paying twice for simply turning up for work. They also feared the negative consequences of employees turning up for work when they were ill.

Some of the limitations of a punitive approach discussed above would also apply to attendance incentives, which are unlikely to work if the wider causes of absence are not simultaneously addressed.

Examples of attendance incentives

In 2004 the Royal Mail introduced a widely publicised incentive scheme alongside a range of other absence control measures, including improved occupational health services and training for line managers. Employees with no sickness over a six-month period were entered into a prize draw to win a new car or holiday vouchers. As a result 37 people won new cars and 75 won £2,000 in holiday vouchers, a further 90,000 winning £150 of holiday vouchers. Unplanned absence during this period reduced from 6.4 per cent to 5.7 per cent (CIPD, 2005b).

The Manchester law firm Pannone – ranked 18th in the *Sunday Times* '100 Best Companies to Work For list' in 2010 – runs an annual reward scheme to thank employees for good attendance. The rewards are quite modest, but employees within the firm who have had no absence within the previous 12 months receive a payment of £100, and those with no more than four days' absence receive £75. This applies only to staff below a certain salary level and is reported as very popular by the Operations Partner. Absence levels within the firm have historically been low, and this is one of a range of measures intended to address short-term absence and encourage employee health and satisfaction (2011c).

LONG-TERM ABSENCE

Most of the absence management strategies considered so far have been primarily aimed at addressing short-term unpredictable absence rather than long-term absence, although elements of some of these approaches apply to all types of absence. CIPD survey data for the past few years consistently reports long-term absence (defined as absence of four weeks or longer) to account for approximately 19 per cent of all absence, although within the public and not-for-profit sectors this is higher, at 26 per cent and 21 per cent respectively (CIPD, 2012i). CBI data (2011) attributes one third of employee absence to long-term conditions and suggests that nearly half of all absence in the public sector is due to long-term ill health. There are clear indications that although work-related physical injury is on the decline, work-related 'psychological distress', including stress, depression and anxiety, remains a significant cause of ill health and absence (Irvine, 2011: 753). Since the CIPD reported in 2011 for the first time that stress was the main cause of long-term absence for both manual and non-manual employees, it would seem that the management of long-term absence should also be a priority for organisations. Government pressure to encourage early return to work following long-term sickness through initiatives such as the 'fit note' is likely to increase as pressures on public welfare spending continue.

Relatively little attention has been paid within the HRM literature to the management of long-term absence and to the effectiveness of attempts made by employers to enhance return to work and continued employment (James et al, 2002). Although ill health is recognised as a significant cause of sickness absence, and especially so in the case of long-term absence, James et al (2002), from their research among HR managers across 30 organisations, concluded that few employers had comprehensive policies and arrangements for handling cases of long-term absence and serious illness. CIPD (2012a) and ACAS (2012b) advice for handling long-term absence revolves around the need to maintain contact with absent employees, the early intervention of occupational health services and the development of return-to-work plans including adjustments to work and phased returns where appropriate.

James et al's (2002) research, however, suggests that these areas are problematic. They found that line managers who had the primary responsibility for keeping in touch with absent employees were inconsistent in their application of policies and unsure of when and how they should maintain contact. Where occupational health services existed, these played a major role in the management of long-term absence – but this role was often surrounded by ambiguity, employers perceiving that they represented the employee's interests rather than the employers', and some employees regarding a referral to occupational health as the start of punitive action. They found that employers in their study were considering adaptations to working time and jobs to facilitate early return to work, but often faced operational difficulties or budgetary constraints in trying to implement them. They noted the need for greater consistency in the handling of long-term absence and recommended a case management approach whereby those with managerial responsibility and specialist expertise should get together to discuss individual cases.

IDS data (2011c) suggests that some organisations may have improved their management of long-term absence in recent years, with widespread recognition of the need to maintain regular contact with absent employees, recognition of the importance of early intervention of occupational health specialists, and a greater focus on rehabilitation and workplace adjustments. The IDS reports on organisations such as East Sussex County

Council where 'attendance management teams' made up of HR, legal and occupational health professionals work with line managers to deal with individual cases of long-term absence in a similar way to James *et al*'s (2002) suggested 'case managers' (IDS, 2011c).

PRESENTEEISM: THE IMPACT OF ABSENCE MANAGEMENT STRATEGIES?

As noted earlier in the chapter, absence rates have shown a steady decrease over the past two decades, and this is undoubtedly due, to some extent at least, to more proactive approaches to the management of absence adopted by employers, although a direct causal link is difficult to establish. At the same time government policy has sought to promulgate the view that work is good for you, with an explicit aim of encouraging people to work while not in full health (Health, Work and Wellbeing Directorate, 2010: 10):

> A key plank of our health, work and wellbeing strategy is to change broader cultural norms around sickness and work, in particular, the erroneous belief that if you are not 100 per cent fit you should not be in work.

This has led to a growth of interest within the HRM literature in the impact of the absence management strategies adopted by organisations and in the phenomenon of *presenteeism*. Defined as 'attending work while ill' (Johns, 2010: 521), there is a lack of conceptual clarity around this now widely used term in that employees coming to work while ill can be seen as both an aspiration and a problem (Irvine, 2011). Much of the interest stems from claims that presenteeism causes greater loss of productivity than absenteeism, leading to the potential for its effective management to be a source of competitive advantage (Johns, 2010).

The research to date mostly focuses on the factors leading to presenteeism and its impact on individuals and organisations. The influences on an employee's decision to attend work, or not, when unwell, have been grouped by many commentators into those relating to the organisation and those relating to the individual (eg Aronsson and Gustafsson, 2005; Grinyer and Singleton, 2000). Baker-McClearn *et al* (2010: 314) summarise these under the headings of 'organisational pressures' and 'personal motivations'. From their interviews with a range of managers and employees within nine UK organisations, they found support for many of the previous research findings. In terms of *organisational pressures*, sickness absence and trigger policies, the role played by HR, return-to-work interviews, management style and workplace culture were all found to be relevant. A common finding was that employees perceived that their organisation's absence management policies compelled them to attend work, and this was especially so where highly punitive approaches – such as withdrawal of sick pay or threat of dismissal – were used. Employees reported finding themselves in a 'lose/lose situation; if they were absent they would be penalised, but if they attended work they would be unable to perform their duties effectively and would suffer too in terms of their health and general wellbeing' (Baker-McClearn *et al*, 2010: 319). This echoed the earlier findings of Grinyer and Singleton (2000), who had conducted research into two UK public sector employment offices. In one of these organisations, where particularly stringent approaches had been adopted, they identified a fear of taking sickness absence, which was possibly leading to longer-term absence. One interviewee, for example, stated (Grinyer and Singleton, 2000: 14):

> Nobody takes the odd day off sick. Even if you are dying, you still come in, because once you've had over a certain – I think it's three – lots of sick, you get hauled in. And even if it's genuine, you still get hauled in for a verbal warning, so people don't tend to take the odd day now, but go for the long term.

Fear of reaching trigger points was particularly widespread in Grinyer and Singleton's research, coupled with feelings of guilt. This frequently led to employees' taking a longer period of absence to ensure that they were fully fit rather than risk having another episode of absence and reaching the trigger point. Baker-McClearn *et al* (2010) found that the role played by the HR department was often perceived to be primarily concerned with implementing the absence management policy and getting people back into work, rather than supporting them. Line managers similarly felt that the rigidity of the procedures did not allow for a sensitive or supportive approach, and conveyed the impression that there was a 'general culture of not believing that employees are ill' (Baker-McClearn *et al*, 2010: 321). Both Johns (2010) and Baker-McClearn *et al* (2010) acknowledge the development of cultures of presenteeism in some organisations, where senior managers set an example by attending work while unwell, sometimes accompanied by long working hours, conveying the impression that it was not the 'done thing' to go off sick.

A number of personal pressures for presenteeism have also been identified through the research. Aronsson and Gustafsson (2005), based on research in Sweden, found that people who perceived that they were irreplaceable, that no one else could do their job, or that the backlog of work on their return from absence would be unmanageable, were more likely to attend when ill. They also identify the notion of *individual boundarylessness*, referring to people who find it hard to say no to others' demands and expectations, and found that this was linked to presenteeism.

Hansen and Andersen (2008), based on their research in Denmark, also found that perceptions of time pressures were an important influence on presenteeism. Some of the research has explored the influence of employee perceptions of control over their jobs and flexibility in organising their working time – the so-called *adjustment latitude* (Johns, 2010). The overall findings have been a little unclear, but Irvine's (2011) research into employees with mental health conditions found that flexible working was perceived by some employees to be helpful in enabling them to manage their work around their illness. Some participants, however, reported that because they had not disclosed their mental health problems to their employer, flexible working enabled them to conceal the problems more easily, and to 'struggle on'.

A further strong personally motivated influence on presenteeism is a feeling of obligation or commitment to fellow team members, clients or the organisation. In one of the organisations studied by Grinyer and Singleton (2000: 13) team work had recently been introduced, and respondents spoke of the additional pressure imposed by this in that 'being the member of a team instilled an obligation to fellow team members, which resulted in a reluctance to take sick leave'. Although they note that this could be viewed as a positive form of pressure to attend by the organisation, some employees commented on the fact that it also led to longer periods of sickness absence and the spreading of sickness around the office when people attended work with infectious illnesses. Other studies have also reported evidence of presenteeism among doctors and healthcare workers resulting from feelings of commitment to patients, colleague and professional image (Dew *et al*, 2005; Aronsson and Gustaffson, 2005). This could be particularly worrying for organisations such as the NHS, in which staff are expected to stay away from work with certain infectious disorders in order to avoid spreading them among patients.

The possible consequences of presenteeism are well summarised by Hansen and Andersen (2008) and Johns (2010). These can include the worsening of physical or psychological health problems through insufficient or no recuperation time, damage to the quality of working life and lowered productivity or performance. However, Baker-McClearn *et al* (2010) note that presenteeism can also be positive. They describe return-to-work arrangements following long-term absence where employees are supported through phased return and adjustments to their duties. Although these could be perceived as bringing people back to work before they are fully recovered, they could also be seen as an attempt to prevent the social isolation that often accompanies long-term absence and to facilitate rehabilitation. This highlights one of the difficulties with absence management, when policies and practices intended to be supportive by management are perceived as threatening by employees (Grinyer and Singleton, 2000).

CRITICAL REFECTION 10.5

1   What are the pressures to attend work in organisations or job roles with which you are familiar?

2   Do these lead to 'presenteeism', and if they do, what impact does this have?

CONCLUSION

What conclusions, then, can be drawn for the effective management of absence? There is evidence that the more proactive approaches now adopted by many organisations are leading to a reduction in absence and therefore cost savings. However, the research also suggests that although this might be going some way to solve the problem of short-term absence, some unintended consequences could ensue, including perverse incentives to take longer spells of absence to avoid hitting trigger points and the problems associated with presenteeism.

The relationship between sickness absence and presenteeism, or the decision to attend work or not when sick, is complex and influenced by a number of social, cultural, organisational and individual factors. Unless account is taken of these underlying influences when designing strategies for managing absence, these are likely to have only a short-term effect and the problem may transfer elsewhere. This could be manifested in other forms of withdrawal, such as lowered performance or staff turnover. It also suggests that an over-simplistic approach to absence management is unlikely to be successful.

It seems reasonable to conclude that absence should be managed as part of a broader, consistent set of performance management and HR strategies which aim to support employees when they are ill, while at the same time creating an environment in which employees want to come to work rather than feel that they are compelled to. The attempts now being made by some organisations to develop more supportive cultures of attendance, with an emphasis on wider employee wellbeing as well as proactive management of absence, might offer some hopeful signs for the future.

FOCUSING ON EARLY INTERVENTIONS AT SOUTH LANARKSHIRE COUNCIL

CASE STUDY 10.5

South Lanarkshire Council prides itself on being one of the best-performing councils in absence management in Scotland. The Council has demonstrated high-level commitment to maximising attendance, and it is a key work objective and focus for all members of the corporate management team. A number of years ago the

Council decided to take a holistic approach to promoting attendance. It established an overarching 'maximising attendance' policy, which, while incorporating a disciplinary route for unacceptable absences, focused in particular on encouraging attendance rather than on punitive measures. Eileen McPake, Personnel Officer, reported: 'We focus first on early interventions to ensure that employees have what they need. If there is still an issue with absence, we feel more comfortable proceeding down a disciplinary route because we have provided all the support we can as an employer.'

One of the main causes of absence among Council employees was psychological ill health (including depression and work- or home-related stress). The Council focused on early interventions to facilitate recovery and reduce the length of absence. Employees who were absent for psychological reasons were immediately visited or contacted by an early intervention officer in order to fully understand the reason for their absence and find out if anything could be done to help, including referring them to a counsellor, if appropriate. The process gave the employee an opportunity to say what would be helpful to them, and enabled the Council to provide support as an employer.

The Council also offered employees cognitive behaviour therapy (CBT), if it was recommended by the Council's occupational health adviser. Over 60 employees had accessed this service since it was launched the previous year and half of them remained at work during the treatment.

The second most common cause of absence among Council employees was musculoskeletal injuries. Waiting-lists to see a GP-referred physiotherapist averaged six to eight weeks in the area. The Council offered its own physiotherapy service through an external provider which could offer treatment in as many days, and this aided recovery and a more speedy return to work.

Managers were trained to conduct what the Council calls a 'brief intervention' interview. These interviews are short, structured conversations around particular health topics. For example, a manager who suspected that an employee had an alcohol problem might approach that employee, advise that their coming in late or change in behaviour has been noticed, and ask what the employee can tell them about that. The structure of the 'brief intervention' interviews gave employees the chance to have their say and take responsibility for improving their wellbeing.

Managers were also required to conduct return-to-work interviews for every absence. Three absences in a year acted as a trigger for a more formal meeting with the manager. Any underlying health issues or forms of support required were discussed. If there were no underlying health issues, managers advised the employee that their attendance was being monitored. If there was a fourth absence within a year, disciplinary procedures might be instigated, although cases were dealt with on an individual basis.

In June 2009, an employee assistance programme was introduced. The introduction of the EAP provided a vital communication tool to create awareness of support available to employees. The Council had a formal partnership agreement with the trade unions, and the health and wellbeing of employees was a key area that they worked on together to achieve positive outcomes.

The excellent attendance record of the Council was facilitated by real commitment from senior leaders. Attendance figures were reported monthly and discussed at executive team meetings. Attendance policy and practices were regularly reviewed and improved upon. The Council is proud of the progress it has made and of the efforts it makes to support the wellbeing of its employees.

Source: adapted from CIPD (2010b)

Questions

1   The approach taken by South Lanarkshire Council incorporates both preventative and punitive elements. How successful do you think this combination might be?

2   What other factors might the Council have to consider to ensure the continued success of the scheme?

EXPLORE FURTHER

Baker-McClearn, D., Greasley, K., Dale, J. and Griffith, F. (2010) 'Absence management and presenteeism: the pressures on employees to attend work and the impact of attendance on performance', *Human Resource Management Journal*, Vol.20, No.3: 311–28

Dunn, C. and Wilkinson, A. (2002) 'Wish you were here: managing absence', *Personnel Review*, Vol.31, No.2: 228–46

Irvine, A. (2011) 'Fit for work? The influence of sick pay and job flexibility on sickness absence and implications for presenteeism', *Social Policy and Administration*, Vol.45, No.7: 752–69

James, P., Cunningham, I. and Dibben, P. (2002) 'Absence management and the issues of job retention and return to work', *Human Resource Management Journal*, Vol.12, No.2: 82–94

McHugh, M. (2002) 'The absence bug: a treatable viral infection?', *Journal of Managerial Psychology*, Vol.17, No.8: 722–38

Nicholson, N. and Johns, G. (1985) 'The absence culture and the psychological contract – Who's in control of absence?', *Academy of Management Review*, Vol.10, No.3: 397–407

Steers, R. M .and Rhodes, S. R. (1978) 'Major influences on employee attendance: a process model', *Journal of Applied Psychology*, Vol.63, No.4: 391–407

CHAPTER 11

International Performance Management

SUE HUTCHINSON

LEARNING OUTCOMES

By the end of this chapter you should be able to:

- describe global trends in performance management

- explain the role that a nation's culture plays in effective performance management

- understand the impact of other contextual factors on global performance management

- understand the importance of managing expatriate performance effectively

- explore the complexities of managing the performance of expatriates

- understand the extent to which performance management practices are converging or diverging internationally.

INTRODUCTION

Most of the principles upon which performance management is based are predominantly US-centric, and this raises questions about its theoretical underpinnings and appropriateness in other cultures (Chiang and Birtch, 2010). Not all the world shares the features of US work culture, which is categorised as 'individualistic' and 'low in power distance', meaning that employees are likely to prefer egalitarian-type decision-making, to value feedback and to be prepared to challenge their boss (Hofstede, 1980). The USA is thus very different from, say, China with its strong collectivist culture, 'high power distance' and acceptance of authority. Here, employees are reluctant to engage in two-way communication, and challenging the boss may be perceived as insubordination and causing a 'loss of face' (Huo and Von Glinow, 1995). In Chapter 3 it was also noted how differences in national culture can influence motivational factors towards work, and how some common Western reward practices – such as individual performance-related pay – might make 'dangerous cultural exports' (Boxall and Purcell, 2011: 73).

In essence, performance management developed in one country may not be suitable in another country's setting. Previous chapters have emphasised that performance issues are context-driven (see, for example, Chapter 2), and in an international setting an additional set of macro-level (eg societal, economic, political and legal) factors come into play. Increased globalisation and the growth in multinational corporations (MNCs) means that organisations have to pay more attention to the application of performance management practices across borders. Complex decisions have to be made, such as whether all countries should adopt the same system or whether local arrangements should apply (standardisation versus localisation). If local decisions take priority, how can a global strategic approach to performance management be adopted which requires a focus on similarities and standardisation on a world-wide basis (Suutari and Tahvanainen, 2002)?

However, this is not only an issue for MNCs. Increasing migration across international borders has increased the diversity of many national labour forces. UN estimates show that in 2010 there were 214 million migrant workers who had moved across national boundaries, compared to 155 million in 1990 – an increase of some 38 per cent in 20 years (Verma and He, 2010). The UK has seen a net increase of migrants since the 1980s, with substantial increases since 1992, and the proportion of the working-age population born overseas is now around 13 per cent (Coleman, 2010). This raises questions about the appropriateness of performance management practices in the domestic setting for multicultural workforces.

Despite the importance of these trends, the academic literature on international performance management is weak and relatively atheoretical and exploratory in nature (Claus and Briscoe, 2009). Although there are accounts of performance management in different countries, our understanding of how it is applied in different cross-national and cross-cultural contexts is poor and largely anecdotal.

This chapter considers the application of performance management from an international perspective, and begins with some global trends. It then considers the role that a nation's culture plays in determining the way performance is managed, before considering other key macro-level influences. The international HRM literature focuses almost exclusively on performance appraisal (eg Gregerson *et al*, 1996; Snape *et al*, 1998; Shen, 2005; Chiang and Birtch, 2010) rather than performance management systems, so that is our focus here. In addition to managing the performance of host (local) country nationals, MNCs must consider the management of expatriates – those on international assignments in foreign operations. These managers are often critical to the success of MNCs, but the literature and practice suggests that expatriate performance management is largely ignored. The chapter examines the limited research that is available in this area, and the practice, before concluding with a discussion about how far performance management practices are converging or diverging internationally.

GLOBAL TRENDS

Individual country accounts suggest a growth in the adoption of performance management practices (see, for example, Varma, Budhwar and DeNisi, 2008). The most comprehensive data on trends from a comparative perspective comes from the Cranet survey, which collects longitudinal data on HR policy and practice from almost 8,000 organisations in over 30 countries. The survey asks three questions on performance management:

- Who is appraised (management, professional, and clerical, manual)?
- Who contributes to the appraisal (next-level manager, employee, subordinate)?
- What are the outcomes of the appraisal (training, promotion, career development, and performance-related pay)?

The picture that emerges from this survey is (Boselie *et al*, 2011; Brewster *et al*, 2011; Cranet, 2005) that:

- There are large differences between countries in the use of appraisal (see Figures 11.1 and 11.2). In twelve countries (Belgium, the Czech Republic, Denmark, France, Greece, Italy, Slovakia, Slovenia, Switzerland, the UK, Canada and the USA) more than 80 per cent of organisations use appraisal systems. However, in four countries (Iceland,

Norway, Sweden and the Turkish Cypriot community) fewer than 50 per cent of organisations use appraisal systems.

Figure 11.1 Average use of appraisal across employee categories (EU countries)

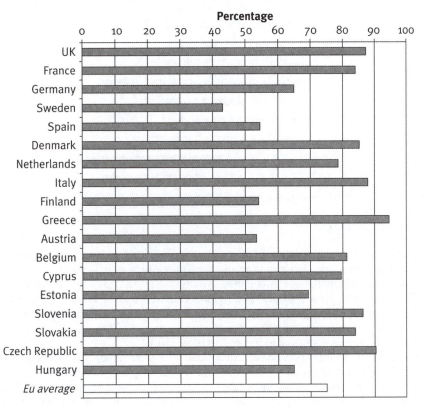

Source: Cranet (2005)

Figure 11.2 Average use of appraisal across employee categories (non-EU European and North America)

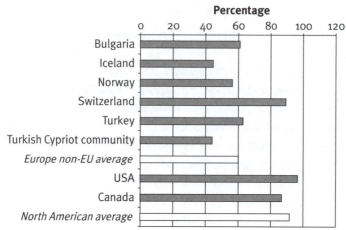

Source: Cranet (2005)

- There was an increase in the use of appraisal systems in all countries for all grades of staff (but particularly clerical and manual staff) between the mid- and late 1990s. The only exception was the use of appraisal systems for professionals in the Netherlands, which remained stable at 82 per cent. In most countries it is the senior people who are more likely to be appraised, although coverage for all grades of staff varied greatly across countries (for example, in 1999 in France just 5 per cent of firms used appraisals for clerical employees, compared to 95 per cent in Sweden).
- The number and proportion of employees who were given the opportunity to contribute to the appraisal process and to 360-degree appraisal increased. There are, however, some striking differences between countries. In Sweden, for example, 90 per cent of firms rely on employee input into the appraisal process, whereas in Japan employee input is just 10 per cent.
- In terms of the purpose of appraisal, defining training needs is the most popular outcome, although informing future career decisions has increased. Pay determination is a major purpose in only a few countries (Italy, Slovenia, Sweden, Norway, the Turkish Cypriot community, Bulgaria and the USA).

The Cranet survey focuses on performance appraisal and can only give a partial snapshot of global trends in performance management. Furthermore, it does not provide explanations for country differences, although there do appear to be contextual differences between countries which are associated with different national cultural norms (Boselie *et al*, 2011). For example, Japan is high in 'power distance' (Hofstede, 1980) whereas Sweden is low in 'power distance', which might explain the variations in employee involvement. This is explored below.

NATIONAL CULTURE

Culture is a rather hazy concept, with many faces and many meanings, but a common conceptualisation is that culture represents the values, belief systems, assumptions and behavioural patterns which differentiate one group of people from another (Aycan, 2005: 1085). In studies, culture is defined and measured through various value dimensions, the best-known being the work of Geert Hofstede (1980, 2001), whose research was based on a large-scale longitudinal study of IBM employees' attitudes in over 50 countries. Hofstede initially identified four dimensions of the differences between national cultures:

- power distance
- uncertainty avoidance
- individualism/collectivism
- masculinity/femininity.

Power distance (PD)

This concerns the extent to which inequalities in the distribution of power are accepted and expected. Cultures high in power distance (eg India, France, Malaysia and Hong Kong) are accepting of an unequal distribution of power and people are respectful of authority. Employees are unlikely to express disagreements with their managers or challenge their superiors because that is considered disrespectful. As Taylor (2011) notes: 'When the boss says "Jump!", people jump' (2011: 234). Management style is likely to be autocratic or paternal, and organisations are hierarchical with centralised decision-making.

In low PD cultures (eg Austria, Germany, Israel), relationships between individuals across hierarchical levels are closer and less formal, and employees are more willing to approach their manager. Management style is likely to be more participative and consultative, and the organisational structure fairly flat or non-hierarchical.

Uncertainty avoidance (UA)

This is associated with the degree to which people feel comfortable with uncertainty, risk-taking and ambiguity. Cultures with high uncertainty avoidance (eg Japan, Greece, France) place greater emphasis on security and do not encourage risk-taking, limiting it with structures, rules and clarity. Low UA cultures (Singapore, Sweden, Britain and Hong Kong) are more likely to encourage risk-taking behaviour, be tolerant of ambiguity and accept innovation and change. Organisations are likely to adopt a decentralised and more flexible structure.

Individualism/collectivism

This reflects the extent to which the interests of the individual (including their immediate family) take precedence over the interests of the group. Strong individualist cultures (eg Britain, the USA and the Netherlands) value personal initiative, choice and achievement. In contrast, in collectivist cultures (eg Pakistan, Peru and Indonesia) group interests (eg social groups or the wider community) take precedence over the individual. Emphasis is given to reducing differences between group members, maintaining group harmony, loyalty, preserving relationships and face-saving. Hofstede found a strong correlation between collectivism and high power distance, which he explained by claiming that in cultures which depend on groups, the people are also dependent on power figures – although there are exceptions, such as France.

Masculinity/femininity

This is to do with the difference cultures place on traditionally 'male' and 'female' values. Masculine cultures (eg Japan, Venezuela, Italy) are associated with values such as assertiveness, ambition, competiveness and material possessions. On the other hand, female cultures (eg the Netherlands, Norway and Sweden) place more value on intrinsic satisfaction such as quality of life, harmony, relationships and care for others.

Based on further research in South-East Asian countries, Hofstede later added a fifth dimension, long-term versus short-term orientation or the 'time horizon' of a society (originally termed 'Confucian dynamism'). China, Japan and other Asian countries score highly on this dimension, characterised by long-term thinking, persistence and perseverance. In contrast, most Western countries score low, with a short-term orientation demonstrated in the achievement of immediate results.

Countries were scored against each of these dimensions, allowing each country to be ranked (see Table 11.1). Britain, for example, is characterised by low power distance, high individualism, masculinity, low uncertainty avoidance and low long-term orientation. Other 'Anglo-Saxon' countries such as the USA, Canada and Australia show a similar pattern, but in Europe there is more variation, indicating that there is no unified European cultural norm. France, for example, is high on power distance and uncertainty avoidance; the Netherlands and Scandinavian countries have a strong feminine culture.

Table 11.1 Hofstede's dimensions by country and ranked position (1 the highest; 53 the lowest)

	Power distance	Individualism	Masculinity	Uncertainty avoidance
Austria	53	18	2	24–25
Chile	24–25	38	46	10–15
Finland	46	17	47	31–32
France	15–16	10–11	35–36	10–15
Germany	42–44	15	9–10	29
Great Britain	42–44	3	9–10	47–48
Greece	27–28	30	18–19	1
Hong Kong	15–16	37	18–19	49–50
India	10–11	21	20–21	45
Israel	52	19	29	19
Italy	34	7	4–5	23
Japan	33	22–23	1	7
Malaysia	1	36	25–26	46
Netherlands	40	4–5	51	35
Portugal	24–25	33–35	45	2
Spain	31	20	37–38	10–15
Sweden	47–48	10–11	52	49–50
Taiwan	29–30	44	32–33	26
USA	38	1	15	43

Source: Hofstede and Bond, 1988
Note: The table shows only selected countries. Some countries were, in any case, excluded from Hofstede's research, such as Russia. East African, West African and Arab countries were listed on a regional rather than individual country basis.

Many criticisms have been levelled at Hofstede's work concerning his conceptualisation of culture (defined as the 'collective programming of the mind'), the dimensions and the methodology (eg McSweeney, 2002; Gerhart and Fang, 2005; Chiang, 2005). Not least is the problem that data was collected from a single company, raising questions about the generalisability of the findings (although Hofstede claimed this was necessary to ensure that organisational specific factors were controlled for and nationality was the key cultural variable). McSweeney (2002, 2009) questions the assumption of cultural homogeneity in one country, when in fact there are wide variations within countries according to regions, social classes, ethnic groups, language, and so on. Spain, Belgium and Switzerland, for example, all have different communities which speak different languages and have different legislation. Even the USA, which is classified as a single cultural unit in Hofstede's work, contains a vast array of different cultural groups. The theory also presents culture as something that is static and durable – but societies can change, and some countries have moved from their original position on the dimensions. Thompson and McHugh (2009) give the example of former Communist countries, traditionally high in power distance, collectivism and uncertainty avoidance, which are now experiencing individualism and becoming accepting of uncertainty. Also, as discussed in the introduction to this chapter, countries are becoming more culturally diverse due to migration.

REFLECTIVE ACTIVITY 11.1

Using Hofstede's cultural dimensions, what are the implications for managing people, including leadership style, for an American-owned MNC that wants to set up a subsidiary in another country in Table 11.1? (Choose any country listed.)

Despite the criticisms of Hofstede, his work seems very plausible, has endured and remains highly influential. Further cultural typologies have been developed by others – for example, Trompenaars and Hampden-Turner (1997), Hall and Hall (1990), Aycan *et al* (2000), and most recently, House *et al*'s (2004) Global Leadership and Organisational Behaviour Effectiveness Research Program (GLOBE). Although some of their dimensions may be different from Hofstede's, their underlying argument remains similar – namely, 'that every culture is held to have a tacit dimension rooted in a subconscious set of beliefs that form the bedrock of national identity' (Edwards and Rees, 2011: 38).

The GLOBE study of 62 societies

House *et al*'s (2004) GLOBE study identifies nine cultural dimensions that influence management practice. Some were based on Hofstede's typology and others were based on other studies (eg Trompenaars and Hampden-Turner, 1997; Kluckhohn and Strodtbeck, 1961; McClelland, 1985).

- *Power distance* – the degree to which members of a collective expect power to be distributed equally
- *Uncertainty avoidance* – the extent to which a society, organisation or group relies on social norms, rules and procedures to alleviate unpredictability of future events
- *Human orientation* – the degree to which a collective encourages and rewards individuals for being fair, altruistic, generous, caring and kind to others
- *Institutional collectivism* – the degree to which organisational and societal institutional practices encourage and reward collective distribution of resources and collective action
- *In-group collectivism* – the extent to which individuals express pride, loyalty and cohesiveness in their organisations and families
- *Assertiveness* – the degree to which individuals are assertive, confrontational and aggressive in their relationship with others
- *Gender egalitarianism* – the extent to which a collective minimises gender inequality

- *Future orientation* – the degree to which individuals engage in future-oriented behaviours such as delaying gratification, planning and investing in the future.
- *Performance orientation* – the extent to which a collective encourages and rewards group members for performance improvement and excellence.

Central to Hofstede's work and those of others is the belief that culture influences leadership style, organisational structures and processes, and the way people are managed. The vast majority of evidence suggests that differences in cultural attitudes do translate into the way HRM is practised (Boxall and Purcell, 2011), and performance management is no exception. There is a growing body of research which shows that practices such as appraisal, performance measurement and performance-related pay are affected by the cultural context (eg Peretz and Fried, 2012; Chiang and Birtch, 2010; Atwater *et al*, 2005; Aycan, 2005; Cascio, 2006). The impact of culture on these practices is considered below.

CULTURAL IMPLICATIONS FOR PERFORMANCE APPRAISAL

In high power distance cultures performance appraisal is more likely to be a top-down judgemental process, and managers rather than other sources (eg peers or subordinates) are more likely to be the main evaluators (Huo and Von Glinow, 1995; Aycan, 2005). Open and frank discussions about performance problems are unlikely to succeed, and challenging managers will be perceived as insubordination and causing loss of face. Upward feedback to managers would be very much against the grain, as would 360-degree feedback. In France, which is high on PD, open criticism of others up the hierarchical line is avoided and appraisals are influenced by an elite system which prevails in society (Barzantny and Festing, 2008). This means that if an individual being appraised is from a more prestigious background, his or her appraisal is likely to be more positive.

In contrast, employees from cultures low in PD are likely to favour a more participative approach and engage in joint discussions with managers to assess performance, set targets, resolve difficulties and plan development needs. Multi-source feedback, which requires a high degree of participation, is more acceptable (Peretz and Fried, 2012). In Germany, the low PD culture manifests itself in a high degree of openness between the rater and ratee in the performance appraisal process, objective-setting is often the result of negotiation, and feedback can include open confrontations (Barzantny and Festing, 2008). Comparing US (low PD) and Hong Kong (high PD) managers, Entrekin and Chung (2001) found that Hong Kong managers preferred a more top-down, less participative, style of appraisal than US managers.

In collectivistic societies, feedback may be expected to be indirect, non-confrontational and subtle, and face-to-face performance interviews are extremely rare (Fletcher and Perry, 2001; Elenkov, 1998). Person-based appraisal schemes are likely to be avoided because of their potential to reveal the shortcomings of other group members and disturb group harmony (Kovach, 1995; Vallance, 1999; Trompenaars and Hampden-Turner, 1997). Employees are likely to prefer group feedback and group training to individual feedback and training (Earley, 1994; van de Vliert *et al*, 2004; Peretz and Fried, 2012). 360-degree feedback tends to be avoided in collectivist cultures because it may disturb group harmony due to the constant monitoring of the behaviour of one's colleagues (Aycan, 2005). On the other hand, individualistic cultures are likely to favour appraisal schemes which focus upon the individual and emphasise individual achievement and recognition.

Cultures which are high in uncertainty avoidance are more likely to rely on formality in the performance appraisal process. Control is necessary in the form of highly structured and standardised rules and procedures to reduce fear of the unknown. Performance feedback is more frequent to ensure that performance expectations are understood and to minimise any uncertainty and misunderstanding (Paik *et al*, 2000). Appraisals are more communication-development-centric because they reduce uncertainty regarding future performance outcomes and rewards (Chiang and Birtch, 2010).

Appraising performance across borders

Chiang and Birtch's (2010) study of appraisal in a multinational context provides further evidence to support the view that appraisal purposes and practices are influenced by cultural differences. Using House *et al*'s (2004) GLOBE dimensions of assertiveness, in-group collectivism, power distance and uncertainty avoidance, their analysis of the banking industry in seven countries (Canada, China-Hong Kong, Finland, Singapore, Sweden, the UK and the USA) found that:

- Low uncertainty avoidance, in-group collectivist and high power distance cultures are more likely to emphasise the evaluative role of appraisal (pay and promotion) in comparison to low PD and high UA cultures (eg Finland and Sweden), which use appraisal for communication-development.
- Frequent formal feedback was more likely to be preferred in high assertive and low in-group collectivist cultures and uncertainty avoidance cultures (eg the UK, the USA and Canada).
- Participation and the use of multi-source ratings are more acceptable in low in-group collectivist (eg the USA and the UK) and high uncertainty avoidance cultures (eg Sweden and Finland).
- Top-down one-way assessment by supervisor and annual formal appraisal is more likely to be found in high power distance and in-group collectivist cultures (eg Hong Kong and Singapore).

Chiang and Birtch (2010) do, however, caution not to oversimplify the influence of culture or make generalisations based solely on cultural stereotypes. Differences in appraisal can also stem from organisational, institutional and economic influences (see Chapter 2 and later in this chapter).

CULTURAL INFLUENCES ON OTHER PERFORMANCE MANAGEMENT PRACTICES

Culture also influences how managers evaluate their subordinates (Varma and Budhwar, 2011). For example, managers in India were found to give significantly higher ratings – above the level warranted – to employees they liked, because of culturally accepted practices such as the need to protect and support members of their in-group (Varma *et al*, 2005). Chinese managers are more likely than Western managers to base performance reviews upon personal attributions, and less on outcomes, and there is also a high degree of subjectivity in their evaluations (Claus and Briscoe, 2009).

Aycan (2005) notes that what constitutes 'good performance' is culture-bound, influencing the choice of performance criteria. Individualistic cultures prefer objective and quantifiable criteria and emphasise individual contribution and personal achievement. In contrast, collectivist cultures emphasise group-based achievement and criteria such as group loyalty, maintenance of harmonious relationships, trustworthiness, awareness of obligations, gratitude, organisational citizenship, conformity and contribution to team maintenance (Aycan, 2005; Brewster *et al*, 2011). Collectivist cultures also expect to put more emphasis on equity (Chiang, 2005).

Schuler and Rogovsky's (1998) study of the link between national culture and pay systems found that nations with high individualistic cultures have a greater focus on paying for performance generally, and a strong focus on individual performance-related pay (PRP). In contrast, countries low in individualism had less of a focus on performance-related pay. Similar findings were found for share ownership and options. They also found that in nations high in uncertainty avoidance pay systems based on seniority and skills were common, and there was less of a focus on individual PRP. More masculine cultures were likely to focus on individual bonuses for most employees. In contrast, more feminine cultures had less of a focus on these payments for non-managerial employees, but not for managers. Differences in power distance were only found on employee share ownership or options.

Culture, however, is by no means the only influence on reward, and there is strong evidence that the prevalence of a reward system is not necessarily consistent with the cultural profile of the country (Brewster *et al*, 2011). In a study of 10 nations Lowe *et al* (2002) found that paying for performance for managers was evenly spread across industrialised and newly-industrialised nations. The 2010 Cranet survey shows that individualised performance-related pay is most common in Switzerland, Greece, Finland and the USA, but least used in the UK, Australia, Cyprus and Japan. Chiang and Birch's (2007) study of reward preferences in four countries (Canada, the UK, Hong Kong-China and Finland) found that although cross-national variation in culture can account for some of the variation in employees' preferences, it is limited in explaining differences. Clearly, other factors, in particular institutional arrangements (eg the role of unions and collective bargaining), and legislation are (more) important influences on reward practice.

 PERFORMANCE MANAGEMENT IN CHINESE CULTURES

CASE STUDY 11.1

China is a strongly collectivist nation which has been influenced by Confucian cultural values that influence the way of work. In particular (Fitzpatrick, 2003):

- The concept of *guanxi* renders relationships extremely important.
- Saving face and building on reciprocal relationships is done by *renquing*, which means doing favours.
- Once you build a relationship, whether through family or work, you work hard to reciprocate favours to keep 'face' or *mianzi*.
- By exercising *bao* (reciprocity), you cannot lose face.
- *Chang bei* reinforces the importance of respect for elders and seniority.

In addition to a strong emphasis on interpersonal relationships and family orientation, there is a respect for age and hierarchy, a need for harmony, and moral cultivation (Tayeb, 2005).

The Chinese version of performance appraisal practices has existed in China for a very long time (Chapter 2), and the strong influence of Chinese culture in performance management practices is confirmed by a number of empirical studies (for example, Hempel, 2001; Snape *et al*, 1998; Entrekin and Chung, 2001; Huo and Von Glinow, 1995). Group-based evaluations and feedback are often preferred to individual evaluations and feedback, and two-way communication and conflict is avoided, emphasising the importance of collectivism, harmony and 'face' in the workplace. Respect for hierarchy, age and seniority means that managers and elders are not challenged in the performance management process, and are given priority in decision-making. Older/more senior people are considered to make a higher-level contribution and add more value to the organisation, which will be reflected in rewards and promotion. Fairness and equity in rewards is also important, especially in the distribution of bonuses. Cooke (2008) reports on how those who were rewarded top prizes had to share their bonuses with their colleagues, or rotate awards, in order to avoid jealousy and resentment. Easterby-Smith *et al*'s (1995) comparative study of Chinese and UK organisations found that appraisal criteria in Chinese organisations focus not only on hard tasks but also on 'moral' and ideological behaviour.

However, as Cooke (2008) points out, changes in cultural outlook are taking place in China, and although the collectivist culture remains strong, there is a discernible trend towards more Western-style performance management practices – such as encouraging individual accountability and initiative in Chinese firms, and the implementation of individual performance-related reward – as the result of changes in China's economic policy since the 1970s (eg Bai and Bennington, 2005; Bailey *et al*, 1997).

OTHER CONTEXTUAL FACTORS

Although national culture is clearly important in understanding the ways in which performance management may need adapting to the local environment, it is important to recognise that institutional differences (eg the state, the legal system, the financial system, religion, the family) also play a significant role (Meyer and Rowan, 1977; DiMaggio and Powell, 1983). Murphy and DeNisi's (2008) framework (Chapter 2) suggests a number of additional macro-contextual factors at the national or regional level, such as the legal framework of the country and technology. In the USA a legal system that makes it possible to challenge employment decisions has meant a focus on results-based measurement approaches which are considered more objective and less prone to challenge, and an emphasis on detailed and specific record-keeping (Murphy and DeNisi, 2008; Pulakos *et al*, 2008). Legislation preventing discrimination in many countries means that schemes have to be carefully designed and documented in order to address issues of accuracy and fairness, and care must be taken to train raters to avoid bias and inconsistent treatment. Sparrow (2008) gives the example of the age discrimination legislation which has impacted on gender-equality schemes in the UK. The recent changes relating to retirement also means that UK organisations have to pay much greater attention to managing their workforce's performance.

Germany's highly regulated legal environment involving extensive labour market institutions of collective bargaining, co-determination and vocational training has strongly influenced performance management systems, which are characterised by a high level of worker input, consensus-building and a long-term career focus (Barzantny and Festing, 2008). In France, the legal environment is considered to have a minimal impact on performance management (Barzantny and Festing, 2008), although it does have the highest level of profit share among manual employees (more than 70 per cent of organisations use profit share) because French law has mandated profit share in all but the smallest private sector organisations (Brewster *et al*, 2007). Employees' protection against dismissal can also influence appraisal practices. In Australia, dismissed employees can use performance appraisal records to challenge decisions to terminate their employment, and employers are advised to retain all documention relating to performance. Employers also have a duty of care to employees with poor performance and are required to conduct and document regular performance assessment by law (De Cieri and Sheehan, 2008). In Turkey, a labour law introduced in 2003 requires employers to carry the burden of inadequate performance in dismissal cases, which has meant that organisations now have to be systematic and objective in their assessment of employees (Aycan and Yavuz, 2008).

Technology can also influence the type of performance information that is collected, how it is used, and the content of appraisals (Murphy and DeNisi, 2008). Access to computer monitoring means that hard output-based measures are more likely to be captured than behaviours. In a call centre environment, for example, it is easier to monitor the number of calls taken, the length of calls, and so on, rather than the quality of service. Technology can also influence who does the rating and the number of raters by making it possible to appraise people who cannot be observed directly, make feedback anonymous, and collate performance information (Chapter 6).

REFLECTIVE ACTIVITY 11.2

What other macro-level contextual factors might influence performance management practices in an international organisation?

Finally, before moving on to the topic of expatriate performance management, consider the global approach to performance management taken by the paper giant Kimberly-Clark, as described in Case Study 11.2.

CASE STUDY 11.2

A GLOBAL APPROACH TO PERFORMANCE MANAGEMENT AT KIMBERLY-CLARK

Kimberly-Clark, the multinational paper manufacturer who produces Andrex toilet paper and Kleenex tissues, introduced a global approach to managing and measuring performance in 2005 which covers all of its white-collar employees working in 68 countries. So that the process was not perceived as North-American-centric, a global team was set up to finalise the design and identify regional and cultural issues. Four principles guided the design: clarity, so that people are setting objectives and know what to do; alignment, so that those objectives are aligned to the business; accountability, so that people are doing what they are supposed to be doing; and differentiation on performance issues. The old system, which relied largely on team leaders' own observations, failed to differentiate between performers, and partly in response to this the new process includes 360-degree appraisal with feedback from customers, peers and direct reports. However, because employees in some cultures – particularly in Asia and South America – find it difficult to make critical comments about their bosses, especially if they could be identified, the

feedback is anonymous. Interestingly, the company found that in North Asia, which covers China and Korea, attitudes towards this approach revealed a generation gap. Younger employees were positive about the process and more willing to give honest feedback, especially about their bosses, compared to older employees. A huge training programme was rolled out on how to operate the performance management system, and this has also encouraged employees of all ages to see the benefits of multi-rater feedback.

The performance management system is web-based and has been translated into different languages, which has helped to address ownership issues among business leaders. The process begins in January each year, when individuals set their own objectives and review them with their team leader. Team leaders can also cascade objectives down to team members. These objectives are recorded on the computerised performance management system, where other people can see them. This helps individuals to perceive how their objectives, and those of others (including their boss), are aligned with the business needs. Quarterly informal discussions are encouraged between the team leader and his or her direct reports in order to review progress. At the end of the year team leaders rate employees on six leadership qualities (ie on their visionary aptitude, their inspirational qualities, their collaborative disposition, their innovative skills, their decision-making ability and their talent-building progress) – and on their results. Calibration sessions are held to make sure that assessments are consistent and fair. A distribution system operates whereby no more than 20 per cent of employees are allocated the top two boxes of the ratings grid, and 5 per cent are placed in the bottom two. Ratings are linked to pay, the top performers getting the highest increases and the people at the bottom getting no increases.

Source: Arkin (2007b)

Questions

1   Are there any potential difficulties with this global approach to performance management?

2   What improvements might you make?

EXPATRIATE PERFORMANCE MANAGEMENT

The management of expatriate staff – employees who are transferred overseas on an international assignment – has received considerable attention in the International HRM literature, although it has largely focused on the selection, adjustment and repatriation of such managers (Gregersen, Hite and Black, 1996). Expatriates are generally assumed to come from the parent or headquarters country, but can also include host-country nationals who are transferred to work outside their home country, and third-country nationals who are from neither the home nor the host country. Regardless of origin, this group of staff plays a pivotal role in the success of MNCs, often holding key positions – but they are among the most expensive people that MNCs employ, and their failure rate is generally considered to be high (Brewster *et al*, 2011). Using 1995 survey data, Forster (2000: 128–9) estimated that the cost of moving a US expatriate to the UK for two years (including selection, training and monitoring) was at least £250,000, excluding the housing costs and other material benefits. Harvey and Moeller (2009) suggest a failure rate in the region of 20 per cent to 40 per cent, although failure rates vary depending on the definition of 'failure' used (eg premature return, reduced effectiveness in the assignment, or adjustment problems) and the nationality of the expatriate (failure rates for Americans, for example, are considerably higher than for Europeans). A survey of US managers undertaking assignments overseas found that 10 per cent to 20 per cent returned before scheduled to do so, and 30 per cent completed the assignment but failed to meet their supervisor's performance expectations (Black and Gregerson, 1999). Although there is a debate about the whole concept of expatriate failure and its value and magnitude (see, for example, Harzing and Christensen, 2004), it is clear that many expatriates are failing to perform effectively. This is also of concern because:

- it can give the organisation a bad image
- relationships with host country networks (eg government officials) may become strained
- there can be a negative impact on the morale of local employees
- organisational performance may be reduced
- there is a shortage of managerial talent capable of operating internationally
- failure can also be costly and traumatic for the international manager and his or her family.

For those who return, repatriation can also be a problem. Surveys suggest that between 10 per cent and 25 per cent of expatriates leave their company within 12 months of repatriation – much higher than for equivalent non-expatriates – and between a quarter and a third of expatriates leave within two years of returning (in Brewster *et al*, 2011). A key issue in repatriation is the management of expectations, particularly surrounding career prospects. Many expatriates, for example, expect to have enhanced their career prospects on their return (and this is often not the case), or lack career direction.

All this points to the importance of managing expatriates' performance effectively. Although a good deal is known about the potential factors that may influence expatriate failure (see the *Activity* below), few studies explore how MNCs should manage the performance of this unique body of managers (Tahvanainen, 2000; Claus and Briscoe, 2009). Effective performance management can help stabilise and improve the experience of expatriation and repatriation, by setting expectations, providing feedback on performance, identifying support, and guiding career and compensation decisions. Also, as Hollinshead (2010) asserts, 'It offers an effective channel for interpersonal communications, thus avoiding the "out-of-sight and out-of-mind" syndrome, and provides a tangible way of mentoring in difficult circumstances, potentially alleviating the risk of expatriate failure' (Hollinshead, 2010: 97).

REFLECTIVE ACTIVITY 11.3

Reasons for expatriate failure

- *Individual* – family issues, unwillingness to be relocated, dual career issues, lack of commitment to assignment, lack of language capabilities, inadequate support for the employee/family
- *Organisational* – lack of career planning, inadequate orientation, inadequate compensation programme, inadequate training programmes
- *Environmental* – emerging markets, restrictions on HR by government, hostility of environment (eg climate, healthcare), cultural taboos (women, minorities)

- *Systematic* – 'centric' IHRM orientations, *ad hoc* case-by-case negotiation with candidate, inadequate career development process during foreign assignment, ineffective performance appraisal system.

Source: adapted from Harvey and Novicevic (2001)

1   Based on this evidence, what initiatives might be introduced to reduce the likelihood of expatriate failure?

THE CONTEXT OF EXPATRIATE PERFORMANCE MANAGEMENT

Expatriate performance management is hugely complex and involves a distinct set of challenges. A wide variety of environmental factors (societal, legal, economic, technical and physical) can affect international assignments that differ considerably from the domestic context (Murphy and Cleveland, 1991; Shen, 2005). The business and working environment is likely to be more intense and intricate; adjustment can be difficult and involve an extended learning curve (Briscoe *et al*, 2012; Hollinshead, 2010). Not only will there be cross-cultural differences in business practices, but a culturally different workforce may have to be managed with different performance expectations and motivations. Employees may be on employment contracts very different from the home country's, and subject to different employment legislation. As Oddou and Mendenhall (2012: 238) observe:

The expatriate manager must walk a tightrope. He must deal with a new cultural work group, learn the ins and outs of the new business environment, possibly determine how to work with a foreign boss, find out what foreign management expects of him, and so on. He must also understand the rules of the game on the home front. It is difficult, and sometimes impossible, to please both.

There are also unique individual factors relating to the competence and personal circumstances of the expatriate (eg the family). The literature suggests that a distinctive set of qualities are required of the overseas manager (see Table 11.2), although it should be noted that most have a strong US bias. (See also Mendenhall and Osland, 2002; Brownell, 2006; Conner, 2000; Yamazaki and Kayes, 2004; and Brewster *et al*, 2011.)

Table 11.2 Key characteristics of expatriate managers

Core areas	Key skills and abilities
Professional and technical	Experience in company Technical knowledge Previous overseas experience Managerial talent Overall experience and education
Relational	Interpersonal skills (eg communication, information-seeking, listening, observation) Maturity and emotional stability Tolerance of ambiguity Flexibility/adaptability Respect Non-judgemental/non-evaluative in interpreting behaviour
Self-maintenance factors	Stress management Resilience Self-assertion – initiative, self-confidence/self-efficacy
Leadership and motivation	Influencing skills and relationship-building Decision-making Initiative Belief in mission Interest in working overseas Congruence with career path
Cultural awareness	Cultural empathy and sensitivity Language skills
Family situation	Stability in family situation Supportive and adaptable partner and family
Other	Perseverance Ability to use humour Sense of politics

Source: adapted from Brewster *et al* (2011) and Yamazaki and Kayes (2004)

CRITICAL REFLECTION 11.1

Consider the list of desirable characteristics for international managers in Table 11.2.

1   Do you think they can be universally applied to all expatriate managers?

2   How practical is it to assess and develop these competencies?

Non-work factors can also impact on performance, particularly the partner/family circumstances. For example, if the partner and/or children are having difficulty adapting to the cultural environment or resistant to moving, it can adversely affect the morale and performance of the expatriate. Research suggests that about three quarters of expatriates are accompanied by at least one family member (Dickmann *et al*, 2006). Alternatively, leaving family members behind can also be stressful and negatively impact on work commitment, job satisfaction and performance.

There is increasing diversity in the types of assignments and roles of international managers, and the traditional idea of the 'international manager' as someone who is a mid-career manager undertaking an international assignment for about three years is now something of a myth (Forster, 2000). International managers are more varied than that and include those who work abroad on short-term assignments (between one and 12 months in length), 'transpatriates' (individuals who operate globally rather than in one specific local culture), international commuters, and those working on virtual assignments which do not require managers to physically relocate (Welch, Worm and Fenwick, 2003).

Suutari and Tahvanainen (2002) argue that the nature of the role (position and task type) will influence the content of performance management practices so that a standardised performance management system is very unlikely to be appropriate for all types of expatriate employees. This is well illustrated in a study of Nokia Telecommunications (Tahvanainen, 2000), the Finland-based MNC, which found that despite a standard performance management system for global use, expatriates' performance was managed differently for different types of expatriates (top managers, middle managers, business establishers, project employees and R&D project personnel). This is illustrated in Table 11.3.

Table 11.3 Performance management variations for different Nokia expatriate employees

	Goal-setting	Performance evaluation	Training and development	Performance-related pay
Top manager	• Mostly self-development goals which are agreed with managers located in another country (at the HQ or area HQ) • Emphasis on clear financial goals	• By manager located in another country	• Expectation that the expatriate raises the issue	• Clear link between performance and incentives
Middle manager	• Manager in host location sets the goals, but many expatriates also have manager at HQ • Goals vary from fairly specific to very specific	• When undertaken, by manager in host location • Satisfactory amount of on-going performance feedback for most	• Discussed and agreed with host location manager • Expatriates engaged in training while on assignment	• All work under an incentive scheme but link between pay and performance often unclear
Business establisher	• Goals agreed with primary manager located within host or home country • Relatively few broad goals	• By primary manager(s) • Satisfactory amount of on-going performance feedback for some	• Discussed and agreed with primary manager • Expatriates have no time for training while on assignment	• Most have an incentive scheme, but link between pay and performance often unclear
Customer project worker	• No formal work-related goals	• Formal evaluation rare; when it occurs is done by host country manager • Insufficient amount of on-going feedback	• Discussed and agreed with administrative manager in home country • Expatriates have no time for training while on assignment	• Entitled to yearly bonuses, but no direct link to individual performance

	Goal-setting	Performance evaluation	Training and development	Performance-related pay
R&D project worker	• Goals set by manager in host location • Goals vary from vague to specific	• By manager in host location • Satisfactory amount of on-going performance feedback	• Discussed and agreed with home country manager • Expatriates have no time for training while on assignment	• Some entitled to bonuses partly linked to individual performance

Source: Tahvanainen (2000)

REFLECTIVE ACTIVITY 11.4

Looking at Table 11.3, what are the main differences in practice between the groups of managers?

What are the implications of these findings for management practice?

Additional problems in managing expatriate performance are (Briscoe *et al*, 2012; Oddou and Mendenhall, 2012):

- parent-country ethnocentrism and a lack of understanding of the foreign culture and environment
- a communication gap between the expatriate and the home/sponsor office because of distance and time differences
- differences in host (local) and home/sponsor country nationals' perceptions of what is an effective performance
- inadequate establishment of performance objectives for foreign operations (ie unclear, contradictory) and the means of recording individual and organisational performance
- the choice of evaluator (home- or host/sponsor-country-based?)
- all too frequent home country indifference to the foreign experience of the expatriate.

The expatriate performance management literature focuses on performance appraisal, addressing questions about the 'what' (what performance criteria should be used?), the 'who' (who does the evaluations?), the 'when' (how often?) and the 'how' (in what format?). These key issues are considered below.

EXPATRIATE PERFORMANCE APPRAISAL

WHAT SHOULD BE EVALUATED?

MNCs cannot assume that standard performance critieria developed in the domestic context will automatically apply to an overseas environment. Firstly, there may be differences between host and home country management's perceptions of what is valued as effective performance. For example, success from the home country's perspective might be improved profitablity of a particular subsidiary in the short term, but in the host country, success might be judged as building up good relationships with local government officials, which could improve business performance in the long term (Harzing and Christensen, 2004). The cultural norms in the host country may mean that behaviours associated with good performance in the parent nation may not be considered appropriate by local managers and employees. Whereas an authoritative and forceful style might be regarded as good leadership behaviour in, say, Asian countries, it can be seen as dysfunctional behaviour in many Western countries where participation and empowerment are valued. Oddou and Mendenhall (2012) cite the example of a US expatriate manager who adopted a participative decision-making style in India but was thought to be rather incompetent by local workers because of the Indian belief that managers, partly due to their social class level, are perceived as experts. A manager should therefore not have to ask for ideas. The wider the cultural gap between home and host country, the greater is the problem and the potential for expatriate role conflict and ineffective management.

Secondly, as already discussed, external constraints can impact on performance (such as currency devaluation, level of economic development, political instability) which are beyond the control of the individual manager, and often difficult to isolate from job-related factors. Moreover, these factors may not be understood by the parent country. Hollinshead (2010) gives the example of an expatriate manager in a Latin American country who spends months successfully avoiding strike action, which gains little recognition in the US parent company unsympathetic to trade unionism. The influence of situational constraints has to be considered in the choice of performance measurements. Typically, more visible measures are used (eg profits, market share, productivity levels), but these output-based measures may ignore the impact of external factors (Chapter 5). For example, a favourable exchange rate may mask underlying operational problems when results are translated back into home country currency, and vice versa (Gregersen *et al*, 1996). Performance measures must also recognise that developing a market in foreign subsidiaries is generally slower and more difficult to achieve than at home (Shen, 2005). When examined out of context, behaviours that may suggest under-performance can be adaptive responses to these various factors that surround expatriate performance (Gregersen *et al*, 1996: 3). For these reasons Gregersen *et al* (1996) and Dowling *et al* (2008) suggest that MNCs should assess 'contextual goals' and use multiple criteria that will allow a more balanced and less biased approach.

Research suggests, however, that MNCs are not likely to use different criteria to evaluate domestic and foreign managers. Although there may be some adjustments depending on country situations, in the main MNCs are more likely to use the same basic performance criteria across their operations (Borkowski, 1999).

WHO SHOULD UNDERTAKE THE EVALUATION?

The key question here is should the rater(s) come from the home country or the host (local) country? The direct line manager may be located in a different country, may never have worked or lived overseas, and may lack the specialist knowledge and understanding of the local situation, and the manager's impact on performance. Any home-country manager undertaking an assessment therefore has to be trained to appreciate the complexities of working and managing in a foreign environment. Geographical differences between manager and assignee also mean that giving feedback – particularly if it is to be on-going and informal – will be problematic. Dowling *et al* (2008) maintain that, in these circumstances, feedback is only viable against hard criteria although, as discussed previously, this approach can ignore the impact of situational constraints. Harzing and Christensen (2004) suggest that assigning a mentor at headquarters with international experience might go some way to alleviating the problem of regular feedback and help signal early problems in performance.

In contrast, host or local country managers will be familiar with the assignee's performance and the local constraints. On the other hand, the host country manager is likely to evaluate expatriate performance from his or her own cultural frame of reference and set of expectations (Oddou and Mendenhall, 2010), and may not understand or appreciate all the issues of working in a foreign country or the way of managing in the parent country. There may also be language barriers.

The ideal situation would seem to be one which has a balance of raters from the host and home country to give a more accurate picture of performance (Black *et al*, 1992; Gregersen *et al*, 1996). Indeed, many MNCs use a matrix management structure for managing international assignees such that a host country manager *and* a home country manager have input into the performance appraisal. Problems can arise, however, if these raters have different perspectives on performance and different agendas, and certain cultural settings may not support the use of multiple raters (see earlier discussion). Gregersen *et al*'s (1996) exploratory study of 58 US MNCs found that 81 per cent used more than one rater when assessing expatriate performance, and that the immedate supervisor is the most common expatriate rater (74 per cent from the host country, and 39 per cent from the home country); and the expatriate as self-rater was the next most common rater. Similarly, Suutari and Tahvanainen's (2002) study of 301 Finnish expatriate managers found that the typical performance rater was a supervisor in the host country (54 per cent), with a third (35 per cent) of cases reporting to the supervisor in the home country and/or the expatriate himself or herself (35 per cent).

FORMAT AND FREQUENCY OF APPRAISAL

In the light of the previous discussion on the unique context and multi-dimensional nature of expatriate performance it seems reasonable to argue that appraisal forms should be customised. Despite this, Gregersen *et al* (1996) found that 76 per cent of respondents used the same standardised appraisal form for expatriate appraisal. Lack of time and resources are potential barriers to customising forms. The researchers also noted that more frequent appraisals relate positively to perceived accuracy of expatriate performance appraisal.

Appraisals have, in addition, to take into account the fact that expatriates normally go through an extended adjustment period in which performance in the job may diminish in the short term (Black and Mendenhall, 1991). Some MNCs do not expect peak performance from expatriates until well into their assignment. For example, Japanese companies do not expect peak performance until the third year of the assignment (Tung, 1984). One of the ways in which organisations can help expatriates prepare and adjust to the international assignment is to provide some induction in the form of pre-training. Although the content and focus of these programmes varies according to the individual and the assignment, at base they might include (Muller-Camen and Brewster, 2008):

- environmental briefings about the host country's political system, the economy, its history, laws, institutions, markets, management processes, etc
- cultural awareness training
- language training – even at a very basic level
- pre-departure visits to the host country
- meeting people who have worked in the country.

Partners and children of expatriate managers might be included in this. Research suggests that cross-cultural training has positive effect, although only a fifth of all organisations provide it (Brewster *et al*, 2011). One of the major difficulties is that the length of time between the decision to go and actually going is often very short. Cross-cultural training during the assignment is also relatively rare (Tarique and Caligiuri, 2004).

MNCS' PRACTICE OF EXPATRIATE PERFORMANCE MANAGEMENT

The evidence suggests that expatriate performance is often treated as an extension of domestic schemes in both US and non-US MNCs (Tung and Varma, 2008; Shih *et al*, 2005; Gregersen *et al*, 1996), or at worst ignored, although it must be remembered that the research is scant. For example, in a study of five MNEs of different country origin (US, Japanese, Dutch, Korean and Taiwanese), Shih *et al* (2005) found that all firms surveyed did not make adjustments to expatriate performance appraisal to take account of host-country conditions. Briscoe *et al* (2012) report on the informality with which firms evaluate the performance of expatriates, quoting survey evidence that 83 per cent of MNEs do not use performance management to measure the success of their international assignees, and many (35 per cent) do not use any type of measurement at all (Briscoe *et al*, 2012: 353). Brewster (1998) found that half of European MNCs had no formal appraisal systems for expatriates. There are, however, exceptions: Finnish MNCs appear to evaluate their expatriates (Suutari and Tahvanainen, 2002). In the main, however, the uniqueness of international assignees appears to be ignored, and MNCs are failing to recognise the context when it comes to the performance management of expatriates – the culture of the host nation, the needs of the assignment, the role the manager will play in the organisation, and so on. In fact, as Fletcher (2008) notes, MNCs seem to prefer to build up strong cultures of their own which can to some extent ameliorate the impact of differences in national cultures of the workforces over time. 'Because there is a set way of doing things in the organisation, it can become the accepted norm for everyone when they have become fully socialised into the organisation' (Fletcher, 2008: 178).

CONVERGENCE OR DIVERGENCE OF PERFORMANCE MANAGEMENT

One of the debates that has dominated the International HRM literature is the extent to which we are witnessing 'convergence' or 'divergence' in IHRM (Sparrow *et al*, 1994; Rowley and Benson, 2002). Convergence assumes that a standard model of HRM will emerge as a result of globalisation and internationalisation, despite national and cultural differences. In other words, some form of 'best practice HRM' will become the norm across the globe. Conversely, divergence supports the notion of 'fit' and argues that HR practices should be adapted to the local environment according to societal and environmental needs (Brewster and Larsen, 2000a).

In the context of performance management, the question is: are US/Western models of performance management becoming the norm in the world, or is the trend towards local adaptation? The empirical evidence is divided, but on balance Briscoe *et al* (2011) and others argue that the divergence theory has greater support. In other words, organisations are likely to adopt performance management systems that are consistent with the societal cultures in which they are embedded. For example, in examining performance appraisals in Hong Kong, Singapore and Taiwan, Paik *et al* (2000) found strong evidence for the divergence perspective. Their results are particularly noteworthy in that they show significant differences among Chinese cluster-based countries, which are often presented as being in the same cultural cluster.

Based on a large longitudinal dataset from multiple countries, Peretz and Fried (2012) also found support for the contingency approach and go a step further by testing for the impact of congruence between societal cultures and performance appraisal practices on two behavioural outcomes – absenteeism and turnover. They found that organisations that adopt practices which fit with the societal cultures in which they are embedded tended to reduce turnover and absenteeism, and that the converse was true – incongruence increased the level of these behavioural outcomes. The strong message, then, is that organisations should adapt appraisal practices to fit the dominant societal culture.

DeNisi *et al* (2008), however, suggest that the global picture points to a degree of convergence in performance management practices, and that as countries become more economically mature, their systems move closer to the types found in the USA and Western Europe (DeNisi *et al*, 2008: 258). Looking at China (see Case Study 11.1), for example, the influence of culture is clear but there is a trend towards more Western-style practices (Cooke, 2008). Based on the evidence of two quite different datasets (Cranet and Global HR Research Alliance), Boselie *et al* (2011) suggest a more complex picture with differences between MNCs and domestic firms in their approach to performance management. MNCs are managing to implement standardised practices in many different country contexts, whereas the activities of domestic firms are more country-specific.

CONCLUSION

This chapter has considered performance management in a global context and discussed the huge difficulties of implementing performance management in different cultural, legal, political and technical environments. The growing internationalisation of business and the increasing diversity in national labour forces makes it important that all organisations consider whether a 'one-size-fits-all' approach to performance management is appropriate for themselves. MNCs are the most obvious organisations affected by these issues, but it is also increasingly important for organisations operating in a single country setting.

Although the empirical research in this area is thin, the conclusion that must be drawn is that a complex set of environmental factors can affect global performance management, and that a scheme developed for one country or one culture may not be suitable in another setting. In other words, a contingency or 'best fit' approach should be adopted which takes account of cultural and institutional differences, plus, in the case of expatriate managers, individual and job-related factors. Organisations should not 'blindly copy something that has worked elsewhere' (DeNisi *et al*, 2008: 260), for to do so can result in ineffective management, reduced performance and damaged relationships. That said, however, it is also important to recognise that other organisational factors influence performance management practice, particularly in MNCs which rely on building up strong organisational cultures of their own.

In their book on global performance management, DeNisi *et al* (2008: 260) sum up the position well:

> Visitors to India will find that the menu at McDonald's does not include its classic hamburgers – instead, the chain sells vegetable burgers. This 'Indianisation' of the hamburger seems to be exactly the approach we need in the area of performance management. As countries develop more sophisticated systems, they should learn from other countries, but also make sure that, where needed, they modify existing programmes to fit with local 'tastes'.

EXPLORE FURTHER

Aycan, Z. (2005) 'The interplay between cultural and institutional contingencies in human resource management practices', *International Journal of Human Resource Management*, Vol.16, No.7: 1083–1119

Boselie, P., Farndale, E. and Paauwe, J. (2008) 'Performance management', in Brewster, C. J. and Mayrhofer, W. (eds) *Handbook of Research on Comparative Human Resource Management*. Cheltenham: Edward Elgar

Brewster, C., Sparrow, P., Vernon, G. and Houldsworth, E. (2011) *International Human Resource Management*, 4th edition. London: CIPD

Chiang, F. F. T. and Birtch, T. A. (2010) 'Appraising performance across borders: an empirical examination of the purposes and practices of performance appraisal in a multi-country context', *Journal of Management Studies*, Vol.47. No.7: 1365–93

Claus, L. and Briscoe, D. B. (2009) 'Employee performance management across borders: a review of relevant academic literature', *International Journal of Management Review*, Vol.11, No.2: 175–96

Gerhart, B. and Fang, M. (2005) 'National culture and human resource management: assumptions and evidence', *International Journal of Human Resource Management*, Vol.16, No.6: 971–86

Gregersen, H. B, Hite, J. M. and Black, J. S. (1996) 'Expatriate performance appraisal in US multinational firms', *Journal of International Business Studies*, Vol.27, No.4: 711–38

Harvey, M. and Moeller, M. (2009) 'Expatriate managers: a historical review', *International Journal of Management Review*, Vol.11, No.3: 275–96

Peretz, H. and Fried, Y. (2012) 'National cultures, performance appraisal practices, and organzational absenteeism and turnover: a study across 21 countries', *Journal of Applied Psychology*, Vol.97, No.2: 448–59

Varma, A., Budhwar, P. S. and DeNisi, A. (2008) *Performance Management Systems: A global perspective*. Abingdon: Routledge

CHAPTER 12

Developing Performance Management

SUE HUTCHINSON

LEARNING OUTCOMES

By the end of this chapter you should be able to:

- critically evaluate the effectiveness of performance management
- make recommendations for improvements to the practice of performance management
- review your own knowledge and understanding of performance management using case-study-based activities.

INTRODUCTION

The purpose of this final chapter is to bring together some of the recurring themes in this book by identifying some of the key difficulties in the practice of performance management, and to propose ways in which the design and operation of such schemes can be improved. The book has examined a wide range of topics and practices reflecting the all-encompassing nature of performance management, and has tried to present a balanced approach to the subject, drawing on the available research evidence and taking into account employer and employee interests. It began by examining the premise that performance can be managed by HR policies, and provided a framework for managing performance which emphasised the need to consider the effectiveness of HRM and its implementation. Accordingly, the book has examined not just the theory of performance management but its practice, and it will be abundantly clear to the reader that there is frequently a gap between what is espoused and what is enacted. Problems in both the design and implementation of performance management suggest that it is not delivering all that it promises. This may partly explain why performance management has received such mixed and strong reactions from managers, employees and academics. As Lawler observed back in 1994, performance management has been one of the 'most praised, most criticised and most debated management practices for decades' (1994: 16), and this remains the case today. Nevertheless, the rise in interest in performance management over the last few decades suggests that organisations believe it can deliver and is an essential tool for high-performing organisations.

This chapter begins by examining the research evidence on the effectiveness of performance management, and then summarises some of the common problems in operationalising performance management, before making some recommendations for improvement. The chapter concludes with some case study activities which should enable students to review their understanding of the subject.

HOW EFFFECTIVE IS PERFORMANCE MANAGEMENT?

The research evidence on performance management *per se* is very thin (Fletcher and Williams, 1996: 170), partly reflecting the difficulties in isolating the impact of performance management from other factors. As noted in Chapter 1, performance is a multi-level phenomenon, and many factors impact on organisational performance which may outweigh any improvements at the individual performance (Den Hartog *et al*, 2004; DeNisi, 2000). At the macro-level, there is a growing body of evidence that shows that HRM policies can impact positively on organisational performance, and this was explored in Chapter 1. There is also some extensive research on the impact of individual performance management practices such as performance appraisal and feedback, goal-setting and performance-related rewards, which has also been explored in earlier chapters. However, as Fletcher and Williams (1996) point out, the research does not adequately address the question of the extent to which multiple elements of performance management are effective in achieving the desired outcomes of improved organisational performance. To address this gap they conducted their own research in nine UK organisations, and found that most elements of performance management contributed to positive employee attitudes, as seen in organisational commitment and job satisfaction. The Audit Commission also found a strong link between effective performance management and employee attitudes in local government (Audit Commission, 1995).

On balance, however, the evidence reveals inconsistent messages regarding the effectiveness of performance management policies (Glendinning, 2002; Biron *et al*, 2011). Research by the Institute of Employment Studies (Strebler, Bevan and Robertson, 2001) found that performance management has limited impact on business performance, lacks a strategic focus and gives conflicting messages between encouragement and control. Pulakos *et al* (2008) claim that performance management is the 'Achilles heel' of HRM, citing survey evidence by Watson Wyatt in the USA which found that only 30 per cent of employees felt that their company's scheme helped to improve performance (Pulakos *et al*, 2008: 105). Haines and St-Onge (2012) report on research that finds that 80 per cent to 90 per cent of human resource professionals consider their performance management system does not improve organisational performance.

The 2009 CIPD survey reveals a more varied but still less than positive picture of HR practitioners' views on what performance management can achieve. The most positive responses are that performance management enables individuals to better understand what they should be doing, 30 per cent agreeing with this statement – although 13 per cent disagree and 57 per cent neither agree nor disagree. Least positive responses concern the impact on employee wellbeing – 29 per cent disagreeing with the statement that performance management can have an impact on employee wellbeing. Just 20 per cent agree that performance management has a positive impact on individual performance (although 59 per cent neither agree nor disagree), and under a quarter (23 per cent) agree that performance management helps line managers manage people better (52 per cent neither agree nor disagree). The significant percentage who 'neither agree nor disagree' to all statements in the survey should not be ignored, however. This suggests either that impact varies within organisations, that respondents do not know the impact (because they do not evaluate their schemes), or that respondents' experiences were relatively immature (ie that schemes had only recently been implemented). Indeed, few organisations seem to evaluate their schemes. For example, just half of respondents to the 2005 CIPD (CIPD, 2005a) survey formally evaluated the effectiveness of their performance management scheme.

Other surveys reveal more encouraging findings. For example, Houldsworth and Jirasinghe's (2006) survey of line managers found considerable satisfaction: some 68 per cent rated performance management as 'very effective to excellent' in their organisation, and three quarters of managers felt that performance measures kept people focused on what was important. A study by E-reward in 2005 revealed mixed but generally positive views about the impact of performance management on organisational performance:

- 32 per cent considered the impact to be 'very significant', and 36 per cent 'fairly significant'
- 10 per cent rated them as 'insignificant'
- more than a fifth (22 per cent) said the impact was 'not known'.

However, the same survey found that half (50 per cent) believed that staff were more demotivated than motivated by performance management, and 45 per cent believed the link between performance management and pay was inappropriate.

What conclusion can we draw from these mixed findings? Certainly, in many organisations performance management is falling short of expectations, with a mismatch between the theory and practice. The literature suggests that the explanation for this gap lies in how performance management is designed and implemented (eg Biron *et al*, 2011; Pulakos *et al*, 2008; Winstanley and Stuart-Smith, 1996; Hendry *et al*, 2000; Grint, 1993), much of that evidence being provided throughout this book. The main challenges that organisations face in operationalising performance management are summarised below

CHALLENGES TO EFFECTIVE PERFORMANCE MANAGEMENT

The key challenges inherent in performance management relate to the following areas:

- difficulties in achieving vertical and horizontal integration (Chapters 1, 2 and 7)
- failure to consider the context (all chapters)
- conflict of purpose (Chapters 2, 6 and 8)
- line management behaviour (Chapters 1, 4, 6, 9 and 10)
- setting performance measurements that are meaningful, accurate, fair and not overly cumbersome or too controlling (Chapter 5)
- rater subjectivity and bias (Chapters 4, 5 and 6)
- making reward allocations (Chapter 8)
- increased bureaucracy, administration and time (Chapter 6)
- the potential for increased control, pressure and stress (Chapters 6, 8 and 9).

Poorly designed and implemented performance management obviously detracts from organisational uses and can have far-reaching consequences (Aguinis, 2009):

- reduced organisational performance
- decreased job performance
- job dissatisfaction and reduced motivation
- increased staff turnover
- the use of false or misleading information
- lower self-esteem
- felt unfairness
- damaged relationships
- increased employee pressure and stress
- increased job insecurity
- wasted money
- unnecessary demands on managers' and employees' time
- increased number and severity of grievances
- increased number of unfair dismissal claims
- a culture of poor performance management.

So how can organisations build more effective performance management? Based on the evidence presented in this book, the following recommendations are proposed. Most of these issues are fully examined in earlier chapters of the book (see the list) and are therefore only summarised here.

RECOMMENDATIONS FOR IMPROVING THE EFFECTIVENESS OF PERFORMANCE MANAGEMENT

INTEGRATE, ALIGN AND CONTEXTUALISE

Performance management is most effective when it aligns individual and team contribution with organisational priorities to provide a 'line of sight' between what an individual does and the organisation's goals. It also requires performance management practices to be aligned with each other to support and reinforce the organisation's strategy. All this is hugely difficult to achieve, and Chapters 2 and 7 highlighted some of the many challenges associated with operationalising strategy at the individual and group levels. Integration of performance management policies is also problematic, and its importance is often ignored in practice. It is not uncommon, for example, to find the 'deadly combination' of individual performance-related pay (IPRP) and teamworking practised together (Chapter 1). Alignment can be supported by a clear vision and/or mission statement, by stated values, a strong culture and organisational climate, and through the development of 'employer branding' (Marchington and Wilkinson, 2012; Bowen and Ostroff, 2004). This was discussed in Chapter 2. The use of competence frameworks can link employee behaviours with organisational strategy and values, and helps integrate performance management policies (Chapter 7).

Integration emphasises the importance of context. A central theme in this book is that performance issues are context-driven, yet many organisations fail to consider the environment in which performance management practices are applied (see, for example, Chapters 1, 2, 5, 8 and 11). Benchmarking against 'best practice' standards within similar organisations or similar sectors fails to contextualise performance management to the particular needs of the organisation and can act as a constraint to more innovative practices (Harris, 2007). The same is true for organisations operating in cross-national settings: a scheme developed for the domestic setting may not be suitable for another location where differences in culture and/or institutional arrangements apply. Thus, performance management schemes cannot be bought 'off the shelf', and all activities – performance measurements, feedback, any allocation of rewards, and the type of training delivered – must be tailor-made and designed and implemented within the context of the organisation, taking into consideration the national and organisational culture, the employee relations climate, organisational structure, sector and size, and the types of employees and the jobs that people do.

CLARIFY AND SIMPLIFY

The issue of how to accommodate the potentially conflicting objectives of development and evaluation has been a recurring theme in this book (see, for example, Chapters 2 and 6). The more traditional evaluative approach with its focus on past performance, making judgements and the allocation of reward, can contradict and undermine a more forward-looking developmental approach. These two approaches also require quite different management skills, and it is well documented that managers are reluctant to judge employees and to differentiate when there is a link with reward. To minimise the potential for conflict, organisations should make clear the aims of performance management and the purpose of any direct link to reward. If a reward allocation is to be made, different dates should be set for the development discussion and for the pay discussion. This prevents the review from being about the individual's pay, with little discussion about development needs.

It has also been noted previously how managers and employees dislike the prescriptive and overly detailed form-filling associated with performance management, regarding it as an administrative burden and time-consuming (Chapter 6). The more detailed, complex and time-consuming the system is, the less likely it is to be used by managers and employees who will be tempted to take short cuts, make snap decisions or avoid the process altogether. Case study research by the Institute of Employment Studies (Brown and Hirsh, 2011) on the implementation of performance management found that all case study organisations were working towards simplifying and clarifying their processes. Keeping it simple makes it easy to operate and understand, can be less formal, and may be more in keeping with the culture of the organisation (see Case Study 12.5 at the very end of this chapter). This could include keeping performance measurements to a minimum and focusing only on the key activities which make a difference (Hendry *et al*, 2000). A proliferation of measurements and targets at all levels of the organisation can be confusing and be a contributory factor to perceptions of control and reduced employee morale. Fewer measures also means greater flexibility (see Case Study 12.5).

ADOPT A BALANCED APPROACH

As Boselie (2010) notes, performance management can often disturb the balance between employer and employee interests by becoming too focused on practices such as performance-related pay, close monitoring and outcomes that serve the employers' interests. He argues that 'to restore the balance an ideal performance management also pays attention to what employees want' (Boselie, 2010: 82) by focusing on development and career opportunities and paying more attention to employee wellbeing, including work–life balance, employment security, autonomy and fixed pay. A more balanced approach helps address the radical critique of performance management, which suggests it is a form of power and control, producing undesirable effects on employees such as undue pressure and stress, and feelings of job insecurity (Chapters 6 and 10).

A more balanced approach can also be achieved by employee involvement and participation, not just in the design of performance management but in the process and evaluation of schemes. Self-appraisals and 360-degree feedback, for example, can give employees a greater sense of ownership and control. Personal development plans are a mechanism to encourage individuals to take more responsibility for their own development, and self-management learning can improve employee morale and motivation. Greater involvement and ownership can also make the process more engaging and increase the likelihood that employees will achieve their own objectives (IDS, 2011a). At Sony Europe, employees have been encouraged to take more responsibility for their own performance in a scheme called My Workstyle (see Case Study 12.1).

MY WORKSTYLE AT SONY EUROPE

CASE STUDY 12.1

Sony Europe Ltd provides manufacturing equipment and devices to aid technology development, design and quality assurance for a range of industries. The company employs 1,400 people in the UK and 4,200 across Europe. In 2010 a new performance management process was introduced which has empowered individuals to take ownership of their own development, and performance is no longer seen as the sole responsibility of line managers. The new process is based on a three-step 'Know me, Focus me, Grow me' model (created by Standard Life Investments) and rebranded and adapted for Sony into My Workstyle. It is supported by a new performance management website, branded with the same name.

Know me is the preparation stage to help employees understand themselves better. Employees are encouraged to complete a 'My profile' section of the appraisal form before their formal review. This is set out to read like a CV. Individuals write about their current role, their strengths and weaknesses, learning preferences, likes and dislikes, and aspirations (eg the job they would like to be considered for in the future). This also helps with succession planning. There are tools available online to help employees learn more about these aspects, such as a 'strengths-finder tool'.

The **Focus me** stage centres on the formal reviews which take place at least twice a year. The company has designed both structured and unstructured appraisal forms to cater for individual preferences because some people find structure constraining. Employees work with their manager to establish and agree a number of SMART objectives (see Chapter 5) which are assessed and rated at the end of the review period. The website gives advice on how to set SMART objectives.

Grow me focuses on the consequences in terms of rewards and development. Employees are given ratings for each of their objectives at the end of the review period and an overall performance rating which is used to determine individual rewards. Managers have to give their reasons for the grades awarded. The appraisal form has a development plan section which links to the Group's global careers site and 60- to 90-minute experiential learning modules which provide employees and managers with quick training sessions on, for example, 'Driving my career' and 'How to get ahead in Sony'.

Source: adapted from IDS (2011a) *The Performance Management Cycle*, HR Study 938

COMMUNICATE

Linked to this is the need to communicate the purpose, process and outcomes of any performance management scheme to employees and managers, since this improves transparency, understanding and helps build an ethical approach to performance management (Winstanley and Stuart-Smith, 1996). Providing information can also enhance co-operation and commitment, improve trust, strengthen the psychological contract and create a stronger sense of accountability. Biron *et al*'s (2011) study based on 16 world-leading firms found that performance management effectiveness improved when organisations clearly communicated performance expectations. They identified three primary communication mechanisms: first, supervisor feedback; second, formal programmes for socialisation which were used for skill development; and third, tools such as an intranet, bulletin boards, group/departmental meetings, internal newsletters, leaflets and excellence awards to keep employees continually updated. Effective communications can also strengthen the manager–employee relationship, which has been shown to be one of the key determinants of successful performance management (Pulakos and O'Leary, 2011) by, for example, improving perceptions of performance management fairness and procedural justice (Beer, 1981; Wexley and Klimoski, 1984).

Also relevant here is the role of information and communication technology, or e-HRM. e-HRM has been defined as 'a way of implementing HR strategies, policies and practices in organisations through a conscious and directed support of and/or with the full use of web-based technology' (Ruël, Bondarouk and Looise, 2004: 281), and offers substantial benefits. For example, e-HRM can improve the efficiency of HR activities by reducing costs and increasing the speed of the process, improve communication, enhance employee involvement and facilitate a more strategic role for HR (Gainey and Klaas, 2008; Parry, 2011).

More specifically effective use of technology can help improve the delivery of performance management and ease the burden on managers. Agreed objectives can be recorded online and tracked throughout the year, and regular review meetings can be automatically scheduled by the system (IDS, 2011a). Emails can provide reminders of the need to provide feedback – particularly helpful for 360-degree feedback when multiple stakeholders are involved. Systems can be used to compare and track performance, identify exceptional performance and provide feedback. Where performance ratings are used, the system may be able to apply any formulas or other criteria to calculate employees' final scores quickly and accurately. These could then be integrated with an online payroll system to determine bonus payments or salary increases. It can also enable faster sharing of information at all levels (organisation, department and team). In absence management technology can be used to record absences online through a centralised notification system, collect accurate absence data, help monitor trends and tackle problems. Technology can also enable learning, training and development (Chapter 7) through, for example, online learning materials and virtual classrooms.

It is important to note, however, that technology only facilitates performance management provided that 'it is controlled, and not in control' (Chase and Fuchs, 2008). Technology as a method of surveillance – as exemplified in call centre environments, where all outputs are measured and telephone conversations listened to and recorded – must be used with caution.

INVEST IN LINE MANAGERS

Line managers play a critical and dominant role in managing performance, and in doing so affect employee perceptions, their attitudes and performance-related behaviours (Chapter 1). The overall quality of the relationship line managers have with their teams can also shape individuals' views of the organisation and the employee relations climate (Chapters 4, 9 and 10). Yet the demands on these managers are considerable. They have to undertake a diverse range of tasks which require quite complex and subtle management skills. This includes setting individual and team objectives in line with the business aims and plan, assessing and rating performance, providing constructive feedback, identifying training and development needs, acting as coach and mentor, and dealing with under-performers. Many managers do not have the skills or confidence to undertake these tasks, nor the motivation and commitment.

Organisational support is needed to equip managers with the ability (A), motivation (M) and opportunity (O) (see Chapter 1) to effectively manage performance. Managers should be selected on the basis of skills and competencies suited to good people management, and job descriptions and persons specifications should clearly reflect the skills and expectations of the role. The Selfridges case (see Case Study 12.2) provides an example of a company which has done just that. Appropriately targeting training (formal and informal) can develop the skills and confidence of line managers (discussed separately below). In some organisations, for example, an effective way of improving appraisal skills is for managers to conduct mock appraisal interviews and critique each other, which shows up good and bad practices. Other forms of training support may additionally be considered. At John Lewis, learning and development advisers help managers identify the training and development needs of their staff as well as provide development opportunities for the managers themselves, including training in leadership skills (Hutchinson and Purcell, 2007).

Job expectations can also be clarified through the performance management process by setting appropriate people management objectives, and this can also encourage ownership of performance management. Multi-source feedback and self-assessment are useful ways of helping managers assess their progress and reinforcing the importance of good performance management. Incentives and recognition for good performance management practice can also motivate managers. Managers should have balanced workloads that take account of the need to allocate time for performance management activities, and team sizes should not be too big. Any reward decisions linked to individual or team performance should be delegated to the line. Calibration meetings are useful if they provide the opportunity to discuss under-performance and identify talent, but should avoid taking authority away from the line manager (Chapter 8). Involving managers in the design of performance management policies – for example, through working parties and project groups or taking part in pilot studies – can also encourage ownership and buy-in to the policies and process.

Chapters 2 and 4 consider some of the ways in which HR specialists can provide active support and advice.

CASE STUDY 12.2

MANAGING THE MANAGERS AT SELFRIDGE'S, MANCHESTER TRAFFORD PARK STORE

In 2001, Selfridge's Trafford Park store made a determined effort to improve the performance of their front-line managers (team leaders) following the results of an employee survey which showed that team leaders were not providing staff with enough support or living the values of the organisation. The first step was to redefine the team leader role to give greater role clarity and more responsibility for people management. The key skills demanded of team leaders were identified as communication, being a team player, resilience, coaching, and the ability to motivate others, all of which were written into the new job description. (Previously, team leaders had been selected primarily on the basis of experience.) The main purpose of the role is to 'motivate, develop and lead the team to deliver excellent customer service and standards'. Key accountabilities cover four areas:

- ensuring excellent customer service
- managing sales associates
- ensuring effective communication and teamworking
- ensuring excellent standards on the shop floor.

The management of sales associates includes performance management, coaching and counselling, working with team trainers, recruitment and selection, and formal and informal disciplinary meetings. The coaching role involves observing sales associates once a week (on a rotational basis) and providing instant feedback. Counselling covers monitoring and managing staff on absence, lateness, attitude and conduct on a monthly basis. Team leaders are also responsible for key performance indicators which are incorporated into their own performance reviews.

The selection criteria for team leaders was changed to reflect the new role. A new appraisal scheme was introduced linked more closely to succession planning, and all team leaders initially received seven days of training. There is a team leader forum which meets twice a month to discuss common issues and problems, particularly concerning their people management role, and selected senior managers (eg HR specialists) can be invited to those meeting to advise on problems. Support is also on hand from assistant sales managers who have responsibility for coaching and developing team leaders on a formal and informal basis.

Source: Hutchinson and Purcell (2003)

PROVIDE TRAINING AND LEARNING OPPORTUNITIES

Effective training is an obvious intervention to build more effective performance management. According to Rankin (2010), management training should be aimed at:

- persuading managers of the importance of performance management
- ensuring that managers have a good working knowledge of the policies and processes
- imparting an understanding of the relationship between performance management and the organisational procedures, including disciplinary and grievance procedures
- helping managers develop the skills and knowledge required for effective performance management, including assertiveness, listening, note-taking and leadership
- equipping managers with the skills and knowledge to conduct performance management in an objective way and in accordance with principles of equal opportunities and diversity.

Training can also improve managers' self-efficacy and confidence in conducting appraisals and make them feel comfortable when dealing with diverse appraisal situations.

It is not only line managers who need training. Studies show that performance appraisal training results in an increase in overall rating accuracy (in Biron *et al*, 2011) and should be offered to all raters (Chapter 6) to minimise the likelihood of rater bias in appraisals (intentional and unintentional). Rating errors such as the 'halo' or 'horns' effect, 'first impressions', the 'contrast effect', the 'central tendency' and stereotyping may lead to inaccurate performance assessments and possibly the wrong people being promoted and rewarded. It may also impact on individuals' perceptions of fairness – in particular, notions of procedural and distributive justice, the motivation to perform – and detract from organisational usefulness (Chapters 3 and 6).

Investment in training is also important because it signals that the organisation considers performance management important and is committed to improving its effectiveness (Biron *et al*, 2011). As suggested in Chapter 4, consideration should be given to making training compulsory, but formal training on its own is likely to be insufficient. Training has to be flexible, combining formal and informal approaches to cater for different learning needs and to utilise the resources available (Chapters 4 and 7). Coaching and mentoring, for example, have been shown to be particularly effective ways of learning and providing support for under-performers (Chapters 7 and 9). Time and resources must also be made available for training to be effective.

MONITOR, REVIEW AND EVALUATE

Performance management practices and processes should be regularly and openly monitored and reviewed against some success criteria, and any necessary improvements identified and implemented. Even good schemes need evaluating for their appropriateness in changing organisational contexts. CIPD (2005a) research shows that the most common method for evaluation is opinion or attitude surveys, followed by informal feedback, formal written feedback and focus groups. Combining hard quantitative data (eg surveys) with soft qualitative data (eg focus groups) can provide valuable and meaningful information on all aspects of performance management, such as the frequency and effectiveness of performance appraisals, perceptions of fairness and equity, appropriateness and clarity of objectives, the motivational impact of performance-related rewards, and how well poor performance is managed. Performance appraisals of line managers can also pick up issues of how effectively managers are delivering their performance management responsibilities.

IMPROVE SENIOR MANAGEMENT INVOLVEMENT AND COMMITMENT

The amount of senior management buy-in will have a direct effect on the success or failure of performance management policies and practices (Glendinning, 2002). According to Biron *et al* (2011), senior management involvement in performance management is important because, firstly, the senior managers outline the future direction of the organisation and can match this to performance management objectives; and secondly, the actions of senior managers are highly visible. Role-modelling behaviour of senior managers is particularly important – it is hard, for example, for line managers to be committed to performance appraisals if their boss is not. Senior managers also set the performance culture and climate by, for example, encouraging a blame-free culture in which managers and employees are not afraid to admit to mistakes and poor performance (Chapter 4). They must also provide clarity regarding which performance targets to prioritise, and can in addition provide line managers with very practical support, such as administrative support for performance appraisals.

CASE STUDIES

This chapter concludes with some case study exercises. There are further case studies, including role-playing exercises, on the companion website.

CASE STUDY 12.3

FIONA AS APPRAISER AND APPRAISEE IN A HEALTHCARE ORGANISATION

Fiona joined the paediatric unit of a healthcare organisation (a large NHS Trust in a city centre) 18 months ago and line manages 25 staff. Her job is stressful and she has complained to her own line manager, informally, about frequently having to take work home at weekends. The organisation has a history of poor performance management but recently tried to introduce a new appraisal scheme based on 360-degree appraisal for all staff. However, the scheme was voluntary, and Fiona's initial enthusiasm for it soon wore off as her workload increased. Like other managers and staff in the organisation, she came to view the exercise as one of form-filling and as a bureaucratic burden. Consequently, only a few of her team have undergone the annual appraisals. Although Fiona has been offered training on conducting appraisals, she has not had the time to go on a course.

Fiona herself has not been formally appraised since she joined, although she has had frequent informal discussions with her line manager about her workload. The organisation has recently set targets for each department as a means of achieving high-quality patient care, and Fiona is required to report monthly on her team's key performance indicators as part of the government targets. Her team is also short-staffed, absence levels are high, and it is hard to recruit good staff. As a result, Fiona often has to cover for absent members of her team and has little time to manage her 25 staff. Dealing with sickness absence is an additional problem, and Fiona feels that return-to-work interviews should be undertaken by the HR team rather than by herself. The staffing problems have resulted in recruiting temporary staff from abroad – but this has added to Fiona's problems because there are personality clashes between some team members and further issues around capability.

Question

1   As the HR manager, what changes would you recommend to the approach to performance management at this NHS Trust?

CASE STUDY 12.4

HR SHARED SERVICE CENTRE

Laura, the employee

You are Laura Simmonds, aged 23, who graduated over a year ago with a degree in psychology. You want a career in HR but have found it difficult to get the type of job you want (at the right salary) partly because you don't have the right level of experience. It's also very competitive out there! In the end you took the only job you were offered, which was in the call centre of an HR shared service centre operation. Working in a call centre wasn't what you had hoped to do – the work is very repetitive, highly structured, with little scope for discretion and responsibility. Worst of all, there is no face-to-face contact with people – which is what you'd thought HR was about!

You have been working for 12 months in the call centre and find the work deadly boring. You passed your six-month probationary review with no problem, but since then the monotony of the work has got to you. However, being a bit of a party-goer, you have thrown yourself into the local rave scene. You don't do drugs but you do drink – if you're honest, probably a lot more than is safe.

Up until now your team leader, Phil, has generally left you alone, but in the past few weeks he's been checking what time you come in and makes sarcastic remarks if you're late. Unfortunately, you have been late quite a few times – and once missed a whole day when you woke up so late that it didn't seem worth coming in at all. You were a bit rude to him on the few occasions when he tried to find out what the reasons were (you might even have said on one occasion that it was 'none of his business'). You also might have been a little bit abrupt to customers on the odd occasion when you had a hangover. In general, however, you think you do your job well and get on with colleagues.

It is now time for your first formal performance review with Phil. But you are not sure what to expect at this meeting. At your probationary review Phil gave you a list of core competences for the role, but no one explained them to you:

- working together
- communicating and influencing
- analysing and using evidence

● managing customers.

These are all skills and behaviours which you feel you excel at. The organisation must surely agree with you on that because you had to demonstrate them in your interview for the role. Still, you don't really care – it's not that important a job, and there don't appear to be any career prospects. You're in half a mind to leave and go off travelling with some friends.

Phil, the team leader

You are Phil, a team leader in the HR call centre for a large organisation where you have worked for three years. Just over a year ago, you were promoted to team leader. At first it was a bit difficult managing some of your former work colleagues, but you think that in general you have coped well with the role and you still go out after work for drinks with everyone, so they must think you're OK. Your team department gets most of the results needed, although your targets fell in the last quarter – but that was probably because of technological problems with the phones. Some of the annual performance reviews are coming up, which you dread. They are just a waste of time and an added burden to what is becoming an increasingly demanding role. Surely this is something HR should be doing? With 15 staff to manage you just don't have time to spend more than 15 minutes or so with each team member. You normally use it to catch up on their personal life (that's what your boss does in your appraisal). You feel you are a good judge of character and don't need the review to find out how everyone is doing. Most people are rating an average score of 3,

which means they all get some small bonus each year. And then there are all the forms that need filling out – which you have to do at home in your spare time and mostly make up. Once they are sent to HR you've no idea what happens to them – they seem to fall into a black hole.

You are due to have a review meeting with Laura Simmonds, who has been with the company for 12 months. The probationary review went OK, and most of the time she seems a good worker. In the last few months, however, she has had four 'lates' and one 'uncertified absence'. You once got your head bitten off when you asked where she was, and was told that it was 'none of your business', so you haven't bothered again. There is also a complaint on file from one customer about 'surly and abrupt' behaviour on the phone, although there were also some complimentary comments.

You might raise the absences at the review meeting – you'll see how much time you have and what sort of mood she seems to be in.

Questions

1   As the HR manager, provide some detailed advice for Phil on how to conduct the performance appraisal.

2   What other recommendations would you make to improve the approach to performance management at this organisation?

You might also like to role-play the performance review, with Phil undertaking the advice from HR.

CASE STUDY 12.5

KEEPING IT SIMPLE AT INNOCENT

Innocent started in 1999 after selling smoothies at a music festival. Since that time the company has grown from three to 250 staff, and now sells a range of products including smoothies, veg pots, juices and kids' drinks. Its mission is 'to make natural, delicious food and drink that helps people live well and die old'. Its values are expressed as 'to be natural, be entrepreneurial, be responsible, be commercial and be generous'.

From the end of 1999 (when there were around 100 staff), Innocent has had a 'people director', who sits on the board, and a 'people strategy' which is integrated in the business. HR policies and procedures have been tailored to the organisation's unique context and values and 'what works around here'. Accordingly, Innocent performance management processes are as simple as possible. For example, everyone has

no more than five objectives, and they aim for the performance review to be summed up on one page. As the people director explained: 'We are an organisation where one of our values is about being natural – ie keeping this as human as possible – and so our review process is as much about a quality conversation as it is about the process and levelling side of it.'

Source: CIPD 2012 and www.innocentdrinks.co.uk

Question

1   Suggest other ways in which performance management practices and processes could fit with the organisation's culture and values. (You might want to look at the Innocent website.)

EXPLORE FURTHER

Biron, M., Farndale, E. and Paauwe, J. (2011) 'Performance management effectiveness: lessons from world-leading firms', *International Journal of Human Resource Management*, Vol.22, No.6, March: 1294–1311

Chase, P. and Fuchs, S. (2008) 'Performance management and appraisal', in Muller-Camen, M., Croucher, R. and Leigh, S. (eds) *Human Resource Management: A case study approach*. London: CIPD

CIPD (2009a) *Performance Management in Action: Current trends and practice*. Available online at: www.cipd.co.uk/binaries/ Performance_management_in_action.pdf

Fletcher, C. and Williams, R. (1996) 'Performance management, job satisfaction and organisational commitment', *British Journal of Management*, Vol.17, No.2: 169–79

Glendinning, P. M. (2002) 'Performance management: pariah or messiah?', *Public Personnel Management*, Vol.31, No.2, Summer: 161–78

Parry, E. (2011) 'An examination of e-HRM as a means to increase the value of the HR function', *International Journal of Human Resource Management*, Vol.22, No.5: 1146–62

Pulakos, E. D. and O'Leary, R. S. (2011) 'Why is performance management broken?', *Industrial and Organisational Psychology*, Vol.4, No.2: 146–64

Rankin, N. (2010) *Good Practice: Performance management*. Good practice guides. London: XpertHR. Available online at: www.xperthr.co.uk

Winstanley, D. and Stuart-Smith, K. (1996) 'Policing performance: the ethics of performance management', *Personnel Review*, Vol.25, No.5: 66–84

XpertHR (2010a) 'Communication: line manager briefing on handling difficult conversations'. Available online at: www.xperthr.co.uk

XpertHR (2010b) 'Communication: line manager briefing on motivation'. Available online at: www.xperthr.co.uk

References

ACAS (1990) *Appraisal-Related Pay*, Advisory Booklet. London: ACAS

ACAS (1997, 2003, 2008) *Employee Appraisal*, Advisory Booklet. London: ACAS

ACAS (2005) *Appraisal Related Pay*. Advisory Booklet. London: ACAS

ACAS (2006) *Pay Schemes*, Advisory Booklet. London: ACAS

ACAS (2009a) *Front Line Managers*, Advisory Booklet. London: ACAS

ACAS (2009b) *Disciplinary and Grievance Procedures*, Code of Practice. London: ACAS

ACAS (2010) *How to Manage Performance*. Available online at: www.acas.org.uk

ACAS (2012a) *Challenging Conversations and How to Manage Them*, Advisory Booklet. London: ACAS

ACAS (2012b) *Health, Work and Wellbeing*, Advisory Booklet. London: ACAS

Achrol, R. (1991) 'Evolution of the marketing organisation: new norms for turbulent environments', *Journal of Marketing*, Vol.55, October: 77–93

Adams, J. S. (1965) 'Inequity in social exchange', in Berkowitz, L. (ed.) *Advances in Experimental Social Psychology*, Vol.2. New York: Academic Press

Adams, K. (1991) 'Externalisation versus specialisation: what is happening to personnel?', *Human Resource Management Journal*, Vol.1, No.4: 40–54

Adler, N. J., Doktor, R. and Redding, S. G. (1986) 'From the Atlantic to the Pacific century: cross-cultural management reviewed', *Journal of Management*, Vol.12, No.1: 295–318

Aguinis, H. (2009) *Performance Management*, 2nd edition. Harlow: Pearson/Prentice Hall International

Alderfer, C. (1972) *Existence, Relatedness and Growth: Human needs in organisational settings*. New York: Free Press

Allen, N. J. and Meyer, J. P. (1990) 'The measurement and antecedents of affective, continuance and normative commitment to the organization', *Journal of Occupational Psychology*, Vol.63: 1–18

Ambrose, M. L. and Kulik, C. T. (1999) 'Old friends, new faces: motivation research in the 1990s', *Journal of Management*, Vol.25: 213–92

Amietta, P. (2000) *I Luoghi dell'Apprendimento: Metodi, strumenti e casi di eccellenza*. Milan: FrancoAngeli

Appelbaum, E., Bailey, T., Berg, P. and Kallenberg, A. L. (2000) *Manufacturing Advantage: Why high-performance work systems pay off*. Ithaca, NY: Cornell University Press

Argyris, C. (1960) *Understanding Organizational Behavior.* Homewood, IL: Dorsey Press

Arkin, A. (2007a) 'Force for good?', *People Management*, Vol.13, No.3, 8 February: 26–9

Arkin. A (2007b) 'From soft to strong (performance management)', *People Management*, Vol.13, No.18, 6 September: 30–3

Armstrong, M. (1999) *A Handbook of Human Resource Management,* London: Kogan

Armstrong, M. (2000) *Rewarding Teams.* Good Practice Series. London: CIPD

Armstrong, M. (2006) *Performance Management: Key strategies and practical guidelines.* London: Kogan Page

Armstrong, M. (2009) *Armstrong's Handbook of Performance Management: An evidence-based guide to delivering high performance.* London: Kogan Page

Armstrong, M. and Baron, A. (1998) *Performance management: the new realities.* London: Institute of Personnel and Development

Armstrong, M. and Baron, A. (2005) *Managing Performance: Performance management in action.* London: CIPD

Arnold, J. and Randall, R. (2010) *Work Psychology: Understanding human behaviour in the workplace*, 5th edition. Harlow: FT/Prentice Hall

Arnold, J., Robertson, I. T. and Cooper, C. L. (1991) *Work Psychology.* London: Pitman

Arnold, J., Silvester, J., Patterson, F., Robertson, I., Cooper, C. and Burners, B. (2005) *Work Psychology: Understanding human behaviours in the workplace*, 4th edition. Harlow: Prentice Hall

Aronsson, G. and Gustafsson, K. (2005) 'Sickness presenteeism: prevalence, attendance-pressure factors, and an outline of a model for research', *Journal of Epidemiology and Community Health*, Vol.47, No.9: 958–66

Arrowsmith, J. and Marginson, P. (2010) 'The decline of incentive pay in British manufacturing', *Industrial Relations Journal*, Vol.41, No.4: 289–311

Arthur, J. B. (1994) 'Effects of human resource systems on manufacturing performance and turnover', *Academy of Management Journal*, Vol.37, No.3: 670–87

Aryee, S., Budhwar, P. S. and Chen, Z. X. (2002) 'Trust as a mediator in the relationship between organisational justice and work outcomes: test of a social exchange model', *Journal of Organisational Behaviour*, Vol.23, No.3: 533–46

Atkinson, C. and Hall, L. (2011) 'Flexible working and happiness in the NHS', *Employee Relations*, Vol.33, No.2: 88–105

Atwater, L. E. (1998) 'The advantages and pitfalls of self-assessment in organizations', in Smither, J. W. (ed.) *Performance Appraisal: State of the art in practice.* San Francisco: Jossey-Bass

Atwater, L. E., Brett, J. F. and Charles, A. C. (2007) 'Multisource feedback: lessons learned and implications for practice', *Human Resource Management*, Vol.46, No.2, Summer: 285–307

Atwater, L. E., Waldman, D., Ostroff, C., Robie, C. and Johnson, K. M. (2005) 'Self–other agreement: comparing its relationship with performance in the US and Europe', *International Journal of Selection and Assessment*, Vol.13: 25–40

Audit Commission (1995) *Paying the Piper, Calling the Tune: People, pay and performance in local government – a management handbook*. London: Audit Commission/HMSO

Aycan, Z. (2005) 'The interplay between cultural and institutional contingencies in human resource management practices', *International Journal of Human Resource Management*, Vol.16, No.7: 1083–1119

Aycan, Z. and Yavuz, S. (2008) 'Performance management in Turkey', in Varma, A., Budhwar, P. W. and DeNisi, A. (eds) *Performance Management Systems: A global perspective*. Abingdon: Routledge

Aycan, Z., Kanungo, R. N., Mendonca, M., Yu, K., Deller, J., Stahl, G. and Khursid, A. (2000) 'Impact of culture on human resource management practices: a 10-country comparison', *Applied Psychology: An International Review*, Vol.49, No.1: 192–221

Bach, S. (2005) 'New directions in performance management', in Bach, S. (ed.) *Managing Human Resources: Personnel management in transition*, 4th edition. Oxford: Blackwell

Bach, S. (2009) 'HRM in the public sector', in Wilkinson, A., Bacon, N., Redman, T. and Snell, S. (eds) *The Sage Handbook of Human Resource Management*. London: Sage

Bai, X. and Bennington, L. (2005) 'Performance appraisal in the Chinese state-owned coal industry', *International Journal of Business Performance Management*, Vol.7, No.3: 275–87

Bailey, J. R., Chen, C. C. and Dou, S. G. (1997) 'Conceptions of self and performance-related feedback in the US, Japan and China', *Journal of International Business Studies*, Vol.28, No.3: 605–25

Bailey, T. (1993) *Discretionary Effort and the Organization of Work: Employment participation and work reform since Hawthorne*. Columbia University, New York, Teachers' College and Conservation of Human Resources

Bailey, T., Berg, P. and Sandy, P. (2001) 'The effects of high-performance work practices on employee earnings in the steel, apparel, and medical electronics and imaging industries', *Industrial and Labor Relations Review*, Vol.54, No.2A: 525–43

Bain, P., Watson, A. Mulvey, G. and Gall, G. (2002) 'Taylorism, targets, and the pursuit of quantity and quality by call centre management', *New Technology, Work and Employment*, Vol.17, No.3: 154–69

Baird, L. and Meshoulam, I. (1988) 'Managing two fits of strategic human resource management', *Academy of Management Review*, Vol.13, No.1: 116–28

Baker-McClearn, D., Greasley, K., Dale, J. and Griffith, F. (2010) 'Absence management and presenteeism: the pressures on employees to attend work and the impact of attendance on performance', *Human Resource Management Journal*, Vol.20, No.3: 311–28

Baldamus, W. (1961) *Efficiency and Effort*. London: Tavistock

Baldwin, T. T. and Ford, J. K. (1988) 'Transfer of training: a review and directions for future research', *Personnel Psychology*, Vol.41, No.1: 63–105

Ball, S. (2003) 'The teacher's soul and the terrors of performativity', *Journal of Education Policy*, Vol.18, No.2: 215–28

Bandura, A. (1986) *The Social Foundations of Thought and Action*. Englewood Cliffs, NJ: Prentice Hall

Bandura, A. (1993) 'Perceived self-efficacy in cognitive development and functioning', *Educational Psychology*, Vol.28: 117–48

Barber, A. E. and Bretz, R. D. (2000) 'Compensation, attraction and retention', in Rynes, S. and Gerhart, B. (eds) *Compensation in Organizations: Progress and prospects*. Frontiers of Industrial and Organizational Science series. San Francisco: New Lexington Press

Barzantny, C. and Festing, M. (2008) 'Performance management in France and Germany', in Varma, A., Budhwar, P. W. and DeNisi, A. (eds) *Performance Management Systems: A global perspective*. Abingdon: Routledge

Barney, J. (1991) 'Firm resources and sustained competitive advantage', *Journal of Management*, Vol.17, No.1: 99–120

Bateman, T. S. and Organ, D. W. (1983) 'Job satisfaction and the good soldier: the relationship between affect and employee "citizenship"', *Academy of Management Journal*, Vol.26: 587–95

Becker, B. E. and Huselid, M. A. (1998) 'High-performance work systems and firm performance: a synthesis of research and managerial implications', *Research in Personnel and Human Resources Management*, Vol.16: 53–101

Becker, B. E., Huselid, M. A., Pickus, P. S. and Spratt, M. F. (1997) 'HR as a source of shareholder value: research and recommendations', *Human Resource Management Journal*, Vol.31, No.1: 39–47

Becker, T. E., Billings, R., Eveleth, D. and Gilbert, N. (1996) 'Foci and bases of employee commitment: implications for job performance', *Academy of Management Journal*, Vol. 39, No.2: 464–82

Becton, J. B., Giles, W. F. and Schraeder, M. (2008) 'Evaluating and rewarding OCBs: potential consequences of formally incorporating organisational citizenship behaviours in performance appraisal and reward systems', *Employee Relations*, Vol.30, No.5: 494–514

Beecroft, A. (2011) *Employment Law*. Government Report. Available online at: www.bis.gov.uk

Beer, M. (1981) 'Performance appraisal: dilemmas and possibilities', *Organizational Dynamics*, Vol.9, No.3: 24–36

Beer, M. and Cannon, M. D. (2004) 'Promise and peril in implementing pay for performance', *Human Resource Management*, Vol.43, No.1: 49–67

Beer, M. and Eisenstat, R. A. (2000) 'The silent killers of strategy implementation and learning', *Sloan Management Review*, Vol.41, No.4, Summer: 29–40

Belfield, R. and Marsden, D. (2003) 'Performance pay, monitoring environments and establishment performance', *International Journal of Manpower*, Vol.24, No.4: 452–71

Bendix, R. (1956) *Work Authority in Industry*. New York: John Wiley & Sons

Bernardin, H. J., Cooke, D. K. and Villanova, P. (2000) 'Conscientiousness and agreeableness as predictors of rating leniency', *Journal of Applied Psychology*, Vol.85: 232–4

Berry, M (2008) 'Generation Y: the hard facts', *Personnel Today*, 14 September

Betcherman, G., McMullen, K., Leckie, N. and Caron, C. (1994) *The Canadian Workplace in Transition*. Kingston, Ontario: IRC Press

Bies, R. J. and Moag, J. S. (1986) 'Interactional justice: communication criteria of fairness', in Lewicki, R. J., Sheppard, B. H. and Bazerman, M. (eds) *Research on Negotiation in Organisations*. Greenwich, CT: JAI

Biggs, J. (1991) *Teaching for Learning: The view from cognitive psychology*. Victoria, Australia: ACER

Biggs, J. and Collis, K. (1982) *Evaluating the Quality of Learning: The SOLO taxonomy*. New York: Academic Press

Biron, M., Farndale, E. and Paauwe, J. (2011) 'Performance management effectiveness: lessons from world-leading firms', *International Journal of Human Resource Management*, Vol.22, No.6, March: 1294–1311

Black, C. (2008) *Working for a Healthier Tomorrow*. London: Department for Work and Pensions. Available online at: www.dwp.gov.uk/docs/hwwb-working-for-a-healthier-tomorrow.pdf [accessed 29 June 2012]

Black, C. and Frost, D. (2011) *Health at Work: An independent review of sickness absence*. London: Department for Work and Pensions. Available online at: www.dwp.gov.uk/health-at-work.pdf [accessed 29 June 2012]

Black, J. S. and Gregerson, H. (1999) 'The right way to manager expats', *Harvard Business Review*, Vol.77, No.2: 52–60

Black, J. S. and Mendenhall, M. (1991) 'The U-curve adjustment hypothesis revisited: a review and theoretical framework', *Journal of International Business Studies*, Vol.22, No.2: 225–48

Black, J. S., Gregersen, H. B. and Mendenhall, M. (1992) *Global Assignments: Successfully expatriating and repatriating international managers*. San Francisco: Jossey-Bass

Blass, E. (2007) *Talent Management: Maximising talent for the whole business*. London: Chartered Management Institute/Berkhamsted: Ashridge Management Consulting

Blau, G. (1999) 'Testing the longitudinal impact of work variables and performance appraisal satisfaction on subsequent overall job satisfaction', *Human Relations*, Vol.52, No.8: 1099–1113

Blau, P. (1967) *Exchange and Power in Social Life*. New York: John Wiley & Sons

Boaden, R., Marchington, M., Hyde, P., Harris, C., Sparrow, P., Pass, S., Carroll, M. and Cortvriend, P. (2008) *Improving Health through Human Resource Management: The process of engagement and alignment*. London: CIPD

Bolino, M. C. and Turnley, W. H. (2008) 'Old faces, new places: equity theory in cross-cultural contexts', *Journal of Organizational Behavior*, Vol.29, No.1: 29–50

Bonoma, T. W. (1976) 'Conflict, cooperation and trust in three power systems', *Behavioural Science*, Vol.21, No.6: 499–514

Borkowski, S. C. (1999) 'International managerial performance evaluation: a five-country comparison', *Journal of International Business Studies*, Vol.30, No.3: 533–55

Borman, W. C. and Motowidlo. S. J. (1993) 'Expanding the criterion domain to include elements of contextual performance', in Schimtt, N. and Borman, W. C. (eds) *Personnel Selection in Organizations*. San Francisco: Jossey-Bass

Boselie, P. (2010) *Strategic Human Resource Management: A balanced approach*. London/ Columbus, OH: McGraw-Hill

Boselie, P., Dietz, G. and Boon, C. (2005) 'Commonalties and contradictions in research on human resource management and performance', *Human Resource Management Journal*, Vol.15, No.3: 67–94

Boselie, P., Farndale, E. and Paauwe, J. (2011) 'Performance management', in Brewster, C. J. and Mayrhofer, W. (eds) *Handbook of Research on Comparative Human Resource Management*. Cheltenham: Edward Elgar

Bourner, T., O'Hara, S. and Webber, T. (2002) 'Learning to manage change in the Health Service', in Brockbank, A., McGill, I. and Beech, N. (eds) *Reflective Learning in Practice*. Aldershot: Gower

Bowen, D. and Ostroff, C. (2004) 'Understanding HRM–firm performance linkages: the role of the "strength" of the HRM system', *Academy of Management Review*, Vol.29, No.2: 203–21

Boxall, P. and Macky, K. (2009) 'Research and theory in high-performance work systems: progressing the high-involvement stream', *Human Resource Management Journal*, Vol.19, No.1: 3–23

Boxall, P. and Purcell, J. (2003) *Strategy and Human Resource Management*. Basingstoke and New York: Palgrave Macmillan

Boxall, P. and Purcell, J. (2008) *Strategy and Human Resource Management*, 2nd edition. Basingstoke and New York: Palgrave Macmillan

Boxall, P. and Purcell, J. (2011) *Strategy and Human Resource Management*, 3rd edition. Basingstoke and New York: Palgrave Macmillan

Boyatzis, R. (1982) *The Competent Manager: A model for effective performance*. New York: John Wiley & Sons

Boydell, T. (1971) *A Guide to the Identification of Training Needs*. London: British Association for Commercial and Industrial Education

Bramley, P. (2003) *Evaluating Training*. London: CIPD

Brammer, S., Millington, A. and Rayton, B. A. (2007) 'The contribution of corporate social responsibility to organizational commitment', *International Journal of Human Resource Management*, Vol.18, No.10: 1701–19

Brandl, J., Madsen, M. T. and Madsen, H. (2009) 'The perceived importance of HR duties to Danish line managers', *Human Resource Management Journal*, Vol.19, No.2: 194–210

Braverman, H. (1974) *Labour and Monopoly Capital: The degradation of work in the twentieth century*. New York: Monthly Review Press

Breaugh, J. A. (1981) 'Predicting absenteeism from prior absenteeism and work attitudes', *Journal of Applied Psychology*, Vol.66, No.5: 555–60

Brender-Ilan, Y. and Shultz, T. (2005) 'Perceived fairness of the mystery customer method: comparing two employee evaluation practices', *Employee Responsibilities and Rights Journal*, Vol.17, No.4, December: 231–43

Brenneman, W. B., Keys, J. B. and Fulmer, R. M. (1998) 'Learning across a living company: the Shell Company's experiences', *Organizational Dynamics*, Vol.27, No.2: 61–9

Brett, J. and Atwater, L. (2001) '360-degree feedback: accuracy, reactions and perceptions of usefulness', *Journal of Applied Psychology*, Vol.86: 930–42

Brewster, C. (1998) 'International HRM: beyond expatriation', *Human Resource Management*, Vol.7, No.3: 31–42

Brewster, C. and Larsen, H. H. (2000a) *Human Resource Management in Northern Europe*. Oxford: Blackwell

Brewster, C. and Larsen, H. H. (2000b) 'Responsibility in human resource management: the role of the line', in Brewster, C. and Larsen, H. H. (eds) *Human Resource Management in Northern Europe*. Oxford: Blackwell

Brewster, C., Sparrow, P., Vernon, G. and Houldsworth, E. (2007) *International Performance Management*, 3rd edition. London: CIPD

Brewster, C., Sparrow, P., Vernon, G. and Houldsworth, E. (2011) *International Performance Management*, 4th edition. London: CIPD

Brinkerhoff, R. O. (2006) 'Increasing impact of training investments: an evaluation strategy for building organisational learning capability', *Industrial and Commercial Training*, Vol.38, No.6: 302–7

Briscoe, D. B., Schuler, R. and Tarique, I. (2012) *International Human Resource Management: Policies and practices for multinational enterprises*, 4th edition. New York: Routledge

Brockett, J. (2009) 'Are bonuses to blame for banking's downward spiral?', *People Management*, Vol.15, No.4, December: 8

Brooke, P. B. (1986) 'Beyond the Steers and Rhodes model of employee attendance', *Academy of Management Review*, Vol.11, No.2: 345–61

Brooke, P. P. and Price, J. L. (1989) 'The determinants of absenteeism: an empirical test of a causal model', *Journal of Occupational Psychology*, Vol.62, No.1: 1–19

Brown, D. and Hirsh, W. (2011) *Performance Management: The implementation challenge*. Brighton: Institute for Employment Studies

Brown, K. G. and Gerhardt, M. W. (2002) 'Formative evaluation: an integrative practice model and case study', *Personnel Psychology*, Vol.55, No.4: 951–83

Brown, K. G. and Sitzmann, T. (2011) 'Training and employee development for improved performance', in Zedeck, S. (ed.) *Handbook of Industrial and Organizational Psychology*, Vol.2. Washington, DC: American Psychological Association

Brown, M. and Lim, V. S. (2009) 'Understanding performance management and appraisal: supervisory and employee perspectives', in Wilkinson, A., Bacon, N., Redman, T. and Snell, S. (eds) *The Sage Handbook of Human Resource Management*. London: Sage

Brown, M., Hyatt, D. and Benson, J. (2010) 'Consequences of the performance appraisal experience', *Personnel Review*, Vol.39, No.3: 375–96

Brownell, J. (2006) 'Meeting the competency needs of global leaders: a partnership approach', *Human Resource Management*, Vol.45, No.3: 309–36

Brumbach, G. B. (1988) 'Some ideas and predictions about performance management', *Public Personnel Management,* Winter: 387–402

Brutus, S., Fletcher, C. and Baldry, C. (2009) 'The influence of independent self-construal on rater self-efficacy in performance appraisal', *International Journal of Human Resource Management*, Vol.20, No.9, September: 1999–2011

Bryson, A. and Freeman, R. B. (2006) 'What voice do British workers want?', Centre for Economic Performance Discussion Paper No.731, London School of Economics

Bryson, A., Pendleton, A. and Whitfield, K. (2009) 'The changing use of contingent pay at the modern British workplace', National Institute of Economic and Social Research Discussion Paper No.319

Bryson, A., Freeman, R., Lucifora, C., Pellizzari, M. and Perotin, V. (2012) 'Paying for performance: incentive pay schemes and employees' financial participation', Centre for Economic Performance Discussion Paper No.1112, London School of Economics

Burgess, S., Ratto, M., Propper, C. and Tominey, E. (2004) 'Incentives in the public sector: evidence from a government agency', University of Bristol CMPO Working Paper Series No.04/103

Burton, J., Lee, T. and Holtom, C. (2002) 'The influence of motivation to attend, ability to attend, and organizational commitment on different types of absence behaviors', *Journal of Managerial Issues*, Vol.14, No.2: 181–97

Byrne, Z. S., Pitts, V. E., Wilson, C. M. and Steiner, Z. J. (2012) 'Trusting the fair supervisor: the role of supervisory support in performance appraisals', *Human Resource Management Journal*, Vol.22, No.2: 129–47

Caldwell, C., Thornton, G. C. and Gruys, M. L. (2003) 'Ten classic assessment center errors: challenges to selection validity', *Public Personnel Management*, Vol.32: 73–88

Caldwell, R. (2003) 'The changing roles of personnel managers: old ambiguities, new uncertainties', *Journal of Management Studies*, Vol.40, No.4: 983–1004

Caldwell, R. (2008) 'HR business partner competency models: re-contextualising effectiveness', *Human Resource Management Journal*, Vol.18, No.3: 275–94

Caligiuri, P. M. (2000) 'The Big Five personality characteristics as predictors of expatriate's desire to terminate the assignment and supervisor-rated performance', *Personnel Psychology*, Vol.53, No.1: 67–88

Cameron, J. (2001) 'Negative effects of reward on intrinsic motivation – a limited phenomenon', *Review of Educational Research*, Vol.71, No.1: 29–42

Campbell, J. P., McCloy, R. A., Oppler, S. H. and Sager, C. E. (1993) 'A theory of performance', in Schmitt, N. and Borman, W. C. (eds) *Personnel Selection in Organizations*. San Francisco: Jossey-Bass

Carnevale, D. G. and Wechsler, B. (1992) 'Trust in the public sector: individual and organisational determinants', *Administration and Society*, Vol.23, No.4: 471–94

Carty, M. (2009a) 'Case study: Flexible benefits boost retention at Subsea 7', *IRS Employment Review*, Issue 921

Carty, M. (2009b) 'Case study: Making team bonuses pay at Fenner Dunlop', *IRS Employment Review*, Issue 914

Cascio, W. F. (1991) *Costing Human Resources: The financial impact of behavior in organizations*. Boston, MA: PWS-Kent

Cascio, W. F. (1998) *Applied Psychology in Human Resource Management*. Upper Saddle River, NJ: Prentice Hall

Cascio, W. F. (2006) 'Global performance management systems', in Stahl, G. K. and Bjorkman, L. (eds) *Handbook of Research in International Human Resource Management*. Cheltenham, UK/Northampton, MA: Edward Elgar

Cawley, B., Keeping, L. and Levy, P. (1998) 'Participation in the performance appraisal process and employee reactions: a meta-analytic review of field investigations', *Journal of Applied Psychology*, Vol.83, No.4: 615–33

CBI (2011) *Healthy Returns? Absence and workplace health*. Survey Report. London: CBI. Available online at: www.cbi.org.uk/2011.05-healthy-returns_-_absence_and_workplace_health_survey_2011.pdf [accessed 2 July 2012]

Chamorro-Premuzic, T. (2007) *Personality and Individual Differences*. Oxford: British Psychological Society/Blackwell

Chang, E. and Hahn, J. (2006) 'Does pay-for-performance enhance perceived distributive justice for collectivistic employees?', *Personnel Review*, Vol.35, No.4: 397–412

Charan, R. (2010) 'Banking on talent (talent management)', *People Management*, 28 October: 2–3

Charan, R., Drotter, S. and Noel, J. (2011) *The Leadership Pipeline: How to build the leadership powered company*, 2nd edition. San Francisco: Jossey-Bass

Chase, P. and Fuchs, S. (2008) 'Performance management and appraisal', in Muller-Camen, M., Croucher, R. and Leigh, S. (eds) *Human Resource Management: A case study approach*. London: CIPD

Chen, H.-C. and Naquin, S. S. (2006) 'An integrative model of competency development, training design, assessment center and multi-rater assessment', *Advances in Developing Human Resources*, Vol.8, No.2: 265–82

Chen, Z., Lam, W. and Zhong, J. A. (2007) 'Leader–member exchange and member performance: a new look at individual-level negative feedback-seeking behavior', *Journal of Applied Psychology*, Vol.92, No.1: 202–12

Chiang, C.-F. and Jang, S. C. (2008) 'An expectancy theory model for hotel employee motivation', *International Journal of Hospitality Management*, Vol.27, No.2: 313–22

Chiang, F. (2005) 'A critical examination of Hofstede's thesis and its application to international reward management', *International Journal of Human Resource Management*, Vol.16, No.9: 1543–63

Chiang, F. F. T. and Birch, T. A. (2007) 'Examining the perceived causes of successful employee performance: an East–West comparison', *International Journal of Human Resource Management*, Vol.18, No.2: 232–48

Chiang, F. F. T. and Birch, T. A. (2010) 'Appraising performance across borders: an empirical examination of the purposes and practices of performance appraisal in a multi-country context', *Journal of Management Studies*, Vol.47, No.7: 1365–93

Cho, Y. and Egan, T. M. (2009) 'Action Learning research: a systematic review and conceptual framework', *Human Resource Development Review*, Vol.8, No.4: 431–62

Churchill, G. A., Ford, N. M. and Walker, O. C. (1976) 'Organizational climate and job satisfaction in the sales force', *Journal of Marketing Research*, Vol.13: 323–32

CIPD (2001) *Performance Through People: The new people management*. London: CIPD

CIPD (2005a) *Performance management*. Survey Report. London: CIPD. Available online at: www.cipd.co.uk/binaries/perfmansr0905.pdf

CIPD (2005b) *Absence Management*. Survey Report. London: CIPD. Available online at: www.cipd.co.uk/hr-resources/survey-reports [accessed 2 July 2012]

CIPD (2007) *Learning and Development*. Survey Report. London: CIPD

CIPD (2008) *Learning and Development*. Annual Survey Report. London: CIPD

CIPD (2009a) *Performance Management in Action: Current trends and practice*. Available online at: www.cipd.co.uk/binaries/Performance_management_in_action.pdf

CIPD (2009b) *Recruitment, Retention and Turnover*. Annual Survey Report. London: CIPD

CIPD (2009c) *Absence Management*. Survey Report. London: CIPD

CIPD (2010a) *Employee Attitudes to Pay*. Annual Survey Report. London: CIPD

CIPD (2010b) *Absence Management 2010: Case studies*. London: CIPD. Available online at: www.cipd.co.uk/hr-resources/survey-reports/absence-management-2010-case-studies.aspx [accessed 3 July 2012]

CIPD (2011a) *Performance Appraisal*. Factsheet. London: CIPD. Available online

CIPD (2011b) *Feedback – 360 degree.* Factsheet, London: CIPD Available online

CIPD (2011c) *Focus on E-Learning.* London: CIPD

CIPD (2011d) *The Coaching Climate.* Survey Report. London: CIPD. Available online at: www.cipd.uk/hr-research/surveyreports [accessed 27 March 2013]

CIPD (2011e) *Absence Management.* Survey Report. London: CIPD. Available online at www.cipd.co.uk/hr-resources/survey-reports [accessed 2 July 2012]

CIPD (2012a) *Absence Measurement and Management.* Factsheet. London: CIPD. Available online at: www.cipd.co.uk/hr-resources/factsheets [accessed 2 July 2012]

CIPD (2012b) *HR Shared Service Centre.* Factsheet, November. Available online [accessed March 2013]

CIPD (2012c) *Learning and Development.* Annual Survey Report. Available online at: www.cipd.co.uk/binaries/5688%20LTD%20SR%20report%20WEB.pdf [accessed 23 September 2012]

CIPD (2012d) *Coaching and Mentoring.* Factsheet. Available online at: www.cipd.co.uk/hr-resources/factsheets/coaching-mentoring.aspx [accessed 8 October 2012]

CIPD (2012e) *E Learning.* Factsheet. Available online at: www.cipd.co.uk/hr-resources/factsheets/e-learning.aspx [accessed March 2013]

CIPD (2012f) *Reward Management.* Annual Survey Report. London: CIPD

CIPD (2012g) *Performance-Related Pay.* Factsheet. London: CIPD

CIPD (2012h) *Discipline and Grievances at Work.* Factsheet. Available online at: www.cipd.uk/hr-resources/factsheets [accessed 27 March 2013]

CIPD (2012i) *Absence Management.* Annual Survey Report. London: CIPD

CIPD (2012j) *Achieving Sustainable Organisation Performance Through HR in SMEs.* Research Insight, June. London: CIPD

CIPD (2013a) *Flexible and Voluntary Benefits.* Factsheet. London: CIPD

CIPD (2013b) *Strategic Reward and Total Reward.* Factsheet. London: CIPD

CIPD (2013c) *Bonuses and Incentives.* Factsheet. London: CIPD

Clancy, M. and Seifert, R. (2000) 'The dynamics of workplace grievances and grievance procedures', in Clancy, M. and Seifert, R. *Fairness at Work? The disciplinary and grievance provisions of the Employment Relations Act 1999.* London: Institute of Employment Rights

Claus, L. and Briscoe, D. B. (2009) 'Employee performance management across borders: a review of relevant academic literature', *International Journal of Management Review,* Vol. 11, No.2: 175–96

Coffield, F., Moseley, D., Hall, E. and Ecclestone, K. (2004) *Learning styles and pedagogy in post-16 learning: a systematic and critical review.* London, Learning and Skills Network. Available online at www.leerbeleving.nl/wp-content/uploads/2011/09/learning-styles.pdf

Coleman, J. (2010) *Employment of Foreign Workers 2007–2009*. London: Office for National Statistics

Colquitt, J. A., Lepine, J. A. and Wesson, M. J. (2009) *Organizational behavior: Essentials for improving performance and commitment in the workplace*. New York: McGraw-Hill/Irwin

Combs, C., Liu, Y., Hall, A. and Kitchen, D. (2006) 'How much do high-performance work systems matter? A meta-analysis of their effects on organisational performance', *Personnel Psychology*, Vol.59, No.3: 501–28

Conner, J. (2000) 'Developing the global leaders of tomorrow', *Human Resource Management*, Vol.39, No.2/3: 147–57

Conway, E. and Monks, K. (2009) 'Unravelling the complexities of high commitment: an employee-level analysis', *Human Resource Management Journal*, Vol.19, No.2: 140–58

Conway, N., and Briner, R. B. (2004) 'Promises, promises', *People Management*, 25 November

Conway, N. and Briner, R. B. (2005) *Understanding Psychological Contracts at Work: A critical evaluation of theory and research*. Oxford: Oxford University Press

Conway, N. and Briner, R. B. (2009) 'Fifty years of psychological contract research: what do we know and what are the main challenges?', in Hodgkinson, G. P. and Ford, J. K. (eds) *International Review of Industrial and Organisational Psychology*, Vol.24: 71–130. Chichester: John Wiley

Cooke, F. L. (2004) 'Public sector pay in China: 1949–2001', *International Journal of Human Resource Management*, Vol.15, No.4/5: 895–916

Cooke, F. L. (2008) 'Performance management in China', in Cooke, F. L. (ed.) *Performance Management Systems: A global perspective*. Abingdon: Routledge

Cooper-Thomas, H., Anderson, N. and Cash, M. L. (2012) 'Investigating organisational socialisation: a fresh look at newcomer adjustment strategies', *Personnel Review*, Vol.41, No.1: 41–55

Cox, A., Higgins, T. and Speckesser, S. (2011) *Management Practices and Sustainable Organisational Performance: An analysis of the European Company Survey*. Dublin: European Foundation for the Improvement of Living and Working Conditions

Coyle-Shapiro, J., Kessler, I. and Purcell, J. (2004) 'Exploring organisationally-directed citizenship behaviour: reciprocity or "It's my job"', *Journal of Management Studies*, Vol. 41, No.1: 85–106

Cranet (2005, 2011) *Survey on Comparative Human Resource Management*. International Executive Report

Cressey, P. and MacInnes, J. (1980) 'Voting for Ford: industrial democracy and the control of labour', *Capital and Class*, Vol.11: 5–33

Cropanzano, R., Bowen, D. E. and Gilliland, S. W. (2007) 'The management of organisational justice', *Academy of Management Perspectives*, November: 34–48

Cunningham, I. and Hyman, J. (1995) 'Transforming the HRM vision into reality: the role of line managers and supervisors in implementing change', *Employee Relations*, Vol.17, No.8: 5–20

Cunningham, I. and Hyman, J. (1999) 'Devolving human resource responsibilities to the line: beginning of the end or a new beginning of Personnel?', *Personnel Review*, Vol.28: 9–27

Currie, G. and Procter, G. (2001) 'Exploring the relationship between HR and middle managers', *Human Resource Management Journal*, Vol.11, No.3: 53–69

Cutler, T. (1992) 'Vocational training and British economic performance: a further instalment of the British labour problem', *Work, Employment and Society*, Vol.6, No.2: 161–83

Cyert, R. M. and March, J. G. (1963) *A Behavioral Theory of the Firm*. Englewood Cliffs, NJ: Prentice Hall

Dai, G., De Meuse, K. P. and Peterson, C. (2010) 'Impact of multi-source feedback on leadership competency development: a longitudinal field study', *Journal of Managerial Issues*, Vol.22, No.2, Summer: 197–219

Daily Telegraph: www.telegraph.co.uk/motoring/news/6173404/Council-offers-traffic-wardens-rewards-for-handing-out-tickets.html [accessed 11 September 2009]

Danford, A., Richardson, M., Stewart, P., Tailby, S. and Upchurch, M. (2005) *Partnership and the High-Performance Workplace – Work and employment relations in the aerospace industry*. Future of Work series. Basingstoke: Palgrave Macmillan

Deci, E. L. (1971) 'Effects of externally mediated reward on intrinsic motivation', *Journal of Personality and Social Psychology*, Vol.18: 105–15

Deci, E. L. and Ryan, R. M. (1985) *Intrinsic Motivation and Self-Setermination in Human Behavior*. New York: Plenum

Deci, E. L., Koestner, R. and Ryan, R. M. (2001) 'Extrinsic rewards and intrinsic motivation in education reconsidered once again', *Review of Educational Research*, Vol.71: 1–27

De Cieri, H. and Sheehan, C. (2008) 'Performance management in Australia', in Varma, A., Budhwar, P. W. and DeNisi, A. (eds) *Performance Management Systems: A global perspective*. Abingdon: Routledge

Delery, J. and Doty, D. (1996) 'Modes of theorizing in strategic human resource management: tests of universalistic, contingency and configurational performance predictions', *Academy of Management Journal*, Vol.39, No.4: 802–35

Den Hartog, D. N., Boselie, P. and Paauwe, J. (2004) 'Performance management: a model and research agenda', *Applied Psychology: An International Review*, Vol.53, No.4: 556–69

DeNisi, S. A. (2000) 'Performance appraisal and performance management: a multi-level analysis', in Kozlowski, S. and Klein, K. J. (eds) *Multilevel Theory, Research and Methods in Organizations*. San Francisco: Jossey-Bass

DeNisi, S. A. and Kluger, N. A. (2000) 'Feedback effectiveness: can 360-degree appraisals be improved?', *Academy of Management Executive*, Vol.14, No.1: 129–39

DeNisi, S. A., Varma, A. and Budhwar, P. S. (2008) 'Performance management around the globe: what have we learned?', in Varma, A., Budhwar, P. W. and DeNisi, S. A. (eds) *Performance Management Systems: A global perspective*. Abingdon: Routledge

Department for Business Innovation and Skills (2012) *Employer's Charter*. Available online at: www.bis.gov.uk and www.gov.uk/government/uploads/.../employerscharter.pdf

Department for Education (2012) *Teachers' Standards*, May 2012. Available online at: www.education.gov.uk/publications

Department for Work and Pensions (2011) 'Ministers call for end to long-term sickness absence as independent review is launched'. DWP press release, 17 February. Available online at: www.dwp.gov.uk/newsroom/press-releases/2011/feb-2011/dwp022-11.shtml

Deutsch, M. (1958) 'Trust and suspicion', *Journal of Conflict Resolution*, Vol.2: 265–79

Dew, K., Keefe, V. and Small, K. (2005) '"Choosing" to work when sick: workplace presenteeism', *Social Science and Medicine*, Vol.60, No.10: 2273–82

Dickmann, M., Doherty, N. and Brewster, C, (2006) 'Why do they go? Individual and corporate perspectives on the factors influencing the decision to accept an international assigment', *International Journal of Human Resource Management*, Vol.19, No.4: 731–51

DiMaggio, P. J. and Powell, W. (1983) 'The iron cage revisited: institutional isomorphism and collective rationality in organizational fields', *American Sociological Review*, Vol.48, No.2, April: 147–60

Dowling, B. and Richardson, R. (1997) 'Evaluating performance-related pay for managers in the National Health Service', *International Journal of Human Resource Management*, Vol.8, No.3: 348–66

Dowling, P. J., Welch, D. E., Festing, M. and Engle, A. L. (2008) *International Human Resource Management: Managing people in a multinational context*, 5th edition. Cincinnati, OH: Cengage Learning

Driscoll, M. (2002) *Web-based training: creating e-learning experiences*, 2nd edition. San Francisco: Jossey-Bass

Drucker, P. (1955) *The Practice of Management*. London: Heinemann

Drucker, P. (1974) *Management: Task, responsibilities, practices*. New York: Harper & Row

Drucker, P. F. (1993) *The Post-Capitalist Society*. New York: Harper Business

Dunn, C. and Wilkinson, A. (2002) 'Wish you were here: managing absence', *Personnel Review*, Vol.31, No.2: 228–46

Earley, P. C. (1994) 'Self or group? Cultural effects of training on self efficacy and performance', *Adminstrative Science Quarterly*, Vol.39, 89–117

Easterby-Smith, M. (1994) *Evaluating Management Development, Training and Education*. Aldershot: Gower

Easterby-Smith, M., Malina, D. and Lu, Y. (1995) 'How culture-sensitive is HRM? A comparative analysis of Chinese and UK companies', *International Journal of Human Resource Management*, Vol.6, No.1: 31–59

Edwards, M. R., Borman, W. C. and Sproul, J. R. (1985) 'Solving the double-bind in performance appraisal: a saga of wolves, sloths, and eagles', *Business Horizons*, No.85309, May–June: 59–68

Edwards, P. K. (1986) *Conflict at Work: A materialist analysis of workplace relations*. Oxford: Blackwell

Edwards, P. K. and Whitston, C. (1989) 'Industrial discipline, the control of attendance and the subordination of labour: towards an integrated analysis', *Work, Employment and Society*, Vol.3, No.1: 1–28

Edwards, P. K. and Whitston, C. (1994) 'Disciplinary practice: a study of railways in Britain 1860–1988', *Work, Employment and Society*, Vol.8, No.3: 317–37

Edwards, P. and Wright, M. (2001) 'High-involvement work systems and performance outcomes: the strength of variable, contingent and context-bound relationships', *International Journal of Human Resource Management*, Vol.12, No.4: 568–85

Edwards, T. and Rees, C. (2011) *International Human Resource Management: Globalization, national systems and multinational companies*, 2nd edition. Harlow: Financial Times/Prentice Hall

Eisenberger, R., Fasolo, P. and Davis-Lamastro, V. (1990) 'Perceived organisational support and employee diligence, commitment and innovation', *Journal of Applied Psychology*, Vol.75, No.1: 51–9

Eisenberger, R., Huntington, R., Hutchinson, S. and Sowa, D. (1986) 'Perceived organisational support', *Journal of Applied Psychology*, Vol.71: 500–7

Eisenberger, R., Huntington, R., Hutchinson, S. and Sowa, D. (1997) 'Perceived organisational support, discretionary treatment, and job satisfaction', *Journal of Applied Psychology*, Vol.82: 812–20

Eisenberger, R., Stinglhamber, F., Vandenberghe, C., Sucharski, I. and Rhoades, L. (2002) 'Perceived supervisor support: contributions to perceived organisational support and employee retention', *Journal of Applied Psychology*, Vol.87: 565–73

Elenkov, S. E. (1998) 'Can American management concepts work in Russia? A cross-cultural comparative study', *California Management Review*, Vol.40: 133–56

Entrekin, L. and Chung, Y. (2001) 'Attitudes towards different sources of executive appraisal: a comparison of Hong Kong Chinese and American managers in Hong Kong', *International Journal of Human Resources Management*, Vol.12, No.6: 965–87

Evans, A. and Palmer, S. (1997) *From Absence to Attendance*. London: IPD

Fang, M. and Gerhart, B. (2012) 'Does pay for performance diminish intrinsic interest?', *International Journal of Human Resource Management*, Vol.23, No.6: 1176–96

Farrell, C. and Morris, J. (2009) 'Still searching for evidence? Evidence-based policy, performance pay and teachers', *Journal of Industrial Relations*, Vol.51, No.1: 75–94

Fay, C. H. and Latham, G. P. (1982) 'Effects of training and rating scales on rating errors', *Personnel Psychology*, Vol.35, No.1: 105–12

Fenton-O'Creevy, M. (2001) 'Employee involvement and the middle manager: saboteur or scapegoat?', *Human Resource Management Journal*, Vol.11, No.1: 24–40

Ferris, G. R., Judge, T. A., Rowland, K. M. and Fitzgibbons, D. E. (1994) 'Subordinate influence and the performance evaluation process: test of a model', *Organizational Behavior and Human Decision Processes*, Vol.58: 101–35

Fitzpatrick, P. (2003) 'Cultural evolution', *People Management*, 16 April

Fletcher, C. (2001) 'Performance appraisal and management: the developing research agenda', *Journal of Occupational and Organizational Psychology*, Vol.74: 473–87

Fletcher, C. (2008) *Appraisal, Feedback and Development: Making performance review work*, 4th edition. Abingdon: Routledge

Fletcher, C. and Baldry, C. (1999) 'Multi-source feedback systems: a research perspective', in Cooper, C. L. and Robertson, I. T. (eds) *International Review of Industrial and Organisational Psychology*, Vol.14. Chichester: Wiley

Fletcher, C. and Perry, E. I. (2001) 'Performance appraisal and feedback: a consideration of national culture and a review of contemporary research', in Anderson, N., Ones, D. S., Singali, H. K. and Viswesvaran, C. (eds) *Handbook of Industrial, Work and Organisational Psychology: Vol.1 – Personnel Psychology*. London: Sage

Fletcher, C. and Williams, R. (1996) 'Performance management, job satisfaction and organisational commitment', *British Journal of Management*, Vol.17, No.2: 169–79

Forster, N. (2000) 'The myth of the "international manager"', *International Journal of Human Resource Management*, Vol.11, No.1: 126–42

Fox, A. (1966) 'Management ideology and labour relations', *British Journal of Industrial Relations*, Vol.4, No.1: 366–78

Fox, A. (1974) *Beyond Contract: Work power and trust relations*. London: Faber & Faber

Fox, A. (1985) *Man Mismanagement*, 2nd edition. London: Hutchinson

Fox, S. and Spector, P. E. (1999) 'A model of work frustration–aggression', *Journal of Organisational Behaviour*, Vol.20: 915–31

Francis, F. and Keegan, A. (2006) 'The changing face of HRM: in search of balance', *Human Resource Management Journal*, Vol.16, No.3: 231–49

Fried, Y. and Ferris, G. R. (1987) 'The validity of the job characteristics model: a meta-analysis', *Personnel Psychology*, Vol.40, No.2: 287–322

Friedman, A. L. (2012) *Continuing Professional Development*. London/New York: Routledge

Fuchs, S. (2010) 'Critical issues in people resourcing (1): reconceptualising employee performance', in Roper, I., Prouska, R. and Na Ayudhya, U. C. (eds) *Critical Issues in Human Resource Management*. London: CIPD

Fulmer, R. M. and Vicere, A. A. (1996) 'Executive development: an analysis of competitive forces', *Planning Review*, Vol.24, No.1: 31–6

Furnham, A. (2004) 'Performance management systems', *European Business Journal*, Vol. 16, No.2: 83–94

Gainey, T. W. and Klaas, B. S. (2008) 'The use and impact of e-HRM: a survey of HR professionals', *People and Strategy*, Vol.31, No.3: 50–5

Garavan, T. N. (2007) 'A strategic perspective on HRD', *Advances in Developing Human Resources*, Vol.9, No.1, February: 11–30

García, M. U. (2005) 'Training and business performance: the Spanish case', *International Journal of Human Resource Management*, Vol.16, No.9: 1691–1710

Gardner, A. C. (2011) 'Goal-setting and gain-sharing: the evidence on effectiveness', *Compensation and Benefits Review*, Vol.43, No.4, July–August: 236–44

Garvin, D. A. (1993) 'Building a learning organization', *Harvard Business Review*, Vol.71, No.4: 78–91

General Dental Council (2012) www.gdc-uk.org/Pages/default.aspx [accessed 13 August 2012]

Gerhart, B. and Fang, M. (2005) 'National culture and human resource management: assumptions and evidence', *International Journal of Human Resource Management*, Vol. 16, No.6: 971–86

Gerhart, B. and Rynes, S. L. (2003) *Compensation: Theory, evidence and strategic implications*. Thousand Oaks, CA: Sage Publications

Gerstner, C. R. and Day, D. V. (1997) 'Meta-analytic review of leader–member exchange theory: correlates and construct issues', *Journal of Applied Psychology*, Vo.82, No.6: 827–44

Giangreco, A., Sebastiano, A. and Peccei, R. (2009) 'Trainees' reaction to training: an analysis of the factors affecting overall satisfaction with training', *International Journal of Human Resource Management*, Vol.20, No.1: 96–111

Gibb, S. (2003) 'Line manager involvement in learning and development: small beer or big deal?', *Employee Relations*, Vo.25, No.3: 281–93

Gibb, S. (2008) *Human Resource Development: Processes, Practices and Perspectives*, 2nd edition. Basingstoke: Palgrave Macmillan

Gibb, S. and Megginson, D. (2006) 'Employee development' in Redman T. and Wilkinson A. (eds) *Contemporary Human Resource Management: text and cases* 2nd edition. Harlow: Pearson

Gilbert, C., De Winne, S. and Sels, L. (2011a) 'The influence of line managers and HR department on employees' affective commitment', *International Journal of Human Resource Management*, Vol.22, No.8: 1618–37

Gilbert, C., De Winne, S. and Sels, L. (2011b) 'Antecedents of front-line managers' perceptions of HR role stressors', *Personnel Review*, Vol.40, No.5: 549–69

Glendinning, P. M. (2002) 'Performance management: pariah or messiah?', *Public Personnel Management*, Vol.31, No.2, Summer: 161–78

Gold, J. and Smith, J. (2010) 'Continuing professional development and lifelong learning', in Gold, J., Holden, R., Iles, P., Stewart, J. and Beardwell, J. (eds) *Human Resource Development: Theory and Practice*. Basingstoke: Palgrave Macmillan

Gould-Williams, J. and Davies, F. (2005) 'Using social exchange theory to predict the effects of HRM practice on employee outcomes: an analysis of public sector workers', *Public Management Review*, Vol.7, No.1: 1–24

Graen, G. B. and Uhl-Bien, M. (1995) 'Relationship-based approach to leadership: development of leader–member exchange (LMX) theory of leadership over 25 years: applying a multi-level, multi-domain approach', *Leadership Quarterly*, Vol.6, No.2: 219–47

Greenberg, J. (1988) 'Equity and workplace status: a field experiment', *Journal of Applied Psychology*, Vol.73: 606–13

Gregersen, H. B., Hite, J. M. and Black, J. S. (1996) 'Expatriate performance appraisal in US multinational firms', *Journal of International Business Studies*, Vol.27, No.4: 711–38

Greguras, G. J., Robie, C., Schleicher, D. J. and Goff, M. (2003) 'A field study of the effects of rating purpose on the quality of multi-source ratings', *Personnel Psychology*, Vol.56: 1–21

Griffeth, R. W., Horn, P. W. and Gaertner, S. (2000) 'Meta-analysis of antecedents and correlates of employee turnover', *Journal of Management*, Vol.26, No.3: 463–88

Griffin, R. W., O'Leary-Kelly, A. and Collins, J. (1998) 'Dysfunctional work behaviours in organisations', in Cooper, C. L. and Rousseau, D. M. (eds) *Trends in Organisational Behaviour*. Chichester: John Wiley & Sons

Grint, K. (1993) 'What's wrong with performance appraisals? A critique and a suggestion', *Human Resource Management Journal*, Vol.3, No.3, Spring: 61–77

Grinyer, A. and Singleton, V. (2000) 'Sickness absence as risk-taking behaviour: a study of organisational and cultural factors in the public sector', *Health, Risk and Society*, Vol.2, No.1: 7–21

Gruman, J. A. and Saks, A. M. (2011) 'Performance management and employee engagement', *Human Resource Management Review*, Vol.21, No.2: 123–36

Guest, D. E. (1997) 'Human resource management and performance: a review and research agenda', *International Journal of Human Resource Management*, Vol.12, No.7: 1092–1106

Guest, D. E. (1999) 'Human resource management: the workers' verdict', *Human Resource Management Journal*, Vol.9, No.3 : 5–25

Guest, D. E. (2007) 'Human resource management and the worker: towards a new psychological contract?', in Boxall, P., Purcell, J. and Wright, P. (eds) *The Oxford Handbook of Human Resource Management*. Oxford: Oxford University Press

Guest, D. E. (2011) 'Human resource management and performance: still searching for some answers', *Human Resource Management Journal*, Vol.21, No.1: 3–13

Guest, D. E. and Conway, N. (1998) *Fairness at Work and the Psychological Contract*. London: Institute of Personnel and Development

Guest, D. E. and Conway, N. (2002) *The State of the Psychological Contract*. London: CIPD

Guest, D. E. and Conway, N. (2004) *Employee Well-being and the Psychological Contract: A report for the CIPD*. London: CIPD

Guest, D. E. and Conway, N. (2011) 'The impact of HR practices, HR effectiveness and a "strong" HR system on organisational outcomes: a stakeholder perspective', *International Journal of Human Resource Management*, Vol.22, No.8: 1686–1702

Guest, D. E. and Hoque, K. (1994) 'The good, the bad and the ugly: employment relations in new non-union workplaces', *Human Resource Management Journal*, Vol.5, No.1: 1–14

Guest, D. E., Michie, J., Conway, N. and Sheehan, M. (2003) 'Human resource management and corporate performance in the UK', *British Journal of Industrial Relations*, Vol.41: 291–314

Guthridge, M., Komm, A. B. and Lawson, E. (2006) 'The people problem in talent management', *McKinsey Quarterly Review*, Vol.76, May–June: 137–52

Guthrie, J. P. (2007) 'Renumeration: pay effects at work', in Boxall, P., Purcell, J. and Wright, P. (eds) *Oxford Handbook of Human Resource Management*. Oxford: Oxford University Press

Haberberg, A. and Rieple, A. (2008) *Strategic Management: Theory and application*. Oxford: Oxford University Press

Hackett, R. D., Bycio, P. and Hausdorf, P. A. (1994) 'Further assessment of Meyer and Allen's three-component model of organisational commitment', *Journal of Applied Psychology*, Vol.79: 15–23

Hackman, J. R. and Oldham, G. R. (1975) 'Development of the job diagnostic survey', *Journal of Applied Psychology*, Vol.60, No.2: 159–70

Hackman, J. R. and Oldham, G. R. (1980) *Work Design*. Reading, MA: Addison-Wesley

Haines, V. Y. and St-Onge, S. (2012) 'Performance management effectiveness: practices or context?', *International Journal of Human Resource Management*, Vol.23, No.6, March: 1158–75

Hales, C. (2005) 'Rooted in supervision, branching into management: continuity and change in the role of first line manager', *Journal of Management Studies*, Vol.42, No.3: 471–506

Hales, C. (2006/7) 'Moving down the line? The shifting boundary between middle and first-line management', *Journal of General Management*, Vol.32, No.2, Winter: 31–55

Hall, D. T. (1984) 'Human resource development and organisational effectiveness', in Fombrun, D., Tichy, M. A. and Devanna, M. A. (eds) *Strategic Human Resource Management*. New York: John Wiley & Sons

Hall, E. and Hall, M. (1990) *Understanding Cultural Differences.* Yarmouth, MA: Intercultural Press

Hamblin, A. C. (1974) *Evaluation and Control of Training.* Maidenhead: McGraw-Hill

Hamel, G. (2012) *What Matters Now: How to win in a world of relentless change, ferocious competition and unstoppable innovation.* New York/Chichester: John Wiley & Sons

Hansen, C. D. and Andersen, J. H. (2008) 'Going ill to work – what personal circumstances, attitudes and work-related factors are associated with sickness presenteeism?', *Social Science and Medicine*, Vol.67: 956–64

Harbison, F. and Myers, C. (1959) *Management in the Industrial World: An international analysis.* London/New York: McGraw-Hill

Harris, K. J., Kacmar, K. M., Zinvuska, S. and Shaw, J. D. (2007) 'The impact of political skill on impression management effectiveness', *Journal of Applied Psychology*, Vol.92: 278–85

Harris, L. (2007) 'Rewarding employee performance: line managers' values, beliefs and perspectives', *International Journal of Human Resource Management*, Vol.12, No.7: 1182–92

Harris, L., Doughty, D. and Kirk, S. (2002) 'The devolution of HR responsibilities – perspectives from the UK's public sector', *Journal of European Industrial Training*, Vol.26, No.5: 218–29

Harrison, R. (2006) *Learning and Development*, 4th edition. London: CIPD

Harrison, R. (2009) *Learning and Development*, 5th edition. London: CIPD

Harter, J., Schmidt, F. and Haynes, T. (2002) 'Business-unit-level relationships between employee satisfaction, employee engagement and business outcomes: a meta-analysis', *Journal of Applied Psychology*, Vol.87, No.2: 268–79

Harvey, J. and Nicholson, N. (1993) 'Incentives and penalties as means of influencing attendance: a study in the UK public sector', *International Journal of Human Resource Management*, Vol.4, No.4: 856–74

Harvey, M. and Moeller, M. (2009) 'Expatriate managers: a historical review', *International Journal of Management Review*, Vol.11, No.3: 275–96

Harvey, M. and Novecevic, M. M. (2001) 'Selecting expatriates for increasingly complex global assignnments', *Career Development International*, Vol.6, No.2: 69–87

Harzing, A.-W. and Christensen, C. (2004) 'Expatriate failure: time to abandon the concept?', *Career Development International*, Vol.9, No.7: 616–26

Health and Safety Executive (HSE) *Case Studies Relating to Musculoskeletal Disorders.* Available online at www.hse.gov.uk/msd/experience.htm

Health, Work and Wellbeing Directorate (HWWD) (2010) *Reforming the Medical Statement.* Available online at: www.dwp.gov.uk/docs/reform-med-stat-govt-response-29jan10.pdf [accessed 2 July 2012]

Heathfield, S. (2007) 'Performance appraisals don't work: what does?', *Journal for Quality and Participation*, Vol.30, No.1: 6–9

Heavey, C., Halliday, S. V., Gilbert, D. and Murphy, E. (2011) 'Enhancing performance: bringing trust, commitment and motivation together in organisations', *Journal of General Management*, Vol.36, No.3: 1–18

Heery, E. (2000) 'Trade unions and the management of reward', in White, G. and Drucker, J. (eds) *Reward Management: Critical perspectives*. London: Routledge

Hempel, P. (2001) 'Differences between Chinese and American managerial views of performance', *Personnel Review*, Vol.30, No.2: 203–26

Hendry, C., Bradley, P. and Perkins, S. (1997) 'Missed: a motivator', *People Management*, 15 May: 20–5

Hendry, C., Woodward, S. and Bradley, P. (2000) 'Performance and rewards: cleaning out the stables', *Human Resource Management Journal*, Vol.10, No.3: 46–62

Hendry, L. and Pettigrew, A. (1990) 'Human resource management: an agenda for the 1990s', *International Journal of Human Resource Management*, Vol.1: 17–43

Heneman, R. L. (1992) *Merit Pay: Linking pay increases to performance ratings*. Reading, MA: Addison-Wesley

Hensel, R., Meijers, F., van der Leeden, R. and Kessels, J. (2010) '360-degree feedback: how many raters are needed for reliable ratings on the capacity to develop competences, with personal qualities as developmental goals?', *International Journal of Human Resource Management*, Vol.21, No.15: 2813–30

Hersey, P. and Blanchard, K. H. (1969) 'Life-cycle theory of leadership', *Training and Development Journal*, Vol.23, No.5: 26–34

Herzberg, F. (1959) *The Motivation to Work*. New York: John Wiley & Sons

Herzberg, F. (1966) *Work and the Nature of Man*. New York: Staples Press

Herzberg, F. (1968) 'One more time: how do you motivate your employees?', *Harvard Business Review*, January–February: 109–20.

Herzberg, F. (1987 reprint) 'One more time: how do you motivate your employees?', *Harvard Business Review*, Vol.65, No.5: 109–20

Heywood, J. S. and Jirjahn, U. (2006) 'Performance pay: determinants and consequences', in Lewin, D. (ed.) *Contemporary Issues in Industrial Relations*. Research Volume. Champaign, IL: Labor and Employment Relations Association

High Pay Commission Report (2011) *Cheques with Balances: Why tackling high pay is in the national interest*. London: Compass/Rowntree Charitable Trust

Hislop, D. (2009) 'Knowledge management and human resource management', in Redman, T. and Wilkinson, A. (eds) *Contemporary Human Resource Management: Text and cases*, 2nd/3rd edition. Harlow: Pearson

HMIC (Her Majesty's Inspectorate of Constabulary) (2000) *On the Record*. London: HMIC

Hofstede, G. (1980) *Culture's Consequences: International differences in work-related values*. Beverly Hills, CA: Sage Publications

Hofstede, G. (2001) *Culture's Consequences. Comparing values, behaviors, institutions, and organizations across nations*, 2nd edition. Thousand Oaks, CA: Sage Publications

Hofstede, G. and Bond, M.H. (1988) 'The Confucious connection from cultural roots to economic growth', *Organizational Dynamics*, Vol 16, No 4: 4–21.

Holbeche, L. (2009) *Aligning Human Resources and Business Strategy*, 2nd edition. Oxford: Butterworth-Heinemann

Hollinshead, G. (2010) *International and Comparative Human Resource Management*. Maidenhead: McGraw-Hill

Home Office (1999) *The Stephen Lawrence Inquiry: Report of an inquiry* by Sir William Macpherson of Cluny, Cm 4262-I, February

Honey, P. and Mumford, A. (1982) *The Manual of Learning Styles*. Maidenhead: Peter Honey

Honey, P. and Mumford. A. (1989) *The Manual of Learning Opportunities*. Maidenhead: Peter Honey

Houldsworth, E. and Jirasinghe, D. (2006) *Managing and Measuring Employee Performance*. London: Kogan Page

House, R. J., Hanges, P. J., Javidan, M., Dorfman, P. W. and Gupta, V. (2004) *Culture, Leadership and Organization: The GLOBE Study of 62 Societies*. Thousand Oaks, CA: Sage Publications

Huczynski, A. and Buchanan, D. (2007) *Organisational Behaviour*. Harlow: Prentice Hall

Huczynski, A. and Fitzpatrick, M. (1989) *Managing Employee Absence for a Competitive Edge*. London: Pitman

Huo, Y. P. and Von Glinow, M. A. (1995) 'On transplanting human resource practices to China: a culture-driven approach', *International Journal of Manpower*, Vol.16, No.9: 3–15

Huselid, M. A. (1995) 'The impact of human resource management practices on turnover, productivity, and corporate financial performance', *Academy of Management Journal*, Vol.38, No.3: 635–872

Huseman, R. C., Hatfield, J. D. and Miles, E. W. (1987) 'A new perspective on equity theory: the equity sensitivity construct', *Academy of Management Review*, Vol.12, No.2, April: 222–34

Hutchinson, S. and Purcell, J. (2003) *Bringing Policies to Life: The vital role of line managers*. London: CIPD

Hutchinson, S. and Purcell, J. (2007) *The role of line managers in reward, and training, learning and development*. Research Report. London: CIPD

Hutchinson, S. and Purcell, J. (2010) 'Managing ward managers for roles in HRM in the NHS: overworked and under-resourced', *Human Resource Management Journal*, Vol.20, No.4: 357–74

Hutchinson, S. and Tailby, S. (2012) 'Strategic HR and the line: how can front-line managers manage?' Paper presented at the 11th World Congress of IFSAM, University of Limerick, Republic of Ireland, 26–29 June

Hutchinson, S. and Wood, S. (1995) *Personnel and the Line: Developing the new relationship.* London: Institute of Personnel and Development

Hutton, W. (2011) *Hutton Review of Fair Pay in the Public Sector: Final report.* London: HM Treasury. Available online at www.hm-treasury.gov.uk/d/hutton_fairpay_review.pdf

Hyman, J. (2000) 'Financial participation schemes', in White, G. and Druker, J. (eds) *Reward Management: A critical text.* London: Routledge

Ichniowski, C., Shaw, K. and Prennushi, G. (1997) 'The effects of human resource management practices on productivity: a study of steel finishing lines', *American Economic Review,* Vol.87, No.3: 291–313

IDS (2003) Microsoft UK – Performance management. HR Studies

IDS (2005) Absence management. HR Studies 810. Available online at: www.idshrstudies.com

IDS (2007) Performance management. HR Studies 839

IDS (2008) Total reward. HR Studies 871

IDS (2009a) Performance management. HR Studies 866

IDS (2009b) Executive coaching and mentoring. HR Studies 897

IDS (2010a) Pay progression. HR Studies 929

IDS (2010b) Changing board incentives: pay for performance. Available online at: www.idshrstudies.com

IDS (2011a) The performance management cycle. HR Studies 938

IDS (2011b) Waitrose – Recruitment. Available online at ids.thomsonreuters.com/hr-in-practice/case-studies

IDS (2011c) Absence management. HR Studies 936. Available online at: www.idshrstudies.com

IDS (2011d) The role of technology in HR. HR Studies 954. Available online at: www.idshrstudies.com

IDS (2012) HR in practice. HR Studies 961

IRS (2008) 'Line managers' role in people management', *IRS Employment Review,* Issue 894

IRS (2009) 'Online induction at RSK Environment Consultancy', *IRS Employment Review,* Issue 935

IRS (2011) 'Performance-related pay: the 2011 XpertHR survey', *IRS Employment Review,* 2 September

Irvine, A. (2011) 'Fit for work? The influence of sick pay and job flexibility on sickness absence and implications for presenteeism', *Social Policy and Administration*, Vol.45, No. 7: 752–69

Isaac, J. E. (2001) 'Performance-related pay: the importance of fairness', *Journal of Industrial Relations*, Vol.43, No.2: 111–23

Iverson, R. D. and Buttigieg, D. M. (1999) 'Affective, normative and continuance commitment: can the right kind of commitment be managed?', *Journal of Management Studies*, Vol.36: 307–33

Iverson, R. D. and Deery, S. J. (2001) 'Understanding the "personological" basis of employee withdrawal: the influence of affective disposition on employee tardiness, early departure and absenteeism', *Journal of Applied Psychology*, Vol.86, No.5: 856–66

Jackman, J. M. and Strober, M. H. (2003) 'Fear of feedback', *Harvard Business Review*, Vol.81, No.4: 101–8

Jackson, B. (1985) *Winning and Keeping Industrial Customers*. Lexington, MA: Lexington Books

James, P., Cunningham, I. and Dibben, P. (2002) 'Absence management: the issues of job retention and return to work', *Human Resource Management Journal*, Vol.12, No.2: 82–94

Jansen, P. and Vloeberghs, D. (1999) 'Multi-rater feedback methods: personal and organisational implications', *Journal of Managerial Psychology*, Vol.14, No.6: 455–76

Jawahar, I. M. (2007) 'The influence of perception of fairness on performance appraisal reactions', *Journal of Labour Research*, Vol.28: 735–54

Johns, G. (2010) 'Presenteeism in the workplace: a review and research agenda', *Journal of Organizational Behavior*, Vol.31, No.4: 519–42

Johnson, A. (2006) 'Orange blossoms', *People Management*, Vol.12, No.21: 57–60

Johnson, S. (1984) 'Merit pay for teachers: a poor prescription for reform', *Harvard Educational Review*, Vol.54, No.2: 175–86

Jones, C. and Saundry, R. (2012) 'The practice of discipline: evaluating the roles and relationship between managers and HR professionals', *Human Resource Management Journal*, Vol.22, No.3: 252–66

Judge, T. A., Martocchio, J. J. and Thoresen, C. J. (1997) 'Five-factor model of personality and employee absence', *Journal of Applied Psychology*, Vol.82, No.5: 745–55

Judge, T. A., Thoresen, C. J., Bono, J. E. and Patton, G. K. (2001) 'The job satisfaction–job performance relationship: a qualitative and quantitative review', *Psychological Bulletin*, No.127: 376–407

Kahn-Freund, O. (1986) 'Labour and the law', in Wedderburn, (Lord) W. *The Worker and the Law*, 3rd edition. Harmondsworth: Penguin

Kalleberg, A., Knoke, D., Marsden, P. and Spaeth, J. (1996) *Organizations in America: Analyzing their structures and human resource practices*. Thousand Oaks, CA/London: Sage

Kaplan, R. S. and Norton, D. P. (1992) 'The balanced scorecard: measures that drive performance', *Harvard Business Review*, January–February: 71–9

Kaplan, R. S. and Norton, D. P. (1993) 'Putting the balanced scorecard to work', *Harvard Business Review*, September–October: 134–47

Kaplan, R. S. and Norton, D. P. (1996a) 'Using the balanced scorecard as a strategic management system', *Harvard Business Review*, January–February: 75–85

Kaplan, R. S. and Norton, D. P. (1996b) *The Balanced Scorecard: Translating strategy into action*. Boston, MA: Harvard Business School Press

Kaplan, R. S. and Norton, D. P. (2001) *The Strategy-Focused Organization*. Boston, MA: Harvard Business School Press

Katz, D. and Kahn, R. L. (1996) *The Social Psychology of Organizations*. New York: John Wiley & Sons

Kaufman, B. E. (1993) *The Origins and Evolution of the Field of Industrial Relations in the United States*. New York: ILR Press.

Kauhanen, A. and Piekkola, H. (2006) 'What makes performance-related pay schemes work? Finnish evidence', *Journal of Management and Governance*, Vol.10, No.2: 149–77

Keegan, A. and Francis, H. (2010) 'Practitioner talk: the changing textscape of HRM and emergence of HR business partnership', *International Journal of Human Resource Management*, Vol.21, No.6: 873–98

Kelly, R. T. (1983) 'Predicting absenteeism from prior absenteeism, attitudinal factors, and nonattitudinal factors', *Journal of Applied Psychology*, Vol.68, No.3: 536–40

Kersley, B., Alpin, C., Forth, J., Bryson, A., Bewley, H., Dix, G. and Oxenbridge, S. (2006) *Inside the Workplace: Findings of the 2004 Workplace Employment Relations Survey*. London: Department of Trade and Industry

Kessler, I. (1994) 'Performance-related pay: contrasting approaches', *Industrial Relations Journal*, Vol.25, No.2, June: 122–35

Kessler, I. and Purcell, J. (1992) 'Performance-related pay: objectives and applications', *Human Resource Management Journal*, Vol.2, No.3: 34–59

Khilji, S. E. and Wang, X. (2006) 'Intended and implemented HRM: the missing linchpin in strategic international human resource management research', *International Journal of Human Resource Management*, Vol.17, No.7: 1171–89

Kidder, P. J. and Rouiller, J. Z. (1997) 'Evaluating the success of a large-scale training effort', *National Productivity Review*, Vol.16, Spring: 79–89

Kinnie, N., Hutchinson, S. and Purcell, J. (2000) 'Fun and surveillance: the paradox of high-commitment management in call centres', *International Journal of Human Resource Management*, Vol.11, No.2: 967–85

Kinnie, N., Purcell, J., Hutchinson, S., Rayton, B. and Swart, J. (2005) 'Satisfaction with HR practices and commitment in the organisation: why one size does not fit all', *Human Resource Management Journal*, Vol.15, No.4: 9–29

Kirkpatrick, D. L. (1967) 'Evaluation of training', in Craig, R. and Bittel, L. (eds) *Training and Evaluation Handbook*. New York: McGraw-Hill

Kirkpatrick, D. L. (1994) *Evaluating Training Programs: The four levels*. San Francisco: Berrett-Koehler

Kluckhohn, F. R. and Strodtbeck, F. L. (1961) *Variations in Value Orientations*. New York: Row, Peterson & Co.

Kluger, A. N. and DeNisi, A. (1996) 'The effects of feedback intervention on performance: a historical review, a meta-analysis', *Psychological Bulletin*, Vol.119, No.2: 254–84

Kochan, T. A. and Barocci, T. A. (1985) *Human Resource Management and Industrial Relations*. Boston, MA: Little Brown

Kohn, A. (1993) 'Why incentive plans cannot work', *Harvard Business Review*, Vol.71, No. 5, Sept–Oct: 54–63

Kolb, D. (1984) *Experiential Learning*. Englewood Cliffs, NJ: Prentice Hall

Kolb, D., Osland, J. and Rubin, I. (1995) *Organizational Behavior: An experiential approach*, 6th edition. Englewood Cliffs, NJ: Prentice Hall

Kovach, R. C. (1995) 'Matching assumptions to environment in the transfer of management practices: performance appraisal in Hungary', *International Studies of Management and Organisations*, Vol.24, No.4: 83–99

Kramer, R. M. (1999) 'Trust and distrust in organisations: emerging perspectives, enduring questions', *Annual Review of Psychology*, Vol.50: 569–98

Kwarteng, K. (MP), Patel, P. (MP), Raab, D. (MP), Skidmore, C. (MP) and Truss, E. (MP) (2012) *Britannia Unchained: Global lessons for growth and prosperity*. Basingstoke: Palgrave Macmillan

Lam, W., Huang, X. and Snape, E. (2007) 'Feedback-seeking behavior and leader-member exchange: do supervisor-attributed motives matter?', *Academy of Management Journal*, Vol.50: 348–63

Landy, F. J. and Conte, J. M. (2010) *Work in the Twenty-First Century: An introduction to industrial and organisational psychology*, 3rd edition. Hoboken, NJ: John Wiley & Sons

Larsen, H. H. and Brewster, C. (2003) 'Line management responsibility of HRM: what is happening in Europe?', *Employee Relations*, Vol.25, No.3: 228–44

Latham, G. P. and Locke, E. A. (2006) 'Enhancing the benefits and overcoming the pitfalls of goal-setting', *Organisational Dynamics*, Vol.35, No.4: 332–40

Latham, G. P. and Pinder, C. C. (2005) 'Work motivation theory and research at the dawn of the twenty-first century', *Annual Review of Psychology*, Vol.56: 485–516

Latham, G. P. and Wexley, K. N. (1977) 'Behavioural observation scales for performance appraisal purposes', *Personnel Psychology*, Vol.30, No.2: 255–68

Latham, G. P., Locke, E. A. and Fassina, N. E. (2005) *Psychological Management of Individual Performance*. London/New York: John Wiley & Sons

Latham, G. P., Sulsky, L. M. and Macdonald, H. (2007) 'Performance management', in Boxall, P., Purcell, J. and Wright, P. (eds) *Oxford Handbook of Human Resource Management*. Oxford: Oxford University Press

Latham, G. P., Skarlicki, D., Irvine, D. and Siegel, J. P. (1993) 'The increased importance of performance appraisals to employee effectiveness in organizational settings in North America', in Cooper, C. L. and Robertson, J. T. (eds) *International Review of Industrial and Organizational Psychology*, Vol.14. New York: John Wiley & Sons

Lawler, E. E. (1971) *Pay and Organizational Effectiveness: A psychological view*. New York: McGraw-Hill

Lawler, E. (1986) *High Involvement Management*. San Francisco: Jossey-Bass

Lawler, E. E. (1990) *Strategic Pay: Aligning organizational strategies and pay systems*. San Francisco: Jossey-Bass

Lawler, E. E. (1994) *Motivation in Work Organizations*. San Francisco: Jossey-Bass

Lawler, E. E. (2002) 'The folly of forced ranking', *Strategy and Business*, Vol.28: 28–32

Lawler, E. E. (2003) 'What it means to treat people right', *Ivey Business Journal*, Nov–Dec: 1–6

Lee, S. H. and Pershing, J. A. (2002) 'Dimensions and design criteria for developing training reaction evaluations', *Human Resource Development International*, Vol.5, No.2: 175–97

Legge, K. (1978) *Power, Innovation and Problem-Solving in Personnel Management*. Maidenhead: McGraw-Hill

Legge, K. (1995) *Human Resource Management: Rhetorics and realities*. Basingstoke: Macmillan

Legge, K. (2005) *Human Resource Management: Rhetorics and realities,* Anniversary edition. Basingstoke: Macmillan

Lepak D. and Snell, S. (1999) 'The human resource architecture: toward a theory of human capital allocation and development', *Academy of Management Review*, Vol.24, No. 1: 31–48.

Levinson, H. (2005) 'Management by whose objectives?', *Harvard Business Review*, Vol. 81, No.1, January: 107–16

Levy, P. E. and Williams, J. R. (2004) 'The social context of performance appraisal: a review and framework for the future', *Journal of Management*, Vol.30, No.6, December: 881–905

Lewis, T. (2011) 'Assessing social identity and collective efficacy as theories of group motivation at work', *International Journal of Human Resource Management*, Vol.22, No.4, Feb–Mar: 963–80

Locke, E. (2003) 'Good definitions: The epistemological foundation of scientific progress', in Greenberg, J. (ed), *Organizational behavior, State of the science*: 415–44. Mahwah, NJ: Lawrence Erlbaum Associates.

Locke, E. A. (1968) 'Toward a theory of task motivation and incentives', *Organizational Behavior and Human Performance*, Vol.3: 157–89

Locke, E. A. (1976) 'The nature and causes of job satisfaction', in Dunnette, M. D. (ed.) *Handbook of Industrial and Organizational Psychology*. Chicago: Rand McNally

Locke, E. A. and Latham, G. P. (1984) *Goal-setting: A motivational technique that works*. Englewood Cliffs, NJ: Prentice Hall

Locke, E. A. and Latham, G. P. (2002) 'Building a practically useful theory of goal-setting and task motivation: a 35-year odyssey', *American Psychologist*, Vol.57, No.9: 705–17

Locke, E. A. and Latham, G. P. (2004) 'What should we do about motivation theory? Six recommendations for the twenty-first century', *Academy of Management Review*, Vol.29, No.3: 388–403

Locke, E. A., Shaw, K. N., Saari, L. M. and Latham, G. P. (1981) 'Goal-setting and task performance 1969–1980', *Psychological Bulletin* (of the American Psychological Association), Vol.90, No.1: 125–52

Locke, E. A., Feren, D. B., McCaleb, V. M., Shaw, K. N. and Denny, A. T. (1980) 'The relative effectiveness of four methods of motivating employee performance', in Duncan, K. D., Gruneberg, M. and Wallis, D. (eds) *Changes in Working Life*. New York: John Wiley & Sons

London, M. L. and Smither, J. W. (1995) 'Can multi-source feedback change perceptions of goal accomplishment, self-evaluations and performance-related outcomes? Theory-based applications and directions for research', *Personnel Psychology*, Vol.48: 803–39

Longenecker, C. O. (1989) 'Truth or consequences: politics and performance appraisals', *Business Horizons*, Vol.32, November–December: 976–82

Longenecker, C. O. (1997) 'Why managerial performance appraisals are ineffective: causes and lesson', *Career Development International*, Vol.2, No.5: 212–18

Longenecker, C. O., Sims, H. P. and Gioia, D. A. (1987) 'Behind the mask: the politics of employee appraisal', *Academy of Management Executive*, Vol.1, No.3: 183–93

Lord, R. G., Hanges, P. J. and Godfrey, E. G. (2003) 'Integrating neural networks into decision-making and motivational theory: rethinking VIE theory', *Canadian Psychology*, Vol.44, No.1: 21–38

Lowe, K. B., Milliman, J., De Cieri, H. and Dowling, P. J. (2002) 'International compensation practices: a 10-country comparative analysis', *Human Resource Management*, Vol.41, No.1: 45–66

Lowry, D. (2002) 'Performance management', in Leopold, J. (ed.) *Human Resources in Organisations*. Harlow: FT/Prentice Hall

Lupton, T. (1963) *On the Shop Floor: Two studies of workshop organisation and output*. Oxford: Pergamon

MacDuffie, J. (1995) 'Human resource bundles and manufacturing performance: organizational logic and flexible production systems in the world auto industry', *Industrial and Labor Relations Review*, Vol.48, No.2: 197–221

Macky, K. and Boxall, P. (2007) 'The relationship between "high-performance work practices" and employee attitudes: an investigation of additive and interaction effects', *International Journal of Human Resource Management*, Vol.18, April: 537–67

MacLeod, D. and Clarke, N. (2009) *Engaging for Success: Enhancing performance through employee engagement*. A Report to Government. London: Department of Business, Innovation and Skills

Mann, S. and Robertson, I. T. (1996) 'What should training evaluations evaluate?', *Journal of European Industrial Training*, Vol.20, No.9: 14–20

Marchington, M. and Grugulis, I. (2000) '"Best practice" human resource management: perfect opportunity or dangerous illusion?', *International Journal of Human Resource Management*, Vol.11, 6 December: 1104–24

Marchington, M. and Wilkinson, A. (2008) *Human Resource Management at Work: People management and development*, 4th edition. London: CIPD

Marchington, M. and Wilkinson, A. (2012) *Human Resource Management at Work*, 5th edition. London: CIPD

Marquardt, M. and Banks, S. (2010) 'Theory to practice: Action Learning', *Advances in Developing Human Resources*, Vol.12, No.2: 159–62

Marsden, D. (2004) 'The role of performance-related pay in renegotiating the "effort bargain": the case of the British public service', *Industrial and Labor Relations Review*, Vol. 57, No.3: 350–70

Marsden, D. (2009) 'The paradox of performance-related pay systems: why do we keep adopting them in the face of evidence that they fail to motivate?', Centre for Economic Performance Discussion Paper No.946, London School of Economics

Marsden, D. and Richardson, R. (1994) 'Performing for pay? The effects of "merit pay" on motivation in a public service', *British Journal of Industrial Relations*, Vol.32, No.2: 243–61

Marsden, D., French, A. and Kubo, S. (2001) *Does Performance Pay Demotivate, and Does It Matter?* London: Centre for Economic Performance, London School of Economics

Martocchio, J. J. (1994) 'The effects of absence culture on individual absence', *Human Relations*, Vol.47, No.3: 243–61

Marton, F. and Ramsden, P. (1988) 'What does it take to improve learning?', in Ramsden, P. (ed.) *Improving Learning: New perspectives*. London: Kogan Page

Marton, F. and Säljö, R. (1976) 'On qualitative differences in learning, II: outcome and process', *British Journal of Educational Psychology*, Vol.46: 4–11

Maslow, A. H. (1943) 'A theory of human motivation', *Psychological Review*, Vol.50: 370–96

Maslow, A. H. (1954) *Motivation and Personality*. New York: Harper & Row

Mather, K. (2011) 'Employment relations and the illusion of trust', in Searle, R. H. and Skinner, D. (eds) *Trust and Human Resource Management*. Cheltenham: Edward Elgar

Maxwell, G. A. and Watson, S. (2006) 'Perspectives on line managers in HRM: Hilton International's UK Hotels', *International Journal of Human Resource Management*, Vol. 17, No.6: 1152–70.

Mayer, R. C., Davis, J. H. and Schoorman, F. D. (1995) 'An integrative model of organisational trust', *Academy of Management Review*, Vol.20, No.3: 709–34

Mayo, A. (2008) 'People-related measures and high-performance HRM', in Muller-Camen, M., Croucher, R. and Leigh, S. (eds) *Human Resource Management: A case study approach*. London: CIPD

Mayo, E. (1933) *The Human Problems of an Industrial Civilization*. New York: Macmillan

McAdams, J. L. (1999) 'Nonmonetary rewards: cash equivalents and tangible awards', in Berger, L. A. and Berger, D. R. (eds) *The Compensation Handbook: A state-of-the-art guide to compensation strategy and design*, 4th edition. New York: McGraw-Hill

McCarthy, D. and Palcic, D. (2012) 'The impact of large-scale employee share ownership plans on labour productivity: the case of Eircom', *International Journal of Human Resource Management*, Vol.23, No.17: 3710–24. Available online at: www.tandfonline.com/doi/pdf/10.1080/09585192.2012.655762

McClelland, D. C. (1961) *The Achieving Society*. Princeton, NJ: Van Nostrand

McClelland, D. C. (1985) *Human Motivation*. Glenview, IL: Scott, Foresman

McConville, T. (2006) 'Devolved HRM responsibilities, middle managers and role dissonance', *Personnel Review*, Vol.35, No.6: 637–53

McDonnell, A. and Gunnigle, P. (2009) 'Performance management', in Collings, D. G. and Wood, G. (eds) *Human Resource Management: A critical introduction*. New York/London: Routledge

McGivering, I. C., Matthews, C. G. J. and Scott, W. H. (1969) *Management in Britain: A general characterisation*. Liverpool: Liverpool University Press

McGovern, F., Gratton, L., Hope-Hailey, V., Stiles, S. and Truss, C. (1997) 'Human resource management on the line?', *Human Resource Management Journal*, Vol.7, No.4: 12–29

McGregor, D. (1957) 'An uneasy look at performance appraisal', *Harvard Business Review*, Vol.35, No.3: 89–94

McGregor, D. (1960) *The Human Side of Enterprise*. New York: McGraw-Hill

McHugh, M. (2002) 'The absence bug: a treatable viral infection?', *Journal of Managerial Psychology*, Vol.17, No.8: 722–38

McSweeney, B. (2002) 'Hofstede's model of national cultural differences and their consequences: a triumph of faith – a failure of analysis', *Human Relations*, Vol.55, No.1: 89–118

McSweeney, B. (2009) 'Dynamic diversity: variety and variation within countries', *Organization Studies*, Vol.30, No.9: 933–57

Mendenhall, M. and Osland, J. S. (2002) 'An overview of the extant global leadership research', Symposium presentation at the Academy of International Business, Puerto Rico, June

Merriman, K. K. (2010) 'Lost in translation: cultural interpretations of performance pay', *Compensation and Benefits Review*, Vol.42, No.5: 403–10

Meyer, J. P. and Allen, N. J. (1991) 'A three-component conceptualisation of organisational commitment', *Human Resource Management Review*, Vol.1: 61–89

Meyer, J. P. and Allen, N. J. (1997) *Commitment in the Workplace: Theory, research, and application*. Thousand Oaks, CA/London: Sage Publications

Meyer, J. P., Stanley, D., Herscovitch, L. and Topolnytsky, L. (2002) 'Affective, continuance, and normative commitment to the organisation: a meta-analysis', *Journal of Vocational Behavior*, Vol.61: 20–52

Meyer, J. P., Paunonen, S. V., Gellatly, I., Goffin, R. and Jackson, D. (1989) 'Organisational commitment and job performance: it's the nature of the commitment that counts', *Journal of Applied Psychology*, Vol.74: 152–6

Meyer, J. W. and Rowan, B. (1977) 'Institutional organizations: formal structure as myth and ceremony', *American Journal of Sociology*, Vol.83: 340–63

Michaels, E., Handfield-Jones, H. and Axelrod, B. (2001) *The War for Talent*. Watertown, MA: Harvard Business School Press

Miles, R. and Snow, C. (1984) 'Designing human resource systems', *Organizational Dynamics*, Summer: 36–52

Milliman, J,. Nason, S., Zhu, C. and De Cieri, H. (2002) 'An exploratory assessment of the purposes of performance in North and Central America and the Pacific Rim', *Human Resource Management*, Vol.41. No.1: 87–102

Milsome, S. (2006) 'Devolving HR responsibilities: are managers ready and able?', *IRS Employment Review*, No.842, 3 March

Milsome, S. (2010) 'The use of absence triggers in managing absence: the 2010 IRS Survey', *IRS Employment Review*, 23 February. Available online at www.xperthr.co.uk

Mohrman, A. M. and Mohrman, S. A. (1995) 'Performance management and "running the business"', *Compensation & Benefits Review*, July–August: 69–75

Morgan, R. and Hunt, S. (1994) 'The commitment–trust theory of relationship marketing', *Journal of Marketing*, Vol.58, No.3: 20–38

Motowidlo, S. J and Van Scotter, J. R. (1994) 'Evidence that task performance should be distinguished from contextual performance', *Journal of Applied Psychology*, Vol.79, No.4: 475–80

Mowday, R., Steers, R. and Porter, L. (1979) 'The measurement of organisational commitment', *Journal of Vocational Behaviour*, Vol.14, No.2: 224–47

Muller-Camen, M. and Brewster, C. (2008) 'International human resource management', in Muller-Camen, M., Croucher, R. and Leigh, S. (eds) *Human Resource Management: A case study approach*. London: CIPD

Mullins, L. (2010) *Management and Organisational Behaviour*, 9th edition. Harlow: FT/ Prentice Hall

Murnane, R. J. and Cohen, D. K. (1986) 'Merit pay and the evaluation problem: why most merit pay plans fail and a few survive', *Harvard Educational Review*, Vol.56, No.1: 1–17

Murphy, K. R. (2008) 'Explaining the weak relationship between job performance and ratings of job performance', *Industrial and Organizational Psychology*, Vol.1: 148–60

Murphy, K. R. and Cleveland, J. N. (1991) *Performance Appraisal: An organizational perspective*. Boston, MA: Allyn & Bacon

Murphy, K. R. and Cleveland, J. N. (1995) *Understanding Performance Appraisal: Social, organizational and goal-based perspectives*. Thousand Oaks, CA: Sage Publications

Murphy, K. R. and DeNisi, A. (2008) 'A model of the appraisal process', in Varma, A., Budhwar, P. W. and DeNisi, A. (eds) *Performance Management Systems: A global perspective*. Abingdon: Routledge

Nadler, D. and Lawler, E. E. (1979) 'Motivation: a diagnostic approach', in Steers, M. and Porter, L. (eds) *Motivation and Work Behaviour*, 2nd edition. New York: McGraw-Hill

Nadler, L. (1970) *Developing Human Resources*. Houston, TX: Gulf

Nadler, L. and Wiggs, G. (1986) *Managing Human Resource Development: A practical guide*. San Francisco: Jossey-Bass

Napier, N. K. and Peterson, R. B. (2001) 'Putting human resource management at the line manager level', *Business Horizons*, January–February: 72–81

Nehles, A. C., van Riemsdijk, M., Kok, I. and Looise, J. C. (2006) 'Implementing human resource management successfully: a first-line management challenge', *Management Review*, Vol.17, No.3: 256–73

Nelson, B. (1994) *1001 Ways to Reward Employees*. New York: Workman

Newton, T. and Findlay, P. (1996) 'Playing God? The performance of appraisal', *Human Resource Management Journal*, Vol.6, No.3: 42–58

Nichols, T. (1986) *The British Worker Question: A new look at workers and productivity in manufacturing*. London: Routledge & Kegan Paul

Nicholson, N. (1977) 'Absence behaviour and attendance motivation: a conceptual synthesis', *Journal of Management Studies*, Vol.14, No.3: 231–52

Nicholson, N. and Johns, G. (1985) 'The absence culture and the psychological contract: who's in control of absence?', *Academy of Management Review*, Vol.10, No.3: 397–407

Nishii, L., Lepak, D. and Schneider, B. (2008) 'Employee attributions of the "why" of HR practices: their effects on employee attitudes and behaviours, and customer satisfaction', *Personnel Psychology*, Vol.61, No.3: 503–45

Nonaka, I. and Takeuchi, H. (1995) *The Knowledge-Creating Company*. Oxford: Oxford University Press

North, R. F. J., Strain, D. L. and Abbott, L. (2000) 'Training teachers in computer-based management information systems', *Journal of Computer-Assisted Learning*, Vol.16, No.1: 163–72

O'Boyle, E. and Aguinis, H. (2012) 'The best and the rest: revisiting the norm of normality of individual performance', *Personnel Psychology*, Vol.65, No.1: 79–119

Oddou, G. R. and Mendenhall, M. E. (2012) 'Expatriate performance management: problems and solutions', in Stahl, G. K., Mendenhall, M. E. and Oddou, G. R. (eds) *Readings and Cases in International Human Resource Management Behavior*, 5th edition. New York: Routledge

Office for National Statistics (ONS) (2012a) *International Comparisons of Productivity: First estimates for 2011*. Available online at: www.ons.org

Office for National Statistics (ONS) (2012b) 'Sickness absence in the labour market', April. Available online at: www.ons.gov.uk

O'Hara, S., Bourner, T. and Webber, T. (2004) 'The practice of self-managed Action Learning', *Action Learning: Research and Practice*, Vol.1, No.1: 29–42

Organ, D. W. (1977) 'Organizational citizenship behavior: it's construct clean-up time', *Human Performance*, Vol.10: 85–97

Organ, D. W. (1988) *Organizational Citizenship Behavior: The Good Soldier Syndrome*. Lexington, MA: Lexington Books

Organ, D. W. and Moorman, R. H. (1993) 'Fairness and organizational citizenship behavior: what are the connections?', *Social Justice Research*, Vol.6: 5–18

Organ , D. W. and Ryan, K. (1995) 'A meta-analytic review of attitudinal and dispositional predictors of organizational citizenship behavior', *Personnel Psychology*, Vol.48, No.4: 775–802

Organ, D. W., Podsakoff, P. M. and Mackenzie, S. B. (2006) *Organizational Citizenship Behavior: Its nature, antecedents and consequences*. Thousand Oaks, CA: Sage Publications

Oyer, P. (2004) 'Why do firms use incentives that have no incentive effects?', *Journal of Finance*, Vol.59: 1619–49

Paauwe, J. (2004) *HRM and Performance: Achieving long-term viability*. Oxford: Oxford University Press

Paauwe, J. and Boselie, P. (2003) 'Challenging strategic HRM and the relevance of the institutional setting', *Human Resource Management Journal*, Vol.13, No.3: 56–70

Paauwe J. and Richardson, R. (1997) 'Introduction to the special issue on HRM and performance', *International Journal of Human Resource Management*, Vol.8, No.3: 257–62

Paik, Y., Vance, C. M. and Stage, H. D. (2000) 'A test of assumed cluster homogeneity for performance appraisal management in four Southeast Asian countries', *International Journal of Human Resource Management*, Vol.11, No.4: 736–50

Pantazis, C. (2002) 'Maximising e-learning to train the twenty-first-century workforce', *Public Personnel Management*, Vol.31, No.1: 21–6

Parry, E. (2011) 'An examination of e-HRM as a means to increase the value of the HR function', *International Journal of Human Resource Management*, Vol.22, No.5: 1146–62

Patterson, M., West, M., Lawthorn, R. and Nickell, S. (1997) 'Impact of people management practices on business performance', *Issues in People Management*, No. 22. London: Institute of Personnel and Development

Peccei, R. (2004) 'Human resource management and the search for the happy workplace', Inaugural Address as Visiting Professor, Research in Management Series, given at Erasmus University, Rotterdam

Pedler, M., Burgoyne, J. and Boydell, T. (1991) *The Learning Company: A strategy for sustainable development*. London: McGraw-Hill

Pendleton, A., Wilson, N. and Wright, M. (1998) 'The perception and effects of share ownership: empirical evidence from employee buy-outs', *British Journal of Industrial Relations*, Vol.36, No.1: 99–124

Pepper, A. A., Gore, J. and Crossman, A. (2012) 'Are long-term incentive plans an effective and efficient way of motivating senior executives?', *Human Resource Management Journal*, Vol.23, No.1, January: 36–51

Peretz, H. and Fried, Y. (2012) 'National cultures, performance appraisal practices, and organzational absenteeism and turnover: a study across 21 countries', *Journal of Applied Psychology*, Vol.97, No.2: 448–59

Perkins, S. and White, G. (2011) *Reward Management*. London: CIPD

Perry, E. L. and Kulik, C. T. (2008) 'The devolution of HR to the line: implication of perceptions of people management effectiveness', *International Journal of Human Resource Management*, Vol.19, No.2: 262–73

Pfeffer, J. (1998a) *The Human Equation: Building profits by putting people first*. Boston, MA: Harvard Business School Press

Pfeffer, J. (1998b) 'Six dangerous myths about pay', *Harvard Business Review*, Vol.67, No. 3: 109–19

Pfeffer, J. and Sutton, R. I. (1999) *The Knowing–Doing Gap: How smart companies turn knowledge into action*. Boston, MA: Harvard Business School Publishing

Pfeffer, J. and Sutton, R. I. (2006) *Hard Facts, Dangerous Half-Truths, and Total Nonsense: Profiting from evidence-based management*. Boston, MA: Harvard Business School Press

Pilbeam, S. and Corbridge, M. (2010) *People Resourcing and Talent Planning: HRM in practice*, 4th edition. Harlow: FT/Prentice Hall

Pinder, C. C. (1998) *Work Motivation in Organizational Behavior*. Upper Saddle River, NJ: Prentice Hall

Plant, R. A. and Ryan, R. J. (1992) 'Training evaluation: a procedure for validating an organization's investment in training', *Journal of Industrial Training*, Vol.16, No.10: 22–31

Polanyi, M. (1966) *The Tacit Dimension*. London: Routledge & Kegan Paul

Pollack, D. and Pollack, L. (1996) 'Using 360-degree feedback in performance appraisal', *Personnel Administration*, Vol.25, No.4: 507–28

Pollitt, D. (2004) 'Tesco pilots scheme to cut unplanned leave of absence: approach wins backing of staff and union', *Human Resource Management International Digest*, Vol.12, No.6: 21–3

Pollitt, D. (2008) 'Driving down sickness absence at First Group: nurse-led system promotes employee health', *Human Resource Management International Digest*, Vol.16, No.2: 26–7

Porter, L. W. and Lawler, E. E. (1968) *Managerial Attitudes and Performance*. Homewood, IL: Irwin-Dorsey Press

Porter, L. W., Steers, R. M., Mowday, R. T. and Boulian, P. V. (1974) 'Organisational commitment, job satisfaction and turnover among psychiatric technicians', *Journal of Applied Psychology*, Vol.59, No.5: 603–9

Porter, M. E. (1985) *Competitive Advantage: Creating and sustaining superior performance*. New York: Free Press

Prendergast, C. (1999) 'The provision of incentives in firms', *Journal of Economic Literature*, Vol.37, No.1, March: 7–63

PricewaterhouseCoopers LLP (2008) *Building the Case for Wellness*. Report for Health, Work and Wellbeing governmental partnership. Available online at www.dwp.gov.uk/docs/hwwb-dwp-wellness-report-public.pdf

PricewaterhouseCoopers LLP (2011) 'One in three workers openly admits to skiving', UK Media Centre. Available online at: www.ukmediacentre.pwc.com/News-Releases/One-in-three-workers-openly-admit-to-skiving-10c8.aspx

Pulakos, E. D. (2009) *Performance Management: A new approach for driving business results*. Oxford/Boston, MA: Blackwell

Pulakos, E. D. and O'Leary, R. S. (2011) 'Why is performance management broken?', *Industrial and Organisational Psychology*, Vol.4, No.2: 146–64

Pulakos, E. D., Mueller-Hanson, R. A. and O'Leary, R. S. (2008) 'Performance management in the United States', in Varma, A., Budhwar, P. W. and DeNisi, A. (eds) *Performance Management Systems: A global perspective*. Abingdon: Routledge

Purcell, J. (1999) 'The search for best practice and best fit in human resource management: chimera or cul de sac?', *Human Resource Management Journal*, Vol.9, No.3: 26–41

Purcell, J. and Hutchinson, S. (2007a) 'Front-line managers as agents in the HRM–performance causal chain: theory, analysis and evidence', *Human Resource Management Journal*, Vol.17, No.1: 3–20

Purcell, J. and Hutchinson, S. (2007b) *Learning and the Line: The role of the line manager in learning and development*. London: CIPD

Purcell, J. and Kinnie, N. (2007) 'HRM and business performance', in Boxall, P., Purcell, J. and Wright, P. (eds) *The Oxford Handbook of Human Resource Management*. Oxford: Oxford University Press.

Purcell, J., Kinnie, N. and Hutchinson, S. (2003) 'Open-minded: inside the black box: an overview', *People Management*, Vol.9, No.10: 30–3

Purcell, J., Kinnie, N., Hutchinson, S., Rayton, B. and Swart, J. (2003) *Understanding the People and Performance Link: Unlocking the black box*. London: CIPD

Purcell, J., Kinnie, N., Swart, J., Rayton, B. and Hutchinson, S. (2008/9) *People and Performance*. Abingdon: Routledge

Raelin, J. A. (2008) *Work-based learning: Bridging knowledge and action in the workplace*. San Francisco: Jossey-Bass

Ramsey, H., Scholarios, D. and Harley, B. (2000) 'Employees and high-performance work systems: testing inside the black box', *British Journal of Industrial Relations*, Vol.38, No.4: 501–31

Randell, G. A. (1989) 'Employee apporaisal', in Sisson, K. (ed.) *Personnel Management in Britain*. Oxford: Blackwell

Randell, G. A. (1994) 'Employee appraisal', in Sisson, K. (ed.) *Personnel Management: A comprehensive guide to theory and practice in Britain*. Oxford: Blackwell

Rankin, N. (2010) *Good Practice: Performance management*. Good practice guides. London: XpertHR. Available online at: www.xperthr.co.uk

Redman, T. (2009) 'Performance appraisal', in Redman, T. and Wilkinson, A. (eds) *Contemporary Human Resource Management: Text and cases*, 3rd edition. Harlow: Pearson

Redman, T. and Matthews, B. P. (1995) 'Do corporate turkeys vote for Christmas? Managers' attitudes toward upward appraisal', *Personnel Review*, Vol.24, No.7: 13–24

Redman, T. and Wilkinson, A. (2009) *Contemporary Human Resource Management: Text and cases*, 3rd edition. Harlow: Pearson

Redman, T. and Wilkinson, A. (2012) *Contemporary Human Resource Management: Text and cases*, 4th edition. Harlow: Pearson

Redmond, L. (2011) 'Measuring up performance reviews', *People Management*, 7 September

Rees, B. (2003) *The Construction of Management: Gender issues and competence techniques in modern organisations*. London: Edward Elgar

Reid, M.A., Barrington, B. and Brown, M. (2007) *Human Resource Development: Beyond training interventions*, 7th edition. London: CIPD

Reilly, P. and Hirsh, W. (2012) 'Obtaining customer feedback on HR: who dares wins', *People Management*, January

Reilly, P., Phillipson, J. and Smith, P. (2005) 'Team-based pay in the United Kingdom', *Compensation and Benefits Review*, Vol.37, No.4, July–August: 54–60

Reilly, P., Tamkin, P. and Broughton, A. (2007) *The Changing HR Function: Transforming HR?* London: CIPD

Renwick, D. (2003) 'Line manager involvement in HRM: an inside view', *Employee Relations*, Vol.25, No.3: 262–80

Renwick, D. W. S. (2009) 'Line managers and HRM', in Redman, T. and Wilkinson, A. (eds) *Contemporary HRM*, 3rd edition. Harlow: Pearson Education

Revans, R. W. (1980) *Action Learning: New techniques for management*. London: Blond & Briggs

Revans, R. W. (1982) *The Origin and Growth of Action Learning*. Bromley: Chartwell-Bratt

Revans, R. W. (1998) *ABC of Action Learning*. London: Lemos & Crane

Rhoades, L. and Eisenberger, R. (2002) 'Perceived organisational support: a review of the literature', *Journal of Applied Psychology*, Vol.87, No.4: 698–714

Rhodes, S. R. and Steers, R. M. (1990) *Managing Employee Absenteeism*. Reading, MA: Addison-Wesley

Ringelmann, M. (1913) 'Research on animate sources of power: the work of man', *Annales de l'Institut National Agronomique*, Vol.12: 1–40

Roberts, G. (1997) *Recruitment and Selection: A competency approach*. London: CIPD

Roethlisberger, F. J. and Dickson, W. J. (1939) *Management and the Worker*. Cambridge, MA: Harvard University Press

Rollinson, D. (2008) *Organisational Behaviour and Analysis: An integrated approach*, 4th edition. Harlow: FT/Prentice Hall

Rollinson, D., Handley, J., Hook, C. and Foot, M. (1997) 'The disciplinary experience and its effects on behaviour: an exploratory study', *Work, Employment and Society*, Vol.11, No. 2: 283–311

Romanowska, J. (1993) 'Employee development through education liaison', *Education and Training*, Vol.35, No.3: 58–71

Roper, I., Prouska, R. and Na Ayudhya, U. C. (2010) *Critical Issues in Human Resource Management*. London: CIPD

Rose, M. (2000) 'Target practice', *People Management*, Vol.6, No.23, Nov–Dec: 44

Rosenfeld, P., Giacalone, R. A. and Riordan, C. A. (2002) *Impression Management: Building and enhancing reputations at work*. London: Thomson Learning

Rousseau, D. (1995) *Psychological Contracts in Organizations: Understanding written and unwritten agreements*. London: Sage.

Rousseau, J. J. (1947) *The Social Contract*. Oxford: Oxford University Press (first published 1762)

Rowley, C. and Benson, J. (2002) 'Convergence and divergence in Asian human resource management', *California Management Review*, Vol.44, No.2, Winter: 90–109

Roy, D. (1952) 'Quota restriction and goldbricking in a machine shop', *American Journal of Sociology*. Vol.57, No.2: 427–42; reprinted in Lupton, T. (ed.) (1972) *Payment Systems*. London: Penguin

Roy, D. (1954) 'Efficiency and "the fix": informal inter-group relations in a piecework machine shop', *American Journal of Sociology*, Vol.60, No.3: 225–66

Ruël, H. J. M., Bondarouk, T. V. and Looise, J. K. (2004) 'E-HRM: innovation or irritation – explorative empirical study in five large companies on web-based HRM', *Management Review*, Vol.15, No.3: 364–80

Saks, A. M. and Burke, L. A. (2012) 'An investigation into the relationship between training evaluation and the transfer of training', *International Journal of Training and Development*, Vol.16, No.2: 118–27

Scambler, G. (2008) *Sociology as Applied to Medicine*, 6th edition. London: W. B. Saunders/Elsevier

Schein, E. (1978) *Career Dynamics: Matching Individual and Organizational Needs*. Reading, MA: Addison-Wesley

Schleicher, D. J., Bull, R. A. and Green, S. G. (2009) 'Rater reactions to forced distribution rating systems', *Journal of Management*, Vol.35, No.4, August: 899–927

Schuler, R. and Jackson, S. (1987) 'Linking competitive strategies with human resource management practices', *Academy of Management Executive*, Vol.1, No.3: 207–19

Schuler, R. and Rogovsky, N. (1998) 'Understanding compensation practice variations across firms: the impact of national culture', *Journal of International Business Studies*, Vol. 29, No.1: 159–77

Sears, D. and McDermott, D. (2003) 'The rise and fall of rank and yank', *Information Strategy: The Executive's Journal*, Vol.19, No.3, Spring: 6–11

Senge, P. M. (1990) *The Fifth Discipline*. London: Century Business

Sharp, R. (2011) 'Performance-related pay: the 2011 XpertHR survey', *IRS Employment Review*, 2 September

Shen, J. (2005) 'Effective international performance appraisals: easily said, hard to do', *Compensation and Beneifts Review*, Vol.37, No.4, July–August: 70–9

Shields, J. (2007) *Managing Employee Performance and Rewards: Concepts, practices, strategies*. Cambridge/Melbourne, Australia: Cambridge University Press

Shih, H. A., Chiang, Y. H. and Kim, I. S. (2005) 'Expatriate performance management from MNEs of different national origins', *International Journal of Manpower*, Vol.26, No. 2: 157–76

Shipton, H. (2006) 'Cohesion or confusion? Towards a typology for organisational learning research', *International Journal of Management Reviews*, Vol.8, No.4: 233–52

Shore, L. M. and Wayne, S. J. (1993) 'Commitment and employee behavior: comparison of affective and continuance commitment with perceived organizational support', *Academy of Management Journal*, Vol.78: 774–80

Shurville, S. J. and Rospigliosi, A. (2009) 'Implementing blended self-managed Action Learning for digital entrepreneurs in higher education', *Action Learning: Research and Practice*, Vol.6, No.1, March: 53–61

Sisson, G. (2001) *Hands-On Training: A simple and effective method for on-the-job training*. San Francisco: Berrett-Koehler

Skinner, D. and Searle, R. H. (2011) 'Trust in the context of performance appraisal', in Searle, R. H. and Skinner, D. (eds) *Trust and Human Resource Management*. Cheltenham: Edward Elgar

Sledge, A., Miles, A. K.. and Coppage, S. (2008) 'What role does culture play? A look at motivation and job satisfaction among hotel workers in Brazil', *International Journal of Human Resource Management*, Vol.19, No.9: 1667–82

Smedley, T. (2010) 'HRD: Cadbury introduce "720-degree feedback"', *People Management*, 22 April

Smith, P. C. and Kendall, L. M. (1963) 'Retranslation of expectations: an approach to the construction of unambiguous anchors for rating scales', *Journal of Applied Psychology*, Vol.47: 149–55

Smither, J. W., London, M. L. and Reilly, R. R. (2005) 'Does performance improve following multi-source feedback? A theoretical model, meta-analysis, and review of empirical findings', *Personnel Psychology*, Vol.58: 33–66

Smither, J. W., London, M. L., Flautt, R., Vargas, Y. and Kucine, I. (2003) 'Can working with an executive coach improve multisource feedback ratings over time? A quasi-experimental field study', *Personnel Psychology*, Vol.56: 23–44

Snape, E. and Redman, T. (2010) 'HRM practices, organizational citizenship behavior, and performance: a multi-level analysis', *Journal of Management Studies*, Vol.47, No.7: 1219–47

Snape, E., Thompson, D., Yan, F. K.-C. and Redman, T. (1998) 'Performance appraisal and culture: practice and attiudes in Hong Kong and Great Britain', *International Journal of Human Resource Management*, Vol.9, No.5: 841–61

Sparrow, P. (2008) 'Performance management in the UK', in Varma, A., Budhwar, P. S. and DeNisi, A. (eds) *Performance Management Systems: A global perspective*. Abingdon: Routledge

Sparrow, P., Schuler, R. and Jackson, S. (1994) 'Convergence or divergence: human resource practices for competitive advantage worldwide', *International Journal of Human Resource Management*, Vol.5, No.2: 267–99

Steers, R. M. and Porter, L. W. (1991) *Motivation and Work Behaviour*, 5th edition. Maidenhead: McGraw-Hill

Steers, R. M. and Rhodes, S. R. (1978) 'Major influences on employee attendance: a process model', *Journal of Applied Psychology*, Vol.63, No.4: 391–407

Stewart, J. and Rigg, C. (2011) *Learning and Talent Development*. London: CIPD

Stiles, P., Gratton, L., Truss, C., Hope-Hailey, V. and McGovern, P. (1997) 'Performance management and the psychological contract', *Human Resource Management Journal*, Vol. 7, No.1: 57–66

Storey, J. (1983) *Management Prerogative and the Question of Control*. London: Routledge & Kegan Paul

Storey, J. (1989) *New Perspectives on Human Resource Management*. London: Routledge

Storey, J. (1992) *Developments in the Management of Human Resources*. Oxford: Blackwell

Storey, J. (2007) *Human Resource Management: A critical text*, 3rd edition. London: Thomson

Strebler, M. T., Bevan, S. and Robertson, D. (2001) *Performance Review: Balancing objectives and content*, Report 370. Brighton: Institute for Employment Studies

Suff, R. (2006) 'Managing underperformance: are line managers up to it?', *IRS Employment Review* 854

Suff, R. (2009) 'Managing underperformance: the 2009 IRS survey', *IRS Employment Review* 915

Suff, R. (2010) 'Benchmarking competencies: the 2010 survey', *IRS Employment Review*, 23 August

Suff, R. (2011a) 'Managing underperformance survey: tools and techniques'. Available online at: www.xperthr.co.uk.

Suff, R. (2011b) 'Absence rates survey 2011: 2.8 per cent of working time lost', *IRS Employment Review*, 28 June. Available online at: www.xperthr.co.uk

Suff, R. (2011c) 'Improving line managers' capability', *IRS Employment Review*

Suutari, V. and Tahvanainen, M. (2002) 'The antecedents of performance management among Finnish expatriates', *International Journal of Human Resource Management*, Vol. 13, No.1, February: 55–75

Swart, J. and Kinnie, N. (2010) 'Organisational learning, knowledge assets and HR practices in professional service firms', *Human Resource Management Journal*, Vol.20, No. 1: 64–79

Swart, J., Mann, C., Brown, S. and Price, A. (2005) *Human Resource Development: Strategy and tactics*. London: Elsevier/Butterworth-Heinemann

Tahvanainen, M. (2000) 'Expatriate performance management: the case of Nokia Telemcommunications', *Human Resource Management*, Vol.39, No.2/3, Summer–Fall: 267–75

Taormina, R. (1999) 'Predicting employee commitment and satisfaction: the relative effects of socialization and demographics', *International Journal of Human Resource Management*, Vol.10: 1060–76

Tarique, L. and Caligiuri, P. (2004) 'Training and development of international staff', in Harzing, A.-W. and van Ruysseveldt, J. (eds) *International Human Resource Management*. Thousand Oaks, CA: Sage Publications

Tasker, J. (2006) 'Tough love: do you have the heart?', *Personnel Today*, 14 February: 24–8

Tayeb, M. H. (2005) *International Human Resource Management: A multinational company perspective*. Oxford: Oxford University Press

Taylor, F. W. (1911) *Principles of Scientific Management*. New York: Harper

Taylor, F. W. (1947) *Scientific Management*. New York: Harper & Bros

Taylor, P., Baldry, C., Bain, P. and Ellis, V. (2003) 'A unique working environment: health, sickness and absence management in UK call centres', *Work, Employment and Society*, Vol.17, No.3: 435–58

Taylor, S. (2010) *Resourcing and Talent Management*, 5th edition. London: CIPD

Taylor, S. (2011) *Contemporary Issues in Human Resource Management*. London: CIPD

Teague, P. and Roche, W. K. (2012) 'Line managers and the management of workplace conflict: evidence from Ireland', *Human Resource Management Journal*, Vol.22: 235–51

Tekleab, A. G., Takeuchi, R. and Taylor, S. M. (2005) 'Extending the chain of relationships among organisational justice, social exchange and employee relations: the role of contract violations', *Academy of Management Journal*, Vol.48, No.1: 145–57

The Economist (2007) 'After smart weapons, smart soldiers'. Available online at: www.economist.com/node/10015844 [accessed 25 October 2007]

The Economist (2012) 'The countdown starts', 18 August. Available online at: www.economist.com/node/21560568 [accessed 22 October 2012]

Thibaut, J. and Walker, L. (1975) *Procedural Justice: A psychological analysis*. Hillsdale, NJ: Lawrence Erlbaum

Thompson, P. and McHugh, D. (2009) *Work Organisations: A critical approach*, 4th edition. Basingstoke: Macmillan

Thornton, G. C. III and Mueller-Hanson, R. A. (2004) *Developing Organizational Simulations: A guide for practitioners and students*. Mahwah, NJ: Lawrence Erlbaum

Tien, F. F. (2000) 'To what degree does the desire for promotion motivate faculty to perform research? Testing the expectancy theory', *Research in Higher Education*, Vol.41, No.6: 723–52

Tietze, S. and Nadin, S. (2011) 'The psychological contract and the transition from office-based to home-based work', *Human Resource Management Journal*, Vol.21, No.3: 318–34

Torrington, D., Hall, L., Taylor, S. and Atkinson, C. (2011) *Human Resource Management*, 8th edition. Harlow: FT/Prentice Hall

Towler, A. J. and Dipboye, R. L. (2001) 'Effects of trainer expressiveness, organization and trainee goal orientation on training outcomes', *Journal of Applied Psychology*, Vol.86, No. 4: 664–73

Townley, B. (1990) 'The politics of appraisal: lessons of the introduction of appraisal into UK universities', *Human Resource Management Journal*, Vol.1, No.2: 27–44

Trompenaars, F. and Hampden-Turner, C. (1997) *Riding the Waves of Culture: Understanding cultural diversity in business*, 2nd edition. London: Nicholas Brealey

Truss, C. (2001) 'Complexities and controversies in linking HRM with organisational outcomes', *Journal of Management Studies*, Vol.38, No.8: 1121–49

Truss, C., Mankin, D. and Kelliher, C. (2012) *Strategic Human Resource Management*. Oxford: Oxford University Press

Tung, R. L. (1984) 'Human resource planning in Japanese multinationals: a model for US firms?', *Journal of International Business Studies*, Vol.15, No.2: 139–49

Tung, R. L. and Varma, A. (2008) 'Expatriate selection and evaluation', in Smith, P. B., Peterson, M. F. and Thomas, D. C. (eds) *Handbook of Cross-Cultural Management Research*. London: Sage

Tyson, S. and Fell, A. (1986) *Evaluating the Personnel Function*. London: Hutchinson

Tyson, S. and Ward, P. (2004) 'The use of feedback technique in the evaluation of management development', *Management Learning*, Vol.35, No.2: 205–23

Tziner, A. and Murphy, K. R. (1999) 'Additional evidence of attitudinal influences in performance appraisal', *Journal of Business and Psychology*, Vol.13: 407–19

Tziner, A., Murphy, K. R. and Cleveland, J. N. (2001) 'Relationships between attitudes toward organisations and performance appraisal systems and rating behaviour', *International Journal of Selection and Assessment*, Vol.9: 226–39

Tziner, A., Murphy, K. R. and Cleveland, J. N. (2005) 'Contextual and rater factors affecting rating behaviour', *Group and Organizational Management*, Vol.30: 89–98

Uhl-Bien, M., Graen, G. B. and Scandura, T. A. (2000) 'Implications of leader–member exchange (LMX) for strategic human resource management systems', in Ferris, G. (ed.) *Research in Personnel and Human Resource Management*, Vol.18: 137–85. Greenwich, CT: JAI Press

UKCES (2009) *High-Performance Working: A synthesis of key literature*. London: United Kingdom Commission for Employment and Skills

Ulrich, D. (1997) *Human Resource Champions: The next agenda for adding value and delivering results*. Cambridge, MA: Harvard Business School Press

Ulrich, D. and Beatty, D. (2001) 'From partners to players: extending the HR playing field', *Human Resource Management*, Vol.40, No.4: 293–307

Ulrich, D. and Brockbank, W. (2005) *The HR Value Proposition*. Boston, MA: Harvard Business School Press

Vallance, S. (1999) 'Performance appraisal in Singapore, Thailand, and the Phillipines: a cultural perspective', *Australian Journal of Public Administration*, Vol.58: 78–95

Vandenberg, R. J., Richardson, H. A. and Eastman, L. J. (1999) 'The impact of high work processes on organisational effectiveness: a second-order latent variable approach', *Group and Organisational Management*, Vol.24, No.1: 300–39 van den Bossche, P., Segers, M. and Jansen, N. (2010) 'Transfer of training: the role of feedback in supportive social networks', *International Journal of Training and Development*, Vol.14, No.2: 81–94

van der Heijden, B. I. J. M. and Nijhof, A. H. J. (2004) 'The value of subjectivity: problems and prospects for 360-degree appraisal systems', *International Journal of Human Resource Management*, Vol.15, No.3: 493–511

van de Vliert, E., Shi, K., Sanders, K., Wang, Y. and Huang, X. (2004) 'Chinese and Dutch interpretations of supervisors' feedback', *Journal of Cross-Cultural Psychology*, Vol.35, No. 4: 417–35

Vansteenkiste, M., Lens, W., de Witte, H. and Feather, N. T. (2005) 'Understanding unemployed people's job search behaviour, unemployment experience and wellbeing: a comparison of expectancy–value theory and self-determination theory', *British Journal of Social Psychology*, Vol.44, No.2: 268–86

van Wanrooy, B., Bewley, H., Bryson, A., Forth, J., Freeth, S., Stokes L. and Wood, S. (2013) *The 2011 Workplace Employment Relations Study: First findings*. London: BIS/ACAS/ESRC/UKCES/NIESR

Varma, A. and Budhwar, P. S. (2011) 'Global performance management', in Harzing, A.-W. and Pinnington, A. H. (eds) *International Human Resource Management*, 3rd edition. London/Thousand Oaks, CA: Sage

Varma, A. and Stroh, L. K. (2001) 'The impact of same-sex LMX dyads on performance evaluations', *Human Resource Management*, Vol.40: 309–20

Varma, A., Budhwar, P. S. and DeNisi, A. (2008) *Performance Management Systems: A global perspective*. Abingdon: Routledge

Varma, A., Pichler, S. and Srinivas, E. S. (2005) 'The role of interpersonal affect in performance appraisal: evidence from two samples – the US and India', *International Journal of Human Resource Management*, Vol.16, No.11: 2029–44

Velada, R., Caetano, A., Michel, J. W., Lyons, B. D. and Kavanagh, M. M. (2007) 'The effects of training design, individual characteristics and work environment on transfer of training', *International Journal of Training and Development*, Vol.11, No.4: 282–94

Verma, A. and He, Q. (2010) 'Global challenges for development of human resources', in Roper, I., Prouska, R. and Na Ayudhya, U. C. (eds) *Critical Issues in Human Resource Management*. London: CIPD

Voelpel, S.C., Leibold, M. and Eckhoff, R. A. (2006) 'The tyranny of the balanced scorecard in the innovation economy', *Journal of Intellectual Capital*, Vol.7, No.1: 43–60

Vroom, V. H. (1964) *Work and Motivation*. New York: John Wiley & Sons

Wahba, M. A. and Bridwell, L. G. (1976) 'Maslow reconsidered: a review of research on the need hierarchy theory', *Organizational Behavior and Human Performance*, Vol.15, No. 2: 212–40

Wahba, M. A. and House, R. (1974) 'Expectancy theory in work and motivation: some logical and methodological issues', *Human Relations*, Vol.27: 121–47

Wall, T. and Wood, S. (2005) 'The romance of HRM and business performance, and the case for big science', *Human Relations*, Vol.58, No.4: 429–62

Warr, P. and Yearta, S. (1995) 'Health and motivational factors in sickness absence', *Human Resource Management Journal*, Vol.5, No.5, September: 33–48

Warr, P. B., Bird, M. W. and Rackham, N. (1970) *Evaluation of Training Management*. Aldershot: Gower

Watson, T. (1980) *Sociology: Work and industry*. London: Routledge & Kegan Paul

Wayne, S. J. and Linden, R. C. (1995) 'Effects of impression management on performance ratings: a longitudinal study', *Academy of Management Journal*, Vol.38: 232–60

Wedderburn, Lord W. (1986) *The Worker and the Law*. London: Butterworth/ Harmondsworth: Penguin

Welch, D. E., Worm, V. and Fenwick, M. (2003) 'Are virtual assignments feasible?', *Management International Review*, Vol.43, Special Issue 1: 95–114

Welch, J. and Welch, S. (2005) *Winning*. New York/London: Harper Business

Wernimont, P. F. (1966) 'Intrinsic and extrinsic factors in job satisfaction', *Journal of Applied Psychology*, Vol.50: 41–50

West, M. (2002) 'A matter of life and death', *People Management*, Vol.8, No.4, 21 February: 30–6

West, M. A., Guthrie, J. P., Dawson, J. F., Borrill, C. S. and Carter, M. R. (2006) 'Reducing patient mortality in hospitals: the role of human resource management', *Journal of Organisational Behaviour*, Vol.27: 938–1002

West, M. A., Borrill, C., Dawson, J., Scully, J., Carter, M., Anelay, S., Patterson, M. and Waring, J. (2002) 'The link between the management of employees and patient mortality in acute hospitals', *International Journal of Human Resource Management*, Vol.13, No.8: 1299–1310

Wexley, K. N. and Klimoski, R. (1984) 'Performance appraisal: an update', in Rowland, K. M. and Ferris, G. D. (eds) *Research in Personnel and Human Resources Management*. Greenwich, CN: JAI Press

Whiddett, S. and Hollyforde, S. (2003) *A Practical Guide to Competences: How to enhance individual and organisational performance*, 2nd edition. London: CIPD

White, M., Hill, S., McGovern, P., Mills, C. and Smeaton, D. (2003) '"High-performance" management practices, working hours and work–life balance', *British Journal of Industrial Relations*, Vol.41, No.2: 175–95

Whitener, E. M., Brodt, S. E., Korsgaard, M. A. and Werner, J. M. (1998) 'Managers are initiators of trust: an exchange relationship framework for understanding managerial trustworthy behaviour', *Academy of Management Review*, Vol.23, No.3: 513–30

Whittaker, S. and Marchington, M. (2003) 'Devolving HR responsibility to the line: threat, opportunity or partnership?', *Employee Relations*, Vol.36, No.3: 245–61

Wilkes, R. and Bates, G. (2010) *Line Manager Briefing on Handling Difficult Conversations*. London: XpertHR

Wimer, S. and Nowack, K. M. (1998) 'Thirteen common mistakes using 360-degree feedback', *Training and Development*, Vol.52, No.5: 69–70

Winchester, D. and Bach, S. (1995) 'The state: the public sector', in Edwards, P. K. (ed.) *Industrial Relations: Theory and practice in Britain*. Oxford: Blackwell

Winstanley, D. and Stuart-Smith, K. (1996) 'Policing performance: the ethics of performance management', *Personnel Review*, Vol.25, No.5: 66–84

Witcher, B.J., and Chau, V.S. (2008) 'Contrasting uses of balanced scorecards: case studies at two UK companies', *Strategic Change,* Vol 17, No.3/4: 101–114.

Wolff, C. (2005) 'Appraisals (2): learning from practice and experience', *IRS Employment Review*, No.829, 12 August: 13–17

Wolff, C. (2010) 'IRS line manager training survey 2010: HR wants compulsory training', *IRS Employment Review*, Issue, 5 May

Wolff, C. (2011) 'How manager training can reduce absence rates: the 2011 XpertHR survey', *IRS Employment Review*, September. Available online at: www.xperthr.co.uk

Wood, S. (1999) 'Human resource management and performance', *International Journal of Management Review*, Vol.1, No.4: 367–413

Wood, S. and de Menezes, L. (1998) 'High-commitment management in the UK: evidence from the Workplace Industrial Relations Survey and the Employer's Manpower Skills Practices Survey', *Human Relations*, Vol.51, No.4: 485–515

Wood, S. and Wall, T. (2007) 'Work enrichment and employee voice in human resource management–performance studies', *International Journal of Human Resource Management*, Vol.18, No.7: 1335–72

Woodruffe, C. (1991) 'Competent by any other name', *Personnel Management*, Vol.23, No.9, September: 30–3

Woodruffe, C. (1993) 'What is meant by a competency?', *Leadership and Organisation Development Journal*, Vol.14, No.1: 29–36

Woods, S. A. and West, M. A. (2010) *The Psychology of Work and Organizations*. New York: Cengage

Worrall, L. and Cooper C. (2012) *The Quality of Working Life 2012: Managers' wellbeing, motivation and productivity*. London: Chartered Management Institute

Wright, P. M. and Gardner, T. M. (2004) 'The human resource–firm performance relationship: methodological and theoretical challenges', in Holman, D., Wall, T., Clegg, C., Sparrow, P. and Howard, A. (eds) *The New Workplace: A guide to the human impact of modern working practices*. London: John Wiley

Wright, P. M. and Nishii, L. (2004) 'Strategic HRM and organisational behaviour: integrating multiple-level analysis', Paper presented at the 'What Next for HRM?' Conference, Rotterdam.

Wright, P. M., Gardner, T. and Moynihan, L. M. (2003) 'The impact of HR practices on the performance of business units', *Human Resource Management Journal*, Vol.13, No.5: 21–36

Wright, P. M., McMahan, G. C. and McWilliams, A. (1994) 'Human resources and sustained competitive advantage: a resource-based perspective', *International Journal of Human Resource Management*, Vol.5, No.2: 301–26

Wright, P., Scott, S. and Jacobsen, P. H. (2004) 'Current approaches to HR strategies: inside-out versus outside-in', *Human Resource Planning*, Vol.27, No.4: 35–47

Wright, P., Gardner, T., Moynihan, L. and Allen, M. (2005) 'The relationship between HR practices and firm performance: examining causal order', *Personnel Psychology*, Vol.58, No.2: 409–46

Wright, P., McMahan, G., Snell, S. and Gerhart, B. (2001) 'Comparing line and HR executives' perceptions of HR effectiveness: services, roles and contributions', *Human Resource Management*, Vol.40: 111–23

Wright, T. (2006) 'The emergence of job satisfaction in organisational behaviour', *Journal of Management History*, Vol.12: 262–77

XpertHR (2010a) 'Communication: line manager briefing on handling difficult conversations'. Available online at: www.xperthr.co.uk

XpertHR (2010b) 'Communication: line manager briefing on motivation'. Available online at: www.xperthr.co.uk

Yamazaki, Y. and Kayes, C. (2004) 'An experiential approach to cross-cultural learning: a review and integration of competencies for successful expatriate adaption', *Academy of Management Learning and Education*, Vol.55, No.4: 927–48

Youndt, M., Snell, S., Dean, J. and Lepak, D. (1996) 'Human resource management, manufacturing strategy, and firm performance', *Academy of Management Journal*, Vol.39, No.4: 836–66

Young, L. and Daniel, K. (2003) 'Affectual trust in the workplace', *Human Resource Management*, Vol.14, No.1: 139–55

Yukl, G., Gordon, A., and Taber, T. (2002) 'A hierarchical taxonomy of leadership behavior: integrating a half-century of behavior research', *Journal of Leadership and Organizational Studies*, Vol.9: 15–32

Zagenczyk, T. J., Gibney, R., Kiewitz, C. and Restubog, S. L. D. (2009) 'Mentors, supervisors and role models: do they reduce the effects of psychological contract breach?', *Human Resource Management Journal*, Vol.19, No.3: 237–59

Zand, D. E. (1978) 'Trust and managerial problem-solving', in Bradford, L. P. (ed.) *Group Development*, 2nd edition. La Jolla, CA: University Associates

Index